D1218295

Agricultural
Household Models

A World Bank Research Publication

Agricultural Household Models

Extensions, Applications, and Policy

Inderjit Singh
Lyn Squire
John Strauss
Editors

Published for The World Bank
THE JOHNS HOPKINS UNIVERSITY PRESS
Baltimore and London

The Johns Hopkins University Press
Baltimore, Maryland 21211, U.S.A.

The World Bank does not accept responsibility for the views expressed herein, which are those of
the authors and should not be attributed to the World Bank or to its affiliated organizations.
The findings, interpretations, and conclusions are the results of research supported by the Bank;
they do not necessarily represent official policy of the Bank.

Library of Congress Cataloging-in-Publication Data
Main entry under title:

Agricultural household models.

"Published for the World Bank."
Bibliography: p.
Includes index.
1. Agricultural laborers—Developing countries—Case
studies. 2. Rural families—Developing countries—Case
studies. 3. Agricultural industries—Developing coun-
tries—Case studies. 4. Developing countries—Rural
conditions—Case studies. 5. Agricultural laborers—
Government policy—Developing countries—Case studies.
I. Singh, Inderjit, 1941-   . II. Squire, Lyn,
1946-   . III. Strauss, John, 1951-   .
IV. International Bank for Reconstruction and
Development.
HD1542.A34   1986   331.7′63′091724   85-45102
ISBN 0-8018-3149-0

Contents

Contributors

Avishay Braverman, Agriculture and Rural Development Department, World Bank, Washington, D.C.

Theodore Graham-Tomasi, Department of Agriculture and Applied Economics, University of Minnesota, Minneapolis, Minn.

Farrukh Iqbal, East Asia and Pacific Country Programs Department, World Bank, Washington, D.C.

Subramanian Janakiram, Consultant, World Bank, Washington, D.C.

Jeffrey S. Hammer, Agriculture and Rural Development Department, World Bank, Washington, D.C.

Ramon E. Lopez, Agricultural Economics Department, University of Maryland, College Park, Md.

Mark M. Pitt, Department of Economics, University of Minnesota, Minneapolis, Minn.

Terry Roe, Department of Agriculture and Applied Economics, University of Minnesota, Minneapolis, Minn.

Mark R. Rosenweig, Department of Economics, University of Minnesota, Minneapolis, Minn.

Terry Sicular, Food Research Institute, Stanford University, Stanford, Calif.

Inderjit Singh, South Asia Projects Department, World Bank, Washington, D.C.

Victor E. Smith, Department of Economics, Michigan State University, East Lansing, Mich.

Lyn Squire, Country Policy Department, World Bank, Washington, D.C.

John Strauss, Economic Growth Center, Yale University, New Haven, Conn.

Acknowledgments

THIS BOOK HAS BENEFITED from the financial support of the World Bank's Research Committee and from the encouragement, suggestions, and help of many people. Special thanks are due to Dennis DeTray, whose invaluable comments led to major improvements in the organization and presentation of the book's materials. Jon Skinner provided very helpful comments on early versions of the material in Part I, which also benefited from the careful reading of Robert Evenson and T. Paul Schultz. We were also greatly assisted by the comments of a review panel.

We owe many thanks to Vicki Macintyre for very able and extremely efficient copyediting. Finally, the book could not have come to fruition without the skills and patience of Arlene Elcock, who not only did much of the typing, but also handled much of the correspondence. Lois Van de Velde also provided invaluable help in typing.

Agricultural
Household Models

Introduction

Inderjit Singh, Lyn Squire, and John Strauss

IN MOST DEVELOPING COUNTRIES, agriculture remains a principal source of income for the majority of the population, an important earner of foreign exchange, and a central concern of government policymakers. One of the great problems for these countries is that efforts to predict the consequences of agricultural policies are often confounded by the complex behavioral patterns characteristic of households in semicommercialized, rural economies. That is to say, most households in agricultural areas produce partly for sale and partly for their own consumption. They also purchase some of their inputs (fertilizer, for example) and provide some (such as family labor) from their own resources. Any change in the policies governing agricultural activities will therefore affect not only production, but also consumption and labor supply. These relations are what analysts attempt to capture in their efforts to model the behavior of agricultural households.

Modeling Agricultural Household Models: Why and How

Agricultural households are the main form of economic organization in developing countries. Roughly 70 percent of the labor force in low-income developing countries was employed in the agricultural sector in 1980. Even in the middle-income developing countries, almost 45 percent of the labor force was so employed (table 1). Although some members of the agricultural labor force are landless laborers, agricultural households, according to the information in table 1, are numerous. Consequently, it

Table 1. *Labor Force in Agriculture, 1980, Selected Developing Economies*

Low-income economies	Percent	Middle-income economies	Percent
All	70	All	44
Malawi	86	Indonesia	55
Bangladesh	74	Nigeria	54
Haiti	74	Egypt	50
China	69	Malaysia	50
India	69	Dominican Republic	49
Sierra Leone	65	Philippines	46
		Korea, Rep. of	34

Note: Low-income economies are those with a 1981 per capita income of less than US$410. Middle-income economies are those with a 1981 per capita income greater than US$410.
Source: World Bank (1983), table 21.

is important to understand and account for their behavior when analyzing government interventions in the rural economy.

Governments in developing countries intervene in the agricultural sector through pricing policies and through investment projects. Policies affecting the prices of agricultural commodities are pervasive (see, for example, Schultz 1978). Such policies can influence production, consumption, marketing, or international trade and may be designed to generate revenue, subsidize urban consumers, secure self-sufficiency, earn foreign exchange, or improve rural incomes. Often the public sector is also the principal provider of infrastructure and other services to the rural economy. Transport, irrigation facilities, and extension services are all frequently provided below cost or free of charge by the public sector. Like pricing policies, investments by the public sector can be expected to have a strong impact on production and incomes in agricultural households.

Why

The manner in which agricultural households respond to interventions is a critical factor in determining the relative merits of alternative policies. If, for example, the price of an important agricultural commodity is increased, will agricultural households sell more? Will the introduction of an improved technology increase the demand for labor? And if so, will that increase be met from the agricultural household's own labor resources or will there be a net increase in the demand for hired labor? Questions such as these are difficult to study without a thorough understanding of the microeconomic behavior of agricultural households. That means it is essential to know what factors determine the level of farm production and the demand for farm inputs, what factors govern consumption and the supply of labor, and how the behavior of the household as a producer affects its behavior as a consumer and supplier of labor, and vice versa.

Agricultural household models are designed to capture these relationships in a theoretically consistent fashion so that the results of the analysis can be applied empirically to illuminate the consequences of policy interventions. Ideally, such models should enable the analyst to examine the consequences of policy in three dimensions. First, it is important to examine the effect of alternative policies on the well-being of representative agricultural households. In this book well-being refers to mean household income or some other measure such as nutritional status. In examining the effect of a policy designed to provide inexpensive food for urban consumers, for example, an agricultural household model would allow the analyst to assess the costs to farmers of depressed producer prices.

Second, the analyst will want to examine the "spillover" effects of government policies on other segments of the rural population. Since most rural investment strategies are designed to increase production, their primary impact is on the incomes of agricultural households and thus some of them may not reach landless households or households engaged in nonagricultural activities. A model that incorporates total labor demand and family labor supply allows the analyst to explore the effects of policy on the demand for hired labor and hence on the rural labor market and the incomes of landless households. Similarly, a model that incorporates consumer behavior allows the analyst to explore the consequences of increased profits for agricultural households on the demand for products and services provided by nonagricultural, rural households (see Anderson and Leiserson 1980). Since the demand for nonagricultural commodities is often thought to be much more responsive to an increase in income than the demand for agricultural staples, this spillover effect may well be important.

Third, the analyst is interested in the performance of the agricultural sector from a multisectoral perspective since agriculture is often an important source of both revenue for the public budget and foreign exchange. In assessing the effects of pricing policy on the budget or the balance of payments, governments are obliged to consider the quantitative responses of agricultural households. Reducing export taxes, for example, may increase earnings of foreign exchange and budget revenues provided households market enough additional production. Since agricultural household models capture both consumption and production behavior, they are a natural vehicle for examining the effect of pricing policy on marketed surplus and hence foreign exchange earnings and budget revenues.

Because of the importance of agricultural households in the total population of developing countries and the significance of agricultural sector
policies, the behavior of agricultural households warrants thorough theoretical and empirical investigation. The analysis of agricultural households has been approached from many different angles, each relevant in
its own way and having its advantages and disadvantages. This volume
reports the results of a large body of work that has followed a similar basic
approach, which we believe offers important policy insight that differs
significantly from the results of more traditional approaches.

How

Since 1975, researchers at the Food Research Institute of Stanford University and at the World Bank have been developing microeconomic
models of farm households that combine producer, consumer, and labor
supply decisions in a theoretically consistent manner. In true subsistence
households, these decisions are made simultaneously. Without access to
trade, a household can consume only what it produces and must rely exclusively on its own labor. A large part of agriculture, however, is made
up of semicommercial farms in which some inputs are purchased and
some outputs are sold. In these circumstances, producer, consumer, and
labor supply decisions are no longer made simultaneously, although they
are obviously connected because the market value of consumption cannot exceed the market value of production less the market value of
inputs.

Imagine a simple agricultural household that produces one crop, say,
rice; has a fixed amount of land; and uses one variable input, labor. The
household consumes some of the rice, and sells some in order to buy a
nonagricultural commodity. In addition to using its own labor, the
household hires labor. Assume further that the household can sell rice at
a fixed price and buy labor at a fixed wage. How does this household
organize its productive activities? Since income contributes positively to
total household utility or satisfaction, the household will attempt to
achieve the largest profit possible from its fixed quantity of land. This
implies that the household will go on hiring labor until the marginal revenue product of labor equals the market wage. The household may not, of
course, achieve maximum profits exactly. Nevertheless, in setting the
level of output and the quantity of inputs, the household will try to approximate the profit-maximizing solution and will therefore require information on prices—in this case, the price of rice and the wage rate—and on
the technological relationships between inputs and outputs. These pieces
of information are sufficient for the household to equate marginal revenue product to the wage. Notice that, in making its farm output and in-

put calculations, the household does not need to know how much rice it plans to consume or how much labor it intends to supply. In other words, the household can make its production decisions independently of its consumption and labor-supply decision. (This proposition was developed by Krishna 1964 and by Jorgenson and Lau 1969.)

Consumption and labor-supply decisions, however, are not independent of production decisions. Consumption and labor supply depend on both prices and income and, although prices are fixed by assumption, income is determined, at least to some extent, by the household's profits from its farming activities. Thus, production decisions determine farm profits, which are a component of household income, which in turn influences consumption and labor-supply decisions. This one-way relation between production on the one hand and consumption and labor supply on the other hand is known as the *profit effect*; it will be referred to frequently throughout the volume.

This result—that the decisionmaking process of the agricultural household has a recursive character is crucial for much of the work summarized in this volume. It is based on the assumption that households are price-takers for every commodity, including labor, that is both produced and consumed by the household. According to this line of reasoning, the amount of, say, rice to be produced can be determined independently of the amount of rice to be consumed because the household can always buy or sell rice at a fixed price. Similarly, the amount of labor applied to rice production can be determined independently of the amount of family labor to be used because the difference can be hired at a fixed wage. The only constraint on rice consumption or family labor supply arises from total household income. The household cannot consume more rice or more leisure (that is, reduce its labor supply and use more hired laborers) than is allowed by its total income. Since the household always prefers more income, it makes sense to maximize profits and then allocate the resulting income to rice—the nonagricultural commodity—and leisure, given the prevailing market prices. With prices fixed, therefore, the two components of the model are related only through income and only in one direction, from the production side of the model to the consumption and labor-supply side.

If production decisions affect prices as well as household income, however, the recursive property of the model is eliminated. If the household's decision to hire a certain amount of labor affects the wage rate, or if its decision to sell a quantity of rice affects the market price, then a theoretically consistent treatment requires that production, consumption, and labor-supply decisions be determined jointly. If we assume there is no labor market, for example, then there is no market wage and the household must equate its demand for labor with its own supply of labor. Despite the absence of a market wage, one can nevertheless focus on the shadow, or virtual, price—this being the price that would just secure the observed equality between the demand and supply of household labor. This price will depend on all the variables that influence household decisionmaking.

More important, since this shadow price will influence production, consumption, and labor-supply decisions, income will no longer be the only connection between the two sides of the model and the recursive property will be lost. Thus if there is an increase in the price of rice, production will increase and hence the demand for labor; at the same time, income will increase and hence the supply of labor will decrease. But, if there is no labor market, the supply and demand of household labor must be balanced. Balance will be achieved only if the shadow price of labor increases. An increase in this price, however, will initiate second-round effects—production, for example, will be reduced in response to the increase in the price of a major input. In fact, when all the interactions are complete, one might observe a net decrease in production, despite the increase in its price. Had the wage been fixed, on the other hand, second-round effects would have been eliminated.

The incorporation of endogenously determined prices obviously complicates the analyst's task considerably. The specification of price determination in output and labor markets, therefore, is important. In output markets, the assumption that households are price-takers may often be warranted. Although many agricultural output markets are characterized by extensive government intervention, for example, price fixing by the government implies that agricultural households are price-takers. Similarly, if prices are determined in world markets, it seems perfectly reasonable to assume that any given agricultural household is a price-taker. Obviously, this assumption should be carefully investigated in each case, but, given the existence of many sellers, the assumption that any individual seller is unable to influence the market price may often be the most plausible description of market behavior.

The household must also be a price-taker in the labor market. Rural wages, however, are less likely to be fixed by government intervention or in international markets. Thus the operation of the labor market becomes an important ingredient in the specification of an agricultural household model. Circumstances will clearly differ from case to case, but two recent surveys of rural labor markets point to the existence of many buyers and many sellers and to the general availability of information on rural wage rates among participants in the labor market (Binswanger and Rosenzweig 1984; Squire 1982). The essential elements of a reasonably competitive market may, therefore, often be found in rural areas. In other words, before proceeding to a more complicated model in which production and consumption are determined simultaneously, one ought to have a compelling argument with supporting empirical evidence to substantiate the notion that the behavior of one agricultural household can be expected to influence the market wage for rural labor in general. Accordingly, most, but not all, of the case studies in this volume treat households as price-takers and consequently develop models of recursive decisionmaking.

The approach to agricultural household modeling adopted here can be better understood if we look at the significance of the profit effect. Consider the effect of an increase in the price of rice. If the decisions of the agricultural household are recursive, then the traditional analysis of farm output supply and input demand using the theory of the firm will yield the same results as those of a fully specified agricultural household model. The same is not true, however, for consumption and labor supply. The traditional approach to consumer-demand analysis would allow for the substitution effect and the income effect of the change in the price of rice. The substitution effect is unambiguously negative. And for a normal commodity such as rice, the income effect can be confidently expected to be negative. The traditional approach, therefore, would predict an unambiguous decrease in the consumption of rice following an increase in its price. An integrated agricultural household model, however, allows for an additional effect—the profit effect.

When the price of rice increases, farm profits increase. This means more household income, which will, of course, tend to increase the demand for rice. In the framework of an agricultural household model, therefore, the demand for rice is subject to two forces pulling in opposite directions. On the one hand, an increase in price will tend to reduce demand as a result of the traditional substitution and income effects of consumer theory. On the other hand, the profit effect associated with the same increase in price will tend to increase demand. The ultimate effect on demand is thus a matter for empirical investigation. In fact, the profit effect could outweigh the other effects and thereby reverse the traditional conclusion. That is, an increase in the price of rice may result in increased demand. The studies reported in this volume provide empirical confirmation of this possibility.

Other examples could be cited. The essential principle, however, remains the same: the consistent incorporation of the profit effect can change the direction and magnitude of results predicted by traditional models of consumption and labor-supply behavior.

Structure of the Analysis

The book consists of two main parts: part I provides an overview of empirical results, policy conclusions, and methodological issues; part II contains a series of recent applications of agricultural household modeling that expands the range of policy issues subject to investigation within this general framework and explores several critical methodological issues.

Part I first presents the basic model of an agricultural household that underlies most of the case studies undertaken so far. The model assumes that households are price-takers and is therefore recursive. The decisions modeled include those affecting production and the demand for inputs and those affecting consumption and the supply of labor. Comparative results on selected elasticities are presented for a number of economies (Japan, the Republic of Korea, Malaysia, Nigeria, Sierra Leone, Taiwan, and Thailand). The empirical significance of the approach is demonstrated in a comparison of models that treat production and consumption decisions separately and those in which the decisionmaking process is recursive. The opening chapter also summarizes the implications of agricultural pricing policy for the welfare of farm households, marketed surplus, the demand for nonagricultural goods and services, the rural labor market, budget revenues, and foreign exchange earnings. In addition, it is shown that the basic model can be extended in order to explore the effects of government policy on crop composition, nutritional status, health, saving, and investment and to provide a more comprehensive analysis of the effects on budget revenues and foreign exchange earnings.

Chapter 2 concentrates on methodological topics, primarily the data requirements of the basic model and its extensions, along with aggregation, market interaction, uncertainty, and market imperfections. The most important methodological issue—the question of the recursive property of these models—is also discussed. Part I concludes with a technical appendix that develops a general model of an agricultural household and formally derives the conditions under which it is appropriate to treat the decisions governing production, consumption, and labor supply recursively. The comparative statics of the general model are derived and the difference between recursive and nonrecursive models is demonstrated by reference to certain well-known models such as the one that incorporates Z-goods (or home-produced goods).

Part II contains nine case studies, each of which extends the basic approach in some new direction. Chapters 3 and 4, for example, describe efforts to disaggregate commodities on both the production and consumption sides of the model. First, Singh and Janakiram use Korean and Nigerian data to demonstrate how a linear programming characterization of production can be used to investigate factors influencing the allocation of resources among several crops within the framework of an agricultural household model. Next, Strauss looks at disaggregation of consumed items. With data from Sierra Leone, he is able to show how a farm-household model can be used to examine the effects of pricing policy for nutritional status. In this application, the profit effect becomes critical because the direct effect of an increase in the price of food on consumption may be offset by an increase in farm profits and hence household income. Strauss provides empirical confirmation of this point.

In chapter 5, Pitt and Rosenzweig extend Strauss's analysis to the relations between food intake and household health and that between health and farm profits. According to their results, farm profits are relatively immune to the health status of the farmer because of access to a well-functioning labor market. Health status can be influenced by prices, however; reductions in the price of sugar, for example, help to increase the incidence of illness, whereas reductions in the prices of vegetables and vegetable oil help to reduce it.

Iqbal extends the model in a completely different direction in chapter 6 by focusing on the household's borrowing decision. Moreover, since he believes that households are not price-takers in the capital market, he is obliged to abandon the recursive characteristic of decisionmaking. Using data for rural India, Iqbal demonstrates that interest rates have an important effect on the amount borrowed. Furthermore, he finds that in previous studies the interest rate variable has often proved insignificant because of misspecification of the borrowing variable.

Most of the case studies up to this point in the book deal with representative households. Policy conclusions drawn from such analyses are potentially misleading for at least two reasons. First, households are different, and therefore simply scaling up the results for a representative household may yield unsatisfactory results. Second, the approach ignores general equilibrium effects. Although the wage may be treated as given for any particular household, for example, if all households increase their demand for labor, the market wage may well be pushed upward.

Two chapters address these issues. Again relying on Sierra Leone data, Smith and Strauss use microsimulation to explore the consequences of policy intervention for different types of households. Their results, reported in chapter 7, show that, although the nutritional benefit of a higher rice price is negligible for the rural population at large, its impact on the poorest households is positive. Moreover, this is a direct outcome of the operation of the profit effect. Low-income households have larger marketed surpluses of rice than other households. As a result, an increase in the price of this crop yields an increase in profits for low-income households that is large enough to offset the direct impact on consumption (and hence nutrition) through the traditional substitution and income effects.

Smith and Strauss also touch on the consequences of an induced increase in the rural wage following an increase in the price of rice. This preliminary effort to incorporate general equilibrium effects is taken one step further by Braverman and Hammer, who in chapter 8 aggregate results at the household level and explicitly incorporate market-clearing conditions in the agricultural household model. In applying the model to Senegal, they assume that the prices of groundnuts, cotton, and rice are fixed by the government and that the market clears through adjustments—exports or imports—in international trade. For millet and maize, however, prices are determined endogenously by the interaction of domestic supply and demand. Endogenous prices for land and labor by region are also modeled. The model must therefore be designed to ensure balance in two output markets and two input markets through price adjustments; furthermore, the production, consumption, and labor-supply decisions of households must be consistent with the newly emerging prices. The authors suggest that in this way, the more important general equilibrium effects in the model are captured.

The work of Braverman and Hammer offers the prospect of a useful tool for policy analysis that strikes a reasonable balance between the need to incorporate general equilibrium effects and the need to meet data and computational requirements. Their work also lends itself to the analysis of issues that often concern policymakers. Consider the effect of a decrease in the producer price of groundnuts, a principal export in Senegal. The government may contemplate such a step because it is anxious to reduce the drain on the budget of large subsidies to groundnut producers. At the same time, however, it may be reluctant to jeopardize export earnings. Braverman and Hammer are able to show that, because of interactions with other markets, much of the reduction in export earnings from groundnuts is offset by other crops, whereas the budget savings from groundnuts are largely untouched by developments in other markets. In addition to results of this kind, their work also yields the usual microeconomic results—household incomes, labor supply, consumption, production—associated with agricultural household models. Their approach, however, allows fully for induced changes in market-clearing prices.

The models described so far have been deterministic. Agricultural production is subject to considerable uncertainty, however. Yields, for example, obviously depend on weather conditions that can be predicted with only a limited degree of accuracy. In chapter 9, Roe and Graham-Tomasi begin the difficult task of incorporating production risk into agricultural household models. They demonstrate that, under certain very restrictive circumstances, the recursive property of agricultural household models survives the incorporation of production risk. These circumstances are the existence of markets for contingent states of the future or, in the absence of such markets, special assumptions concerning the household's utility function. That recursiveness of production and consumption decisions might depend on preferences in addition to markets makes the case of risk quite different from the certainty case. Roe and Graham-Tomasi work out an example using a particular utility function and using illustrative data from the Dominican Republic. They show for this case that the problem becomes separable using certainty equivalent income to replace income. They also show that when the analyst ignores risk in computing comparative statics an extra income effect, which counters the profit effect, is omitted. This is because a rise in price raises the variance of profits, so that certainty equivalent income falls for risk-averse households.

In principle, agricultural household modeling is relevant for economic agents other than households provided a discrete, decisionmaking unit can be identified. In an imaginative application to a Chinese collective in chapter 10, Sicular demonstrates that the general approach can be used to analyze the behavior of a group of farm households. Sicular explores the behavior of a Chinese production team subject to various state-imposed quotas and restrictions. One consequence of these restrictions—such as those on labor-market participation—is that Sicular is obliged to abandon the recursive property characteristic of most studies of agricultural households. In the absence of adequate data on consumption, Sicular focuses on the production side of the model. The consumption-production interaction is then introduced by constraining production decisions so that certain optimal levels of consumption by commodity are achieved. Within this framework, Sicular is able to show the consequences of state-imposed restrictions on production and marketing by comparing the results of a restricted model with those of an unrestricted one.

The volume comes to a close in chapter 11 with a discussion of one of the first attempts to address statistically the appropriateness of the recursive characterization of decisionmaking common to most agricultural household models. Lopez argues that production, consumption, and labor-supply decisions may be interdependent because of differences in preferences for off-farm and on-farm work or because of the costs of commuting associated with off-farm work. Having demonstrated analytically that in these circumstances the agricultural household model can no longer be treated recursively, Lopez uses data from Canada to test statistically whether or not the nonrecursive model is preferred to the recursive one. The results of this exercise do not support the use of a recursive model. The quantitative differences in the elasticities estimated by the two models are substantial. For example, the elasticity of total labor supply is 0.04 in the nonrecursive model compared with 0.19 in the recursive one. Although the particular reasons advanced by Lopez in favor of a nonrecursive model may not seem especially relevant to developing countries, the general thrust of his work is clearly important, and further tests using data from developing countries are warranted. (Chapter 2 of this volume contains an evaluation of Lopez's results for future work on agricultural household models.)

It may be useful to conclude these introductory remarks with a brief reader's guide. The reader who is interested in understanding the basic idea behind agricultural household models and who wants a review of the main empirical results and policy conclusions should read chapter 1. The reader who wants to go beyond this and see how the basic model might be extended to a much wider range of policy issues should also read the case studies on crop-composition, nutrition, health, borrowing, and government deficits in chapters 3, 4 and 7, 5, 6, and 8, respectively. Finally, the reader whose interests are methodological and who wants to identify areas for further research should read chapter 2, the technical appendix to part I, and the case studies on aggregation, general equilibrium effects, production risk, market imperfections, and nonrecursive models in chapters 7, 8, 9, 10, and 11, respectively. Although progress to date on agricultural household modeling has been substantial, much remains to be done to substantiate the orders of magnitude of critical elasticities and the policy conclusions emerging from existing studies and to incorporate additional decisions and realism into the models.

References

Anderson, Dennis, and Mark Leiserson. 1980. "Rural Nonfarm Employment in Developing Countries." *Economic Development and Cultural Change*, vol. 28, pp. 227–48.

Binswanger, Hans, and Mark Rosenzweig. 1984. *Contractual Arrangements, Employment and Wages in Rural Labor Markets in Asia.* New Haven, Conn.: Yale University Press.

Jorgenson, Dale, and Lawrence Lau. 1969. "An Economic Theory of Agricultural Household Behavior." Paper read at 4th Far Eastern Meeting of the Econometric Society, Tokyo, Japan.

Krishna, Raj. 1964. "Theory of the Firm: Rapporteur's Report." *Indian Economic Journal*, vol. 11, pp. 514–25.

Schultz, Theodore W. *Distortion of Agricultural Incentives.* 1978. Bloomington, Ind.: University of Indiana Press.

Squire, Lyn. 1981. *Employment Policy in Developing Countries: A Survey of Issues and Evidence.* New York: Oxford University Press.

World Bank. 1983. *World Development Report.* Washington, D.C.

Part I

An Overview of Agricultural Household Models

1

The Basic Model: Theory, Empirical Results, and Policy Conclusions

Inderjit Singh, Lyn Squire, and John Strauss

THE BASIC MODEL PRESENTED HERE is the analytical framework used in most of the early empirical efforts to investigate the behavior of agricultural households. A more general analytical framework is described in the appendix to part I. Many of the case studies presented in part II illustrate how the basic model can be expanded to treat a wider range of policy issues and how it can be modified to reflect more accurately the realities of agricultural production. For the present, however, attention is focused on fundamentals.

The Basic Model

For any production cycle, the household is assumed to maximize a utility function:

(1-1) $$U = U(X_a, X_m, X_l)$$

where the commodities are an agricultural staple (X_a), a market-purchased good (X_m), and leisure (X_l). Utility is maximized subject to a cash income constraint:

$$p_m X_m = p_a(Q - X_a) - w(L - F)$$

where p_m and p_a are the prices of the market-purchased commodity and the staple, respectively, Q is the household's production of the staple (so that $Q - X_a$ is its marketed surplus), w is the market wage, L is total labor input, and F is family labor input (so that $L - F$, if positive, is hired labor and, if negative, is off-farm labor supply).

The household also faces a time constraint—it cannot allocate more time to leisure, on-farm production, or off-farm employment than the total time available to the household:

$$X_l + F = T$$

where T is the total stock of household time. It also faces a production constraint or production technology that depicts the relation between inputs and output:

$$Q = Q(L, A)$$

where A is the household's fixed quantity of land.

In this presentation, various complexities have been omitted. For example, other variable inputs—fertilizer, pesticide—have been omitted and the possibility that more than one crop is being produced has also been ignored. In addition, it has been assumed that family labor and hired labor are perfect substitutes and can be added directly. Production is also assumed to be riskless. Finally, and perhaps most importantly, it will be assumed that the three prices in the model—p_a, p_m, and w—are not affected by actions of the household. That is, the household is assumed to be a price-taker in the three markets and, as argued in the Introduction, this will result in a recursive model. At various points in this volume, each of these assumptions will be abandoned, but for much of the discussion in this chapter they will be retained.

The three constraints on household behavior can be collapsed into a single constraint. Substituting the production constraint into the cash income constraint for Q and substituting the time constraint into the cash income constraint for F yields a single constraint of the form

(1-2) $$p_m X_m + p_a X_a + w X_l = wT + \pi$$

where $\pi = p_a Q(L, A) - wL$ and is a measure of farm profits. In this equation, the left-hand side shows total household "expenditure" on three items—the market-purchased commodity, the household's "purchase" of its own output, and the household's "purchase" of its own time in the form of leisure. The right-hand side is a development of Becker's concept of full income in which the value of the stock of time (wT) owned by the household is explicitly recorded. The extension for agricultural households includes a measure of farm profits ($p_a Q - wL$) with all labor valued at the market wage, this being a consequence of the assumption of price-taking behavior in the labor market. Equations 1-1 and 1-2 are the core of all the studies of agricultural households reported in this volume.

In these equations, the household can choose the levels of consumption for the three commodities and the total labor input into agricultural production. We therefore need to explore the first-order conditions for maximizing each of these choice variables. Consider labor input first. The first-order condition is:

(1-3) $$p_a \partial Q/\partial L = w.$$

That is, the household will equate the marginal revenue product of labor to the market wage. An important attribute of this equation is that it contains only one endogenous variable, L. The other endogenous variables—X_m, X_a, X_l—do not appear and therefore do not influence the household's choice of L. Accordingly, equation 1-3 can be solved for L as a function of prices (p_a and w), the technological parameters of the production function, and the fixed area of land. This result parallels that described in the Introduction in that production decisions can be made independently of consumption and labor-supply (or leisure) decisions.

Let the solution for L be

(1-4) $$L^* = L^*(w, p_a, A).$$

This solution can then be substituted into the right-hand side of the constraint (equation 1-2) to obtain the value of full income when farm profits have been maximized through an appropriate choice of labor input. We could, therefore, rewrite equation 1-2 as

$$p_m X_m + p_a X_a + w X_l = Y^*$$

where Y^* is the value of full income associated with profit-maximizing behavior. Maximizing utility subject to this new version of the constraint yields the following first-order conditions:

(1-5) $$\partial U/\partial X_m = \lambda p_m$$

$$\partial U/\partial X_a = \lambda p_a$$

$$\partial U/\partial X_l = \lambda w$$

and

$$p_m X_m + p_a X_a + w X_l = Y^*$$

which are the standard conditions from consumer-demand theory.

The solution to equation 1-5 yields standard demand curves of the form

(1-6) $$X_i = X_i(p_m, p_a, w, Y^*) \qquad\qquad i = m, a, l.$$

That is, demand depends on prices and income. In the case of the agricultural household, however, income is determined by the household's production activities. It follows that changes in factors influencing production will change Y^* and hence consumption behavior. Consumption behavior, therefore, is not independent of production behavior. This establishes the recursive property of the model described in the Introduction.

To complete this section, we derive the "profit effect" also mentioned in the Introduction. Assume that the price of the agricultural staple is increased. What is the effect on consumption of the staple? From equation 1-6,

$$(1\text{-}7) \qquad \frac{dX_a}{dp_a} = \frac{\partial X_a}{\partial p_a} + \frac{\partial X_a}{\partial Y^*} \frac{\partial Y^*}{\partial p_a}.$$

The first term on the right-hand side is the standard result of consumer-demand theory and, for a normal good, is negative. The second term captures the profit effect. A change in the price of the staple increases farm profits and hence full income. From equation 1-7,

$$\frac{\partial Y^*}{\partial p_\alpha} dp_\alpha = \frac{\partial \pi}{\partial p_\alpha} dp_\alpha = Q \, dp_\alpha.$$

That is, the profit effect equals output times the change in price and is, therefore, unambiguously positive. As noted in the Introduction, the positive effect of an increase in profits—an effect that is totally ignored in traditional models of demand—will definitely dampen and may outweigh the negative effect of standard consumer-demand theory.

Estimation Issues

Given a recursive model, a set of output-supply and variable input-demand functions (equation 1-4) and a set of commodity-demand equations including leisure or labor supply (see equation 1-6) can be derived from the household's equilibrium. The output supplies and input demands are functions of input and output prices and of farm characteristics (including fixed inputs). They are derived from a profit function that obeys the usual constraints from the theory of the firm: homogeneity of degree one in prices, and convexity with respect to prices. The commodity demands are functions of commodity prices, full income, and possibly household characteristics (see below). When full income is held constant, these demands satisfy the usual constraints of demand theory: adding up to total expenditure; zero homogeneity with respect to prices and exogenous income; and symmetry and negative semidefiniteness of the Slutsky-substitution matrix. These results can be used as a guide when specifying the model for estimation.

If estimation is to be carried out by econometric means, errors have to be added to the model. The issues involved in specifying a sensible error structure are outside the scope of this chapter. For simplicity, suppose the errors are added to the demand and output-supply equations. If for a given household the errors on the input-demand and output-supply equations are uncorrelated with the errors on the commodity-demand equations, the entire system of equations is statistically block recursive. In this case, profits will be uncorrelated with the commodity-demand disturbances so that the latter equations may be consistently estimated as a system independent from the output-supply and input-demand equations. The practical advantage of estimating the demand and production sides of the model separately is that far fewer parameters need to be estimated for each. This can be important if the equations are nonlinear in parameters and have to be estimated using numerical algorithms, since expense is greatly reduced and tractability increased. Thus models with greater detail can be estimated.

Even though demand-side and production-side errors are uncorrelated, errors on different commodity-demand equations may still be correlated, as might errors of different output-supply and input-demand equations. This is intuitively plausible. Moreover, it is a necessary condition for the commodity-demand equations, since they must satisfy the adding-up constraint; that is, expenditures must add up to full income. If this constraint is to be met for every household, the errors, or a linear combination of them, must add up to zero for each household so that the result is nonzero correlations. This result is well known and is one reason for estimating either the commodity-demand equations or the output-supply and input-demand equations as a system: accounting for the error covariances will improve the statistical efficiency of the estimates. A second reason for estimating these equations as a system (or, more properly, two separate systems, one for the commodity demands and one for the output supplies and input demands) is to account for cross-equation parameter restrictions. These will occur because these equations are derived from a common optimizing problem. In particular, the adding up and the Slutsky symmetry constraints will impose certain cross-equation constraints on commodity-demand parameters, which, if used (and if they are correct), will again improve the statistical efficiency of the estimates. These advantages are well known and have given rise to an econometric literature on estimation of demand systems (see, for example, Brown and Deaton 1972; Barten 1977; Deaton and Muellbauer 1980).

One does not have to estimate a system of equations, since single, reduced-form equations can be consistently estimated as well. This will be advantageous when the underlying model is not recursive (see chapter 2).

The disadvantage of this approach is that it is usually not possible to solve for the reduced form analytically. Consequently, one cannot take full advantage of economic theory in imposing (or testing) parameter restrictions, although some of the restrictions may be readily apparent. Nevertheless, it is possible to specify what variables belong in the reduced form and thus to estimate a least squares approximation to it. In general, by not imposing parameter restrictions one sacrifices only statistical efficiency, and not consistency.

Even if the underlying model is recursive, estimating a single equation may be advantageous because it can economize data requirements. To estimate a complete set of commodity-demand, output-supply, and input-demand equations requires an enormous amount of data on consumption expenditures and prices for farm and nonfarm commodities; on household time allocation to on-farm and off-farm work and related wages; and on inputs and outputs of the production activities. To estimate a single equation, however, the analyst needs data on only one endogenous variable and the proper exogenous variables, but not on all the endogenous variables. (Other aspects of estimation—data requirements, specification of variables—are discussed in chapter 2.)

Empirical Results

The first empirical studies to give estimates of agricultural household models (Lau, Lin, and Yotopoulos 1978; Yotopoulos, Lau, and Lin 1976; Kuroda and Yotopoulos 1978, 1980; Adulavidhaya and others 1979; Adulavidhaya, Kuroda, Lau, and Yotopoulos 1984; and Barnum and Squire 1978, 1979a, b) are econometric studies that specify separable models and that estimate commodity demands and either output supply and input demands or a production function. They are highly aggregative on the demand side and use one agricultural commodity produced and consumed by the household (our X_a), one nonagricultural commodity that can only be purchased (our X_m), and leisure (our X_l). Kuroda and Yotopoulos decompose leisure into leisure of family members who work on the farm and leisure of these working off the farm. Those working off the farm are therefore different people with different labor quality than those working on the farm. To make the model separable they also implicitly assume hired labor is used on the farm. All the studies provide more detail on the production side and thus allow for several variable and fixed inputs.

Lau, Lin, and Yotopoulos (1978) look at Taiwanese household data averaged by farm size and by region for each of two years. Kuroda and Yotopoulos (1978, 1980) use cross-sectional household data from Japan, also grouped by farm size and by region. Adulavidhaya and others (1979, 1984) use cross-sectional household data from Thailand, but the cross sections differ for the production and consumption sides of the model. This approach considers that the two sets of households behave identically and is possible only because the model is recursive. Otherwise, data on the same set of households would be necessary. Barnum and Squire (1978, 1979a, b) use cross-sectional household data from the Muda River Valley in Malaysia. Both the Malaysian and Thai households practice monoculture (rice cultivation), so that aggregation on the production side is not a problem. It was possible to estimate price elasticities for Taiwan, Japan, and Thailand because prices vary by region (and over time in Taiwan). In Malaysia only, wages vary. By making sufficiently strong assumptions about preferences, however, price elasticities could be calculated.

These four studies use the systems approach to estimate commodity demands. Lau, Lin, and Yotopoulos (1978), Kuroda and Yotopoulos (1980), and Adulavidhaya and others (1984) use the Linear Logarithmic Expenditure System (LLES), whereas Barnum and Squire (1979a, b) use a Linear Expenditure System (LES). The LLES is derived from a translog indirect utility function that is homogeneous of degree minus one in prices. This implies that every expenditure elasticity with respect to full income is one—which is a restrictive assumption, particularly if one specifies many commodities. That fact that LLES is linear in parameters, however, makes estimation simpler. The LES is derived from an additive utility function, the Stone-Geary. It has fewer parameters to estimate than an LLES, but is nonlinear in parameters. Since the system is additive, Engel curves must be linear and no Hicks-complementarity between commodities is allowed for. As is true for the LLES, these conditions become less restrictive when commodities are highly aggregated. According to Deaton (1978), however, additivity should be rejected even then.

In all of these studies, household characteristics such as total size and its distribution are regarded as fixed, but they do affect commodity demands. The effects of demographic variables on demand can be modeled in different ways. Lau, Lin, and Yotopoulos (1978), for example, enter household characteristics as separate arguments into the utility function. This implies that they will be independent variables in the expenditure as well as indirect utility functions. Barnum and Squire use linear translation (see Pollak and Wales 1981) to enter household characteristics. This involves subtracting commodity-specific indices from each commodity in the utility function—that is, $U(X_0 - \gamma_0, \ldots, X_n - \gamma_n)$, where the X_i's are consumption of commodity i, and the γ's are the translation parameters that depend linearly on household characteristics. The associated indirect utility function looks like $V(p, Y - \Sigma_{i=1}^{n} p_i \gamma_i)$. In other words, everywhere that full income, Y, appears, one subtracts the sum of the values of these commodity indices (the p_i's being prices). Consequently, in this specification, the effect of household characteristics comes through full income. Other specifications of household characteristics are possible and perhaps are preferable. (For an excellent review, see Pollak and Wales 1981.

When demographic variables are used, an LLES share equation is given by

$$-\frac{p_j X_j}{Y} = \alpha_j + \sum_{k=1}^{n} \beta_{jk} \ln \frac{p_j}{Y} + \sum_{l=1}^{r} \sigma_{jl} \ln a_l$$

$$\sum_{j=1}^{n} \alpha_j = -1; \quad \sum_{k=1}^{n} \beta_{jk} = 0, \forall_j; \quad \sum_{j=1}^{n} \sigma_{jl} = 0, \forall_l$$

where p_j, X_j, and Y are defined as before, a_l is the lth household characteristic, and the α's, β's, and σ's are parameters to be estimated. An LES expenditure equation with linear translating is given by

$$p_j X_j = p_j(\theta_j + \gamma_j) + \beta_j[Y - \sum_{i=1}^{n} p_i(\theta_i + \gamma_i)], \quad \sum_{j=1}^{n} \beta_j = 1.$$

Here the β's are the (constant) marginal budget shares, the θ's are parameters, and the γ's are the translation parameters that are a linear function of household characteristics, that is, $\gamma_i = \Sigma_{l=1}^{r} \sigma_{il} a_l$.

For the production side, Yotopoulos, Lau, and Lin (1976), Kuroda and Yotopoulos (1978), and Adulavidhaya and others (1979) estimate a profit function and associated input demand functions, which are derived from a Cobb-Douglas production function. Barnum and Squire (1978, 1979a) estimate a Cobb-Douglas production function directly since they do not have the necessary price data to estimate the dual functions.

Two other studies must be included here since they also estimate complete systems on both the demand and production sides. One, by Singh and Janakiram (see chapter 3), is based on Korean and Nigerian data, and the other, by Strauss (chapter 4), looks at data from Sierra Leone. Singh and Janakiram specify a linear expenditure system for the consumption side and use a linear program to model the production side; Strauss characterizes consumption behavior by a quadratic expenditure system and production behavior by a multiple output production function in which outputs are related by a constant elasticity of transformation and inputs by a Cobb-Douglas function.

As can be seen from table 1-1, the seven studies are nearly evenly split in their findings concerning the consumption of the agricultural commodity: four report a positive own-price elasticity and three a negative one. The magnitudes of both positive and negative elasticities are small. The positive response indicates that the profit effect has more than offset the traditional negative effect predicted by standard consumer-demand theory. For consumption of market-purchased goods, the most important result is the strongly positive cross-price elasticities. This result also attests to the strength of the profit effect in increasing total expenditure. The reported elasticities suggest that the level of farm incomes and the availability of nonfarm goods are important determinants of responsiveness. Sierra Leone, for example, has a much lower elasticity than the East Asian economies.

Elasticities of marketed surplus are strongly positive, whereas those for labor supply are negative. The positive elasticities of marketed surplus indicate that, even where the profit effect is strong enough to make consumption response positive, the total output response is always large enough to offset increased household consumption. The negative responses for labor supply suggest a strong profit effect and reflect the empirical fact that leisure is a normal good. (Other results are summarized in appendix tables 1A-1–1A-4.)

Table 1-1. *Selected Elasticities: Response to Changes in the Price of the Agricultural Commodity*

Economy	Agricultural commodity	Consumption of agricultural good	Consumption of market-purchased goods	Marketed surplus	Labor supply
Taiwan	Farm output	0.22	1.18	1.03	−1.54
Malaysia	Rice	0.38	1.94	0.66	−0.57
Korea, Rep. of	Rice	0.01	0.81	1.40	−0.13
Japan	Farm output	−0.35	0.61	2.97	−1.01
Thailand	Farm output	−0.37	0.51	8.10	−0.62
Sierra Leone	Rice	−0.66	0.14	0.71	−0.09
Northern Nigeria	Sorghum	0.19	0.57	0.20	−0.06

Do Agricultural Household Models Matter?

Agricultural household models integrate production and consumption decisions in rural farm households. As a result, they require a complex theoretical structure as well as a considerable amount of data for empirical estimation. The studies summarized here attest to the fact that, both theoretically and empirically, such models are difficult and costly to estimate. Is the effort justified? Can practitioners make do with far simpler techniques that have been traditionally used to model farm behavior— that is, with techniques that do not allow for even a recursive relation between the supply and demand sides? If our interest is empirical, we must ask whether agricultural household models, which account for the interdependence of production and consumption decisions, provide estimates of elasticities that are quite different from what could have been obtained otherwise. If we are interested in policy, we must ascertain whether the differences in these elasticity estimates have different policy implications from those that would have been arrived at by traditional methods. In this section we consider the empirical significance of agricultural household models.

As noted earlier, the distinctive feature of agricultural household models is that they include the profit effect (equation 1-7). When we compare elasticities with and without the profit effect (see table 1-2), the results clearly establish the empirical significance of agricultural household models. The estimates of the elasticity of demand with respect to

Table 1-2. *Selected Response Elasticities under Varying and Constant Profits*

Economy	Agricultural commodity		Nonagricultural commodity		Labor supply	
	A^a	B^b	A^a	B^b	A^a	B^b
With respect to agricultural price						
Taiwan	−0.72	0.22	0.13	1.18	0.21	−1.59
Malaysia	−0.04	0.38	−0.27	1.94	0.08	−0.57
Korea, Rep. of	−0.18	0.01	−0.19	0.81	0.03	−0.13
Japan	−0.87	−0.35	0.08	0.61	0.16	−1.00
Thailand	−0.82	−0.37	0.06	0.51	0.18	−0.62
Sierra Leone	−0.74	−0.66	−0.03	0.14	0.01	−0.09
Northern Nigeria	−0.05	0.19	−0.14	0.57	0.03	−0.06
With respect to wage rate						
Taiwan	0.14	−0.03	0.05	−0.12	−0.12	0.17
Malaysia	0.06	−0.08	0.29	−0.35	−0.07	0.11
Korea, Rep. of	0.16	0.01	0.77	0.05	0.00	0.11
Japan	0.29	0.15	0.39	0.25	0.15	0.45
Thailand	0.57	0.47 ·	0.62	0.52	0.08	0.26
Sierra Leone	0.47	0.37	0.78	0.57	0.14	0.26
Northern Nigeria	0.06	0.02	0.04	0.01	0.01	0.01

a. Holding profits constant.
b. Allowing profits to vary.

own-price not only differ significantly in the cases of Japan, Thailand, and Sierra Leone, for example, but they also change sign in the case of Taiwan, Malaysia, Korea, and northern Nigeria. Thus, whereas traditional models of demand, as we would expect, predict a decline in own-consumption in response to an increase in agricultural commodity prices, for four cases, the agricultural household models predict an increase. This is because the profit effect—which is the result of the increase in income when crop prices are raised—offsets the negative price effects. Farm households end up increasing their own consumption as prices are raised. Whether or not the amounts they offer on the market will be reduced will depend on the elasticity of output, which we know remains positive in these cases (see table 1-1). The marketed surplus response, however, is dampened by the profit effect.

The differences in the elasticity of demand for nonagricultural goods with respect to the price of agricultural goods are also striking. The elasticities change sign in four cases, and in the other three cases the magnitudes are much larger when the profit effect is included. Whereas cross-price elasticities estimated using traditional demand models tend to be low or negative because of negative income effects, the estimates obtained with the agricultural household model are positive and large because of the positive profit effect. The elasticities of household labor supply with respect to the price of the agricultural good also differ greatly. In the traditional demand models, an increase in the price of the agricultural good reduces the consumption of both that good and leisure, and thus implies an increase in the family work effort (table 1-2). In contrast, agricultural household models predict a negative response of household labor supply to increased output prices because households are willing to take a part of their increased incomes in increased leisure, thereby reducing their work effort. Consequently, any increase in the demand for labor in agricultural production will have considerable spillover effect on the demand for hired labor.

Although fewer signs change when responses to agricultural wage rates are examined, the magnitudes change. In traditional demand models, an increase in the wage rate implies an increase in real household incomes, which induces a positive-demand response with respect to agricultural and nonagricultural goods and a negative or inelastic response where household labor supply is concerned. In agricultural household models these effects are partly offset because an increase in wages also affects the production side and reduces total farm incomes. As a result, demand responses for both agricultural and nonagricultural goods are either dampened or totally offset (as in Taiwan and Malaysia), and labor supply response becomes positive or more elastic.

Looking at the market (or off-farm) labor-supply responses of landed and landless households in rural India, Rosenzweig (1980) provides a different type of evidence that agricultural household models matter. After separately estimating reduced-form market-supply equations for landless and agricultural households, Rosenzweig compares coefficients between the two groups and finds that twenty-one out of twenty-two comparisons conform to the predictions of the agricultural household framework. For instance, the off-farm male labor response of landless households to increases in the market male wage is less than for agricultural households, as would be predicted because of the negative profit effect of raising male wages.

Furthermore, agricultural household models provide other elasticities that are not even defined for models that focus exclusively on consumption behavior. These are the elasticities of demand with respect to nonlabor input prices and stocks of fixed factors of production, including land and farm technology (see table 1-3). Although the absolute magnitudes are small in most cases, the important point is that they have no counterpart in models that do not integrate production and consumption. Thus, despite the fact that traditional demand models can predict demand responses to output prices, they tell us nothing about such responses to changes in the fixed factors of product or technology. Similarly, traditional supply models can predict supply responses to changes in output

Table 1-3. *Selected Response Elasticities with Respect to Variable Input Prices and Fixed Factors*

Economy	Agricultural commodity	Nonagricultural commodity	Marketed surplus	Labor supply
With respect to fertilizer price[a]				
Taiwan	−0.11	−0.11	−0.24	0.18
Malaysia	−0.03	−0.18	−0.15	0.05
Korea, Rep. of	−0.05	−0.23	−0.34	0.04
Japan	−0.03	−0.03	−0.09	0.07
Thailand	−0.03	−0.03	−0.41	0.05
With respect to land				
Taiwan	0.46	0.46	1.00	−0.77
Malaysia	0.26	1.37	1.15	−0.41
Korea, Rep. of	0.10	0.49	0.81	−0.08
Japan	0.19	0.19	0.96	−0.43
Thailand	0.11	0.11	1.48	−0.19
Sierra Leone	0.01	0.02	0.02	−0.01
Northern Nigeria	0.10	0.16	0.06	−0.08

a. Fertilizer is barely used in the Sierra Leone and northern Nigeria samples and therefore was not modeled.

and input prices or in fixed factors of production and technology, but they fail to tell us anything about the demand responses to these exogenous factors. Agricultural household models therefore provide a vital link between the demand and supply-side responses to exogenous policy changes. Although these links can be established informally between traditional supply-and-demand models, in agricultural household models they are handled directly within a consistent theory and framework of estimation.

When should a full agricultural household model be used? The answer is that, since the profit effect is its distinguishing feature, such a model is appropriate when the profit effect is likely to be important. Notice, however, that changes in some exogenous prices have a small effect on farm profits. The profit effect is much more important in Malaysia than in Sierra Leone (table 1-6), for example, partly because the effect of a price change on profits is much larger in Malaysia, where a 10 percent increase in output price results in a 16 percent increase in profits. In Sierra Leone, the same percentage increase in output price increases profits by only 2 percent.

Second, even if profits are affected by an exogenous price increase, they may be only a small part of full income (equation 1-2), and it is full income that appears in the demand equations. For our sample of economies, the share of profits in full income ranges from 0.5 in Malaysia to only 0.2 in Thailand. It follows that a given percentage increase in profits will have a much greater impact on total income in Malaysia than in Thailand.

Finally, the effect of full income on demand varies among commodities. It is much more important in the case of nonagricultural commodities than agricultural ones, for example, since the demand for agricultural commodities tends to be inelastic with respect to income. In Malaysia, the elasticity of demand for rice with respect to full income is only 0.52 compared with 2.74 for market-purchased goods. As a result, the profit effect is much more significant in the case of nonagricultural goods (table 1-6).

These remarks suggest that, if profits are relatively insensitive to producer prices and constitute a relatively small part of full income and if consumption of a particular item is relatively insensitive to full income, then an agricultural household model will not necessarily make our analysis more accurate. This proves to be the case, for example, with the elasticity of demand for agricultural goods with respect to changes in producer prices in Sierra Leone, although it is not true for low-income households in that study (see chapter 4). If these three conditions are reversed, however, a full agricultural household model is of critical importance, as the elasticity of demand for nonagricultural goods with respect to producer prices in Malaysia reveals.

Policy Results

Agricultural household models provide insight into three broad areas of interest to policymakers: the welfare or real incomes of agricultural households; the spillover effects of agricultural policies onto the rural, nonagricultural economy; and, at a more aggregate level, the interaction between agricultural policy and international trade or fiscal policy. The potential role of agricultural household models in this respect becomes evident when we look at these three dimensions in a "typical" agricultural policy such as taxing output (either through export taxes or marketing boards) in order to generate revenue for the central exchequer and simultaneously subsidizing a significant input (usually fertilizer) to restore, at least in part, producer incentives. The model could just as easily be applied to other policies, but this particular combination has been adopted by many developing countries and illustrates well the type of issue that can be analyzed within the framework of the agricultural household model.

Consider, first, the effect of pricing policy on the welfare or real full income of a representative agricultural household. For some price changes—for example, a change in the price of fertilizer—the resulting change in nominal full income is an accurate measure of the change in real income since the prices of all consumer goods have remained unchanged. In other cases, however, the commodity in question may be both a consumer good and a farm output or input. If the price of, say, an agricultural staple is increased, the household will benefit as a producer but lose as a consumer. As long as the household is a net producer of the commodity, its net benefit will be positive (see the appendix to part I). Nevertheless, to quantify the net gain to the household, one must allow for both the positive effect coming through farm profits and the negative effect coming through an increase in the price of an important consumer good.

Table 1-4 presents estimates of the elasticities of real full income with respect to changes in output price and fertilizer price for the six studies examined earlier. For marginal changes, the decrease in real income following an increase in the price of the agricultural output equals marketed surplus times the price increase, and the increase following a reduction in the price of an input equals the quantity of the input times the price reduction. Thus, if prices, marketed surplus, and full income are known, these elasticities can be calculated without reference to price and income elasticities. For nonmarginal changes, however, it would be necessary to

Table 1-4. *Effect on Real Income of Changes in Output and Fertilizer Prices*

Economy	Response to output price	Response to fertilizer price
Taiwan	0.90	−0.11
Malaysia	0.67	−0.07
Korea, Rep. of	0.40	−0.10
Japan	0.34	−0.03
Thailand	0.10	−0.03
Sierra Leone	0.09	—
Northern Nigeria	0.12	—

— Not applicable. Fertilizer is barely used in the Sierra Leone and northern Nigeria samples and therefore was not modeled.

use information on the underlying structure of preferences to calculate equivalent or compensating variation.

The percentage change in real income among the six countries under consideration is less than the percentage change in either the output price or the fertilizer price (table 1-4). In addition, it appears that the loss in real income arising from a given percentage reduction in the output price can be offset only if the price of fertilizer is reduced by a much larger percentage. In Malaysia, for example, a 10 percent reduction in output price would reduce real income by almost 7 percent, whereas a 10 percent reduction in the price of fertilizer would increase real income by only about 1 percent. This difference arises from the relative magnitudes of marketed surplus and fertilizer use. Thus, if policymakers are interested primarily in the welfare of agricultural households, intervention in output markets is likely to be much more important than intervention in the markets for variable, nonlabor inputs.

Policymakers are also concerned with the welfare of rural households that do not own or rent land for cultivation. Landless households either sell their labor to land-operating households or else engage in nonfarm activities (see, for example, Anderson and Leiserson 1980). Although governments have few policy instruments by which to improve the welfare of these households directly, price interventions and investment programs directed at land-operating households have spillover effects that may (or may not) be beneficial for these households. What can agricultural household models tell us about these effects?

An increase in the price of an important agricultural staple will obviously hurt households that are net consumers of that item. The direct effect of a price increase will therefore be unambiguously negative for landless households and nonfarm households. The policymaker thus faces a dilemma: if he wants to improve incentives and increase the incomes of agricultural households, he does so at the expense of other rural households. There are, however, offsetting indirect effects. If the price of the agricultural commodity is increased, for example, agricultural households increase their demand for total—hired and family—farm labor and reduce the supply of family labor; that is, they increase their leisure time (see table 1-5). As a result, the demand for hired labor can be expected to increase substantially to the benefit of landless households. In Malaysia, the reported elasticities of labor demand (1.61) and labor supply (0.57) imply an elasticity of demand for hired labor of 10.9. Although this figure in part reflects the initial small percentage of hired labor in total labor (19 percent), it nevertheless implies a substantial change in labor market conditions and would undoubtedly exert upward pressure on rural wage rates and would thereby offset, at least to some extent, the negative consequences, among landless households, of higher prices for agricultural commodities.

The policy implications of these findings are particularly significant because they also shed light on the extent to which the positive gains from technological improvements trickle down via the labor market to the rural landless. It is now widely accepted that the technological innovations associated with the green revolution (improved seeds, increased use of fertilizers and pesticides, increased irrigation and cropping intensity) have

Table 1-5. *Spillover Effects of Changes in Output and Fertilizer Price*

Economy	Labor demand	Labor supply	Consumption of nonagricultural goods
Output price			
Taiwan	2.25	−1.54	1.18
Malaysia	1.61	−0.57	1.94
Korea, Rep. of	0.57	−0.13	0.81
Japan	1.98	−1.01	0.61
Thailand	1.90	−0.62	0.51
Sierra Leone	0.14	−0.09	0.14
Northern Nigeria	0.12	−0.06	0.23
Fertilizer price[a]			
Taiwan	−0.23	0.18	−0.22
Malaysia	−0.12	0.05	−0.18
Korea, Rep. of	−0.12	0.04	−0.23
Japan	−0.13	0.07	−0.03
Thailand	−0.11	0.05	−0.03

a. Fertilizer is barely used in the Sierra Leone and northern Nigeria samples and therefore was not modeled.

had a great deal to do with increasing the demand for total labor, but the concern has been whether this increased demand would do much for hired labor, most of which comes from the smallest farms and the landless. The empirical findings show that it could. When an increase, either in the fixed factors of production or technologies, boosts farm incomes, the amount of family (household's own) labor effort tends to decline (see table 1-7). Therefore any increase in the demand for total labor means an even larger increase in the demand for hired labor. The labor supply-and-demand elasticities emerging from empirical applications of agricultural household models provide strong support for the view that trickle-down effects are both positive and significant.

A second indirect effect of increased output prices is a significant increase in the demand for nonagricultural goods (see table 1-5). The response elasticity is positive and greater than 1 in two economies (Taiwan and Malaysia) and is positive and greater than 0.5 in all economies except Sierra Leone, though for low-income households in Sierra Leone it is also high (0.9). Some of this demand will be for imports and urban-produced commodities. But a large part will be for rurally produced goods and services and will therefore increase demand for the output of nonfarm, rural households. Any increase in farm profits, whether caused by a price change or a technological improvement, can be expected to lead to a substantial increase in the demand for goods and services produced by nonagricultural households. Thus, spillover effects through output markets will, at least in part, offset the negative effects on nonfarm households of an increase in agricultural prices and will ensure that the benefits of technological improvements are dispensed throughout the rural community.

Table 1-5 also traces through the effects of a change in the price of fertilizer. The results suggest that changes in fertilizer prices can be made without generating large negative or positive spillover effects.

As mentioned earlier, governments often tax agricultural output in order to generate revenue and at the same time subsidize essential inputs such as fertilizer in order to restore production incentives. In this way, they hope to achieve self-sufficiency or earn foreign exchange. Can agricultural household models shed light on these and other policy options? Indeed, the information they provide with respect to the effect of pricing policy on marketed surplus and fertilizer demand can be used as inputs in calculations of self-sufficiency, balance of payment effects, and budgetary effects.

If a government's primary concern is self-sufficiency, it needs to know the marketed surplus available for procurement. When we look at the elasticity estimates for agricultural production, consumption, and marketed surplus (table 1-6), two points become clear. First, even where con-

Table 1-6. *Response of Output, Consumption, Marketed Surplus, and Input Demand to Price Changes*

Economy	Agricultural output	Agricultural consumption	Marketed surplus	Fertilizer demand
Output price				
Taiwan	1.25	0.22	1.03	2.25
Malaysia	0.61	0.38	0.66	1.61
Korea, Rep. of	1.56	0.01	1.40	1.29
Japan	0.98	−0.35	2.97	1.98
Thailand	0.90	−0.37	8.10	1.90
Sierra Leone	0.11	−0.66	0.71	—
Northern Nigeria	0.30	0.19	0.20	—
Fertilizer price[a]				
Taiwan	−0.23	−0.11	−0.23	−1.23
Malaysia	−0.13	−0.03	−0.15	−1.13
Korea, Rep. of	−0.30	−0.05	−0.34	−1.10
Japan	−0.13	−0.03	−0.09	−1.13
Thailand	−0.11	−0.03	−0.41	−1.11

— Not applicable.

a. Fertilizer is barely used in the Sierra Leone and northern Nigeria samples and therefore was not modeled.

sumption responds positively to an increase in the price of the agricultural commodity because of the profit effect, marketed surplus still responds positively. Where the consumption response is negative, the elasticities of marketed surplus are positive and large (see, for example, the case of Thailand). Governments can therefore use pricing policy in the output market to increase the marketed surplus even when it is unable to set consumer and producer prices independently. Second, efforts to offset disincentives in output markets through fertilizer subsidies will not be effective unless the fertilizer price is reduced by a much greater percentage than the output price.

Rough estimates of the effect of pricing policies on budget revenues and foreign exchange can also be derived from table 1-6. Assume, for example, that the output is exported and that the fertilizer is imported. According to table 1-10, an increase in output price will induce an increase in marketed surplus available for export, but only at the expense of increased use of fertilizer. The net foreign exchange effect, therefore, is given by the difference between the revenues from exporting the agricultural output and the costs of importing additional fertilizer. Similarly, if the output is taxed and fertilizer is subsidized, one can perform a similar calculation to arrive at a rough estimate of the net impact on the budget. In fact, the framework of the agricultural household model is highly flexible and can be adapted to fit many other circumstances and issues. One of the purposes of this volume is to present some of the extensions that have recently been tested (see chapters 3, 4, 5, 6, and 7).

Some Extensions

Most of the early work on agricultural household models ignored questions of choice among competing crops. These studies either examined monocultures or else treated farm output as an aggregate. Several important policy issues, however, are concerned with the *choice among alternative crops*. Many governments, for example, are concerned with the effect of export taxation on production when export crops compete with food crops destined for the domestic market. Similarly, if fertilizer intensity varies among crops, price-induced changes in the composition of output may have significant effects on the demand for fertilizer. The demand for hired labor can also be influenced by changes in crop composition.

The basic agricultural household model can be modified easily to accommodate multiple crops. Thus a production function for a single crop can be replaced with an implicit production function linking inputs and outputs:

$$G(Q_1, \ldots Q_n, V_1, \ldots V_m, A_1, \ldots A_k) = 0$$

where Q represents output, V is variable inputs, and A is fixed factors. Provided the household is a price-taker in the relevant markets, the introduction of multiple outputs does not affect the recursive property of the model. Two of the studies covered in this volume—those by Singh and Janakiram and by Strauss—allow specifically for multiple crops.

This is an important policy extension since pricing policies are often oriented around specific commodities, but other crops will likely be affected as well. These studies cover three countries: the Republic of Korea, Nigeria, and Sierra Leone, and in each case cover crops grown primarily for consumption, for sale, and crops both consumed and exchanged. The countries cover three dissimilar environments. In Korea, farm households are well integrated into product and factor markets. Crops are grown under irrigated conditions and in single stands. Considerable technological advance has occurred in rice production, with a consequent high-level use of purchased inputs. In addition, there are many sources for nonfarm incomes. Households in Sierra Leone are also fairly well integrated into product and labor markets, but the level of income is far lower than for Korean households. There has been little technological change in paddy rice (or other crop) production so there is little use for nonpurchased inputs. Irrigation is nonexistent and crops are grown in mixtures. Households in the state of Kaduna in northern Nigeria are far more isolated from factor and product markets. Production is mostly for subsistence, and intercropping is widespread. Northern Nigeria is also a semiarid area, in contrast to Korea and Sierra Leone, so production risk is important (see chapter 9).

Table 1-7 reports own- and cross-price elasticities both for output supplies and marketed surpluses for households in the three countries. In all cases, the cross-price elasticities of output supply are very small, despite the crop disaggregation. For these studies, then, the need for comprehensive pricing policies is not evident. Korean households show a far greater own price output responsiveness than their northern Nigerian or Sierra Leone counterparts, which may be partly explained by the higher level of infrastructural development and the greater market integration in Korea.

The cross-price responses of marketed surpluses are small for the Sierra Leone case, but not negligible, and they are miniscule for the Korean and northern Nigerian samples. This reflects the very small cross-price elasticities both of output supply and commodity demands in the latter two studies. Again, the overwhelming impact of a commodity pricing policy is predicted by these studies to be on that commodity, without large spillover effects. It was necessary to disaggregate commodities in order to reach such a conclusion.

Table 1-7. *Cross-Price Elasticities of Supply and Marketed Surplus*

Economy	With respect to price of	Supply			Marketed surplus		
Korea,		*Rice*	*Barley*	*Soybeans*	*Rice*	*Barley*	*Soybeans*
Rep. of	Rice	1.56	−0.00[a]	0.00[a]	1.4	−0.00[a]	−0.00[a]
	Barley	−0.00[a]	0.50	−0.00[a]	−0.00[a]	0.50	−0.00[a]
	Soybeans	0.04	−0.10	−0.10	−0.03	−0.15	0.06
Nigeria		*Sorghum*	*Millet*	*Groundnuts*	*Sorghum*	*Millet*	*Groundnuts*
	Sorghum	0.30	−0.00[a]	−0.20	0.25	−0.00[a]	0.04
	Millet	−0.00[a]	0.25	−0.05	−0.00[a]	0.18	−0.07
	Groundnuts	−0.00[a]	−0.00[a]	0.18	−0.00[a]	−0.00[a]	0.09
Sierra Leone		*Rice*	*Rootcrops*	*Oil palm*	*Rice*	*Rootcrops*	*Oil palm*
	Rice	0.11	0.01	0.00[a]	0.71	0.06	−0.03
	Root crops and other cereals	0.02	0.10	0.00[a]	−0.08	0.46	−0.29
	Oil palm products	0.00[a]	0.00[a]	0.02	−0.05	−0.02	0.44

a. Insignificantly small.

Commodity disaggregation may also be important if calorie content varies among commodities and if governments are interested in the *nutritional status* of agricultural households. Strauss (chapter 4) shows how the basic model can be elaborated to investigate the effect of pricing policy on caloric intake. In his model, the utility function (see equation 1-1) becomes

$$U = U(X)$$

where X is a vector of consumer goods, including food items, nonfood items, and leisure. Caloric intake (K) can then be calculated from

$$K = \sum_i a_i X_i \qquad\qquad i = 1 \cdots m$$

where a_i is the calorie content of a unit of the ith food and $X_i, i = 1 \cdots m$ are quantities of different food items.

With this extension, Strauss demonstrates that price changes exert a considerable effect on caloric intake and that the profit effect plays a significant role. One might expect that an increase in the price of an important food item would probably have a negative impact on caloric intake. According to table 1-8, however, in most cases, an increased price results in increased caloric intake because of an increase in profits. That is to say, even if the consumption of such a commodity declines, the extra profits can be used to purchase increased quantities of other foodstuffs, with the result that overall caloric intake will respond positively. Strauss is also able to demonstrate an important point regarding the distribution of calories among income groups in Sierra Leone: even if a price increase causes a reduction in the caloric intake of middle-income and high-income households (see the case of rice in table 1-8), the intake of low-income households is increased. This suggests that, if policymakers are concerned primarily with the nutritional status of low-income households, price increases for major food items may prove to be beneficial. Increases in the prices of food items toward, say, world prices may improve the nutri-

Table 1-8. *Response of Caloric Intake to Price Changes in Sierra Leone*

Food	Elasticity of caloric intake		
	Low income	Middle income	High income
Rice	0.19	−0.24	−0.20
Root crops and other cereals	0.43	0.13	0.11
Oils and fats	0.27	−0.03	−0.21
Fish and animal products	0.48	0.23	0.05
Miscellaneous foods	0.14	0.01	−0.01

tional status of low-income households and provide appropriate signals for resource allocation. The usual equity-growth tradeoff may be absent in this case.

Policymakers are interested in nutritional status presumably because it affects health and may also affect productivity at the individual level. Pitt and Rosenzweig (chapter 5) take the analysis one step further, therefore, and examine the interaction between *prices, health, and farm profits* in the context of an agricultural household model. To do so, they incorporate a health variable directly in the utility function (people prefer to be healthy) and in the production function (a healthy individual is more productive). To complete their model, they introduce a production function for health:

$$H = H(X_a, X_m, X_l, Z)$$

which says that health (*H*) depends on consumption (X_a and X_m) and hence on nutrition, leisure (or work effort, X_l), and a vector (Z) of other factors that affect health, some of which are chosen by the household (boiling water) and some of which are community-level services (well water).

When this model is applied to data from Indonesia, it is found that a 10 percent increase in the consumption of fish, fruit, and vegetables reduces the probability of illness by 9, 3, and 6 percent, respectively, whereas a 10 percent increase in the consumption of sugar increases the probability of illness by almost 12 percent. These results suggest that increases in consumption cannot automatically be assumed to contribute to health since the composition of consumption may also change in a manner detrimental to health.

In addition to estimating the health production function, Pitt and Rosenzweig also estimate a reduced-form equation that produces a direct link between prices and health. They show that a 10 percent reduction in the prices of vegetables and vegetable oil will decrease the probability of the household head being ill by 4 and 9 percent, respectively, whereas the same percentage reduction in the prices of grains and sugar will increase the probability of illness by 15 and 20 percent, respectively, albeit from a very low base. These results are calculated with profits held constant, however. In principle, when profits are allowed to vary, some of these results may be modified. In this particular application the coefficient on farm profits proved statistically insignificant. The results reported above are therefore reasonably accurate measures of the total effect of price changes on health.

Changes in health may also affect productivity and farm profits. Pitt and Rosenzweig demonstrate for their sample, however, that the effects of ill-health on labor supply are not reflected in reduced farm profits when households have recourse to an active labor market. Thus, although family labor supply is significantly reduced by illness, total labor input, and hence farm profits, remain unaffected. In other words, in this Indonesian sample the benefits of improved health (or the costs of a deterioration in health) in agricultural households will be reflected in household income— if at all—only through labor-market supply.

Most of the policy issues mentioned thus far have been static in nature and have been couched in a single-period framework. Iqbal's work (chapter 6) represents a significant departure from previous studies in that it introduces another period to accommodate *borrowing, saving, and investment* decisions. Since governments and multinational agencies devote substantial quantities of funds to rural credit programs, this particular extension makes it possible to apply agricultural household models to a new set of policy issues of considerable importance in many countries.

In the first period of Iqbal's two-period model, the household may borrow and invest in farm improvements. In the second period, the loan must be repaid with interest and the household enjoys higher farm profits as a result of its investment in period one. Accordingly, the single full-income constraint is replaced by two full-income constraints, one for each period:

$$\Pi(K_1) + w_1 T_1 + B = C_1 + I$$

and

$$\Pi(K_1 + I) + w_2 T_2 = C_2 + B(1 + r[B])$$

where K_1 is capital in period one and I is investment, so that $K_1 + I$ is capital in period two. B is borrowing in period one and $B(1 + r[B])$ is repayment in period two. C is the value of consumption of goods and leisure. Iqbal draws a parallel between his treatment of household savings and borrowing and the treatment of own-consumption and marketed surplus or family labor supply and hired labor in the standard agricultural household model. He notes that the recursive property of the standard model carries over to his two-period extension, provided the household can borrow at a fixed rate of interest. In his application to Indian households, Iqbal argues that the interest rate is influenced by household borrowing decisions (r is a function of B in the second-period constraint) and therefore he adopts a nonrecursive specification.

Iqbal finds that borrowing is significantly reduced by increases in the interest rate, the elasticity being -1.2. His results support the view that interest rate policy can have a marked effect on the level of debt held by farmers. Iqbal also shows that farmers owning more than three hectares are highly sensitive to the interest rate, whereas the coefficient on borrowing by farmers owning less than three hectares is statistically insignificant. It follows that the elimination or reduction of subsidies to programs providing agricultural credit may serve the dual purpose of increasing efficiency in the capital market and simultaneously improving equity, since the reduction in borrowing by "large" farmers will exceed that by "small" ones.

As noted earlier, governments are also interested in the effects of agricultural pricing policy on more aggregate economic variables such as *budget deficits and foreign exchange earnings*. In Senegal, for example, agricultural products generate 70 percent of total export earnings, and deficits arising from the government's policy on agricultural pricing amount to more than 20 percent of government expenditure and 2 percent of GDP. Changes in agricultural prices can therefore be expected to have a considerable impact on these aggregates. Indeed, concern with the existing levels of foreign exchange earnings and a budget deficit may be the primary motivation for changing pricing policy in many countries. The government of Senegal has explored a number of ways, including pricing policy, to promote the production and consumption of millet in order to reduce imports of rice and hence improve the country's balance of payments.

The effect of pricing policy on foreign exchange and budget revenues discussed earlier in the chapter is further illuminated by Braverman and Hammer (chapter 8) through their addition of market-clearing conditions (for the major outputs and inputs) to the basic model. The changes in consumption, production, or labor supply at the household level following any change in an exogenous variable can then be aggregated and fed into the market-clearing equations. In some cases, the market is cleared through adjustments in international trade, and prices remain fixed at levels determined by the government, that is,

$$Q(\bar{p}_a) = X_a(\bar{p}_a) + E$$

where E represents net exports. In this event, a change in production or consumption has an immediate effect on foreign exchange earnings. Alternatively, the market may clear through adjustments in price, that is,

$$Q(p_a) = X_a(p_a).$$

Now a policy-induced change in production or consumption will bring about a change in price, which will generate second-round effects on production and consumption.

In their application to Senegal, Braverman and Hammer assume the first form of marketing clearing (quantity adjustment) for cotton, groundnuts, and rice and the second form (price adjustment) for maize and millet. The second-round effects flowing from induced changes in the prices of maize and millet are captured fully in their model. Table 1-9 provides a sample of their policy results. Compare, first, the effect of reducing the price of groundnuts or increasing the price of fertilizer on the deficit arising from the government's agricultural pricing policy. Both policies reduce the deficit. The reduction in the price of groundnuts, however, has a relatively small effect on net foreign exchange earnings (mainly because a reduction in rice imports offsets reduced exports), although it reduces the real incomes of farmers in the groundnut basin by almost 6 percent. Although an increase in the price of fertilizer causes a larger fall in net export earnings (in reflection of the fertilizer intensity of export crops), farm incomes are reduced by only 1 percent. This example illustrates the policy tradeoffs that can be explored within the framework of Braverman and Hammer's extension. It also confirms a point made earlier—that to be effective, changes in the prices of inputs such as fertilizer must be much larger than changes in the prices of the main outputs.

Another important point regarding the formulation of policy in Senegal is that the government has been eager to reduce imports of rice and hence save foreign exchange by increasing domestic production of rice and increasing consumption of domestic substitutes such as millet. How can this goal be achieved? One possibility is to increase the producers' price of rice. Such a measure does indeed reduce rice imports (by 7 percent), but net foreign exchange earnings fall (by 4.5 percent), because in order to increase rice production, farmers switch out of export crops (see table 1-9). The desired result, an increase in net foreign exchange earnings, fails to materialize because of substitution possibilities in production. In this case, failure to recognize substitution possibilities produces a

Table 1-9. *Effect of Agricultural Pricing Policy in Senegal*
(percentage change)

Policy	Real income, groundnut basin	Export earnings	Government deficit
15 percent decrease in producer price of groundnuts	−5.7	−1.9	−18.1
100 percent increase in price of fertilizer	−1.1	−5.2	−10.4
50 percent increase in producer price of rice	0.2	−4.5	−0.1
50 percent increase in consumer price of rice	−4.7	−0.2	−34.8

perverse result. In other situations, however, policy may be designed to take advantage of substitution possibilities. The government might increase the consumer price of rice in the hope that people would change their pattern of consumption in favor of millet. According to Braverman and Hammer's analysis, however, such a policy would have little impact on net export earnings, so that in this case a reliance on substitution possibilities would have been misplaced (see table 1-9).

These examples from the work of Braverman and Hammer illustrate the importance of placing agricultural household models in a multimarket framework, particularly where foreign exchange earnings and government revenues are of concern. Because the expansion of one crop is usually detrimental to another crop, changes in the quantities of internationally traded items and in the quantities of taxed or subsidized items will influence the overall impact of policy on foreign exchange and government revenue even if a change in a government-controlled price in one market leaves the prices in all other agricultural markets unchanged. More generally, changes in government-controlled prices will induce changes in other prices so that even measures of output response, labor supply response, consumer response, and changes in farm profits will have to allow for general equilibrium effects (see chapter 2). Thus the multimarket extension may well emerge as the most useful vehicle for generating relevant policy results from agricultural household models.

Appendix: Detailed Elasticities from Studies of Agricultural Household Models

The four tables in this appendix are on the following pages.

Table 1A-1. Elasticities of Agricultural Commodity Consumption

Economy	Commodity	Total expenditure	Commodity price				Fixed factors				Scale technology factor
			Own	Nonfarm	Wage	Fertilizer price	Workers	Dependents	Land	Capital	
Taiwan	Farm goods	n.a.	0.22	0.29	−0.03	−0.11	0.84	0.43	0.46	0.04	n.a.
Malaysia	Rice	n.a.	0.38	−0.15	−0.08	−0.03	0.44	0.23	0.26	n.a.	0.42
Japan	Farm goods	n.a.	−0.35	0.31	0.15[a]	−0.03	0.07[b]	0.14	0.19	0.07[c]	n.a.
Thailand	Farm goods	n.a.	−0.37	0.05	0.47	−0.03[d]	0.70	−0.16	0.11	0.10	n.a.
Korea, Rep. of	Rice	0.57	0.01	n.a.	0.01	−0.05	n.a.	n.a.	0.10[e]	n.a.	0.002[f]
Sierra Leone	Rice	0.52	−0.66	0.13	0.37	—	0.26[g]	0.13[h]	0.01	0.04	0.11
Northern Nigeria	Sorghum	1.80	0.19	n.a.	0.02	—	n.a.	n.a.	n.a.	n.a.	n.a.

n.a. Not available.

— Not applicable. Fertilizer was barely used by the Sierra Leone and northern Nigeria samples and therefore was not modeled.

a. Farm wages.

b. On-farm workers.

c. Machinery.

d. Price index of fertilizer, seed, and chemicals.

e. Average farm size.

f. With respect to increased tiller capacity.

g. Males 15 years and older.

h. Children 10 years and younger.

43

Table 1A-2. *Elasticities of Nonagricultural Commodity Consumption*

Economy	Total expenditure	Commodity prices				Fixed factors				
		Own	Agricultural commodity	Wage	Fertilizer price	Workers	Dependents	Land	Capital	Scale technology factor
Taiwan	n.a.	−0.58	1.18	−0.12	−0.11	0.84	0.0	0.46	0.04	n.a.
Malaysia	n.a.	−0.77	1.94[a]	−0.35	−0.18	−0.06	−0.05	1.37	n.a.	2.21
Japan	n.a.	−0.97	0.61	0.25[b]	−0.03	−0.12[c]	0.02	0.19	0.07[d]	n.a.
Thailand	n.a.	−0.89	0.51	0.52	−0.03[e]	0.69	−0.29	0.11	0.10	n.a.
Korea, Rep. of	2.76	−0.87	0.81[a]	0.05	−0.23	n.a.	n.a.	0.49[f]	n.a.	0.01[g]
Sierra Leone	1.18	−0.93	0.14[a]	0.57	n.a.	0.41[h]	0.09[i]	0.02	0.10	0.27
Northern Nigeria	3.30	n.a.	0.57[j]	0.01	n.a.	n.a.	n.a.	n.a.	n.a.	n.a.

n.a. Not available.
a. Price of rice.
b. Farm wage.
c. On-farm workers.
d. Machinery.
e. Price index of fertilizer, seed, and chemicals.
f. Average farm size.
g. With respect to tiller capacity.
h. Males 15 and older.
i. Children 10 and younger.
j. With respect to sorghum price.

44

Table 1A-3. *Elasticities of Agricultural Commodity-Marketed Surplus*

| Economy | Commodity | Commodity prices | | Wage | Fertilizer price | Fixed factors | | | | Scale technology factor |
		Own	Nonfarm			Workers	Dependents	Land	Capital	
Taiwan	Farm goods	1.03	-0.05	-0.95	-0.24	-0.13	-0.07	1.00	0.08	n.a.
Malaysia	Rice	0.66	n.a.	-0.55	-0.15	0.09	-0.50	1.15	n.a.	1.85
Japan	Farm goods	2.97	-0.13	-0.77[a]	-0.09	-0.03[b]	-0.06	0.96	0.37[c]	n.a.
Thailand	Farm goods	8.10	-0.12	-3.62	-0.41[d]	-1.72	0.39	1.48	1.44	n.a.
Korea, Rep. of	Rice	1.40	n.a.	n.a.	-0.34	n.a.	n.a.	0.81	n.a.	n.a.
Sierra Leone	Rice	0.71	-0.12	-0.49	n.a.	-0.21[e]	-0.12[f]	0.02	0.11	0.32
Northern Nigeria	Sorghum	0.20	n.a.	n.a.	n.a.	n.a.	n.a.	0.06	n.a.	n.a.

n.a. Not available.
a. Farm wage.
b. On-farm workers.
c. Machinery.
d. Price index of fertilizer, seed, and chemicals.
e. Males 15 and older.
f. Children 10 and younger.

Table 1A-4. Elasticities of Labor Supply

Economy	Type of labor	Commodity prices					Fixed factors				
		Agricultural commodity	Nonfarm commodity	Farm wage	Off-farm wage	Fertilizer price	Workers	Dependents	Land	Capital	Scale technology factor
Taiwan	Total	-1.54	0.58	0.17	n.a.	0.18	1.27	0.20	-0.77	-0.06	n.a.
Malaysia	Total	-0.57[a]	0.24	0.11	n.a.	0.05	0.62	0.12	-0.41	n.a.	-0.65
Japan	Farm	-1.01	0.30	0.45	-1.97	0.07	-0.89[h]	0.34	-0.43	-0.17[c]	n.a.
Thailand	Total	-0.62	0.10	0.26	n.a.	0.05[d]	0.94	-0.28	-0.19	-0.19	n.a.
Korea, Rep. of	Total	-0.13[a]	n.a.	0.11	n.a.	0.04	n.a.	n.a.	-0.08[c]	n.a.	-0.002[f]
Sierra Leone	Total	-0.09[a]	-0.05	0.26	n.a.	n.a.	0.55[g]	0.13[h]	-0.01	-0.05	n.a.
Sierra Leone	Off-farm	-4.42[c]	-1.85	17.18	n.a.	n.a.	14.36[g]	3.78[h]	-0.94	-4.90	n.a.
Northern Nigeria	Total	-0.06	n.a.	0.10	n.a.	n.a.	n.a.	n.a.	n.a.	n.a.	n.a.

n.a. Not available.

a. Price of rice.

b. On-farm workers.

c. Machinery.

d. Price index of fertilizer, seed, and chemicals.

e. Average farm size.

f. With respect to tiller capacity.

g. Males 15 and older.

h. Children 10 and younger.

References

Adulavidhaya, Kamphol, Yoshimi Kuroda, Lawrence Lau, Pichit Lerttamrab, and Pan Yotopoulos. 1979. "A Microeconomic Analysis of the Agriculture of Thailand." *Food Research Institute Studies*, vol. 17, pp. 79–86.

Adulavidhaya, Kamphol, Yoshimi Kuroda, Lawrence Lau, and Pan Yotopoulos. 1984. "The Comparative Statics of the Behavior of Agricultural Households in Thailand." *Singapore Economic Review*, vol. 29, pp. 67–96.

Anderson, Dennis, and Mark Leiserson. "Rural Nonfarm Employment in Developing Countries." *Economic Development and Cultural Change*, vol. 28, pp. 227–48.

Barnum, Howard, and Lyn Squire. 1978. "Technology and Relative Economic Efficiency." *Oxford Economic Papers*, vol. 30, pp. 181–98.

_____. 1979a. "An Econometric Application of the Theory of the Farm Household." *Journal of Development Economics*, vol. 6, pp. 79–102.

_____. 1979b. *A Model of an Agricultural Household*. Washington, D.C.: World Bank.

Barten, Anton. 1977. "The Systems of Consumer Demand Functions Approach: A Review." *Econometrica*, vol. 45, pp. 23–52.

Brown, Alan, and Angus Deaton. 1972. "Surveys in Applied Economics: Models of Consumer Behavior." *Economic Journal*, vol. 82, pp. 1145–1236.

Deaton, Angus, and John Muellbauer. 1980. *Economics and Consumer Behavior*. Cambridge, Mass.: Cambridge University Press.

Kuroda, Yoshimi, and Pan Yotopoulos. 1978. "A Microeconomic Analysis of Production Behavior of the Farm Household in Japan: A Profit Function Approach." *The Economic Review* (Japan), vol. 29, pp. 116–29.

_____. 1980. "A Study of Consumption Behavior of the Farm Household in Japan: An Application of the Linear Logarithmic Expenditure System." *The Economic Review* (Japan), vol. 31, pp. 1–15.

Lau, Lawrence, Wuu-Long Lin, and Pan Yotopoulos. 1978. "The Linear Logarithmic Expenditure System: An Application to Consumption Leisure Choice." *Econometrica*, vol. 46, pp. 843–68.

Pollak, Robert, and Terence Wales. 1981. "Demographic Variables in Demand Analysis." *Econometrica*, vol. 49, pp. 1533–51.

Yotopoulos, Pan, Lawrence Lau, and Wuu-Long Lin. 1976. "Microeconomic Output Supply and Factor Demand Functions in the Agriculture of the Province of Taiwan." *American Journal of Agricultural Economics*, vol. 58, pp. 333–40.

2

Methodological Issues

Inderjit Singh, Lyn Squire, and John Strauss

A NUMBER OF IMPORTANT METHODOLOGICAL ISSUES arise from the empirical literature on agricultural household models. Perhaps foremost among these is the question of the empirical validity of recursive models. Some would argue (see Lopez chapter 11) that the principle of separability cannot be applied in some cases. (Separable and recursive are used interchangeably here.) Nonseparability may be important when modeling certain phenomena, for instance when sales and purchase prices differ for the same commodity, or when markets are incomplete, as they might be in the face of risk and incentive problems. The first question to consider, then, is to what extent nonseparability is justified in agricultural household modeling.

Nonseparability

Nonseparability affects empirical farm-household modeling in two ways: it changes the comparative statics, and it renders statistically inconsistent the usual demand-and-supply parameter estimates. The comparative statics of a general, one-period nonseparable model are derived in the appendix to part I, where it is shown that a virtual (or shadow) price will exist if a commodity has an incomplete market or if the household is at a corner (that is, if it consumes all of its output). This virtual price will be endogenous to the household, and, if the commodity is both produced and consumed, the shadow price will be a function of both preferences and technology.

In Lopez's model (chapter 11), for instance, on-farm and off-farm labor are imperfect substitutes in the household utility function. Members care differentially whether they work for themselves or for others. In addition, Lopez assumes that family and hired labor are imperfect substitutes in the farm production function. Because of these two assumptions, his model is nonseparable; households have a supply of on-farm and off-farm labor, but, at the given market farm wage rate, it is unlikely that the supply of household on-farm labor will equal the demand for household farm labor. Since households will equate the two, they will act as if they faced a virtual farm wage different from the market wage. This virtual farm wage is derived implicitly from equating household on-farm household labor supply and demand. It is therefore a function of both consumption-related and production-related variables and is endogenous to the household. Meanwhile, if interior solutions are assumed, off-farm labor-supply decisions will respond to the market off-farm wage, and hired-in farm labor demand will respond to the market farm wage. Hence, the virtual farm wage will be a function of both market-farm and off-farm wages.

The comparative statics will have extra terms similar to those derived in the appendix to part I because the virtual farm wage will now change in response to exogenous variables. If the researcher wrongly believed the model to be separable, elasticity calculations would be in error, even if utility and production function parameters were known, because the virtual price would be wrongly treated as constant. How important this omission will be depends on the responsiveness of the virtual price to the changing exogenous variable and on the responsiveness of the variable of policy interest to changes in the virtual price. These magnitudes can often be guessed.

In Lopez's model, for example, the response of the uncompensated virtual farm wage (see the appendix for the distinction between uncompensated and compensated virtual prices) to an exogenous change in, say, the off-farm wage is likely to be positive. As the off-farm wage increases, there will be a positive substitution effect on the virtual farm wage, provided off-farm and on-farm work are substitutes in the utility function. This results from an upward shift of the on-farm labor-supply function (if utility is held constant) that accompanies the increase in the off-farm wage. In addition, full income rises with the off-farm wage rate, which, if we assume negative income effects on labor supply, should shift the on-farm labor-supply function still further upward. The responsiveness of the virtual farm wage will depend on the magnitudes of the shifts of the on-farm labor-supply function and on the steepness of the household farm-labor-demand functions. If family and hired labor are close substitutes, farm demand for household laborers should be elastic, and the resulting effect of the off-farm wage on the virtual farm wage should be small. This is clearly an empirical question, however.

If the policymaker is interested in the effect of a change in the off-farm wage on off-farm labor supply, the next step is to investigate the responsiveness of off-farm labor supply to a rise in the virtual farm wage. This should be negative because, if utility is held constant, off-farm labor supply will respond negatively to the virtual farm wage (if we assume substitutability). Income effects will be nonexistent because household farm-labor demand equals on-farm labor supply. This suggests that ignoring the endogeneity of the virtual farm wage in Lopez's model will create an upward bias in the off-farm labor-supply elasticity with respect to the off-farm wage rate, providing the true model parameters are known.

True model parameters are not known, however, and if a nonseparable model is wrongly estimated as separable, parameter estimates will be inconsistent. In general, the magnitude of the inconsistency cannot be determined analytically and as yet there is no Monte Carlo experimental evidence in this regard. Consequently, the magnitude of the statistical bias for estimating a separable model when a nonseparable model is valid is not known. Of course, the combined effects of parameter inconsistency and missing terms in the comparative statics may reinforce or offset each other. The one piece of evidence on the combined effect—that provided by Lopez—suggests that total labor supply (off-farm plus on-farm labor) is much less responsive to a simultaneous change in off-farm and on-farm market wage rates when a nonseparable model is being used. This finding is consistent with the previous arguments concerning off-farm elasticity. The nonseparable model yields a total labor-supply elasticity of 0.04, whereas the separable model indicates an elasticity of 0.19. Standard errors are not provided, however, so it is not clear how much of the difference is attributable to imprecision in the estimates.

It seems intuitively clear that, if the changing exogenous variable and the variable of policy interest are far removed from the market that is cleared by a virtual price, the issue of separability becomes less important. In the above example, the exogenous variable was a wage rate, the variable of policy interest was labor supply, and the virtual price was also a wage rate. In these circumstances, the difference between a separable specification and a nonseparable specification is likely to be at its greatest. Consider a different example, say, the consequences for marketed surplus when the price of the agricultural output changes. Output price will have three effects on the virtual farm wage rate. First, the farm-labor-demand schedule will be raised, and this will put upward pressure on the virtual wage. Second—provided on-farm labor and the agricultural commodity are substitutes—the income-compensated on-farm labor-supply schedule will be raised. This shift will probably be small, however, since the degree of substitutability between on-farm labor and food, far removed variables, is likely to be low. Third, an increased farm output price will have an effect on real full income in proportion to the marketed surplus of output. Provided this surplus is positive, the labor-supply schedule will shift upward still further. All three effects will tend to push the virtual on-farm wage higher.

The higher virtual farm wage will reduce output supply and increase consumption of the farm output. The effect on consumption is likely to be small, however, coming as it will through substitution effects between farm-labor and farm-output consumption. (Remember there will be no income effects from the induced rise in the virtual farm wage since on-farm labor demand equals its supply in this model.) Consequently, the difference between a separable and nonseparable specification, when we are considering the effect of the price of the agricultural output on marketed surplus, is likely to be confined to the effect on output of an induced rise in the on-farm virtual wage. The size of the increase will depend largely on the responsiveness of labor demand to output price and of on-farm labor supply to income. Accordingly, before abandoning separability, the analyst should carefully consider the interaction among changes in exogenous variables, changes in the virtual price, and changes in the variables of policy interest.

A few more points should be noted concerning potential generalizations from Lopez's paper. First, the data are aggregate, being at the level of the census division in Canada. To treat an average of households as if it were a single household requires special assumptions concerning the utility function. Lopez assumes quasi homotheticity, which results in linear Engel curves. Likewise, the commodities are highly aggregated, with all consumption (both food and nonfood) being grouped together; off-farm and on-farm labor constitute the other groups.

One reason for the limited commodity disaggregation on the demand side is the high cost of estimating such a nonseparable model, even with only three commodities. Lopez's model is highly nonlinear in parameters; thus, if many equations were involved, it would be very difficult to estimate them with maximum likelihood techniques. As an alternative, equations could be consistently estimated by subgroups, for instance, by those from the production side and those from the consumption side, provided instrumental variables techniques (such as nonlinear three-stage least squares) were used to account for endogeneity of certain variables (for example, profits in the commodity-demand equations). The use of subgroups could reduce the expense of estimation at the cost of some statistical efficiency, but the procedure would still be expensive. Estimating separable models is in general a much more tractable problem; hence it is useful to know roughly what is lost by incorrectly specifying a separable model.

Unfortunately, it is impossible to assess the overall importance of separability, and, even in a specific case such as Lopez's, a useful prognosis is not readily apparent to practitioners. For some types of analyses, the basic model will probably be a good approximation, but under what conditions? The most that can be said at present is that it may be possible to assess the bias in comparative statics caused by ignoring nonseparability, as was done in this section, but even then, the potential bias depends upon the hypothetical sources of the nonseparability, which the analyst will in general know only imperfectly.

Applications of Nonseparability: Differing Sales and Purchase Prices

Given the strong policy and empirical focus of the agricultural household literature, it makes sense that methodological interest in nonseparability should be directed at specific circumstances in which reasonable models ought to be nonseparable. The example of differing preferences for on-farm and off-farm work is a possible source of nonseparability, but its empirical relevance in developing countries is not clear. As Lopez argues, differential preferences for on-farm and off-farm labor can arise from transportation costs of off-farm labor. Although Lopez does not use some of the testable implications of that idea (such as differing transportation costs across households leading to differing labor supply decisions), he does illustrate how differences between sales and purchase prices can affect the basic assumptions used in formulating a model.

Differences between sales and purchase prices can arise because of commodity heterogeneity. For instance, the quality of food consumed out of home production may differ from that of market-purchased food. Some of these differences may be related to different degrees of processing or other embodied market services. In a dynamic model under risk, demands for home-produced and market-purchased food might differ because of differing attitudes toward risk. Allowing this kind of commodity heterogeneity seems to be a reasonable way to model the household effects of certain government infrastructural investments such as roads.

Alternatively, sales and purchase prices might differ for labor. One potential reason might be the higher costs of supervising hired labor because of incentive problems connected with short-run fixed wage contracts. Such moral-hazard problems could give rise to imperfect substitutability between hired and family labor. Though it need not. Quality-adjusted units of labor could be perfect substitutes. In this case, quality-adjusted sales and purchase prices do not differ, and separability of the basic agricultural household model is unaffected.

Whether commodity heterogeneity results in nonseparability depends on whether the household chooses a corner solution for which supply equals demand. For instance, if a household consumes its entire food production, market-purchased food being an imperfect substitute, then a virtual price for home-produced food exists, which in general will be higher than the sales price of food. This will affect the comparative statics, as explained earlier (also see the appendix). If the household sells some of its food output, however, the market sales price is the appropriate opportunity cost. The same idea is applicable in the hired-versus-family labor case. In many data sets, there will be households both at corners and at interior solutions. Since being at corners is a household choice, it must be modeled as such statistically (see Wales and Woodland 1983; Lee and Pitt 1984). Given current econometric theory and software, only a few corner solutions (two to three per household, at the most) can be handled simultaneously.

Another view is that different sales and purchase prices do not result from commodity heterogeneity, since the commodities are perfect substitutes without adjusting for quality. This might result from transport costs, abstracting from any quality differential caused by the transport. In this case, the budget constraint has a different slope, depending upon whether the commodity is to be sold or purchased on net balance.

The two cases are portrayed in figure 2-1. Take first the case that family labor is an imperfect substitute for hired labor. Output is also consumed. In this case, family labor cannot be purchased, so the budget constraint is the segment BD, just being tangent from the right to the production possibilities frontier at point B. There exists a virtual, or shadow, wage that would cause the household to supply labor just up to point B. If this virtual price is greater than the market wage, then the household will not sell any labor on the market, choosing a point on the segment OB of production function at which its marginal rates of substitution and marginal product are equated.

In the case in which a price wedge exists between sales and hiring wage of labor (there being no quality differences between hired and family labor), the budget constraint will look like the segments CA and BD. The smaller the price wedge, the closer the two segments will lie, joining as one line in the limit with no price differential. In this case, a household may be on the budget segment CA as a net hirer of labor, on the segment BD as a net seller of labor, or on the portion AB of the production func-

Figure 2.1. *Effect of Differing Sales and Purchase Prices of Labor on Revenue Constraint*

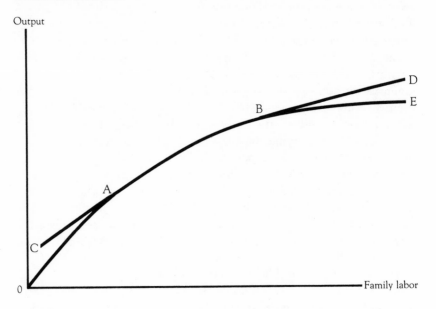

Output

D

E

B

A

C

0   Family labor

tion. Thus three regimes exist, whereas in the imperfect substitutes case, there are only two. Now two comparisons of virtual with market wages must be made to determine which segment the household chooses.

If the virtual price of labor at point A is greater than the market wage, then labor will be hired, the household being on the CA segment. If the virtual wage at point B is less than the market wage, then labor will be sold, and the household located on segment BD. Otherwise the household will be self-sufficient in labor, equating marginal rates of substitution with marginal product.

This problem resembles the nonconvex budget constraint arising from nonproportional income taxes, which has been described in the literature. Some of the econometric methods that exist to handle this case (see Heckman and MaCurdy 1981) are applicable here.

Applications of Nonseparability:
Incomplete and Interlinked Markets and Risk

Despite the growing literature on interlinkage (for example, Bardhan 1984; Binswanger and Rosenzweig 1984), studies of empirical modeling of agricultural households have not yet considered the interlinking of markets that may result from incomplete markets. The fact that households may be rationed in the credit market because of potential default (Stiglitz and Weiss 1981) will affect their behavior in other markets. Credit rationing may give rise to share tenancy (Jaynes 1982), with tenants borrowing from landlords. Access to land rental markets may be constrained by ownership of draft animals in cases where no rental markets exist for such animals. Renting out land may serve to secure more draft animals. The nonseparability thereby induced will give rise to several phenomena: for example, land lease or rental decisions may be affected by the stock of household laborers as households adjust land holdings to family size, or labor-supply decisions may be affected by land ownership through virtual prices as well as through income.

In the case of credit rationing, the interest rate charged to the household will be a function of how much has been borrowed, as well as of other household characteristics (see chapter 6). Furthermore, the effective wage rate may be affected by the number of hired laborers if supervision costs per worker are not constant. Such imperfections in markets will also result in nonseparability.

Underlying many of the discussions of incomplete markets and market interlinkages is the notion of risk. Although risk in one market is not a sufficient condition to cause such linkages, it is an important ingredient in the case of share tenancy (Newbery and Stiglitz 1979). Bardhan and Srinivasan (1971) use an agricultural household model in which land can be sharecropped and households maximize expected utility. Their model, although it incorporates risk, has a one-period framework, as do most models in the market-linkage literature. Yet, this approach ignores the time dimension that is crucially related to risk.

The only truly dynamic model under risk is that formulated by Roe and Graham-Tomasi (chapter 9), who model risks in farm production, not in prices. The separability results they obtain are not only instructive, but they also alert one to certain strong assumptions that have to be made if the result is to stand. Clearly, if perfectly competitive markets exist for future contingencies as well as for other markets, and given product homogeneity, risk can be completely diversified away and so does not present a problem. If contingent markets do not exist, then special assumptions must be made about preferences and about the distribution of yields in addition to markets before separability can result. Given their multiperiod framework, Roe and Graham-Tomasi must assume a perfectly competitive market to exist for a financial asset. This assumption, on top of the assumptions for one-period static models, would result in separability in an intertemporal model without risk, as Iqbal (chapter 6) points out. Adding risk, however, requires further assumptions concerning preferences. Providing households maximize expected utility, risk neutrality along with the previously maintained assumptions plus a perfectly competitive financial market would ensure separable production and consumption decisions.

Under risk aversion, Roe and Graham-Tomasi show that if the utility function is additively separable over time, with each period's subutility function being of negative exponential form (as is often assumed in the risk literature), if the exponents are functions that are homothetic with respect to consumption bundles (including leisure) and if production risk is multiplicative and normally distributed, then separability results. In this very special case, the household behaves as if it first maximizes certainty equivalent full income with respect to input and output choices (which is equivalent to maximizing expected utility of full income), and then maximizes utility subject its budget constraint, in which certainty equivalent full income appears.

In this special case, the profit effect of a change in farm output price has two counteracting components, since it is certainty equivalent full income that is changing in response to output price. An increase in farm output price raises mean profits but also increases its variance. The first effect is analogous to the usual profits effect. The second effect, however, acts to reduce certainty equivalent full income for risk averters, thus counteracting the positive effect on mean profits. Indeed, the combined profit effect of an increase in output price is no longer unambiguously positive, particularly if yields are sufficiently risky.

Past literature on the behavior of the pure firm under risk (for instance, Roumasset, Boussard, and Singh 1979) assumed that firms maximize expected utility of profits; this idea is consistent with a farm household framework, given risk aversion, under these special assumptions, but not necessarily under more general conditions. Without any restrictions on preferences other than a utility function—which is additively separable over time—Roe and Graham-Tomasi show that, conditional upon the optimal consumption bundle, the first-order conditions for expected utility maximization are identical to those of the pure firm maximizing expected utility of profits. Embedded in these first-order conditions, however, are the levels of optimal commodity consumption, which are unknown, and therefore input choices do depend in general upon consumption bundles.

As noted, markets for contingent claims (that is, for consumption in each period as a function of the realized state of the world), are absent in this model. Given possibilities for complete diversification of production risk, attitudes toward risk will not matter in the determination of production choices (whereas they do in Roe and Graham-Tomasi's model). Although complete risk diversification may not be possible in developing country agriculture, some means of diversification do exist; these range from investment in human capital (through education and migration) to investment in livestock or other physical assets to the formation of larger households, and so on. Clearly, this initial attempt at incorporating risk does not allow for such possibilities.

The assumption of a perfect financial asset market is one of the points of departure for the literature on incomplete and interlinked markets discussed above. If the interlinkage literature is correct, then the separability assumption under risk will not apply. Since much of this literature is theoretical, further empirical research is needed to define the nature of interlinked markets.

A second set of problems arises when we consider the particular specification of Roe and Graham-Tomasi's model, especially their assumption that the period-specific subutility function is homothetic. This restriction on preferences is implied by either constant absolute or constant relative risk aversion (Stiglitz 1969). Although this may be an empirically tractable assumption, the homotheticity assumption is overly strong since it restricts all income elasticities to unity.

Furthermore, this model overlooks possible randomness in future prices. Roe and Graham-Tomasi assume that future prices are known by households but that future production is random. Yet there may be circumstances in which production instability will cause price instability. In all agricultural household modeling, the data on relative prices must vary over observations, say, regions, if commodity-demand systems are to be estimated. If markets are well integrated so that local production disturbances do not affect local prices and regional price variation is sufficiently great, then local production uncertainty is consistent with local price certainty. Regional prices may vary because of other factors, however, such as government prescriptions on interregional trade or extremely poor transportation facilities, which may make invalid a small region assumption (so that local production does affect local prices).

Incorporating random prices into the agricultural household model is likely to be a more complicated task and will probably involve private storage decisions (see Wright 1979) as well as price expectations formation (see Eckstein 1983).

In addition, just as in the literature on the pure firm under risk, assumptions concerning what decisions can be made before uncertainty is resolved may vary and thus can greatly affect the analytical results. In Roe and Graham-Tomasi's model, all input decisions are made before the uncertainty is resolved.

Applications of Nonseparability: Household Production Activities

For many policy applications, it will be necessary to consider both household production activities and agricultural production activities. When this new dimension is added to the model, separability will in some cases be affected. Pitt and Rosenzweig (chapter 5) argue that whether farm production decisions can be modeled independently of other decisions— such as health inputs, consumption, and labor supply—depends on the nature of the hired labor market and the degree of substitutability between hired and family labor. Provided the two types of labor are perfect substitutes, separability between farm production and other decisions still holds because household demand for a certain quantity of a particular quality of labor can be met by hiring at a constant wage in the market. Consequently, the health of family laborers does not affect demand for healthy labor time. Clearly this would not be true if family and hired labor were imperfect substitutes.

A current concern of many policymakers is how to estimate the impacts of policy instruments such as food prices and health and education projects on health outcomes of individual farm-household members. For some policies, it may be important to estimate certain household production processes empirically, such as the relationship between food intakes, other health inputs, and health outcomes (see chapter 5). If estimates of the health technology are to be consistent, attention must be given to the fact that certain health inputs—such as food consumed, time devoted to health care, or boiling water—are household decisions. This is an important area for future research.

Even if policymakers only need reduced-form estimates of policy impacts, it will be important to disaggregate male and female time use and wages. This has not been done in typical farm-household modeling (Rosenzweig 1980 is an exception), but is important in this context because of specialization by gender in certain household activities. If health time care is female-labor intensive, for example, the effects on health outcomes within the household will differ between a rise in female wages and a rise in male wages. The substitution effect of an increase in female wages should lead to a greater decline in health than would the substitution effect of an equivalent increase in male wages. Of course, income effects will also be important and will tend to raise the demand for health. The importance of distinguishing male and female wages when evaluating impacts of policies on household nonmarket, nonfarm activities is one of the principal messages of the literature on the so-called new household economics that needs to be incorporated into household production activities of farm households as well.

Multimarket Analysis

If agricultural household models are to be used for policy analysis, inter-market relations need to be accounted for because of their potential importance. Such an accounting requires moving toward a general equilibrium analysis. Yotopoulos and Lau (1974) suggested some types of macrolevel models that might be useful, but they did not have the data needed to test their ideas. Barnum and Squire (1979) and Smith and Strauss (chapter 7) allow rural wages to be endogenously determined by equilibrating net labor demand (supply) among agricultural households with net labor supply (demand) in the rest of the economy.

Even if a limited amount of market interaction is allowed, certain results are significantly affected. Barnum and Squire find that in Malaysia increases in the price of rice cause such a large increase in the rural wage rate that output supply and marketed surplus of rice are both lowered in response. Consumption of paddy still increases, but by a smaller amount than when wages are exogenous. Smith and Strauss show that the partial equilibrium results for Sierra Leone stand up in sign but not in magnitude. Marketed surplus of rice remains positive, but the magnitude of the arc elasticity is more than halved, from 0.75 to 0.3.

Of course, the wage rate may not be the only endogenous price. Other prices may be endogenous as a result of government trade policies (for example, import or export quotas) or because of high transportation costs. Which prices should be allowed to equilibrate will differ, of course, for each application.

Braverman, Ahn, and Hammer (1983) examine agricultural pricing policies in Korea that were expected to reduce deficits in the government's Grain Management Fund and Fertilizer Fund. This study allows the price of the traditional variety of rice and rural wages to be endogenous while prices of high-yielding rice, barley, and fertilizer are government controlled. Effects of policy changes are traced through to government budgets, incomes of different classes of rural and urban households, national income, and marketed surpluses. The model's equations are based on agent optimizing behavior. For the rural sector, there are commodity and labor-demand and labor-supply equations derived from an agricultural household model using the Almost Ideal Demand System (Deaton and Muellbauer 1980) and the translog profit function. Urban commodity demands are also derived using an Almost Ideal Demand System. Finally, market-clearing equations are specified, and it is through these that specific government policies can be analyzed. For instance, the traditional rice market in Korea is modeled as a closed system in which urban demand equals rural marketed surplus. For a high-yielding variety of rice, imports are allowed, and the government supports the producer price above the world market price and subsidizes urban consumers. Because the structure of the model is general, it can be adapted to a variety of country and policy contexts. Indeed, a number of such adaptations have been reported: in Senegal (see chapter 8), Sierra Leone (Braverman, Hammer, and Jorgenson 1983), Cyprus (Braverman, Hammer, and Jorgenson 1984), and Malawi (Kirchner, Singh, and Squire 1984).

Several problems with respect to specification and data arise in those models. The basic model demands a great deal of data, as does the agricultural household model. Ideally, parameters should be econometrically estimated before being used in the simulation, but this ideal will not always be feasible because of the poor quality or lack of data. Hence, in practice, parameters are estimated, borrowed from other studies, or assumed. The system of equations is then solved at one point in time, and the solved values are compared with actual values for the economy at that particular moment. If the difference is too large in some sense, parameters are then changed iteratively until a desired closeness of simulated to actual values is achieved. Once a baseline simulation has been achieved, policy experiments can be simulated and sensitivity analysis of some small number of parameters performed. The lack of appropriate data manifests itself in parameters that may be imprecise. The sensitivity of the model's policy should therefore be carefully investigated. The Korea study, for example, has a relatively large number of parameters estimated from real world data. In the Senegal study, by contrast, many parameters are assumed and others (for instance, the price elasticities) are drawn from weak sources. This situation is largely a reflection of the stage of development of the data collection agencies in Korea versus those in Senegal. The assessment of the sensitivity of policy results to unprecise parameters is therefore especially important in the Senegalese model. This analysis of sensitivity leads to different conclusions for different variables of policy interest, and for different parameters. Parameters more directly related to the policy outcomes of interest will need to be estimated more precisely. In Senegal, for example, the effect of a 50 percent increase in the consumer price of rice on net foreign exchange earnings from agriculture depends critically on the assumed cross-price elasticity between the price of rice and millet consumption. Under high elasticity, much more millet is consumed, millet prices go up, and acreage is switched from groundnuts, the export crop, to domestically consumed millet. A low elasticity raises foreign exchange from agriculture, as tariffs from rice are increased, whereas rice consumption falls off only slightly. For government deficits in the agricultural sector, the elasticity assumptions make much less difference. Although less government tariff revenue is gained from increased consumer prices of rice when rice price elasticities are assumed to be high, the subsidies to groundnut producers drop because fewer groundnuts are produced—more acreage being switched over to millet than in the low-elasticity case.

Another practical problem has to do with how these models are solved numerically. If the model is set up in levels—for instance, if the quantities of rice demanded by rural households are a function of prices, wage, full income, and so on—the system of equations is highly nonlinear, and requires a great deal of time and expertise to solve. If the nonlinear system is totally differentiated, however, the resulting linear approximation will be relatively easy to solve with existing computer hardware. Nonetheless there is a tradeoff here because the approximation will be good only for variable values close to the baseline values, and policy analysts may be interested in the effects of large changes in certain variables, in which case the differentiated system may approximate the real world poorly. It is obviously a relatively simple matter to test the reliability of linear approximations by comparing their results with those of fully specified models. This is a high priority for future research and could be easily accomplished using some of the existing multimarket models.

A further problem that arises in model specification but that is not peculiar to multimarket models has to do with the Almost Ideal Demand System, which allows commodities to be inferior goods, but only permits a limited amount of nonlinearity in the Engel curves. It also restricts Engel curves to zero intercepts. Although this might be intuitively acceptable, real world incomes, appropriately measured, are sufficiently far from zero so that extending an approximation to an Engel curve in the relevant region will generally result in a nonzero intercept. If the functional form used to fit the Engel curve has sufficient curvature, this will be less of a problem. As already noted, however, the Almost Ideal Demand System does not have much curvature. The consequences of this are twofold: Engel curve slopes may be badly estimated even at the sample mean, and changes in the slopes as income changes may be missed. These consequences will be most damaging when the real Engel curves are very nonlinear, as might be expected when commodities are more highly disaggregated. This problem can be solved by using Engel curves with more curvature or by introducing nonzero intercepts, or both. Clearly both can be easily incorporated into multimarket analysis. Deaton (1982) has introduced quadratic income terms into the Almost Ideal Demand System, and Strauss (1982) has used the quadratic expenditure system of Howe, Pollak, and Wales (1979). Moreover, Gorman (1981) has shown that, in general, a second-order polynomial in income is as general as one can be in modeling Engel curves and yet still be consistent with utility maximization.

A common approach in macroeconomic work, also followed by Braverman and Hammer in their analyses, is to treat an aggregate of consumers (and producers) as an individual. For example, to relate aggregate commodity consumption to prices and average income, individual Engel curves must be both linear and parallel, as is well known. Otherwise the distribution of income will also affect aggregate consumption. If the concept of representative income (which is not average income) is used, where representative income depends on the income distribution and possibly on prices, then somewhat more general behavior can be accommodated.

Smith and Strauss (chapter 8) simulate outcomes for individual households in the Sierra Leone sample, as do Lau and others (1981) for the Taiwan sample. Knowledge of the regional sampling proportions allows the authors to convert the outcomes for individual households into regional and finally national aggregates. Comparing arc elasticities between this method of microsimulation and that using the representative household, Smith and Strauss find some large differences for both commodity-demand and output-supply elasticities. For example, a 10 percent increase in the price of rice raises the total national production of rice by only 1 percent when a representative household approach is used, compared with 3.4 percent under microsimulation. Rural rice consumption drops 6½ percent with the representative household approach, but only 5 percent with microsimulation. Although the results depend on both the data and the commodity-demand and output-supply specifications, they suggest that care should be taken when simulations are performed with functional forms that do not admit of perfect aggregation. As Smith and Strauss also point out, microsimulation allows the analyst to examine distributional effects of policies more readily. Braverman and Hammer come part way toward distributional disaggregation by allowing for representative households of different income classes (for Korea) or for different regions (Senegal).

Data Requirements and Implications for Data Collection

To estimate a complete agricultural household model, the analyst must have an extensive set of data on consumption expenditures (market purchased and subsistence), labor supply (possibly broken down by sex), farm and nonfarm outputs, purchased and household-supplied variable inputs, fixed farm assets, basic demographic characteristics, and prices, both for consumption and production inputs, including wages. It is obviously a massive undertaking to obtain data of reasonable quality on this scale for a single household. That is why comparatively few such data sets have been collected. Sample size clearly has to be traded off against both data comprehensiveness and quality. Empirical studies conducted to date indicate, however, that massive sample sizes, which many cross sections contain, are not needed to obtain plausible estimates of the structure of the basic farm household.

The precise nature of the potential tradeoffs between sample size, comprehensiveness, and quality is not entirely clear. In separable models, for example, commodity-demand and production-side equations can be estimated on different sets of data as long as each can be considered representative of the area in question, as would be the case if each were from a probability sample. Adulavidhaya and others (1984) did precisely this in the Thailand study. Such a data collection strategy may be more expensive than using common households, however, if increasing returns to scale exist in the collection techniques. Nevertheless, existing, less comprehensive sets of data can be combined. In particular, it is possible to supplement prototypical farm management surveys with a special household budget survey in which prices are also collected.

If complete nonseparable models are to be estimated, then this collection strategy is no longer viable because data are needed for both consumption and production activities on identical households. Many countries today conduct household budget surveys and farm management surveys. If the surveys could be coordinated so that household coverage could at least overlap, and if some price and wage data could be added, the information available for policy analysis would greatly increase. The payoff would be sizable—since such policy analyses could be built on much better quality data.

One potential way to reduce the costs of collecting comprehensive data on a moderately sized group is to obtain samples from only a limited number of geographical areas. This would be a grave mistake in farm-household modeling because then very little price variation would appear in the data. Yet the analyst relies on just such a variation in prices to explain differing consumption and production patterns. Unfortunately, many existing farm management surveys suffer from this very problem. Although household budget surveys may cover an adequate number of geographic regions, they often omit any price or wage data.

If longitudinal data are collected, then less geographical dispersion will be necessary because prices will vary over time. Indeed, longitudinal data on households circumvent a possible problem in the use of purely cross-sectional data—that is, that geographical price variation will be a proxy for other regional variables that might affect consumption or production outcomes. Collecting such panel data can be expensive, and some households may drop out of the survey in a systematic way.

Alternatively, for separable models, it would be possible to use time-series cross-sectional data (which do not follow identical households over time) as long as each cross section was from a representative sample. In that case, households would have to be averaged in groups, for example, by size of land owned within each geographic region. The observations for analysis would then be the group averages. Such a procedure was used by Lau, Lin, and Yotopoulos (1978). The problem with this approach is that the group average may no longer behave as if it were a single household; that is, the distribution of income or assets within the group may also matter. This problem was covered above (see also Deaton and Muellbauer 1980 for an excellent survey).

A different type of aggregation problem has to do with the grouping of commodities and the computation of group price indices. Several studies—for instance those in Taiwan, Japan, and Thailand—assume that all households in a region face the same prices for disaggregated commodities, but allow the weights used in forming the indices to vary for each observation (household group). This technique enables the analyst to derive household (or household group) specific prices. At the same time, it introduces two potentially serious problems: a spurious variation in prices, and a price index endogenous to the household. Suppose that every household in a market area (say, a region) faced the same set of prices for each disaggregated commodity (that is, for different qualities of the same aggregate commodity). Even with a common utility function, different households will buy different amounts of each quality of the aggregate commodity because of differences in full income and in household characteristics. Since the weights used are the share of household expenditure on a particular commodity, the weights will differ by household. Thus the price variation seen by the researcher will be spurious. In addition, these aggregate prices are endogenous to the household since expenditure decisions are endogenous. The endogeneity of prices would have to be accounted for in the estimation procedure in order to produce consistent statistical estimates, but the identifying instruments are lacking. All the variables that might affect the choice of quality are already included in the demand equations, so there would not seem to be any instruments left. Consequently, the analytical framework would have to be reformulated, for instance, into a model of probabilistic choice (see, for example, McFadden 1981). A more practical approach, if choice of quality is not the main focus of the research, is to use regional average weights rather than household specific weights when constructing the price indices. This approach is used in the Sierra Leone and Indonesian studies, among others. Even by averaging the expenditure-share weights over a region, however, it may not be possible to eliminate endogeneity if regions and full incomes are highly correlated.

Although, ideally, prices should be collected for all items consumed by a sample's households, this is both an impractical and unnecessary step in many cases. For the empirical analysis, the researcher will decide on the level of commodity disaggregation and will compute price indices for each group. In practice, prices will probably be required only for the most important items (with respect to budget shares) for each group, but all groups must be covered. If price indices cannot be computed for some groups, price and income elasticities can still be estimated in separable models, but strong assumptions will then have to be made about household preferences. If, for instance, we assume additivity of the direct utility function, as the Linear Expenditure System does, then all price elasticities can be estimated, although not every parameter will be identified. Barnum and Squire (1979) use this property of the LES to estimate all the price and income elasticities in a separable model for data from the Muda River valley in Malaysia when the only price variation in the data set applies to wages. Given the empirical evidence that contradicts some of the implications of the LES (such as additivity of the utility function and linear Engel curves), this is arguably a poor substitute for complete group price coverage. (See Deaton 1978 for a discussion of empirical evidence on additivity; Strauss 1982 for a strong rejection of linear Engel curves for farming households.)

Some comprehensiveness of data may be sacrificed if estimating a complete agricultural household model is not the objective of the analysis. It may be that only one or a few structural or reduced-form equations are of interest. To estimate reduced-form equations, the analyst needs data on all the exogenous variables, of course, but not on all endogenous variables. Moreover, certain details may not be necessary. To estimate health reduced-form equations, for instance, Pitt and Rosenzweig only need data on farm profits (subtracting out the value of family labor as well as purchased inputs), and not on specific input usage. Provided it is easier to obtain expenditure data on inputs rather than quantity data, this is a smaller information requirement. Note, however, that data on consumption prices are needed, even though the focus is on health outcomes. Consequently, it is not enough to collect data on only health outcomes, prices of health inputs (for example, doctor's fees, distance to health facilities, and so on), and an appropriate definition of income such as farm profits (that part of income uncorrelated with that equation's statistical error term) in order to obtain consistent estimates of the reduced-form health equation.

Iqbal, for example, does not need detailed data on consumption expenditure or input usage to estimate his reduced-form borrowing function. Of course, more complete data would have aided the analysis since fewer proxy variables would have been needed, and the interpretation of the coefficients of those contaminated variables would have been cleaner (for instance, the family size variable represents life cycle decisions, but it also affects current full income).

Furthermore, the traditional farm production, cost, or profit-function analysis is concerned only with a subset of the relevant household equations. This traditional analysis, as already noted, is acceptable as long as one is working with a separable farm-household model. In that case, detailed consumption expenditure and price data are not needed. If one is dealing with a nonseparable model, however, estimating even reduced-form output-supply equations will require prices of consumption commodities.

How comprehensive the data set should be depends on whether the goal is to estimate the complete farm-household system or just some parts of it. What data can be reasonably omitted also depends on whether structural or reduced-form equations are being estimated, and whether the household model assumes separability.

As for what can be accomplished with different degrees of shortfall from an ideal quality of data, that question has been only partly answered in the existing studies. Clearly, data sets do not have to be perfect—they never are—and in fact much insight has been gained from data that are far from perfect in quality. Yet even these imperfect data sets are extensive in their variable coverage and contain geographical, and in some instances time-series variations in prices.

Agenda for Future Research

To organize an agenda for future research, we must first distinguish between issues of household behavior and issues of policy analysis. (In making this delineation, we are not judging the relative importance of each group of issues, both of which are very important.) The first question in the household behavior category is what difference it makes if basic elasticity calculations wrongly assume separability. As we have seen, there is little evidence with which to answer this question. Moreover, the question itself is inherently difficult because the answer is likely to depend on how nonseparability enters the model, and there are many possible ways. Thus it may be more fruitful to pursue certain types of nonseparability that are suggested by the policy issue of interest and by the economic institutions that characterize the data set.

With respect to the basic, static model, one of the most important sources of nonseparability is likely to involve commodity heterogeneity, whether for consumption commodities or labor inputs. Such heterogeneity may lead to differing sales and purchase prices for the same commodity (whether there is a quality difference will need to be carefully considered since it leads to differences in modeling, as argued earlier). For labor, potential differences between family and hired labor, or between male, female, and child labor may be important (the latter distinction approaches the issue of intrahousehold distribution, treated below).

In some cases, but not all, it will be important to consider household production activities, not only for health issues, as noted earlier, but also for issues such as fertility and household composition. Although household production activities need not lead to nonseparability between farm production and household consumption, they may. Even if they do not, problems may arise in dealing with intrahousehold distribution, whether a reduced-form, or black box, approach is used in which the intrahousehold allocation mechanisms are not modeled explicitly, or whether more structural approaches are employed. In the black box approach, it will be crucial to account differentially for the effect of male and female opportunity costs on intrahousehold distribution (at least between sexes), as do Pitt and Rosenzweig.

One of the weak areas in the overall farm-household literature is the lack of empirical results on savings and investments. The little work that has been done (for example, that of Iqbal) has used a static framework. No study, except the one by Roe and Graham-Tomasi, has attempted a truly dynamic analysis, and very few longitudinal data sets exist to analyze these issues. Although this type of dynamic analysis could be carried out by ignoring risk, this consideration surely adds a great deal. Within such a framework, the analyst is able to consider not only issues connected with savings and investments (and perhaps their composition), but also those having to do with the adoption of new technologies. Most work on technology adoption under risk (for example, Feder, Just, and Zilberman 1985) has ignored the composition side of household activities and has modeled the household as maximizing expected utility of wealth or income. As Roe and Graham-Tomasi show, the assumptions justifying this approach may be rather restrictive. Much remains to be done in this area; to begin with, much more empirical work is needed, some of the rather restrictive assumptions such as homothetic preferences need to be relaxed, and price risk should be added. Unfortunately, the empirical work will not be easy and may well involve tackling the household model by parts rather than estimating a giant model, which is bound to be enormously expensive to test.

Just how restrictive are the assumptions underlying separability in dynamic models under production risk? This is an area in which the market interlinkage literature and the agricultural household literature intersect. Much more empirical work needs to be done on the true nature of rural labor, credit, and land markets in developing countries. In some areas of the world, farm-household models having a fixed land area will be very poor approximations. Investigating the determinants of land lease and sales behavior within the framework of an agricultural household model is likely to prove highly interesting, even if only reduced-form equations or a subset of structural equations are estimated. In other areas, credit may be rationed for some households and the effects of this on consumption and investment will have to be accounted for. All these issues are theoretical possibilities. Just how prevalent they are empirically is an important question with important consequences for farm-household modeling.

These aspects of household behavior must be considered whether one is attempting to improve the realism of agricultural household models or to model certain policy issues. Some other important research issues have to do with multimarket modeling and tradeoffs that can be made between the quality of data and cost.

A high priority for multimarket policy analysis will be to experiment with less costly solution algorithms and to investigate the adequacy of approximation with a fully differentiated system. In the absence of better-quality data, sensitivity analysis will remain quite important, but it would also be interesting to see just how much difference better-quality data would make.

The realism of the farm-household models used in multimarket analyses could be enhanced by introducing more highly nonlinear Engel curves, for example, and this would be a useful extension, although probably a less important one than the extensions noted above. Somewhat lower on the priority list would be experimenting with disaggregation (microsimulation). Since microsimulation will raise the computational costs of finding equilibrium, it will be important to have some idea of what is lost by wrongly treating groups of households as if they are individual households.

Finally, we need to know whether better-quality data would greatly affect elasticity estimates and which types of data are most crucial. If data on farm profits are gathered in one-time retrospective interviews, for example, will this vastly reduce the quality of estimates compared with a much more intensive (for example, biweekly or monthly) effort to obtain detailed input data, including information on family labor, and output data? These questions have been addressed to some extent by those who collect farm management or household expenditure surveys separately. They are of particular concern in agricultural household modeling since the expense of past surveys has discouraged many from undertaking this kind of analysis.

References

Adulavidhaya, Kamphol, and others. 1984. "The Comparative Statics of the Behavior of Agricultural Households in Thailand." *Singapore Economic Review*, vol. 29, pp. 67–96.

Bardhan, Pranab. 1984. *Land, Labor and Rural Poverty*. New York: Columbia University Press.

Bardhan, Pranab, and T. N. Srinivasan. 1971. "Cropsharing Tenancy in Agriculture: A Theoretical and Empirical Analysis." *American Economic Review*, vol. 51, pp. 48–64.

Barnum, Howard, and Lyn Squire. 1979. *A Model of an Agricultural Household*. Washington, D.C.: World Bank.

Binswanger, Hans, and Mark Rosenzweig, eds. 1984. *Contractual Arrangements, Employment, and Wages in Rural Labor Markets in Asia*. New Haven, Conn.: Yale University Press.

Braverman, Avishay, C. Y. Ahn, and Jeffrey Hammer. 1983. *Alternative Agricultural Pricing Policies in Korea: Their Implications for Government Deficits, Income Distribution, and Balance of Payments*. World Bank Staff Working Paper no. 621. Washington, D.C.

Braverman, Avishay, Jeffrey Hammer, and Erika Jorgenson. 1983. "Agricultural Taxation and Trade Policies in Sierra Leone." World Bank Country Policy Department Paper. Washington, D.C.

_____. 1984. "An Economic Analysis of Reducing Input Subsidies to the Livestock Sector in Cyprus." World Bank Country Policy Department Paper. Washington, D.C.

Deaton, Angus. 1978. "Specification and Testing in Applied Demand Analysis." *Economic Journal*, vol. 88, pp. 524–36.

Deaton, Angus, and John Muellbauer. 1980. *Economics and Consumer Behavior*. Cambridge, Mass.: Cambridge University Press.

Eckstein, Zvi. 1984. "A Rational Expectations Model of Agricultural Supply." *Journal of Political Economy*, vol. 92, pp. 1–19.

Feder, Gershon, Richard Just, and David Zilberman. 1985. "Adoption of Agricultural Innovations in Developing Countries: A Survey." *Economic Development and Cultural Change*, vol. 33, pp. 255–98.

Heckman, James J., and Thomas MaCurdy. 1981. "New Methods for Estimating Labor Supply Functions: A Survey." In *Research in Labor Economics*, vol. 4. Edited by R. Ehrenberg. New York: JAI Press.

Jaynes, Gerald, 1982. "Production and Distribution in Agrarian Economies." *Oxford Economic Papers*, vol. 34, pp. 346–67.

Kirchner, James, I. J. Singh, and Lyn Squire. 1984. "Agricultural Pricing and Marketing Policies in Eastern Africa." World Bank. Processed.

Lau, Lawrence, Wuu-Long Lin, and Pan Yotopoulos. 1978. "The Linear Logarithmic Expenditure System: An Application to Consumption Leisure Choice." *Econometrica*, vol. 46, pp. 843–68.

Lau, Lawrence, Pan Yotopoulos, Erwin Chou, and Wuu-Long Lin. 1981. "The Microeconomics of Distribution: A Simulation of the Farm Economy." *Journal of Policy Modeling*, vol. 3, pp. 175–206.

Lee, Lung-Fei, and Mark Pitt. 1984. "Microeconometric Models of Consumer and Producer Demand with Limited Dependent Variables." Economic Development Center Bulletin no. 84–4. University of Minnesota, Minneapolis.

McFadden, Daniel. 1981. "Econometric Models of Probabilistic Choice." In *Structural Analysis of Discrete Data with Econometric Applications*. Edited by C. Manski and D. McFadden. Cambridge, Mass.: MIT Press.

Muth, Richard. 1966. "Household Production and Consumer Demand Functions." *Econometrica*, vol. 34, pp. 699–708.

Newbery, David, and Joseph Stiglitz. 1979. "Sharecropping, Risk Sharing, and the Importance of Imperfect Information." In *Risk, Uncertainty and Agricultural Development*. Edited by J. Roumasset, J. M. Boussard, and I. J. Singh. New York: Agricultural Development Council.

Pollak, Robert, and Michael Wachter. 1975. "The Relevance of the Household Production Function for the Allocation of Time." *Journal of Political Economy*, vol. 83, pp. 255–77.

Roumasset, James, Marc Boussard, and Inderjit Singh. 1979. *Risk, Uncertainty and Agricultural Development*. New York: Agricultural Development Council.

Stiglitz, Joseph. 1969. "Behavior toward Risk with Many Commodities." *Econometrica*, vol. 37, pp. 660–67.

Stiglitz, Joseph, and Andrew Weiss. 1981. "Credit Rationing in Markets with Imperfect Information." *American Economic Review*, vol. 71, pp. 393–410.

Strauss, John. 1982. "Determinants of Food Consumption in Rural Sierra Leone: Application of the Quadratic Expenditure System to the Consumption-Leisure Component of a Household-Firm Model." *Journal of Development Economics*, vol. 11, pp. 327–53.

Wales, Terence, and A. D. Woodland. 1983. "Estimation of Consumer Demand Systems with Binding Non-Negativity Constraints." *Journal of Econometrics*, vol. 21, pp. 263–285.

Wright, Brian. 1979. "Effects of Ideal Production Stabilization: A Welfare Analysis under Rational Behavior." *Journal of Political Economy*, vol. 87, pp. 1011–33.

Yotopoulos, Pan, and Lawrence Lau. 1974. "On Modeling the Agricultural Sector in Developing Economies." *Journal of Development Economics*, vol. 1, pp. 105–27.

Appendix

The Theory and Comparative Statics of Agricultural Household Models: A General Approach

John Strauss

THIS APPENDIX DEVELOPS the basic model of the agricultural household introduced in chapter 1. The recursive property and comparative statics are derived first. The concept of a shadow or virtual price is then explicitly defined, and it is shown how the response of the virtual price to exogenous variables can be obtained. It turns out that with a minimum of assumptions this response can be signed. Next, these results are used to examine the comparative statics of various farm-household models, when the household faces virtual rather than parametric prices. During this exercise, the difference in the comparative statics between recursive and nonrecursive models becomes clear. The next section presents the outline of a model in which the market for labor is absent. This follows the earliest modeling of an agricultural household, by Chayanov, and its later technical development by Japanese economists (for example, Nakajima). Models that incorporate Z-goods are subsequently discussed, along with the previously neglected topic of models with certain types of commodity heterogeneity, which lead to corner solutions. Finally, conditions under which agricultural household models are recursive are summarized.

A Basic Model: The Household as Price-Taker

All prices in the static model developed here are taken as exogenous. Assume the household maximizes its utility subject to its constraints. Three constraints are specified at first: a production function, a time, and a budget constraint. Since agricultural household models have not generally been used to address issues of intrafamily distribution (Pitt and Rosenzweig explore some of the conceptual problems involved), a household utility function is assumed to exist. Let

(IA-1) $$U(X_1, \ldots, X_L)$$

be the utility function, which is well behaved: quasi-concave with positive partial derivatives. The arguments are household consumption of commodity i, with X_L denoting total leisure time. Clearly, the X_i's can be a vector of commodity consumption for different members of the family as well. For instance, we might want X_L to include male, female, or children's leisure time separately. We could also allow household characteristics such as number of members to enter the utility function separately. As long as these are viewed as fixed, this will not change the analysis.

Utility is maximized subject to a budget constraint:

(IA-2) $$Y = \sum_{i=1}^{L} p_i X_i$$

where Y is the household's full income (see equation [IA-3]), and the p_i's are commodity prices (p_L being the wage rate). Full income of an agricultural household equals the value of its time endowment, plus the value of the household's production less the value of variable inputs required for production of outputs, plus any nonwage, nonhousehold production income such as remittances:

(IA-3) $$Y = p_L T + \sum_{j=1}^{M} q_j Q_j - \sum_{i=1}^{N} q_i V_i - p_L L + E$$

where

T = time endowment
Q_j = output, for $j = 1, \ldots, M$
V_i = nonlabor variable inputs, for $i = 1, \ldots, N$
L = labor demand
q_j = price of Q_j
q_i = price of V_i
E = exogenous income.

For the moment, it is assumed that L is total labor demanded by the household, both family and hired, which are assumed to be perfect substitutes, an assumption we relax later in the discussion on partly absent markets.

Outputs and inputs are related by an implicit production function

(IA-4) $$G(Q_1, \ldots, Q_M, V_1, \ldots, V_N, L, K_1, \ldots, K_0) = 0$$

where K_i's are fixed inputs. This is a general specification that allows for separate production functions for different outputs, or for joint production. G is assumed to satisfy the usual properties for production functions: it is quasi-convex, increasing in outputs and decreasing in inputs.

If the household maximizes utility (IA-1) subject to its full-income (IA-2 and IA-3) and production-function (IA-4) constraints and to prices (p, q) being fixed, then the household's choices can be modeled as recursive decisions, even though the decisions are simultaneous in time (Jorgenson and Lau 1969; Nakajima 1969). The household behaves as though it maximizes the revenue side of its full income, equation (IA-3), subject to its production-function constraint, and then maximizes utility subject to its full-income constraint, equation (IA-2). Since neither the value of endowed time nor exogenous income are household choice variables, maximizing full income is equivalent to maximizing the value of outputs less variable inputs (that is, profits).

To see that the model is separable between revenue and expenditure, the comparative statics are examined. Let the household consume three commodities: leisure, X_L; a good that is purchased on the market, X_m; and a good, X_a, produced by the household. (Obviously all these scalars could just as well be vectors.) The household uses labor, L, another variable input, V, and a fixed input K to produce both Q_a and another crop, Q_c. All Q_c is sold on the market (a commercial crop). The Lagrangian function can be written as

(IA-5) $\pounds = U(X_L, X_m, X_a) + \lambda[p_L T + (q_c Q_c + p_a Q_a - p_L L - q_v V)$
$+ E - p_L X_L - p_m X_m - p_a X_a] + \mu G(Q_c, Q_a, L, V, K).$

If we assume interior solutions, the first-order conditions are:

(IA-6)
$$\frac{\partial \pounds}{\partial X_L} = U_L - \lambda p_L = 0$$

$$\frac{\partial \pounds}{\partial X_m} = U_m - \lambda p_m = 0$$

$$\frac{\partial \pounds}{\partial X_a} = U_a - \lambda p_a = 0$$

$$\frac{\partial \pounds}{\partial \lambda} = p_L(T - X_L - L) + q_c Q_c + p_a(Q_a - X_a)$$
$$- q_v V - p_m X_m + E = 0$$

$$\frac{1}{\lambda}\frac{\partial \pounds}{\partial Q_c} = q_c + \frac{\mu}{\lambda} G_c = 0$$

$$\frac{1}{\lambda} \frac{\partial \pounds}{\partial Q_a} = p_a + \frac{\mu}{\lambda} G_a = 0$$

$$\frac{1}{\lambda} \frac{\partial \pounds}{\partial L} = -p_L + \frac{\mu}{\lambda} G_L = 0$$

$$\frac{1}{\lambda} \frac{\partial \pounds}{\partial V} = -q_v + \frac{\mu}{\lambda} G_v = 0$$

$$\frac{\partial \pounds}{\partial \mu} = G(Q_c, Q_a, L, V, K) = 0.$$

Totally differentiating (IA-6),

(IA-7)

$$
\begin{bmatrix}
U_{LL} & U_{Lm} & U_{La} & -p_L & 0 & 0 & 0 & 0 & 0 \\
U_{mL} & U_{mm} & U_{ma} & -P_m & 0 & 0 & 0 & 0 & 0 \\
U_{aL} & U_{am} & U_{aa} & -p_a & 0 & 0 & 0 & 0 & 0 \\
-p_L & -p_m & -p_a & 0 & 0 & 0 & 0 & 0 & 0 \\
0 & 0 & 0 & 0 & \frac{\mu}{\lambda}G_{cc} & \frac{\mu}{\lambda}G_{ca} & \frac{\mu}{\lambda}G_{cL} & \frac{\mu}{\lambda}G_{cv} & G_c \\
0 & 0 & 0 & 0 & \frac{\mu}{\lambda}G_{ac} & \frac{\mu}{\lambda}G_{aa} & \frac{\mu}{\lambda}G_{aL} & \frac{\mu}{\lambda}G_{av} & G_a \\
0 & 0 & 0 & 0 & \frac{\mu}{\lambda}G_{Lc} & \frac{\mu}{\lambda}G_{La} & \frac{\mu}{\lambda}G_{LL} & \frac{\mu}{\lambda}G_{Lv} & G_L \\
0 & 0 & 0 & 0 & \frac{\mu}{\lambda}G_{vc} & \frac{\mu}{\lambda}G_{va} & \frac{\mu}{\lambda}G_{vL} & \frac{\mu}{\lambda}G_{vv} & G_v \\
0 & 0 & 0 & 0 & G_c & G_a & G_L & G_v & 0
\end{bmatrix}
\begin{bmatrix}
dX_L \\
dX_m \\
dX_a \\
d\lambda \\
dQ_c \\
dQ_a \\
dL \\
dV \\
d\left(\frac{\mu}{\lambda}\right)
\end{bmatrix}
=
\begin{bmatrix}
\lambda dp_L \\
\lambda dp_m \\
\lambda dp_a \\
\psi \\
-dq_c \\
-dp_a \\
dp_L \\
dq_v \\
0
\end{bmatrix}
$$

where $\psi = -(T - X_L - L)dp_L + X_m dp_m - (Q_a - X_a)dp_a - dE - Q_c dq_c + V dq_v - \mu/\lambda\, G_k dk$. When differentiating the budget constraint we have substituted

$$-\frac{\mu}{\lambda} (G_c dQ_c + G_a dQ_a + G_L dL + G_v dV)$$

for

$$q_c dQ_c + p_a dQ_a - p_L dL - q_v dV.$$

This equals $\mu/\lambda\, G_k\, dK$ since $G(\cdot) = 0$. This system of equations is block diagonal, as can easily be seen from equation system (IA-7). The first set of equations, corresponding to the upper left block of the bordered Hessian matrix, gives the solution for commodity demands and the marginal utility of full income. The second (lower right) set of equations gives the solution for output supplies, variable input demands, and the associated multiplier. The assumptions concerning the utility and production functions ensures that second-order conditions are met. Hence, the two decision problems can indeed be solved recursively, despite their simultaneity in time.

Equation (IA-7) demonstrates the principal message of the farm-household literature, that farm technology, quantities of fixed inputs, and prices of variable inputs and of outputs do affect consumption decisions. Given recursiveness, however, the reverse is not true. Preferences, prices of consumption commodities, and income do not affect production decisions. Output supply responds positively to own-price at all times owing to the quasi-convexity assumption on the production function, $\partial Q_c/\partial q_c > 0$. The price of the cash crop, q_c, will be related to consumption of the purchased commodity, X_m, through changed income. From equation (IA-7) it can be seen that

$$\frac{\partial X_m}{\partial q_c} = Q_c \frac{\partial X_m}{\partial E}.$$

Likewise, changes in quantities of fixed inputs, K, will affect income, hence the consumption of X_m:

$$\frac{\partial X_m}{\partial K} = \frac{\mu}{\lambda} G_K \frac{\partial X_m}{\partial E}.$$

Assuming X_m is a normal commodity, increments to fixed inputs or to the cash crop price will induce higher consumption of X_m. For commodities that are also produced by the household, own-price effects are

(IA-8)
$$\frac{\partial X_a}{\partial p_a} = \left.\frac{\partial X_a}{\partial p_a}\right|_U + (Q_a - X_a)\frac{\partial X_a}{\partial E}.$$

Thus, a change in the price of X_a has the usual negative substitution effect, and an income effect that is weighted by net sales (or marketed surplus) of X_a, not consumption of X_a. The income effect is positive for a net seller and negative for a net buyer. In consequence, for net sellers, consumption of X_a might respond positively to changes in its own price even though it is a normal good.

The income effect for a farm household has an extra term, $Q_a(\partial X_a/\partial E)$, as compared with the pure consuming household. This extra effect is introduced when the profits component of full income is raised; hence it can be referred to as a profit effect. To see this, note that from equation (IA-3) $dY = T dp_L + d\pi + dE$, where π = profits, the value of outputs less the value of variable inputs. From equation (IA-3) and the first-order conditions,

$$d\pi = Q_c dq_c + Q_a dp_a - L\, dp_L - V\, dq_v + \frac{\mu}{\lambda} G_k dK.$$

Thus, the fourth element of the right-hand side of equation (IA-7) may be expressed as

$$\psi = -(T - X_L)dp_L + X_m dp_m + X_a dp_a - d\pi - dE.$$

It is then clear that the Marshallian demand for food can be written as

$$X_a(p_L, p_m, p_a, q_c, q_v, K, E) \quad \text{or as} \quad X_a(p_L, p_m, p_a, \pi, E)$$

with profits replacing nonlabor variable input prices and fixed inputs. The comparative statics are then

(IA-8a)
$$\left.\frac{\partial X_a}{\partial p_a}\right|_\pi = \left.\frac{\partial X_a}{\partial p_a}\right|_U - X_a \frac{\partial X_a}{\partial Y}$$

which is identical to the pure consumer case, while

(IA-8b)
$$\frac{\partial X_a}{\partial p_a} = \left.\frac{\partial X_a}{\partial p_a}\right|_U - X_a \frac{\partial X_a}{\partial Y} + \frac{\partial X_a}{\partial Y} \frac{\partial \pi}{\partial p_a}.$$

Since $\partial \pi / \partial p_a = Q_a$, from above, the extra effect does indeed come through changing farm profits. The comparative statics for leisure

(IA-9)
$$\frac{\partial X_L}{\partial p_L} = \left.\frac{\partial X_L}{\partial p_L}\right|_U + (T - X_L - L)\frac{\partial X_L}{\partial Y}$$

are similar. The income effect is weighted by household labor supply minus labor demand (marketed surplus of labor), not by household labor supply. Assuming that leisure is a normal good makes a backward-bending supply curve less likely than if the household were solely a supplier of labor.

Deriving Virtual (Shadow) Prices

To explore the consequences of making prices endogenous to the household, it will be convenient to use duality results to express the equilibrium of the household. We can define the full-income function as the maximization of equation (IA-3) with respect to outputs and variable inputs subject to the production function, (IA-4), and can write

(IA-10)

$$Y = \Lambda(q_c, p_a, p_L, q_v, K, T, E) = p_L T + \pi(q_c, p_a, p_L, q_v, K) + E.$$

The full-income function is the sum of the value of endowed time, a restricted (or short-run) profits function, and exogenous income. The profits function has the usual properties—for example, it is convex in all prices. For the expenditure side of full income, we can define an expenditure function as the minimum expenditure (equation IA-2) required to meet a specified level of utility, $e(p_L, p_m, p_a, \overline{U})$. It obeys the usual properties; in particular it is concave in prices, and the partial derivatives with respect to price are the Hicksian (compensated) demand functions.

Now we are in a position to relax our assumption that prices are fixed market prices. The household's equilibrium is characterized by equality between the household's full-income function, Λ, and its expenditure function, e, where the expenditure function is evaluated at the utility level achieved at the household's optimum. This condition will hold whether or not households face given market prices. Now suppose that a household is constrained to equate consumption with production for some commodity(ies). One possible reason for this would be nonexistence of a market. Consequently, the household's equilibrium will be characterized by a set of additional conditions—equality of household demand and household supply for each commodity for which there is no market (see Dixit and Norman 1980, who use these conditions to characterize an economy under autarky). This second set of equilibrium conditions implicitly defines a set of virtual prices—or shadow prices (Neary and Roberts 1980; Deaton and Muellbauer 1980, chapter 4.3), which, if they existed, would induce the household to equate supply and demand for these commodities.

These virtual prices are not taken parametrically by the household as market prices are; rather, they are determined by the household's choices. From the household's equilibrium, it can be seen that they will be a function of market prices, time endowment, fixed inputs, and either exogenous income or utility. (They will also be a function of fixed household characteristics if these are introduced into the model.) Consequently, these prices depend on both the household's preferences and its production technology. Changes in market prices will now affect behavior directly, as before, and indirectly through changes in the virtual prices. Some mechanism of identifying the consequences of this additional effect is therefore needed to illuminate the significance of one's assumptions regarding price formation. That mechanism will be the comparative statics of the virtual price, which will now be developed.

Suppose, for the moment arbitrarily, that there exists no market for labor. The household equilibrium is characterized by

(IA-11) $e(\bar{p}_L^*, p_m, p_a, \bar{U}) = \bar{p}_L^* T + \pi(q_c, p_a, \bar{p}_L^*, q_v, K) + E$

$\qquad e_L(\bar{p}_L^*, p_m, p_a, \bar{U}) = T + \pi_L(q_c, p_a, \bar{p}_L^*, q_v, K)$

where $e_L = \partial e / \partial p_L^*$ and likewise $\pi_L = \partial \pi / \partial p_L^*$. The second equation gives the Hicksian leisure demand on the left-hand side and time endowment minus labor demand on the right. From this equation, $\bar{p}_L^*$, the compensated virtual price, can be solved for as

(IA-12) $\qquad\qquad\qquad \bar{p}_L^* = \bar{p}_L^*(p_m, p_a, q_c, q_v, K, U).$

Note that the utility level is being held constant, and not exogenous income. Alternatively, the Marshallian leisure demand

$$X_L(p_L^*, p_m, p_a, p_L^* T + \pi + E)$$

can be set equal to time minus labor demand, and a solution obtained:

(IA-13) $\qquad\qquad\qquad p_L^* = p_L^*(p_m, p_a, q_c, q_v, K, E).$

To relate the functions $\bar{p}_L^*$ and p_L^*, a somewhat different expenditure function is needed. Let

$e'(p_L, p_m, p_a, q_c, q_v, K, T, \bar{U}) =$

(IA-14) $\displaystyle\min_{\substack{X_L, X_m, X_a \\ Q_c, Q_a, L, V}} p_L X_L + p_m X_m + p_a X_a - p_L T - q_c Q_c - p_a Q_a$

$\qquad\qquad\qquad + p_L L + q_v V \quad \text{st } U(\cdot) = \bar{U} \text{ and } G(\cdot) = 0.$

This represents the minimum exogenous income, E, necessary to achieve utility level $\bar{U}$, given the production function and prices. It is clear that e' meets all the conditions that a regular expenditure function does, and that

(IA-15) $e'(p_L, p_m, p_a, q_c, q_v, K, T, \bar{U}) =$

$\qquad\qquad\qquad e(p_L, p_m, p_a, \bar{U}) - p_L T - \pi(q_c, p_a, p_L, q_v, K).$

In equation (IA-13), if exogenous income E is evaluated at e' (hence full income, Y, at e) then Marshallian leisure demand equals the Hicksian demand and $p_L^* = \bar{p}_L^*$. Using this equality

(IA-16) $\qquad \dfrac{\partial \bar{p}_L^*}{\partial Z} = \left.\dfrac{\partial p_L^*}{\partial Z}\right|_E + \dfrac{\partial p_L^*}{\partial E}\dfrac{\partial e'}{\partial Z} \qquad Z = p_m, p_a, q_c, q_v, K.$

With utility constant, the response of the virtual price can be expressed in terms of second partial derivatives of the expenditure and profit functions. Using the implicit function rule and equation (IA-11),

(IA-17) $\dfrac{\partial \bar{p}_L^*}{\partial Z} = -(e_{LZ} - \pi_{LZ})/(e_{LL} - \pi_{LL}) \qquad Z = p_m, p_a, q_c, q_v, K.$

The denominator is unambiguously negative owing to the concavity of the expenditure function and the convexity of the profits function. The numerator can be either sign, but often the sign will be determinate if one is willing to assume that commodities are substitutes or complements in consumption or production. For instance, if $Z = p_m$, the price of the market-purchased commodity, X_m, the numerator is $-e_{Lm}$, which is negative if leisure and X_m are substitutes. If $Z = p_a$, the numerator is $\pi_{La} - e_{La}$. The first term is the response of output of X_a to wage, which should be negative. The second term is negative if leisure and X_a are substitutes. For an input price, q_v, the numerator is π_{Lv}, which can be positive or negative, depending on whether labor and input V are gross substitutes or complements.

Equation (IA-17) is a basic result that will be used repeatedly in the subsequent discussion to illuminate the effects of totally or partly absent markets. It allows one to sign the partial derivatives of the compensated virtual price, making this device useful in looking at the comparative statics. Moreover, it allows one to compare directly models that make differing assumptions about the nature of prices the household faces.

The sign of the response of the compensated virtual price, $\bar{p}_L^*$, to exogenous variables can be given an intuitive interpretation. If, for instance, the price of the cash crop rises, the demand schedule for labor should shift upward. Given that other market prices, fixed inputs, and utility are constant, the virtual wage has to rise in order to reequate compensated labor supply with demand. Such a rise will lower labor demand along the new schedule, while raising compensated, or Hicksian, labor supply.

The virtual prices are functions of both household preferences and production technology. Because these prices help to determine both consumption and production choices—they belong in both the expenditure and the full-income functions—the household commodity demands will depend on production technology, both through the virtual price and through full income. Output supplies and input demands will depend on preferences through the virtual price. If, however, the household faces only market prices or if it faces a virtual price for a commodity that is consumed but not produced (or vice versa), then production choices will not depend on household preferences, but consumption choices will depend on production technology through full income. The model is then recursive.

Models with Absent Markets: Labor

In the historical development of agricultural household models, partially autarkic behavior has been very important. One of the earliest models can be traced to the Russian economist A. V. Chayanov (1925) (see Millar 1970 for a reinterpretation). Chayanov was concerned with explaining the allocation of labor between work and leisure in Russian peasant households given his observation that virtually no hired labor was used in farm production activities. He recognized that such households were not simply maximizing profits as in the theory of the firm; rather, they had a subjective equilibrium in which they equated the marginal utility of household consumption with the marginal utility of leisure. His analysis was embellished by a group of Japanese economists, notably Tanaka (1951) and Nakajima (1957), during the 1950s and 1960s. Nakajima (1969), in particular, gave the model currency among English-speaking economists. He not only gave a mathematical formulation to Chayanov's model, but also proposed some additional models. Nakajima's (1969) model of a pure commercial family farm without a labor market assumed that households sold all of their output and purchased commodities from the market, and that they produced the output with family labor and a fixed amount of land. He also allowed for the possibility of a minimum subsistence consumption requirement as well as a target income. In a different version (his semisubsistence family farm), he allows the family to consume some of its output, and in another version introduces two outputs. Similar models of peasant households were advanced by Mellor (1963) and Sen (1966) and by economic anthropologists such as Fisk and Shand (1969). These models are thus special cases of the general form of the agricultural household model developed here.

These models in which the family supplied all of its labor were used primarily to explore the effects on labor supply (and hence output, since family labor was assumed to be the only variable input) of changes in different variables. The effect of output price was of particular interest because of the seemingly perverse possibility that output might respond negatively to output price. This might occur if the income effect, resulting in more leisure demand, was large enough. Nakajima showed that an exogenous increase in land input might also reduce output, because it too would have an income effect on leisure. Nakajima separated the response of labor supply to output price into substitution and income effects, showing that the income-compensated response of labor supply to output price was positive. Sen showed that output response to output price could be negative, and that there could be no output response to the withdrawal of family workers if the remaining family laborers worked sufficiently hard to offset the reduced number of hours worked as workers were withdrawn. This required that the virtual wage (or its ratio to output price, Sen's real cost of labor) be constant, as would be the case in

Sen's model if the marginal utilities of both income and leisure were roughly constant.

The possibility of a negative response of labor demand (and of output supply) to output price at the household level is dependent on the constrained equality of labor demand and labor supply. At the market level labor demand might respond negatively to output price if wage is bid up sufficiently (see Barnum and Squire 1980). If markets exist for all commodities, then the model is recursive and labor demand will respond positively to output price as long as it is not an inferior input. Nakajima noted this when discussing his model with a labor market and a cash crop. Both Jorgenson and Lau (1969) and Krishna (1964, 1969) proposed separable semisubsistence models in which labor is marketed and output is partly consumed at home. Jorgenson and Lau's study has formed the basis on which most of the empirical work to date has been conducted.

Consumption and Leisure Responses

The difference that absence of a labor market makes to the comparative statics of leisure and commodity demand can easily be seen by using the notion of a virtual wage. Write the Marshallian demand as

$$X_i[p_L^*, p_m, p_a, p_L^* T + \pi(q_c, p_a, p_L^*, q_v, K) + E], \quad i = L, M.$$

Differentiate this with respect to q_c to obtain

(IA-18)
$$\frac{\partial X_i}{\partial q_c} = \frac{\partial X_i}{\partial p_L^*} \frac{\partial p_L^*}{\partial q_c} + Q_c \frac{\partial X_i}{\partial Y} \quad i = L, M.$$

Cash output price has two effects on the demand for leisure or for the market purchased good: it has an income effect by changing profits (the second term), and it changes the virtual price for labor. Clearly, when the household is a price-taker in the labor market, the latter effect is zero.

Equation (IA-18) can be decomposed into substitution and income effects, which will help in signing the uncompensated changes in the demand for leisure and the market-purchased commodity. First, it can be shown that the uncompensated effect with respect to the virtual wage equals the compensated effect. To do this, it will be useful to equate Marshallian and Hicksian demands by evaluating full income, Y, and e and the virtual wage at $\bar{p}_L^*$ (that is, if both hold utility constant):

(IA-19) $X_i[\bar{p}_L^*, p_m, p_a, e(\bar{p}_L^*, p_m, p_a, U)] = X_i^c(\bar{p}_L^*, p_m, p_a, U)$
$$i = L, M.$$

Differentiating both sides of (IA-19) with respect to the cash crops price, q_c, and using $\partial e/\partial \bar{p}_L^* = X_L$ results in

(IA-20) $\qquad \dfrac{\partial X_i}{\partial p_L^*}\bigg|_Y \dfrac{\partial \overline{p}_L^*}{\partial q_c} + X_L \dfrac{\partial X_i}{\partial Y} \dfrac{\partial \overline{p}_L^*}{\partial q_c} = \dfrac{\partial X_i^c}{\partial p_L^*} \dfrac{\partial \overline{p}_L^*}{\partial q_c} \qquad i = L, M.$

Since

(IA-21) $\qquad \dfrac{\partial X_i}{\partial p_L^*} = \dfrac{\partial X_i}{\partial p_L^*}\bigg|_Y + (T - L)\dfrac{\partial X_i}{\partial Y}$

and since labor supply equals labor demand, so that $X_L = T - L$, it can be shown by means of equation (IA-20) that $\partial X_i/\partial p_L^* = \partial X_i^c/\partial p_L^*$. Thus the income effect of a change in the virtual wage equals zero, which is intuitive since the net marketed surplus is zero when no labor market exists.

The term $\partial p_L^*/\partial q_c$ in equation (IA-18) can be made more transparent by noting from (IA-16) that

$$\dfrac{\partial p_L^*}{\partial q_c} = \dfrac{\partial \overline{p}_L^*}{\partial q_c} + Q_c \dfrac{\partial p_L^*}{\partial E} \qquad \left(\text{recall that } \dfrac{\partial e'}{\partial q_c} = -Q_c\right).$$

When this is substituted into (IA-18), one obtains

(IA-22) $\qquad \dfrac{\partial X_i}{\partial q_c} = \dfrac{\partial X_i^c}{\partial p_L^*} \dfrac{\partial \overline{p}_L^*}{\partial q_c} + Q_c\left(\dfrac{\partial X_i}{\partial Y} + \dfrac{\partial X_i}{\partial p_L^*} \dfrac{\partial p_L^*}{\partial E}\right) \qquad i = L, M$

(IA-22a) $\qquad\qquad = \dfrac{\partial X_i^c}{\partial p_L^*} \dfrac{\partial \overline{p}_L^*}{\partial q_c} + Q_c \dfrac{\partial X_i}{\partial E} \qquad\qquad i = L, M.$

Equations (IA-22) and (IA-22a) show the decomposed income and substitution effects. They also clarify the significance of one's view regarding the labor market. If the labor market does exist, then the household faces market prices so the substitution effect—the first term in (IA-22a)—is zero and the entire effect of the change in output price is captured by the income effect $[Q_c(\partial X_i/\partial Y)]$. This is positive, providing leisure or the purchased commodity are normal goods. When the labor market is absent, a substitution effect is caused by the change in the income-compensated virtual wage. Using equation (IA-17), we can rewrite this substitution effect as

(IA-23) $\qquad \dfrac{\partial X_i^c}{\partial p_L^*} \dfrac{\partial \overline{p}_L^*}{\partial q_c} = e_{Li}\pi_{Lc}/(e_{LL} - \pi_{LL}) \qquad i = L, M.$

If the compensated virtual wage rises—that is, if $\pi_{Lc} < 0$, in equation (IA-23)—then there is a substitution away from leisure or toward the purchased commodity (if it is a substitute for leisure). The income effect comes in two parts: first, a traditional looking income effect, and, second, a substitution-type effect due to an induced change in the uncompensated virtual wage, p_L^*. This two-part income effect is identical to equation (IA-24) of Neary and

Roberts (1980), once their equation (IA-19) has been substituted in. From equation (IA-22), we can see that when leisure is normal, $\partial p_L^*/\partial E > 0$, the income effect is smaller for leisure and larger for purchased goods (if we assume substitutability with leisure) when the labor market does not exist than when it does. An increase in exogenous income raises the uncompensated virtual wage, and this increase induces a substitution away from leisure or toward the purchased commodity. If we assume that the entire income effect is positive, the net effect of a rise in output price q_c on leisure is indeterminant, but it will be positive for the purchased commodity. This is the same result, of course, as is obtained by both Nakajima (1969) and Sen (1966).

Output Responses

If labor is the only variable input, then the sign of output response to output price must be the opposite to the leisure response. More generally, we can write output supply Q_c as

$$Q_c = \frac{\partial \pi}{\partial q_c} (q_c, p_a, p_L^*, q_v, K)$$

consequently,

(IA-24)
$$\frac{\partial Q_c}{\partial q_c} = \pi_{cc} + \pi_{cL} \frac{\partial p_L^*}{\partial q_c}.$$

The first term is the output-supply response when the virtual wage is fixed, and is positive. The second term is negative, if we assume that output responds negatively to the virtual wage ($\pi_{cL} < 0$), so that the sign of the entire expression is indeterminant. It is possible to show that when household utility is held constant, the response is positive. (See Lopez 1980 for a somewhat different demonstration of this.) Substituting for $\partial p_L^*/\partial q_c$ from equation (IA-16),

(IA-25)
$$\frac{\partial Q_c}{\partial q_c} = \left(\pi_{cc} + \pi_{cL} \frac{\partial \bar{p}_L^*}{\partial q_c} \right) + Q_c \pi_{cL} \frac{\partial p_L}{\partial q_c}.$$

The first two terms are the response of output supply when utility is held constant. The third term is an income effect, which is negative if π_{cL} is negative. The second term equals $\pi_{cL}^2/(e_{LL} - \pi_{LL})$, so it is negative. However, summing it with π_{cc} gives a nonnegative quantity because the function e' (equation [IA-15]) is concave in prices, so that

$$\frac{\partial^2 e'}{\partial q_c^2} \frac{\partial^2 e'}{\partial p_L^{*2}} - \left(\frac{\partial^2 e'}{\partial q_c \partial p_L^*} \right)^2 \geq 0.$$

Straightforward algebra shows that this expression is simply the first two terms in equation (IA-25) multiplied by $-\partial^2 e'/\partial p_L^{*2}$. The magnitude of π_{cL} and consequently the likelihood of a negative output response will be influenced by the number of variable inputs and the partial elasticity of substitution between labor and these other inputs. Presumably, the more inputs and the more substitutable they are, the less negative π_{cL} will be and the more likely will be a positive response to output price. Clearly, when the virtual wage is exogenous to the household, output response will be positive and greater than when the virtual wage is endogenous.

If the household consumes some of the output for which price is changing, Q_c, the comparative statics have an additional substitution effect, and the income effect is weighted by net output sold (marketed surplus) and not by total output:

$$(IA\text{-}26) \qquad \frac{\partial X_i^c}{\partial p_a} = \frac{\partial X_i^c}{\partial p_a}\bigg|_{\bar{p}_L^*} + \frac{\partial X_i^c}{\partial p_L^*}\frac{\partial \bar{p}_L^*}{\partial p_a} \qquad i = L, M, A.$$

Again using equation (IA-17), $\partial \bar{p}_L^*/\partial p_a = (\pi_{aL} - e_{aL})/(e_{LL} - \pi_{LL})$, which is positive if Q_a and leisure are substitutes. Deriving the comparative statics as before, one finds

$$(IA\text{-}27) \qquad \frac{\partial X_i}{\partial p_a} = \left(\frac{\partial X_i^c}{\partial p_a}\bigg|_{p_L^*} + \frac{\partial X_i^c}{\partial p_L^*}\frac{\partial \bar{p}_L^*}{\partial p_a}\right)$$

$$+ (Q_a - X_a)\left(\frac{\partial X_i^c}{\partial p_L^*}\frac{\partial p_L^*}{\partial E} + \frac{\partial X_i}{\partial Y}\right) \qquad i = L, M, A$$

$$(IA\text{-}27a) \qquad \frac{\partial X_i}{\partial p_a} = \frac{\partial X_i^c}{\partial p_a} + (Q_a - X_a)\frac{\partial X_i}{\partial E} \qquad i = L, M, A.$$

The substitution effect for leisure demand can be of either sign. It is not necessarily positive, even if X_a and leisure are substitutes holding the virtual wage constant. The income-compensated response of X_a can also be of either sign when the wage is virtual, since an increase in the price, p_a, will increase the compensated virtual wage leading to a substitution toward X_a. The substitution effect for X_a will be less negative than when the labor market exists, as Neary and Roberts (1980) found in the pure rationing case. The income effect has an extra term, which for X_a and X_m is positive if leisure is a substitute and is negative for leisure demand.

Marketed Surplus Responses

If we examine the response of marketed surplus of X_a, $Q_a - X_a$, to change in p_a, we obtain from (IA-25), (IA-16), and (IA-27)

$$\frac{\partial(Q_a - X_a)}{\partial p_a} = \left(\frac{\partial Q_a}{\partial p_a}\bigg|_{\bar{p}_L^*} + \frac{\partial Q_a}{\partial p_L^*}\frac{\partial \bar{p}_L^*}{\partial p_a} - \frac{\partial X_a^c}{\partial p_a}\bigg|_{\bar{p}_L^*} - \frac{\partial X_a^c}{\partial p_L^*}\frac{\partial \bar{p}_L^*}{\partial p_a}\right)$$

(IA-28) $$+ (Q_a - X_a)\left(\frac{\partial Q_a}{\partial p_L^*}\frac{\partial p_L^*}{\partial E} - \frac{\partial X_a^c}{\partial p_L^*}\frac{\partial p_L^*}{\partial E} - \frac{\partial X_a}{\partial Y}\right).$$

The first four terms (in brackets) hold utility constant, and therefore comprise the substitution effect. It is straightforward to see that this effect equals

$$-\frac{\partial^2 e'}{\partial p_L^{*2}}\left[\frac{\partial^2 e'}{\partial p_a^2}\frac{\partial^2 e'}{\partial p_L^{*2}} - \left(\frac{\partial^2 e'}{\partial p_a \partial p_L^*}\right)^2\right]$$

and consequently is nonnegative (remember that e' is concave in prices). The last term equals

$$(Q_a - X_a)\left(\frac{\partial Q_a}{\partial E} - \frac{\partial X_a}{\partial E}\right)$$

and so is the income effect that should be negative if marketed surplus is positive and X_a is a normal good. Consequently, marketed surplus of X_a might respond positively or negatively to an increase in its own price. Comparing this result with that when the labor market exists, one can see that the extra substitution effects will be negative if X_a and leisure are substitutes, since the compensated virtual wage will then rise. The extra income effects should also be negative, so that a greater possibility exists of obtaining a negative own-price response of marketed surplus of X_a.

The comparative statics with respect to changes in p_m, q_v, K, and T are similar to equation (IA-22), except that the response of the compensated virtual wage is different, as is the term weighting the income effect. Specific formulae are left for the interested reader to derive.

Models with Absent Markets: Z-Goods

The market that one assumes not to exist clearly does not affect the foregoing argument. Hence, the existence of a labor market is a necessary but not a sufficient condition for an agricultural household model to be separable. *All markets must exist for separability,* although this is not a sufficient condition, as is discussed in the next section. Historically, economists thought that the labor market was the one least likely to exist for peasant farms. That view has been changing, however, since active rural labor markets have been found according to several studies (Rosenzweig 1978; Spencer and Byerlee 1977; Bardhan 1979; Squire 1981; Binswanger and Rosenzweig 1984), although they are not necessarily perfectly competitive ones. More recent studies have focused on the nonexistence of a market for so-called Z-goods. This was first formalized by Hymer and Resnick (1969), who refer to Z-goods as nonagricultural, nonleisure activities. In general the commodities Hymer and Resnick refer to, such as food processing and metalworking, are commodities for which small-scale rural industries have been found to exist (Anderson and Leiserson 1980; and Liedholm and Chuta 1976). Z-goods, however, refer equally as well to nontraded outputs of household production activities such as the number and quality of children, home maintenance, or food preparation. In this way, the household production models of Becker (1965) and Gronau (1973, 1977) can be incorporated into agricultural household models.

Hymer and Resnick (1969) were concerned with the increasing specialization of agricultural household activities, which they saw as occurring over time and resulting in an increasing marketed surplus from agricultural households. Rather than focus on the leisure-labor tradeoff, they concentrated on the Z-goods-food tradeoff. In terms of the general model specified here, households produce foods, Q_a, which they consume and sell the surplus in exchange for manufactured commodities, X_m. They produce Z-goods, our L, which they consume entirely at home, $L = X_L$. Labor supply does not enter their model, but implicitly it is assumed to be fixed in amount and to be equal to labor demand; thus it is not a choice variable. In terms of this model, labor is one of the fixed inputs, K, and it does not appear in the utility function. Alternatively, leisure can enter the utility as a fixed factor, similar to other fixed household characteristics such as household size and age distribution. In this case, the expenditure function will include leisure as a conditioning variable just as a short-run cost or profit function includes fixed inputs.

There are no other variable inputs, $V = 0$, nor does there exist a cash crop, $Q_c = 0$. These assumptions imply that the product transformation curve between foods and Z-goods has the usual downward-sloping, concave shape. Consequently, to find the sign of the effect of a change in the price of foods, p_a, on the output of foods, only the effect on demand (hence supply) of Z-goods needs to be considered, $\partial X_L / \partial p_a$, which is given by equation (IA-27). The substitution effect can be of either sign. If Z-goods and foods are substitutes, a rise in food prices will increase Z-goods consumption when the compensated virtual price of Z-goods is held constant. This will force up the virtual price, however, and lead to a substitution away from Z-goods consumption. The income effect is weighted by the marketed surplus of foods, which is presumed to be positive. Hymer and Resnick assume that Z-goods consumption is inferior and that the combined substitution effect is small, so that the net effect of a rise in the price of foods will be a fall in the consumption (and production) of Z-goods, and hence a rise in food production. Of course, if foods are consumed by the household, the food consumption response to food price needs to be examined before what happens to marketed surplus of foods can be judged. As seen from equation (IA-28), marketed surplus of food can either rise or fall in response to an increase in food price, provided the household has a positive marketed surplus and Z-goods are normal (so $\partial p_L^*/\partial E > 0$). However, if Z-goods are inferior, then its virtual price falls when exogenous income rises, so that production of foods rises and compensated consumption of foods falls (provided foods and Z-goods are substitutes), making it more likely that the response of marketed surplus is positive.

The Hymer and Resnick assumption that leisure and labor demand are not choice variables can be relaxed. If it is assumed that no labor market exists, then two virtual prices exist, one for labor and one for household Z-goods. There are thus two equality constraints on supply and demand rather than one. Alternatively, the labor market may be assumed to exist.

As an alternative to the Hymer and Resnick interpretation, Z-goods might be interpreted as being synonymous with household production activities. The original work of Becker (1965), Lancaster (1966), and Muth (1966) emphasizes that the commodities that yield household utility are produced within the household by goods purchased in the market and by labor. In terms of this general model, X_c is a vector of commodities consumed and produced in the home. Market-purchased inputs are denoted by V ($X_m = 0$), and labor demand, L, is a vector of time allocated to the production of each commodity. Leisure usually is not considered, so total time is the sum of time spent in household production, plus market work. It is often assumed that Z-goods production is not joint and that it exhibits constant returns to scale. If no fixed inputs exist, the supply (and profit) functions will be ill-defined so that shadow (or implicit) prices cannot be defined in terms of equality between household supply and demands. Rather, they are defined implicitly by the partial derivatives of the cost functions with respect to output (Pollak and Wachter 1975). However if fixed inputs do exist, or the production functions are strictly convex, shadow (or virtual) prices can be implicitly defined from the equality of household demand and supply functions.

An elaboration of the household production framework by Gronau (1973) provides results almost identical to the model of Hymer and Resnick. Gronau's model amounts to relabeling food consumption as leisure and food production as labor demand. He, too, has a market-purchased and a home-produced (Z) commodity, with home production using labor and purchased inputs. As in the Hymer and Resnick model, a virtual price exists for the home-produced (Z) good. If no labor is supplied to the market, there will exist a virtual (shadow) wage as well, and the analysis is comparable to the Hymer and Resnick model when labor is a choice variable but no market for it exists. In a subsequent study, Gronau (1977) assumes that the market-purchased and the household-produced commodities are perfect substitutes in consumption and so may be added. As long as market purchases are positive and labor is sold on the market, this model is recursive. If labor is not sold on the market, a virtual (shadow) price for labor exists, and if market purchases of the home-produced commodity are zero, a virtual price for it exists. Huffman and Lange (1982) have a slightly different version of Gronau's model in which the household is explicitly an agricultural household. The household jointly produces a farm and a household commodity (X_c and X_a), selling the former and consuming the latter. Labor is sold on the market, but the only market purchases are for production inputs. A virtual price exists for the household commodity and the model is not separable. If, however, the farm and household commodities have separate production functions and fixed inputs could only be allocated to one enterprise, the model would be recursive between farm production decisions and the rest.

Partly Absent Markets: Commodity Heterogeneity

Even if all markets exist, households may face a virtual price that depends on both production technology and household preferences, so that again an agricultural household model would not be recursive. This can occur because markets are partly absent or because constraints are institutionally imposed (see Sicular, chapter 10, for an analysis of such constraints imposed on a production team in the People's Republic of China). In particular, a household may be able to sell a commodity but not buy it, or vice versa. If this commodity is both consumed and produced by the household, then the household's optimum may be at a corner at which consumption equals production. Such corner solutions are likely to occur especially when commodities are heterogeneous. For example, hired and family labor may be imperfect substitutes because of extra monitoring or search costs of hired labor. On-farm and off-farm labor may give different levels of disutility (see Lopez, chapter 11). Alternatively, a commodity consumed out of home production may have a different quality than the same commodity purchased on the market, and thus sales and purchase prices may differ.

Households can sell and consume family labor or home production, but they cannot purchase them. This suggests that, at the market price, supply might be less than demand, which is not possible. For such corner solutions, the commodity in question has a virtual price that would equate supply and demand. The virtual price will be higher than the market price provided that the compensated marketed surplus responds positively to price.

If households have preferences between on-farm and off-farm labor, then even if hired and family labor are perfect substitutes in production there may exist excess supply of on-farm labor at the market wage, in which case the virtual wage will be lower.

It should be clear that the comparative statics for these equilibria are identical to those considered earlier for the cases in which no market exists. Also, if these corner solutions are not binding, then the model is separable, the market prices being the opportunity costs. This will complicate empirical work since, if such heterogeneity exists, a sample is likely to include both households at corners and households at interior solutions.

Recursive Conditions Summarized

This appendix has reviewed the comparative statics of some basic, static agricultural household models. A key modeling issue is under what circumstances a model is recursive. This is very important for applied empirical work since it makes the problem far more tractable (see chapter 1). It has been shown that a sufficient condition for recursiveness is that all markets exist for commodities that are both produced and consumed, with the household being a price-taker in each one, and that such commodities are homogeneous. As long as households can buy or sell as much as they want at given prices, production and consumption decisions can be treated as if they were sequential, production decisions being made first, even though they may be made simultaneously. Such strong conditions are not necessary, however. In particular, the homogeneity assumption can be dropped. In this case, however, the agricultural household model remains recursive only if the household does not choose to be at a corner for a commodity that it both produces and consumes (for example, consuming all of its output). If a corner solution is chosen, then a virtual price exists, which is a function of both preferences and technology, so that the household's decision is no longer separable. Note that even in the case of heterogeneity, it is still necessary to assume that all markets exist and that prices are given to households to achieve recursiveness. If even one market does not exist (for a commodity that is consumed and produced), then recursiveness from production to consumption decisions breaks down.

Historically, nonrecursive agricultural household models were thought to be relevant, primarily because labor markets were presumed not to exist. As more has been learned about rural labor markets in developing countries, this assumption has become increasingly questioned. This does not mean that empirically relevant models have to be recursive, but the reasons for nonrecursiveness need to be clearly spelled out (see chapter 2).

References

Anderson, Dennis, and Mark Leiserson. 1980. "Rural Nonfarm Employment in Developing Countries." *Economic Development and Cultural Change*, vol. 28, pp. 227–48.

Bardhan, Pranab. 1979. "Wages and Unemployment in a Poor Agrarian Economy: A Theoretical and Empirical Analysis." *Journal of Political Economy*, vol. 87, pp. 479–500.

Barnum, Howard, and Lyn Squire. 1980. "Predicting Agricultural Output Response." *Oxford Economic Papers*, vol. 32, pp. 284–95.

_____. 1979. *A Model of an Agricultural Household*. Washington, D.C.: World Bank.

Becker, Gary. 1965. "A Theory of the Allocation of Time." *Economic Journal*, vol. 75, pp. 493–517.

Binswanger, Hans, and Mark Rosenzweig, eds. 1984. *Contractual Arrangements, Employment and Wages in Rural Labor Markets: A Critical Review*. New Haven, Conn.: Yale University Press.

Chayanov, A. V. 1925. "Peasant Farm Organization." Moscow: Cooperative Publishing House. Translated in *A. V. Chayanov: The Theory of Peasant Economy*, ed. D. Thorner, B. Kerblay, and R. E. F. Smith. Homewood, Ill.: Richard Irwin, 1966.

Deaton, Angus, and John Muellbauer. 1980. *Economics and Consumer Behavior*. Cambridge, Mass.: Cambridge University Press.

Dixit, Avinash, and Victor Norman. 1980. *Theory of International Trade: A Dual, General Equilibrium Approach*. Cambridge, Mass.: Cambridge University Press.

Fisk, E. K., and K. T. Shand. 1969. "The Early Stages of Development in a Primitive Economy: The Evolution from Subsistence to Trade and Specializations." In *Subsistence Agriculture and Economic Development*, ed. C. F. Wharton, Jr. Chicago: Aldine.

Gronau, Reuben. 1973. "The Intrafamily Allocation of Time: The Value of the Housewives' Time." *American Economic Review*, vol. 68, pp. 634–51.

_____. 1977. "Leisure, Home Production and Work: The Theory of the Allocation of Time Revisited." *Journal of Political Economy*, vol. 85, pp. 1099–1124.

Huffman, Wallace, and Mark Lange. 1982. "Farm Household Production: Demand for Wife's Labor, Capital Services and the Capital-Labor Ratio." Yale University Economic Growth Center Discussion Paper no. 408. New Haven, Conn.

Hymer, Stephan, and Stephen Resnick. 1969. "A Model of an Agrarian Economy with Nonagricultural Activities." *American Economic Review*, vol. 59, pp. 493–506.

Jorgenson, Dale, and Lawrence Lau. 1969. "An Economic Theory of Agricultural Household Behavior." Paper read at 4th Far Eastern Meeting of the Econometric Society.

Krishna, Raj. 1964. "Theory of the Firm: Rappoteur's Report." *Indian Economic Journal*, vol. 11, pp. 514–25.

_____. 1969. "Comment: Models of the Family Farm." In *Subsistence Agriculture and Economic Development*, ed. C. F. Wharton, Jr. Chicago: Aldine.

Lancaster, Kelvin. 1966. "A New Approach to Consumer Theory." *Journal of Political Economy*, vol. 74, pp. 132–57.

Liedholm, Carl, and Enyinya Chuta. 1976. *The Economics of Rural and Urban Small-Scale Industry in Sierra Leone*. African Rural Economy Working Paper no. 14. East Lansing: Michigan State University.

Lopez, Ramon. 1980. "Economic Behaviour of Self-Employed Farm Producers." Ph.D. dissertation, University of British Columbia, Vancouver.

Mellor, J. 1963. "The Use and Productivity of Farm Labor in Early Stages of Agricultural Development." *Journal of Farm Economics*, vol. 45, pp. 517–34.

Millar, J. 1970. "A Reformulation of A. V. Chayanov's Theory of the Peasant Economy." *Economic Development and Cultural Change*, vol. 18, pp. 219–29.

Muth, Richard. 1966. "Household Production and Consumer Demand Functions." *Econometrica*, vol. 34, pp. 699–708.

Nakajima, Chihiro. 1957. "Over-Occupied and the Theory of the Family Farm." *Osaka Daigaku Keizaigaku*, vol. 6.

_____. 1969. "Subsistence and Commercial Family Farms: Some Theoretical Models of Subjecture Equilibrium." *Subsistence Agriculture and Economic Development*. Edited by C. F. Wharton, Jr. Chicago: Aldine.

Neary, J., and K. Roberts. 1980. "The Theory of Household Behavior under Rationing." *European Economic Review*, vol. 13, pp. 25–42.

Pollak, Robert, and Michael Wachter. 1975. "The Relevance of the Household Production Function for the Allocation of Time." *Journal of Political Economy*, vol. 83, pp. 255–77.

Rosenzweig, Mark. 1978. "Rural Wages, Labor Supply, and Land Reform." *American Economic Review*, vol. 68, pp. 847–61.

_____. 1982. "Agricultural Development, Education and Innovation." In *The Theory and Experience of Economic Development*. Edited by M. Gersovitz and others. London: George Allen & Unwin.

Sen, Amartya K. 1966. "Peasants and Dualism with and without Surplus Labor." *Journal of Political Economy*, vol. 74, pp. 425–50.

Spencer, Dunstan, and Derek Byerlee. 1977. *Small Farms in West Africa: A Descriptive Analysis of Employment, Incomes and Productivity in Sierra Leone*. African Rural Economy Program Working Paper no. 19. East Lansing: Michigan State University.

Squire, Lyn. 1981. *Employment Policy in Developing Countries: A Survey of Issues and Evidence*. New York: Oxford University Press.

Tanaka, Osamu. 1951. "An Equilibrium Analysis of Peasant Economy." *Nogyo Keizai Kenkyu (Journal of Rural Economics)*, vol. 22.

World Bank. 1983. *World Development Report*. New York: Oxford University Press.

Part II

Case Studies

3

Agricultural Household Modeling in a Multicrop Environment: Case Studies in Korea and Nigeria

Inderjit Singh and Subramanian Janakiram

A CONSIDERABLE AMOUNT of both theoretical and applied work has now been done to develop integrated models of behavior for the agricultural household such as those attested to by many studies in this volume. Most of the models to date have been econometric in nature, however, and have treated only single farm outputs on the production side. The decision concerning crop composition has been neglected. It is obviously important to treat multiple crop outputs on the production side of these models because family farms in developing countries are seldom specialized single-crop farms; instead they grow a variety of outputs, some mainly to meet family consumption needs, and others mainly for the market in varying degrees. Of course, linear programming models have been used extensively to analyze the allocation of resources between various competing crops on the farm, but these generally neglect the interdependence between production and consumption decisions that characterize family farms. This chapter outlines an approach that extends the theory of the agricultural household to multicrop economies by using programming models to characterize production decisions. Other chapters in this volume use multiple-output production functions (see chapters 4 and 7).

Farm-household data from two quite dissimilar environments, Korea and Nigeria, are used to illustrate the use of this approach in multicrop environments. The empirical results from this study are therefore of considerable interest. In Korea family farms are highly integrated into rural factor and product markets and, though not fully commercial, they produce mainly for the market. It is a multicrop environment in which a number of outputs are grown under irrigated conditions, which allow considerable control over expected outcomes. Crops are seasonal but are grown in single-crop stands. In addition, there are many sources of non-farm incomes for rural households engaged in farm production. In contrast, farms in the state of Kaduna in northern Nigeria (where the data for this study were collected) are more isolated from factor and product markets and produce primarily for home-subsistence needs. Although these farms are semicommercial and hence linked to factor and product markets, there are few opportunities for off-farm incomes. But most important, the region is semiarid. Thus a great deal of uncertainty exists about expected outcomes that depend upon weather. To hedge against this type of uncertainty, farmers plant a variety of crops, but intercropping is the dominant mode, and crops planted in rotation of various mixtures are the rule and single crop stands are the exception.

This difference in environments leads to behavioral differences that might result in different models. The approach taken here, however, is to use the same model for both sets of households, although the implementation is somewhat different in the two cases. The differences in the empirical results are fairly pronounced: the Nigerian households are more responsive to income where consumption is concerned, but less responsive to prices and to land where outputs and marketed surpluses are concerned. Given that the Nigerian households are far more subsistence oriented, poorer, and in a more land abundant environment than their Korean counterparts, these results are not surprising.

There are several advantages to integrating programming with econometric techniques. First, many economists who deal with development projects in rural areas tend to focus on farm activities rather than production functions when they analyze farm behavior. This is partly because they are primarily interested in cost-benefit analysis and thus tend to collect data for that purpose, which are easier to relate to a set of farm activities than to inputs and outputs that are related through some form of production function. The data collected for cost-benefit analysis can be readily adapted for linear programming models. To do so, in many cases, we need only to specify the objective function with an optimizing rule and organize the data into a set of farm activities with associated inputs, cost outputs, and returns. The widely used modeling routine called FARMOD that the World Bank uses, for example, calculates parametric changes to be made in the budget data used for cost-benefit analysis and thus makes it possible to calculate rates of return under varying assumptions. These data have been readily adapted for use in programming models of representative farms.

Second, project economists find it easier to work with an embodied technology as defined by activities than with a disembodied technology as represented in a production function. Thus, for example, it is easier to deal with an activity associated with "a high-yielding variety sown with tillers and tubewells" and to differentiate this from the activity of sowing a traditional variety with hand labor than it is to work with a production function in which technological change is captured by a constant coefficient that is higher for a set of observations in which "high-yielding varieties sown with tillers" have been included. The two are conceptually similar (and given certain functional forms, the one can be mapped into the other). Nonetheless, technology choices are treated more explicitly in linear programming models and are easier to understand than production functions. Furthermore, activity analysis allows one to examine the impact of technology changes in a piecemeal manner. Thus, for example, the impact of new varieties can be separated from that of mechanization, whereas this is more difficult to do with econometric techniques and decomposition methods unless all the relevant data are available.

Finally, programming models provide a link between the project economists, who usually rely on budget data in their analyses and confine their work almost exclusively to examining production-side effects, and the macroeconomists, who use aggregate data and are more concerned with the broader effects throughout the economy. This link cannot be established unless the analysis done with farm budget data at the representative farm level is linked with demand analysis by tracing the impact of farm-level production changes on farm-sector incomes.

The Theoretical Model

The model of household behavior developed in this chapter extends the basic model set out in chapter 1 to multicrop economies. It describes a semicommercial family farm that operates in competitive product and factor markets, and thus production and consumption decisions are separable. This characterization seems to be quite suitable for the Korean sample. In rural Korea, product and factor markets are well developed and agricultural households are active participants in all markets. For the northern Nigeria sample, as will be seen, this characterization is less appropriate. Because that region is semiarid, production risks are much more important and product and factor markets are far less active, at least during some parts of the years. To model production risk and absent markets is beyond the scope of this chapter, however. (See chapter 9 for an explicit model of an agricultural household under production risk.)

The planning horizon for the model is assumed to be a single crop year. Thus decisions that relate to the total supply of household factors of production—such as family labor force, area of land operated, and other farm implements or animals—are treated as given. The fixed and quasi-fixed endowments available to the household are fixed in the short run. Similarly, it is assumed that the household has already made its decisions concerning the desired level of savings. The model therefore focuses on the short-run allocation of expenditures to different goods (including farm goods for own-consumption and leisure and the allocation of fixed and variable inputs to different production activities. It is also assumed that any incomes from nonfarm and nonwage sources are given and determined exogenously. (That is, any incomes from transfers or other than farm and labor assets are given.)

Further, it is assumed that there are markets for agricultural and other types of labor and that all households participate in labor markets either as buyers or sellers of labor, or both, and that family labor and hired labor are perfect substitutes. Thus the use of family time and the disposal of outputs are determined with reference to market wages and prices. In input and output markets, the household is assumed to be a price-taker. In addition, it is assumed that production is riskless, that land, if rented, is rented on the basis of fixed rents, and that there are no contractual arrangements that might lead to nonstandard profit-maximizing conditions.

With these points in mind, the model can be formulated as follows:

For any production cycle, the agricultural household is assumed to maximize the utility function.[1]

(3-1) $$\max U = U(\chi) = U(\chi_a, \chi_m, \chi_l)$$

subject to:

(3-2) $$[1]'A_i \le \bar{R}_i \qquad\qquad i = 1, \ldots K$$

and

(3-3) $$p'\chi = \pi'A + Z + E$$

where χ is a $(h \times 1)$ vector of items consumed, composed of a vector of agricultural staples (χ_a), a vector of market-purchased goods (χ_m), and leisure (χ_l) and where

    $[1]'$ is an $(l \times n)$ unit vector;

    A_i is an $(n \times 1)$ vector of land use by crop and technologies on the ith type of land (or other quasi-fixed resource); and A is an $(m \times 1)$ vector of A_i;

    $\bar{R}_i$ is the maximum available quantity of the ith type of land (or quasi-fixed resource);

    p' is a $(1 \times h)$ vector of prices of consumed goods including leisure;

π' is a $(1 \times m)$ vector of net returns to fixed factors (after labor costs have been excluded), by crop, technology, and land type;

Z is Becker's concept of full income and equals the market value of total time available to the household plus any (net) nonlabor income.

E is any nonfarm, nonlabor (that is, exogenous) income.

The model thus has h consumption goods (of which one is leisure), k types of land, n crops, and m $(= k \times n)$ different possible crop combinations or activities by land type and technology. The household is assumed to maximize its utility function subject to a land constraint by quality or type (for example, lowland, upland, irrigated, or unirrigated) and a combined income and time constraint. The consumption of family leisure is included on the left-hand side of equation (3-3) and is valued at the market wage. The total (family and hired) labor input into crop production, again valued at the market wage, is included on the right-hand side of equation (3-3) in the determination of π. The household is a net buyer and seller of labor, depending on whether total time available less time allocated to leisure is less than or greater than the total labor requirement in production.

It is assumed that technology is linear. Thus for the rth crop on the ith type of land we have

$$(3\text{-}4) \qquad \pi_{ir} = p_r c_{ir} - \sum_j q_j b_{irj}$$

where p_r is the price of the rth crop (and hence the rth consumption good), c_{ir} is the yield of the rth crop on the ith type of land, q_j is the price of the jth input, and b_{irj} is the jth input requirement per unit of the ith type of land for the rth crop. As noted above, the total (family and hired) labor requirement is one of the inputs.

Forming the Lagrangian expression, we have

$$(3\text{-}5) \quad \max L = U(\chi) - \lambda(p'\chi - \pi'A - Z) + \sum v_i(\bar{R}_i - [1]'A_i).$$

If we note that all χ's and λ's (the marginal utility of income) are positive, the first-order Kuhn-Tucker conditions are

$$(3\text{-}6) \qquad U_\chi - \lambda p' = 0$$

$$(3\text{-}7) \qquad p'x - \pi'A - Z = 0$$

$$(3\text{-}8) \qquad \lambda\pi' - V \le 0$$

$$(3\text{-}9) \qquad IA[\lambda\pi' - V] = 0$$

$$(3\text{-}10) \qquad \bar{R}_i - [1]'A_i \ge 0 \qquad\qquad i = 1, \ldots k$$

(3-11) $$V_i[\bar{R}_i - [1]'A_i] = 0 \qquad i = 1, \ldots k$$

where V is an $(m \times 1)$ vector of V_i and I is a unit matrix.

Equations (3-6) and (3-7) correspond to the standard first-order conditions of consumer-demand theory. Equations (3-8)–(3-11) represent the production side of the model. If equation (3-10) is binding for the ith type of land, then $V_i \geq 0$ represents the shadow price (in terms of utility) of that type of land. If for the rth crop $\lambda\pi_{ir} \leq V_i$, the rth crop will not be grown on the ith type of land. For the sth crop, however, assume that $\lambda\pi_{is} = V_i$. In this event, the ith type of land will be allocated completely to the sth crop. The model thus produces the standard result of complete specialization by land type. The results also indicate that the production side of the model can be solved independently of the value of λ (the marginal utility of income). Since $V_i = \lambda\pi_{is}$, where s is the most profitable crop, a comparison between V_i and $\lambda\pi$ for any $r \neq s$ is not affected by the value of λ; λ is a scalar that can be canceled out, the allocation of land to competing crops being determined exclusively by a comparison of profitability at market prices. If, on the other hand, equation (3-10) is not binding for the ith type of land, that type of land is not cultivated. Once again the solution is independent of λ. Just as for the basic model, this one may therefore be treated as a block recursive one, in which production decisions are first determined by profit maximization and then the consumption decisions are determined by utility maximization, given the level of maximized profits.

The demand side of the model is specified to conform to the linear expenditure system. Both the functional form and the estimation of the demand system are described fully in Barnum and Squire (1979).

Model Results for Agricultural Households in Korea and Nigeria

The linear expenditure system for agricultural households in Korea and Nigeria has been estimated for six commodity groups. In the case of Korea, the commodities are paddy, barley, other farm produce, market-purchased food items, market-purchased nonfood items, and labor supply. In the Nigerian case, the commodity groups are millet, sorghum, other farm produce, market-purchased food items, market-purchased nonfood items, and labor supply. The estimated parameters of the linear expenditure systems are not of direct interest, but a selected set of own-price and expenditure elasticities estimated from these parameters are shown in table 3-1. The results are generally consistent with expectations.

Table 3-1. *Selected Household Demand Elasticities from Korea and Nigeria*

Elasticity	Korea (1970)	Nigeria (1976)
Own-price		
Main crop[a]	−0.18	−0.05
Market purchased nonfood goods	−0.87	−0.6
Labor supply	0.0	0.01
Expenditure		
Main crop[a]	0.57	1.8
Market purchased non food goods	2.76	3.3
Labor supply	−0.45	−0.5

a. The main crop is rice for Korea and sorghum for Nigeria.

The own-price demand elasticities in Nigerian households are somewhat less elastic than for households in Korea, as is to be expected from the relative levels of market integration and production for own-consumption in the two regions. The higher expenditure elasticities in the Nigerian case are somewhat unexpected, but not in any way contrary to theory or other evidence in view of the low level of incomes in Nigeria and the general desire for consumer goods, which are relatively scarce in rural areas of Nigeria compared with Korea. The elasticities of family labor supply are also as expected and are not much different in the two cases.

An important test of the production side of the models is the ability of the linear programming (LP) models to predict the actual observed cropping patterns among farm households. For northern Nigeria, in contrast to Korea, the predicted cropping pattern and profit levels did not conform well to the data. Several crops, the most important being groundnuts and cowpeas, did not come into the solution algorithm. Overspecialization and farm profits that were too high were being predicted. This is a common problem when farm-production choices in which risk is an important consideration are being modeled (see Roumasset, Boussard, and Singh 1979). Another possible factor is the sharp seasonal movement of prices, which are not being captured by the model. Prices are considerably greater in the dry season, when more foods are purchased, than they are after harvest, when foods are eaten out of own-production. This price differential provides an incentive to produce more and to store it, rather than have to buy at high prices later in the year. These considerations, which are much less important for Korea than for Nigeria, are not captured by the model used here.

To capture some of these issues, although not in a rigorous fashion, we introduced the LES estimates of the minimum amounts of farm-produced outputs retained for home consumption as constraints in the programming model.[2] Of these constraints, those for sorghum and millet were not binding, whereas those for relatively less important crops such as groundnuts and cowpeas were. A comparison of the observed and predicted values from the two LP models are presented in table 3-2. They suggest a fairly accurate specification of the production side of the models, given that the Nigerian results are dependent on the constraints imposed iteratively from the demand side of the models. In the Korean case, the models underpredict the areas devoted to potatoes and miscellaneous grains relative to other crops; in the case of Nigeria, the underprediction is for the millet-groundnut-vegetable and the maize-cowpea intercropping activities. In view of the complexity of the cropping patterns in the two regions (three sowing seasons and two land types in Korea and very complex intercropped mixtures year round in Kaduna province in Nigeria), the models perform fairly well.

The real test of the quantitative significance of using the agricultural household modeling approach, however, comes from a comparison of own- and cross-price demand elasticities in two sets of calculations: first, when household and farm behavior are treated separately and the responses of the endogenous variables are estimated under the assumption that farm profits are exogenous; and, second, when household and farm behavior are considered to be interdependent and the responses of endogenous variables to exogenous price changes incorporate changes in

Table 3-2. *Observed versus Predicted Values of Farm Production from the Linear Programming Models, Korea and Nigeria*
(percent)

Cropping pattern	Observed	Predicted
Korea (1970)		
Rice	40.7	43.1
Barley mixtures	28.2	32.8
Miscellaneous grains	4.2	1.0
Pulses	12.2	12.1
Potatoes	6.1	1.5
Vegetables	8.6	9.5
Total	100.0	100.0
Nigeria (1976–77)		
Sorghum-cowpea-groundnut intercrop	54.2	51.4
Millet-groundnut-vegetable intercrop	17.7	15.6
Millet-cotton-maize intercrop	21.8	23.0
Maize-cowpea intercrop	6.3	10.0
Total	100.0	100.0

farm profits that result from changes in the exogenous variables. These two sets of demand elasticities are shown in table 3-3 for both Korea and Nigeria. (All the elasticities calculated for the integrated model are, of course, arc elasticities because the production side of the model is an LP model for which only discrete parametric changes can be made. These arc elasticities are calculated simply by carrying out the parametric changes in the LP models and calculating the changes in profits (and incomes) that result and then calculating the demand side changes that correspond to the changes in farm incomes.)

The first thing to note is that the elasticities from the integrated models are significantly different. In the Korean case, of the twelve elasticities for which comparisons are reported, half have a different sign altogether and two others having the same sign differ significantly in magnitude. In the Nigerian case, of the twelve comparisons possible, two-thirds have

Table 3-3. *A Comparison of Selected Arc Elasticities to Test the Significance of Integrating Household Production and Consumption Decisions, Korea and Nigeria*

| | Elasticity of | | | | | |
| | Own-consumption of rice | | Nonfood purchases | | Labor supply | |
With respect to	I	II	I	II	I	II
Korea (1970)						
Price of rice	−0.18	0.01	−0.19	0.81	0.03	−0.13
Price of barley	0.00	0.06	−0.02	0.30	0.00	−0.05
Price of other crops	0.00	0.12	0.00	0.57	0.00	−0.09
Wage rate	0.16	0.01	0.77	0.05	0.00	0.11

| | Own-consumption of millet | | Own-consumption of sorghum | | Nonfood purchases | | Labor supply | |
	I	II	I	II	I	II	I	II
Nigeria (1976–77)								
Price of millet	−0.08	0.07	−0.25	0.08	−0.15	0.23	0.08	−0.02
Price of sorghum	−0.09	0.19	−0.05	0.19	−0.14	0.57	0.03	−0.06
Wage rate	0.03	0.01	0.06	0.02	0.04	0.01	0.01	0.10

Note: The first set of elasticities in the rows marked (I) are computed on the assumption that farm profits (π) are constant. The second set of elasticities in the rows marked (II) are computed on the assumption that farm profits (π) are variable. Changes in farm profits (π) are estimated by using the linear programming production model to trace the impact of discrete changes in exogenous variables. The first set of elasticities corresponds to the linear expenditure system alone and the second set to the integrated model.

Table 3-4. *Selected Elasticities to Illustrate the Impact of Changes in Farm Technology and Costs on Household Demand in Integrated Models, Korea (1970)*

	With respect to							
Elasticity of	*Wage rate*	*Seed costs*	*Fertilizer and pesticide costs*	*Interest rate on working capital*	*Power tiller capacity*[a]	*Paddy land available*	*Upland available*	*Average farm size*
Own-consumption of rice	0.0097	−0.0111	−0.0484	−0.0155	0.0019	0.0691	0.0334	0.1013
Food purchases	0.0156	−0.0179	−0.078	−0.025	0.0031	0.1114	0.0538	0.1632
Nonfood purchases	0.047	−0.054	−0.2349	−0.0754	0.0094	0.3353	0.1620	0.4913
Labor supply	0.105	0.0088	0.0383	0.0123	−0.0015	−0.0547	−0.0264	−0.0802

a. Obtained by increasing the capacity of power tillers available per household; the elasticity should be read as a percentage change in the endogenous variable for a 1 percent change in the available tiller capacity.

different signs and the rest differ in magnitude. What accounts for this difference?

Consider, for example, the own-price consumption elasticities of the main crops grown by agricultural households—rice in Korea and sorghum in Nigeria. Both these crops are the most important food items (and hence nutrition source) in the consumption bundle and the most important crops on the farms. Traditional demand theory would suggest that the own-consumption of these crops would decrease if their prices were increased (the estimated elasticities are −0.18 and −0.05 for rice and sorghum, respectively), a result totally consistent with theory if agricultural households are to be treated solely as consumers. The integrated models, however, predict that own-consumption of these commodities will increase (the estimated elasticities are 0.01 and 0.19 in this case).

Consider another example, that of the elasticities of family labor supply with respect to the wage rate. Again, in traditional demand theory, an increase in wage rates implies an increase in real household incomes, and the result is a negative or inelastic response of household labor supply. (These elasticities are not significantly different from zero for both Korea and Nigeria.) These effects are offset in the case of the integrated agricultural household models because an increase in agricultural wages also affects farm costs on the production side and reduces total farm incomes. As a result, labor-supply responses become positive or more elastic. (This is the case with an elasticity of 0.11 and 0.1 in Korea and Nigeria, respectively.)

Another set of elasticities can be estimated only for the integrated models—those with respect to input costs and other technological changes in farm production. This point can be illustrated for Korea by the selected set of elasticities in table 3-4. The Korean model is more appropriate for illustration purposes because it is much richer on the production side owing to the widespread adoption of new high-yielding varieties, the extensive use of nonfarm inputs in agriculture, and the use of irrigation and tillers. The Kaduna region in Nigeria has seen few of these technological innovations, nor is the use of nonfarm inputs significant.

Consider, first, the elasticities with respect to the costs of seeds, fertilizers, and pesticides. As input costs go up, the model correctly predicts that farm incomes and hence outlays on all commodities will be reduced and work effort on part of households will be increased. Increased tiller capacities or the availability of additional land (of different qualities) or increases in family size, which increases farm-family labor, have the opposite effects. Similarly, with increased input costs, farm incomes are reduced and thus the amount of family labor supply forthcoming from the households increases, whereas increases in the capacities of land and quasi-fixed inputs have just the opposite effect because household incomes are increased. Without an integrated framework that treats both production and consumption decisions, it would not be possible to trace these effects from the production side to the demand side of household behavior.

The power of the integrated models can also be illustrated by the elasticities of supply and marketed surplus of the main crop, and the elasticities of labor demand and fertilizer demand (the main own- and purchased inputs) in response to output and input prices and land quantity (a simple proxy for farm size). As both output prices and land quantity lead to increased farm incomes, outputs, marketed surplus, and input demands increase, as expected (see table 3-5). In contrast, an increase in fertilizer price leads to a decline in all these endogenous responses, again as expected. When the magnitudes of these responses are compared, the Korean households are far more responsive than those in the Nigerian sample. Given the differences in environment, level of institutional development, and degree of subsistence, this is not surprising.

Another set of elasticities shows the importance of modeling multicrop environments using the LP models. The cross-price supply and marketed surplus elasticities shown in tables 3-6 and 3-7 cannot be estimated in single-crop models that can only provide own-price elasticities (that is, only the diagonal elements). These results are intrinsically interesting because they show that, in Korea, rice complements soybeans because they

Table 3-5. *Selected Arc Elasticities from the Integrated Models, Korea and Nigeria*

	With respect to		
Elasticity of	*Price of rice*	*Fertilizer price*	*Land quantity*
Korea (1970)			
Marketed surplus of rice	1.4	−0.34	0.81
Output of rice	1.56	−0.30	0.9
Total labor demand	0.57	−0.12	0.3
Fertilizer demand	1.29	−1.10	0.6
	Price of sorghum	*Land quantity*	
Nigeria (1976–77)			
Output of sorghum	0.30	0.08	
Marketed surplus of sorghum	0.20	0.06	
Total labor demand	0.12	0.02	

Table 3-6. *Selected Cross-Price Arc Elasticities of Supply of Agricultural Outputs in the Integrated Models, Korea and Nigeria*

With respect to the price of	Elasticity of supply of		
	Rice	Barley	Soybeans
Korea (1970)			
Rice	1.56	−0.0[a]	+0.0[a]
Barley	−0.0[a]	0.5	−0.0[a]
Soybeans	0.04	−0.1	0.1
	Sorghum	Millet	Groundnuts
Nigeria (1976–77)			
Sorghum	0.3	−0.0[a]	−0.2
Millet	−0.0[a]	0.25	−0.5
Groundnuts	−0.0[a]	−0.0[a]	0.18

a. Insignificantly small.

Table 3-7. *Selected Cross-Price Arc Elasticities of Marketed Surplus of Agricultural Outputs in the Integrated Models, Korea and Nigeria*

With respect to the price of	Elasticity of marketed surplus of		
	Rice	Barley	Soybeans
Korea (1970)			
Rice	1.4	−0.0[a]	−0.0[a]
Barley	−0.0[a]	0.5	−0.0[a]
Soybeans	−0.03	−0.15	0.06
	Sorghum	Millet	Groundnuts
Nigeria (1976–77)			
Sorghum	0.25	−0.0[a]	−0.04
Millet	−0.0[a]	0.18	−0.07
Groundnuts	−0.0[a]	−0.0[a]	0.09

a. Insignificantly small.

can be grown in rotation. Thus, increased rice prices also increase soybean output. Barley, however, competes with rice and the cross-price supply elasticity is negative. In Nigeria, groundnuts compete with both sorghum and millet for farm resources, even though they are mainly grown in mixtures with millet and other vegetables. The small cross-price supply elasticities also reveal that the main crops generally dominate the cropping patterns in such a manner that the substitution effects on the production side are insignificant.

Policy Implications

A number of important policy issues can be examined within the framework of the models developed here. The empirical results from these studies have important policy implications for at least four broad sets of issues.

Pricing and Food Procurement Policies

In most developing countries, the government is involved in one way or another in setting producer or consumer prices for foodgrains and in food procurement operations. Any analysis of what these government interventions are likely to achieve must take into account not only the response of rural and urban consumers to prices, but also that of producers, for it is the supply response of the latter that determines the extent to which procurement operations are likely to be successful in fetching forth the desired marketed surplus. But what if the producers themselves constitute a large part of the consumers in rural areas, as is the case with peasant households in most developing countries? Will increased prices increase production and marketed surplus, and if so, by how much? What impact will this have on the nutritional status of rural households?

Because these issues are important, both the Korean and Nigerian governments have tried to (a) keep prices low for urban and rural consumers; (b) provide adequate incentives for farm production; and (c) assure adequate farm incomes. An additional concern in Korea has been to shield producers and consumers from large price fluctuations. These often turn out to be conflicting goals and the determination of what policies to follow depends upon the tradeoffs among alternative objectives. But to evaluate the impact of pricing policies, we need a way of predicting at least three sets of responses: (i) the multiple output responses, given the complex set of relative factor and product prices, resource requirements, and constraints faced by producers at the farm level; (ii) the consumption response of farming households, including their own-consumption; and (iii) the consumption responses of nonfarm rural and urban households to any changes in output or input prices.

Our models provide direct information to the first two components. Consider the own- and cross-price elasticities of rice and sorghum, the two most important food items (and hence nutrition sources) in both Korea and Nigeria. The results from the integrated models suggest that the consumption of both rice and sorghum among rural farming households is likely to increase marginally (the relevant elasticities are 0.01 and 0.19, respectively). Although the predicted output responses of these crops are higher—much more so for Korea (the output elasticities are 1.56 for rice and 0.3 for sorghum)—the increase in household consumption dampens this response, so that the response of marketed surpluses is lower (the relevant elasticities are 1.4 for rice and 0.2 for sorghum in table 3-3). The differences in the estimated responses for marketed surplus in Korea and northern Nigeria suggest much less scope for government pricing policy in generating food production in northern Nigeria, a finding that is consistent with the relatively low levels of technology there.

Similarly, the cross-price demand elasticities are not only positive for other food crops, but are also positive and fairly high for nonfood purchases. This suggests that although raising farm output prices may have a negative impact on the nutritional status of nonfarming rural households, it has a positive impact on agricultural households. The net impact in rural areas depends, of course, upon the relative weights of the two groups in the rural population. In both Korea and Nigeria, farming households are by far the most dominant, and hence increased output prices are likely to enhance the nutritional status in rural areas.

The cross-price effects are both on the production and consumption side. Thus, for example, increased sorghum prices in Nigeria reduce the production of groundnuts and millet as sorghum displaces them in the crop mix, but increased prices, because they increase incomes, have a positive effect on their consumption. An opposite effect occurs when input prices are increased. Thus a 10 percent increase in fertilizer prices in Korea reduces the fertilizer demand by 11 percent and the output of rice by 3 percent, but as incomes decline, so does own-consumption of rice (by 0.1 percent). The decline in the marketed surplus is the outcome of these two offsetting effects. It is important to be able to trace this type of production-consumption interaction in evaluating the impact of input subsidy policies.

The ability to predict accurately the marketed surplus response to government pricing policies is an essential ingredient in developing effective procurement programs and in evaluating their costs and their impact on different groups of the population. Government procurements often determine the level of food imports (exports), which in turn affect foreign exchange.

Farm Technologies and Farm Employment

If rapid technological change in the agricultural sector is both land intensive and labor saving, what is the likely impact on the demand for labor? More important, how will family versus hired labor be affected by this increased demand? This matter is of great interest to policymakers, especially in areas where rural households rely upon wage employment as a major source of income. Such households include not only the landless but also small and marginal farmers with very small land holdings. How would such households fare under different pricing policies and techno-logical regimes? We cannot provide an answer to these questions unless we can establish how agricultural households respond to technological changes in allocating family labor to farm production. Our results pro-vide some insight.

To begin with, all land intensification programs in Korea and Nigeria definitely increase the demand for total labor. The demand for hired la-bor increases at an even higher rate. This is because increased land avail-ability, by increasing farm incomes, also decreases the supply of family labor. The slack is taken up by the increased demand for hired labor. Thus, land-intensification strategies greatly increase the employment op-portunities for rural wage earners. The same effect occurs when new high-yielding varieties are introduced because they also increase the demand for total labor inputs (not shown), but, by increasing income, they in-crease the demand for hired labor even faster.

The impact of labor-displacing technologies such as power tillers on hired labor in Korea is more complicated, however. We have used para-metric changes in the LP model to trace the changes. The results show that, on one hand, the tillers displace labor and thus reduce the total labor demand (the relevant elasticity not shown in the tables is -0.025; that is, a 1 percent increase in tiller capacity reduces total labor demand by 0.25 percent). On the other hand, they also substantially increase farm incomes so that the supply of family labor to farm production is reduced (the relevant elasticity is -0.0015). The net effect on hired labor is posi-tive and the relevant elasticity is 3.8! This is because a small reduction in family labor, which accounts for nearly 96 percent of the total labor use in Korean farming households (using the mean farm size of 1.89 hectares in the sample), means a large increase in the demand for hired labor, even though the total demand for labor has decreased.

Pricing Policies and Farm Employment

Nonfarm households may also benefit considerably from increased wages and employment opportunities related to increased output prices because they not only increase output and the demand for total labor, but they also decrease the supply of family labor as profits and incomes increase. The demand for hired labor thus increases faster than the demand for total labor as farmers use more labor per unit of output. The relevant elasticities for labor demand with respect to the prices of the main crops are 0.57 for Korea and 0.12 for Nigeria; for labor supply, they are −0.13 for Korea and −0.06 for Nigeria. Once again, these relationships are stronger in Korea than in Nigeria.

These results have important policy implications because they show that benefits of new technologies spill over into increased employment for rural wage earners. Increased output prices may also have the same impact, but whether or not they result in a net gain in welfare for the landless depends on two offsetting effects—on the one hand, they obtain increased employment (and perhaps increased wages and incomes, depending on how tight rural labor markets are and how they operate), but, on the other hand, they face higher prices for farm goods because they respond as pure consumers (not having any land at all, by definition, they are not affected by the production side of the model). The debate over which effects dominate is still going strong, and these models can help address the issues more clearly with the relevant empirical elasticities.

Nonfarm Employment and Demand Linkages

Ultimately, the question of what happens to the demand for the labor of the landless cannot be resolved by looking at the demand for farm labor only. The extent to which agricultural growth *induces* employment in the rural nonfarm sector and the industrial sector depends upon the extent to which the growth (and distribution) of farm incomes increases the demand for nonfarm consumer goods and services. How do technological change and changes in farm output prices affect this demand? Our results show that this demand increases tremendously. The elasticities of demand for nonfarm purchased goods in response to increased output prices is positive, as expected, but the expenditure elasticity of demand for these goods is both positive and very high (2.76 in Korea and 3.3 in Nigeria). Thus, as farm incomes and farm employment increase, so does the final demand for nonfarm and industrial goods. Our results allow us to explicitly trace these final demand linkages from the production changes all the way to changes in the final demand for nonfarm goods. Expenditure elasticities for nonfarm goods in the order of 2.5–3.0 as predicted by our results mean that a 10 percent increase in farm and rural incomes would increase the demand for nonfarm goods by about 20 to 30 percent.

Farm household incomes in Korea grew at an annual rate of 5 percent (at constant prices) between 1965 and 1976. The implied growth in demand for nonfarm products is 14 percent per annum. This has, of course, been the reason why high rates in the growth of the labor force in Korea have not been accompanied by unemployment or underemployment. The growth in farm employment generates secondary induced effects that lead to the rapid growth of nonfarm employment. If this is accompanied by high rates of outmigration to the urban sector in response to growing employment opportunities, as in the case of Korea (and Nigeria more recently), real rural wage rates rise quite rapidly and rural poverty is substantially reduced. This linkage between high rates of agricultural growth accompanied by high rates of growth in nonfarm employment and reduced incidence of rural poverty can also be found in other developing economies—most notably, Taiwan and the Indian and Pakistani Punjabs.

The policy implications of the results discussed here illustrate the importance of developing an integrated approach to modeling agricultural household decisions in a multicrop environment.

Conclusions

This chapter extends the theory of an agricultural household to multi-crop environment and provides results for two rather diverse agricultural regions at quite different levels of development. The results clearly indicate the value of such models in tracing the impact of price, technology, and other policy changes in rural areas that are dominated by peasant households that make production and consumption decisions jointly. They also clearly show the quantitative significance of using this approach, as the predicted responses differ not only in magnitude but also in direction when compared with the traditional approaches to demand and supply response.

The approach to modeling agricultural household behavior described here has several limitations, however. Most of these stem from the simplifying assumptions made in developing the theoretical framework. The two that are most troubling (at least for the Nigerian context) are the way in which labor markets are handled and the risk-free environment posited for household decisions. Although evidence shows that most rural households operate in rural factor markets—particularly in labor markets, where they are both buyers and sellers of labor—considerable evidence also shows that these markets are interlinked. Thus, credit, land, and labor contractual relations may not be independent. This linkage implies that the standard type of profit-maximization conditions used here may not hold. This is the case, for example, where tenancy prevails and labor contracts are conditional on land contracts. In such cases the theories would have to be extended and reformulated.

The assumption of a risk-free environment is also a matter of some concern, especially when intercropping decisions are being modeled, as in the case of Nigeria. We know that intercropping is a response to risk in environments with uncertain rainfall. Clearly, the production side of the models could be improved by incorporating risk. This can be done by either using the focus-loss method developed by Boussard and Petit (1967) or by using one or another version of the mean-variance approaches to risk programming. The one that has proved fairly robust is the one developed by Hazell (1971). The real challenge, however, is to integrate this explicitly into an expected utility-maximization framework. An initial attempt in this direction is made by Roe and Graham-Tomasi (see chapter 9). An integrated approach that would both remove the assumptions of independent factor markets and include uncertainty remains a challenge to future research work.

The ultimate value of the modeling approach developed in this chapter lies in its ability to use farm management and farm family budget data that can be collected by project economists and that are often readily available for the analysis of a number of important policy issues. Thus, despite their limitations, these models should find increasing use in project and policy work.

Appendix: Data Sources

The data for Korea are from a series of extensive farm household surveys carried out by the Ministry of Agriculture and Fisheries beginning in 1962. The surveys took in farms that were included in a representative national random sample of farm households throughout the country. As far as possible, the same households were surveyed each year, except when replacements were necessary owing to death, retirement, or migration of the farm operators. From 1962 to 1973, the surveys included approximately 1,200 farm households each year. (The number was increased to 2,500 in 1974.) These surveys cover data on farm production (including area planted to rice and other information on farm operations and expenditures) as well as household data (including family size, labor use, household expenditures, and other sources of income).

We used 1970 data to estimate the linear expenditure systems and derive the parameters for the programming models. After accounting for missing variables and data errors, we had a sample of 524 households. In addition, we used data from the *Yearbook of Agriculture and Forestry*, 1971, to test cropping patterns from a nationwide survey. The survey data appear in the *Report on the Results of Farm Household Economy Survey and*

Production Cost Survey of Agricultural Products (various years) published by the Ministry of Agriculture and Fisheries. The data were made available to us through the courtesy of The National Agricultural Research Institute, Seoul, and the data tapes were provided by the Department of Agricultural Economics and Rural Sociology, Ohio State University.

The Nigerian data come from three large agricultural projects funded by the World Bank. The project areas—Funtua, Gombe, and Gusau—are in the state of Kaduna. So that progress in these project areas could be monitored, a Monitoring and Evaluation Unit was funded under the Bank projects and given the responsibility of collecting farm-level production and expenditure data. The project areas lie in the semidry northern region of Kaduna state and are populated mainly by the Hausa and Fulani. The predominant crops in the region are sorghum, millet, groundnuts, cowpeas, and cotton. More than half the area in this region is cultivated mainly by hand in a mixed intercropping system with practically no modern inputs.

The projects began in 1975 and we were able to obtain data for the 1976–77 cropping season. This information consisted of household size, family labor use, farm income and expenditures, and household expenditures. The data were collected on a *weekly* basis for 42 weeks and covered some 24 villages and 24 households in each village. After validation, a sample size of 312 households from the Funtua project area was selected and the data for the 1976–77 cropping year were used for analysis (for details, see World Bank, 1980).

Notes

1. This model was first presented in a study by Ahn, Singh, and Squire (1981), where the results from the Korean study were first reported.

2. Using the Stone-Geary form of the utility function $U = \Sigma U_i = n \Sigma \beta_i \ln(\chi_i - \gamma_i)$, where χ_i is the per capita consumption of the ith commodity, n the number of family members, and $\beta_i \gamma_i$ the parameters. The estimates of γ_i can be interpreted as minimum amounts retained for own-consumption.

References

Ahn, Choong Yong, Inderjit Singh, and Lyn Squire. 1981. "A Model of an Agricultural Household in Multi-crop Economy: The Case of Korea." *The Review of Economics and Statistics*, vol. 63, no. 4 (November), pp. 520–25.

Barnum, Howard N., and Lyn Squire. 1979. *A Model of an Agricultural Household: Theory and Evidence.* Washington, D.C.: World Bank.

Boussard, Jean Marc, and Michele Petit. 1967. "Representation of Farmer's Behavior under Uncertainty with Focus-Loss Constraint." *Journal of Farm Economics*, vol. 49, no. 4, pp. 869–80.

Hazell, P. B. R. "A Linear Alternative to Quadratic and Semi-Variance Programming for Farm Planning Under Uncertainty." 1971. *American Journal of Agricultural Economics*, vol. 53, no. 1, pp. 53–62.

Roumasset, James, Jean Marc Boussard, and Inderjit Singh, eds. 1979. *Risk, Uncertainty and Agricultural Development*. New York: Agricultural Development Council, New York.

World Bank. 1980. "The Monitoring and Evaluation of the Funtua, Gusau, and Gombe Agricultural Development Projects: A Guide to Statistical Tabulations." West African Region Projects Department. Washington, D.C.

4

Estimating the Determinants of Food Consumption and Caloric Availability in Rural Sierra Leone

John Strauss

THE NUTRITIONAL WELL-BEING OF HOUSEHOLDS, particularly those with low incomes, has become an important consideration for governments of developing countries. Policy planners seldom have much indication of how different policies will affect household food consumption and thereby nutritional well-being, however, particularly among agricultural households. For such households, a change in price or technology, by affecting profits from home production, will shift the budget constraint and thereby result in a profit effect (see chapter 1). The resultant increase in foods consumed may lead to increased or decreased nutrient availability at the household level.

To explore the effects of prices and of income on household nutrient (hereafter) calorie availability, disaggregation of foods is required. The model estimation reported in this chapter does just that. Consumption and marketed surplus responses are estimated for five food items, nonfoods, and labor supply for rural households in Sierra Leone. The responses are obtained by means of a farm-household model with multiple outputs. The data are from a cross-sectional survey of households in rural Sierra Leone. Since price variation for all commodities exists by region, it is possible to estimate complete systems of commodity demand and of output-supply and variable input demands.

The basic farm-household model, which has already been estimated, assumes that households produce a single crop (Lau, Lin, and Yotopoulos 1978; Barnum and Squire 1979). These earlier studies used demand sys-

Note: The research described in this chapter was funded under USAID contract no. AID/DSAN-C-0008.

tems that impose severely restrictive assumptions concerning the effect of full income on expenditures (see chapter 1). Although such assumptions as linear Engel curves may not be completely unreasonable when a high level of commodity aggregation is used, they seem questionable when one is interested in more disaggregated commodities.

This study uses a Quadratic Expenditure System (QES), which allows for quadratic Engel curves. Demographic variables are explicitly incorporated into the model to allow for a richer specification than can be obtained by means of per capita variables. Output and variable input allocation is determined by a system of output-supply and input-demand equations. These equations are derived from a multiple output production function assumed to be separable between outputs and inputs—constant elasticity of transformation is assumed for outputs and Cobb-Douglas for inputs. Thus the analyst is able to use regional price data and can avoid problems of endogeneity with respect to variables on the right-hand side, which would be encountered if a multiple-output production function were estimated directly. Household specialization in production is such, however, that some commodities are not produced by some households. If the censored nature of the data is ignored, parameter estimates become inconsistent. Perhaps this is one reason why econometric approaches to estimating the production side of multiple-output farm-household models have not previously been attempted. (See chapter 3 for a discussion of the use of linear programming to determine crop allocation in a multiple-output agricultural model.)

The results of the study show that for most crops, the own-price effects on consumption remain negative when profits are allowed to vary. Cross-price consumption elasticities are both positive and sizable. Marketed surplus elasticities are sizable, even for the lowest-income households. Elasticities of caloric availability with respect to total expenditure are found to be large, and vary little by expenditure group. Price elasticities of calorie availability are generally positive, though very small, except for the price of the staple food, rice, for which the calorie elasticities are moderately negative. This exception has several important policy implications.

Policy Issues

The potential effect of government policies that operate on the nutritional well-being of rural households in Sierra Leone through prices and income can be explored. These may be targeted to specific groups, or not. Nonprice interventions such as food fortification or direct feeding programs are not addressed here. The farm-household model provides the responses of food consumption to prices and income needed to derive the nutritional effects of government policies. Only partial equilibrium effects are investigated in this study (for some limited general equilibrium effects, see chapter 7).

The principal symptoms of nutritional problems in rural Sierra Leone seem to be underweight and stunted linear growth for age, and anemia. In a national nutrition survey (University of California 1978), almost one-third of rural children aged 0–5 were found to be underweight (weighed less than 80 percent of the expected weight for a reference child of the same age), and slightly more than one-fourth of rural children in the same age group were found to be stunted (less than 90 percent of the expected height of a reference child of the same age). Anemia was found to affect roughly half of the rural children.

This study focuses on calorie availability to the household in the light of evidence that caloric deficiency is a serious problem and of Sukhatme's (for example, 1970) work indicating that protein deficiency tends to be accompanied by calorie deficiency, and protein sufficiency by calorie sufficiency. Two important issues for government policymakers are, first, the degree of responsiveness of calorie availability to changes in income, and, second, the calorie elasticities with respect to food prices.

There is some controversy regarding the calorie elasticity with respect to income. Reutlinger and Selowsky (1976) believe 0.15 and 0.3 to be the relevant bounds. Behrman and Wolfe (1984) find this elasticity to be around 0.05 for households in Nicaragua. If these low estimates are correct, then programs attempting to increase caloric intake by increasing incomes are unlikely to be successful. Rather, programs targeted at specific groups are likely to be more cost effective in this case than general pricing policies or policies focusing on income generation. Even if higher estimates are correct, very large income interventions may be required when caloric targets are substantially greater than existing intakes. The following are estimates reported for some other areas: 0.3 to 0.5 for a sample of northeast Brazilian households (Ward and Sanders 1980); upwards of 0.5 for all households and 0.6 for low-income households in Colombia (Pinstrup-Andersen and Caicedo 1978); and an average of about 0.5 for rural households and as high as 0.75 for low-income households in Indonesia (Timmer and Alderman 1979). The food coverage in the Timmer and Alderman study is incomplete, but the authors argue that their estimates may be a lower bound to the true elasticities since the omitted foods (dairy products, meats, eggs, fish) are likely to be income elastic and high in calories per kilogram. In addition, Pitt (1983) finds an income elasticity of roughly 0.8 for rural Bangladesh households. The fact that the income elasticity falls for higher-income households in several of these studies may help to explain why these estimates vary.

Estimates of elasticities of calorie availability with respect to prices of goods for rural households are rare. Some estimates exist for elasticities of calories with respect to calorie price. In general, the price of a calorie depends on prices of foods and on caloric intake. Since caloric intake results from a household choice, calorie price is endogenous to the household. Many econometric estimates of this elasticity are thus suspect, since they do not account for the endogeneity of calorie price. In addition, it makes sense to inquire about the calorie responsiveness to food prices since these prices correspond much more directly to government policy than do calorie prices. Pitt's (1983) estimates are generally negative but small in magnitude, except for rice, the staple crop in Bangladesh, for which the estimates (around -0.5) are sizable. A shortcoming of Pitt's study is that production data are lacking and thus the farm-household aspect of the problem is not properly accounted for. Whether his price elasticities of caloric intake would remain negative when profits are varied in response to price changes is unclear.

Model Specification and Estimation

Model Specification

The model used is a static, separable, semisubsistence farm-household model (see chapter 1 for a detailed review). Assume that each household has a well-behaved utility function with arguments being household consumption of various goods and of leisure. Goods may be either produced or bought or sold in the market, and labor may be bought or sold in the market. Goods are produced using labor, land, and fixed capital.[1] Land is assumed to be fixed in total amount but must be distributed between uses. A time constraint exists equating household leisure plus labor time to total time available. Finally, a budget constraint exists equating the value of net product transactions plus exogenous income plus the value of net labor transactions to zero. Product prices and wages are exogenous to the household, and markets are assumed to be perfectly competitive. Family and hired labor are assumed to be perfect substitutes, as are consumption from home production and market purchases. Under these assumptions, the household behaves as though its production and consumption decisions are separable, the differences between quantities produced and consumed being bought or sold on the market.

A Quadratic Expenditure System (QES) is used for the demand side of the model (see Howe, Pollak, and Wales 1979). A closed-form solution for the direct utility function cannot in general be obtained analytically. For the Linear Expenditure System (LES) special case, the direct utility function is additively separable. For small departures from the LES special case, there are presumably small departures from additivity in the direct utility function. What the direct utility looks like for large departures from the LES is not clear, however, nor is it clear how to measure large departures since the utility function is ordinal.

The QES meets the neoclassical restrictions (except for the negative semidefiniteness of the Slutsky matrix) and is parsimonious in parameters, yet is not so restrictive as some other systems. In particular, it allows for quadratic Engel curves and inferior goods. The QES is actually a class of demand systems that are derived from a class of indirect utility functions (Howe, Pollak, and Wales 1979; for more details, see Strauss 1982). This model uses the indirect utility function

$$(4\text{-}1) \quad V = -\prod_{k=1}^{N} p_k^{a_k}/(E + p_N T + \pi - \sum_{k=1}^{N} p_k c_k) + \prod_{k=1}^{N} p_k^{(a_k - d_k)}$$

$\sum_{k=1}^{N} a_k = \sum_{k=1}^{N} d_k = 1$, where leisure is treated as the Nth good. The c_k, d_k, and a_k are parameters to be determined from the data[2] and

$\quad E \equiv$ exogenous income,
$\quad p_k \equiv$ prices of goods, $k = 1, \ldots, N - 1$,
$\quad p_N \equiv$ price of labor,
$\quad T \equiv$ total time available to the household,
$\quad \pi \equiv$ short-run profits $=$ value of all outputs less the value of variable inputs (including family labor).

The term $E + p_N T + \pi$ is the household's full income, which is "spent" on consumption of goods and of leisure. Consistent with the farm-household model, full income has replaced the more commonly used total expenditure in the indirect utility function. The demand functions can be derived by Roy's identity, again replacing total expenditure by full income in the derivations. The expenditure functions are given by

$$(4\text{-}2) \quad p_i X_i = p_i c_i + a_i (p_N T + \pi + E - \sum_{k=1}^{N} p_k c_k)$$

$$- (a_i - d_i) \prod_{k=1}^{N} p_k^{-d_k}(p_N T + \pi + E - \sum_{k=1}^{N} p_k c_k)^2 \quad i = 1, \ldots, N$$

$\quad X_i \equiv$ consumption of good i, $i = 1, \ldots, N - 1$
$\quad X_N \equiv$ household leisure.

This has as a special case the linear expenditure system, provided $a_i = d_i, \forall_i$.

Equation 4-2 is an expenditure equation for total household expenditure on good i. It is specified independently of household characteristics such as size and age distribution. Such characteristics may enter the utility function as separate goods (see Lau, Lin, and Yotopoulos 1978) or they may enter in other ways. In this discussion, household characteristics are entered into the demand system by the translation method. The indirect utility function associated with this specification is $V(p, E + \pi + P_N T - \Sigma_{k=1}^{N} p_k b_k)$, where the b_k are commodity specific translation parameters. Thus, everywhere that full income appears in the indirect utility function (1) and the demand function (2), one subtracts from it the sum of values of these commodity indices (see note 4).[3] Using a linearly homogeneous specification for the translation parameters,

$$b_i = \sum_{r=1}^{R} \sigma_{ir} z_r,$$

where $z_r, r = 1, \ldots, R$ are household characteristics and the σ_{ir}'s are parameters.

Total time available to the household, T, is also modeled as being dependent on household characteristics. This circumvents the need to impose values for γ, such as a male having exactly 16 hours per day available for work and leisure. Let

$$T = \sum_{r=1}^{S} \gamma_r m_r$$

where $m_r, r = 1, \ldots, S$ are household characteristics (some possibly identical to the z_r's) and the γ's are parameters. With N commodities, R translation demographic variables, and S demographic variables for total time, this system has at most $(3 + R)N - 2 + S$ parameters to estimate. If some of the z_r's and m_r's are identical there will be fewer parameters since in that case we may combine parameters as

$$p_N \sum_{r=1}^{R'} m_r (\gamma_r - \sigma_{Nr}),$$

where $R' \equiv$ the number of common m's and z's. Clearly, only the difference $\gamma_r - \sigma_{Nr}$ is identified, not both parameters separately.

The production side is specified by assuming that the production function is separable into all outputs as a group and all inputs as a group. This means fewer parameters need to be estimated than when separate production functions are assumed for each output. Such parsimony will be important in view of the estimation difficulties encountered later. In addition, jointness probably exists for at least some of the outputs (there is intercropping); for those that may be nonjoint, the data are inadequate to pursue that approach. For example, some households report no capital or labor use for fishing and animal product activities, yet report positive outputs. Many households reporting zero production of nonfoods report positive labor use to produce nonfoods. When inputs are aggregated, as is done here, into total labor, total capital, and total land, there is a greater chance that such errors will cancel each other out than when using disaggregated inputs. A constant elasticity of transformation (CET) function was used to specify the outputs (see Powell and Gruen 1968) and a Cobb-Douglas function to specify the inputs. This gives the production function as

$$(4\text{-}3) \qquad \left(\sum_{i=1}^{N-1} \delta_i Q_i^\rho \right)^{1/\rho} = \alpha\, L_T^{\beta_L} A^{\beta_A} K^{\beta_K},$$

$Q_i \equiv$ production of good i, $i = 1, \ldots, N-1$,
$L_T \equiv$ labor demand (family plus hired),
$A \equiv$ total land area,
$K \equiv$ capital flow.

The δ_i's, β_i's, and ρ are parameters, with $\rho > 1$ to ensure convexity. The constant elasticity of transformation between outputs is $1/(\rho - 1)$. This production function requires one of two normalizations, either $\alpha = 1$ or $\Sigma_i\, \delta_i = 1$.

Maximizing profits subject to (3) (normalizing $\alpha = 1$) and to A, and K being fixed, the output-supply and labor-demand equations are

$$(4\text{-}4) \qquad Q_i = \beta_L^{\beta_L/1-\beta_L} \delta_i^{-1/(\rho-1)} p_i^{1/(\rho-1)}$$

$$\left(\sum_k \delta_k^{-1/(\rho-1)} p_k^{\rho/(\rho-1)} \right)^{(\rho\beta_L-1)/\rho(1-\beta_L)}$$

$$(A^{\beta_A} K^{\beta_K})^{1/(1-\beta_L)} p_N^{[-\beta_L/(1-\beta_L)]}$$

$$\qquad\qquad\qquad\qquad\qquad i = 1, \ldots, N-1$$

$$L_T = (A^{\beta_A} K^{\beta_K})^{[1/(1-\beta_L)]} \beta_L^{[1/(1-\beta_L)]} p_N^{[-1/(1-\beta_L)]}$$

$$\left(\sum_i \delta_i^{-1/(\rho-1)} p_i^{\rho/(\rho-1)} \right)^{(\rho-1)/[\rho(1-\beta_L)]}.$$

Data and Model Estimation

The data are from a cross-sectional survey of households in rural Sierra Leone conducted during the 1974–75 cropping year (May–April). Sierra Leone was divided into eight geographical regions chosen to conform with agroclimatic zones, and those were used to stratify the sample. Within these regions, three enumeration areas were randomly picked and the households within each were sampled. Households were visited twice each week to obtain information on production, sales, and labor use, among other variables. Half the households were visited twice during one week per month to obtain market-purchase information.

Prices vary regionally in Sierra Leone because of poor transportation facilities. Relative price variation may arise in the face of such difficulties because transportation costs differ by commodity and some regions specialize in providing different commodities because of soil and climate characteristics, and because some commodities become nontradables across regions. (See Jones [1972] and Mutti et al. [1968] for evidence on poor market integration in Sierra Leone.)

The QES was estimated using seven commodities, three demographic variables for the translation parameters, and three for total time available to the household. The commodities are rice, root crops and other cereals, oils and fats, fish and animal products, miscellaneous foods, nonfoods, and labor supply (see table 4A-1). Household size, children younger than 10, and a dummy equal to 1 if the household lived in the northern region were the variables used for the translation parameters; persons older than 10 years, females older than 15, and children aged 11–15 were the variables used to model total time. (In this sample, children younger than 10 did not work and so were excluded.) These variables were chosen partly on the basis of single-demand equation estimation (for details, see Strauss 1982).[4] The number of parameters is forty-two.

One must assume that demand-side and production-side disturbances are uncorrelated in order to consistently estimate parameters of the demand system separately from the production system. Otherwise, profits will be correlated with demand-side disturbances and thus parameter estimates will be inconsistent. (For details of the specification of the disturbances, the estimation procedures, and the parameter estimates see Strauss 1982).

Wald tests were conducted for different hypotheses. A test of whether the LES special case ($a_i = d_i$, $\forall_i$) holds was rejected under the 0.005 level. Tests of the demographic parameters were highly significant. Household characteristics—notably size, age distribution, and location in the northern regions of Sierra Leone—do affect consumption.

The system of output-supply and input-demand equations, equation (4-4), derived from a constant elasticity of transformation–Cobb-Douglas (CET-CD) multiple-output production function, are modified to allow the δ_i parameters to vary for households living near the capital, Freetown. That is, $\delta_i = \delta_{i0} + \delta_{i1} D$, where $D = 1$ for such households. These households are primarily fishing households, and are quite unlike other households in their production characteristics (though this is not true of their consumption characteristics). A statistical problem emerges because many households do not produce several of the six outputs. Three households do not produce rice, nineteen produce no root crops and other cereals, twenty-four no oils and fats, thirty-five no fish and animal products, twelve no miscellaneous foods, and fifty-nine no nonfoods. Hence, if error terms are added to equation (4-4), the estimates of these equations will be inconsistent, since the error terms have a nonzero mean and are not normally distributed. This problem can be overcome by using a Tobit approach.[5] When this is done, the system of output supplies and labor demand is estimated using numerical maximum likelihood techniques (see Strauss 1984a for details and parameter estimates).

Consumption, Labor Supply, and Marketed Surplus Responses

Now that the demand system and production system components of the farm-household model have been estimated separately, the model can be examined in its entirety. Consumption demand may be written $X_i = f(p, z, p_N T(m) + \pi(p, A, K))$, where $p \equiv$ prices, $z \equiv$ household characteristic variables affecting taste, $T \equiv$ time available to the household, $m \equiv$ household characteristic variables determining T (some of which may be identical to some of those in z), and $\pi \equiv$ profits. Differentiating with respect to p_j,

$$(4\text{-}5) \qquad \frac{p_j}{X_i} \frac{\partial X_i}{\partial p_j} = \frac{p_j}{X_i} \frac{\partial X_i}{\partial p_j}\bigg|_{d\pi = 0} + \frac{p_j \partial X_i \partial \pi}{X_i \partial \pi \partial p_j}.$$

The first term is simply the usual uncompensated elasticity of demand of good i with respect to price j. The second term is what might be called the profit effect in elasticity form.

When deriving profit effects, we need $\partial X_i / \partial \pi$, which is easily found from the marginal expenditures out of full income derived from the QES estimates. The more commonly used shares of marginal expenditure are reported here, however (see table 4-1).[6] These estimates are reported at mean values for a representative low-, middle-, and high-expenditure household as well as for the sample mean values. The dividing lines between expenditure groups are less than 350 Leones total expenditure, between 350 and 750 Leones inclusive, and greater than 750 Leones. In 1974-75 one Leone = US$1.1. The sample sizes for these groups are 44, 51, and 53, respectively. From table 4A-2, it is evident that the lower expenditure group faces lower prices for root crops and other cereals and for nonfoods, but higher prices for oils and fats and fish and animal products. Household size tends to be smaller for the lower expenditure group, as does the proportion of family members younger than 10 years.

Table 4-1. *Shares of Marginal Total Expenditure, Sierra Leone*
(percent)

| | Expenditure group | | | |
Commodity	Low	Middle	High	Mean
Rice	0.22	0.16	0.02	0.13
Root crops and other cereals	0.03	0.06	0.12	0.07
Oils and fats	0.13	0.20	0.36	0.23
Fish and animal products	0.13	0.11	0.07	0.11
Miscellaneous foods	0.09	0.07	0.04	0.07
Nonfood	0.40	0.40	0.39	0.39

Note: Partial derivative of commodity expenditure with respect to total income divided by partial derivative of total expenditure with respect to total income. Evaluated at expenditure group means using QES with regional dummy. See table 4A-2 for definitions of expenditure groups.

The shares generally seem to be plausible. The share for rice declines with higher total expenditure, as one would expect, although the 0.02 share for high expenditure households seems a little low. The low share for root crops and other cereals is not surprising, although one would not have expected the marginal share to rise with expenditure. Middle- and high-expenditure households tend to be in areas where the root crops and other cereals commodity group contains a relatively high proportion of cereals. If the marginal propensity to consume other cereals (mostly sorghum) is higher than for cassava, this result is possible. For all expenditure groups, the marginal share is less than the estimated average share. Thus, the estimated average share for root crops and other cereals is declining for each of the representative low-, middle-, and high-expenditure households. The fact that both marginal and average shares are higher for high-expenditure households than for middle- or low-expenditure households is due to the fact that the Engel curve shifts upward (the slope shifts as well) when it is evaluated at higher-expenditure groups. This is possible since prices and household characteristics (Engel curve shifters) are different for different expenditure groups (see table 4A-2). In addition, the marginal share for root crops and other cereals is not negative at our mean evaluation points. This is interesting because many observers have hypothesized that cassava and sorghum may be inferior goods for higher-income groups in West Africa.

Uncompensated price elasticities of demand (the first term in equation [4-5]) are reported in table 4-2. For rice, the own-price elasticity declines in absolute value with expenditure group. Part, but not all, of this is due to the fact that income effect declines with expenditure group. This is

Table 4-2. *Demand Elasticities with Respect to Price, Profits Constant, Sierra Leone*

Price	Expenditure group	Commodity						
		Rice	Root crops and other cereals	Oils and fats	Fish and animal products	Miscellaneous foods	Nonfoods	Household labor
Rice	Low	-1.26	-0.16	-0.23	0.02	0.03	-0.01	0.01E-1
	Middle	-0.78	-0.13	-0.31	0.02	0.02	-0.02	0.01E-1
	High	-0.45	-0.12	-0.38	0.05	0.07	-0.04	0.01
	Mean	-0.74	-0.10	-0.29	0.03	0.03	-0.03	0.01
Root crops and other cereals	Low	-0.02	-0.15	-0.02	-0.02	-0.02	-0.02	0.01
	Middle	-0.02	-0.26	-0.04	-0.02	-0.01	-0.02	0.01
	High	-0.01	-0.31	-0.02	-0.01	-0.01	-0.01	0.01
	Mean	-0.01	-0.22	-0.02	-0.02	-0.01	-0.02	0.01
Oils and fats	Low	0.04	0.04	-0.82	0.05	0.03	0.05	-0.02
	Middle	0.01E-1	0.04E-1	-1.10	0.02E-1	0.01E-1	0.04E-1	-0.02E-1
	High	-0.01E-1	0.05E-1	-1.25	0.02E-1	0.01E-1	0.01	-0.03E-1
	Mean	0.04E-1	0.01	-0.97	0.01	0.01	0.01	-0.01

Fish and animal products	Low	0.02	−0.08	−0.12	−1.29	0.01	−0.01	0.01E−1
	Middle	0.03	−0.06	−0.15	−0.92	0.01	−0.01	0.03E−1
	High	0.06	−0.05	−0.15	−0.81	0.04	−0.03E−1	−0.04E−1
	Mean	0.04	−0.04	−0.12	−0.95	0.02	−0.01	0.01E−3
Miscellaneous foods	Low	0.01	−0.06	−0.10	−0.03E−1	−0.99	−0.01	0.04E−1
	Middle	0.01	−0.06	−0.14	−0.03E−1	−0.60	−0.02	0.01
	High	0.04	−0.04	−0.14	0.02	−0.63	−0.02	0.01
	Mean	0.02	−0.04	−0.11	0.03E−1	−0.71	−0.02	0.01
Nonfoods	Low	0.10	−0.16	−0.21	0.06	0.06	−1.17	−0.01
	Middle	0.07	−0.16	−0.36	0.02	0.03	−0.90	0.01
	High	0.14	−0.12	−0.38	0.07	0.08	−1.05	−0.04E−1
	Mean	0.09	−0.11	−0.30	0.04	0.05	−1.01	−0.04E−1
Labor	Low	1.30	0.72	1.81	1.30	1.03	1.39	−0.06
	Middle	0.56	0.48	1.53	0.71	0.44	0.74	0.09
	High	0.20	0.31	1.16	0.43	0.31	0.65	0.28
	Mean	0.47	0.34	1.25	0.67	0.47	0.78	0.14

Note: Calculated at mean for each expenditure group.

Table 4-3. *Demand Elasticities with Respect to Price, Profits Variable, Sierra Leone*

Price	Expenditure group	Commodity						
		Rice	Root crops and other cereals	Oils and fats	Fish and animal products	Miscellaneous foods	Nonfoods	Household labor
Rice	Low	−0.44	0.47	1.21	0.93	0.69	0.93	−0.32
	Middle	−0.67	0.02	0.15	0.18	0.12	0.16	−0.11
	High	−0.44	−0.04	−0.12	0.10	0.10	0.07	−0.06
	Mean	−0.66	−0.01	0.06	0.17	0.12	0.14	−0.09
Root crops and other cereals	Low	0.47	0.23	0.84	0.52	0.38	0.54	−0.18
	Middle	0.12	−0.07	0.52	0.17	0.11	0.20	−0.12
	High	0.01E−1	−0.15	0.56	0.11	0.06	0.23	−0.14
	Mean	0.11	−0.06	0.53	0.19	0.13	0.25	−0.14
Oils and fats	Low	0.40	0.32	−0.19	0.45	0.32	0.46	−0.16
	Middle	0.08	0.11	−0.79	0.11	0.06	0.13	−0.07
	High	0.02E−1	0.05	−1.08	0.03	0.02	0.08	−0.04
	Mean	0.06	0.08	−0.73	0.10	0.07	0.13	−0.07

Fish and animal products	Low	0.73	0.46	1.12	−0.51	0.59	0.80	−0.28
	Middle	0.28	0.29	0.90	−0.57	0.23	0.40	−0.24
	High	0.07	0.08	0.30	−0.71	0.10	0.19	−0.12
	Mean	0.20	0.17	0.61	−0.68	0.20	0.35	−0.20
Miscellaneous foods	Low	0.24	0.12	0.30	0.25	−0.80	0.25	−0.09
	Middle	0.09	0.05	0.19	0.11	−0.53	0.11	−0.07
	High	0.05	0.02	0.08	0.07	−0.60	0.07	−0.05
	Mean	0.08	0.03	0.14	0.10	−0.65	0.11	−0.06
Nonfoods	Low	0.22	−0.06	0.01	0.20	0.16	−1.03	−0.05
	Middle	0.11	−0.10	−0.18	0.08	0.07	−0.82	−0.03
	High	0.14	−0.08	−0.26	0.09	0.10	−0.99	−0.05
	Mean	0.13	−0.07	−0.16	0.10	0.09	−0.93	−0.05
Labor	Low	0.74	0.29	0.82	0.76	0.57	0.75	0.16
	Middle	0.43	0.29	0.97	0.52	0.33	0.52	0.22
	High	0.19	0.20	0.78	0.35	0.26	0.50	0.38
	Mean	0.37	0.21	0.82	0.50	0.36	0.57	0.26

Note: Calculated at mean for each expenditure group.

certainly not surprising. Root crops do not seem to be price responsive. The relative unresponsiveness of total household labor supplied to wage rate changes (-0.06 to 0.28) is not really surprising either, since this is measuring total supply, not its allocation between uses. The negative sign for the low expenditure group is due to the income effect and gives some slight evidence for a backward-bending supply curve.

The cross-price effects with respect to the price of rice are negative, except for fish and miscellaneous foods. This is to be expected because the large budget share of rice leads to a relatively large income effect.

Income-compensated price elasticities of demand are reported in Strauss (1982). Two points are worth noting here. First, negative semidefiniteness of the Slutsky substitution matrix was tested after estimation and was found to hold for 113 out of 138 observations and for all three expenditure group averages, as well as the sample average. Second, the compensated own-price elasticities tended to be sizable.

Price elasticities of demand when profits are allowed to vary (equation [4-5]) are reported in table 4-3. In deriving these elasticities, care has to be taken to obtain consistent estimates of $\partial \pi / \partial p_j$ (see Strauss 1984a) because of the censoring in the data. A comparison with table 4-2 tests the significance of the agricultural household model approach. The total own-price effects for commodities remain negative when profit effects are added, except for root crops and other cereals at the low-expenditure group. However, the profit effect does change the magnitudes of the price elasticities. An interesting consequence, especially for the low-income households, is that the total own-price elasticities for several commodities such as rice, oils and fats, and fish and animal products no longer drop in absolute value with higher expenditure levels. This is because the profit effects— when expressed as an elasticity—are larger, often much larger, for the lowest expenditure households. There are two reasons why profit effects tend to decline with higher total expenditure levels. First, for some goods, marginal expenditures out of full income decline with higher expenditure (see table 4-1). Second, because the profit effect is an elasticity, it decreases as expenditure levels increase, because mean consumption levels increase. Thus, when expressed as a marginal change, the profit effect does increase with expenditure group for some commodities, for instance, for oils and fats and root crops and other cereals.

Labor Supply

For labor supply, the own-price elasticity is positive for all expenditure groups. Although income effects might tend to cause the supply curve to bend backward, as it does for low-expenditure households, the profits effect partly offsets this, since higher wages imply lower profits. The labor-supply elasticity with respect to the wage increases with expenditure group, since the classical substitution effects increase with expenditure group.

In general, the total cross-price effects on labor supply are negative. The positive signs of the cross-price effects, when profits are held constant, are reversed because of the profit effect. Cross-price responses generally decline with expenditure group for the same reason as before, namely that the profit effect decreases. The cross-price effects on labor supply are negative since leisure is a normal good. The cross-price effects on commodity consumption with respect to the wage rate are smaller in magnitude than when profits are constant, but remain positive. An increased wage rate decreases profits and therefore decreases expenditure on goods. However, a comparison of the uncompensated and compensated elasticities shows that the (positive) income effect exceeds the (negative) profits effect.

Marketed Surplus

Price elasticities of marketed surpluses can be written as

$$(4\text{-}6) \qquad \frac{p_j}{|MS_i|} \frac{\partial MS_i}{\partial p_j} = \frac{Q_i}{|MS_i|} \frac{p_j}{Q_i} \frac{\partial Q_i}{\partial p_j} - \frac{X_i}{|MS_i|} \frac{p_j}{X_i} \frac{\partial X_i}{\partial p_j}.$$

It is a weighted difference of output elasticities and of *total* (profits variable) price elasticities of quantities consumed. The weights are the ratio of quantity produced to surplus, for production, and quantity consumed to surplus, for consumption. The marketed surplus elasticities with respect to changes in the production technology or household characteristic variables (which will only affect consumption) may be similarly derived.

Price elasticities of marketed surplus are presented in table 4-4. Given the Tobit estimation of the production side, $\partial E(Q_i)/\partial p_j$ is used in the first term of equation (4-6) and $\partial E(\pi)/\partial p_j$ in the second (see Strauss 1984a). Also, the divisor is the absolute value of marketed surplus. This is used so that one can easily recognize the sign of $\partial MS_j/\partial p_j$, that is, whether production increases more or less than consumption.

If the sign of the elasticity is positive and the net surplus is positive, then an increase in price will result in more being sold on the market. If the elasticity is positive and the household is a net purchaser (a negative surplus), then an increase in price will lead to less being purchased on the market. A negative elasticity and a positive surplus will lead to less being sold to the market and negative elasticity, and a negative surplus means more will be purchased. (Quantities of marketed surpluses by expenditure group are given in table 4A-4.)

Table 4-4. *Price Elasticities of Marketed Surplus, Sierra Leone*

Price	Expenditure group	Commodity						
		Rice	Root crops and other cereals	Oils and fats	Fish and animal products	Miscellaneous foods	Nonfoods	Household labor
Rice	Low	0.89	0.66	−0.32	−1.05	−0.47	−1.00	−18.45
	Middle	0.73	0.05	−0.04	−0.23	−0.09	−0.17	−5.74
	High	0.75	0.04	0.09	−0.12	−0.03	−0.08	−1.31
	Mean	0.71	0.06	−0.03	−0.72	−0.05	−0.15	−4.42
Root crops and other cereals	Low	−0.11	3.10	−0.31	−0.70	−0.34	−0.58	−7.53
	Middle	−0.09	0.37	−0.17	−0.23	−0.09	−0.21	−5.54
	High	0.02	0.39	−0.40	−0.10	0.02	−0.25	−3.09
	Mean	−0.08	0.46	−0.29	−0.73	−0.04	−0.27	−6.61
Oils and fats	Low	−0.08	0.06	0.79	−0.58	−0.27	−0.50	−7.09
	Middle	−0.07	−0.01	0.29	−0.19	−0.07	−0.14	−2.56
	High	−0.02E−1	−0.01	0.78	−0.04	−0.07E−1	−0.09	−0.58
	Mean	−0.05	−0.02	0.44	−0.44	−0.04	−0.14	−2.35

Fish and animal products	Low	−0.18	0.04	−0.41	2.15	−0.56	−0.86	−10.84
	Middle	−0.22	0.03	−0.29	1.81	−0.22	−0.43	−10.56
	High	−0.09	0.02	−0.21	1.33	−0.01	−0.21	−2.56
	Mean	−0.16	0.02	−0.33	5.94	−0.08	−0.38	−8.80
Miscellaneous foods	Low	−0.05	0.11	−0.09	−0.32	1.97	−0.27	−4.22
	Middle	−0.06	0.03	−0.06	−0.13	1.29	−0.12	−3.77
	High	−0.06	0.03	−0.05	−0.07	0.49	−0.08	−1.36
	Mean	−0.06	0.04	−0.08	−0.34	0.81	−0.12	−3.44
Nonfoods	Low	−0.07	0.08	0.03E−1	−0.30	−0.17	1.12	−1.59
	Middle	−0.09	0.02	0.06	−0.14	−0.09	0.88	−1.24
	High	−0.21	0.04	0.19	−0.12	−0.04	1.08	−0.80
	Mean	−0.12	0.04	0.09	−0.52	−0.06	1.01	−1.85
Labor	Low	−1.22	−5.45	−1.49	−3.30	−2.37	−0.83	27.41
	Middle	−0.58	−0.60	−0.37	−2.02	−1.29	−0.56	16.41
	High	−0.42	−0.54	−0.58	−0.93	−0.44	−0.55	8.57
	Mean	−0.49	−0.72	−0.51	−5.82	−0.78	−0.62	17.18

All the own-price elasticities are positive and some are reasonably high. The positive sign is not surprising since the only total price elasticity of quantity consumed that is positive (a necessary condition to obtain a negative marketed surplus response) is for root crops and other cereals, and it is only positive when evaluated at the average for low-expenditure households. The mean own-price elasticity for rice, the major staple, is 0.71, which is comparable to the elasticity of 1.03 reported for an aggregate agricultural commodity (Lau, Lin, and Yotopoulos 1978) and to the elasticity reported for rice, 0.66 (Barnum and Squire 1979). The price elasticity of marketed surplus tends to decline at higher expenditure levels, largely because the absolute value of marketed surplus, part of the denominator, increases at higher expenditure levels. The low marketed surplus is the reason for the high magnitude of the own-price elasticity for root crops and other cereals among low-expenditure households. If absolute changes in kilograms marketed due to an infinitesimal proportionate increase in price were shown, they would be roughly equal for the low- and middle-expenditure groups, and would rise for the high-expenditure group. Nonetheless, low expenditure households do seem to respond in their marketed surplus to price, contrary to the allegations of many. This is a very important policy conclusion, since many governments rely in their policies only on larger farms to be responsive in their marketed output. This supposition is often used to rationalize policies that discriminate against or have a benign neglect of small holders. In the Sierra Leone case, it is worth noting that the response of marketed surplus comes largely through changes in consumption rather than changes in output (see Strauss 1984b). This may reflect the low level of agricultural technology and infrastructure development in Sierra Leone.

For household labor, the extremely large (positive) values of the marketed surplus (off-farm labor) elasticity with respect to wage rate are simply the result of the very small base, the average household being nearly self-sufficient in labor when labor sold and labor hired are netted out over a period of a year. The absolute change in hours supplied to the market will not be so large. These off-farm labor results contrast markedly with those reported by Rosenzweig (1980). He separated male and female labor supply (which are combined here using relative wages as weights) and found the former's marketed surplus responds negatively to wage.

The cross-price elasticities of marketed surplus tend to be negative because of the strong profit effect in the cross-price elasticity of demand. Indeed, when profits are held constant, most of the cross-price elasticities are positive. For instance, the elasticity of oils and fats surplus to rice price is 0.32 when profits are held constant but -0.32 when it varies (see

Strauss 1984b). The profit effect of an increase in the price of rice will lead to an increase in the consumption of oils and fats. Sales of oils and fats will consequently decrease.

Some of the magnitudes of the cross-price elasticities are fairly large. Again, this is caused by the strong profit effect on consumption. The magnitudes do tend to fall with the higher expenditure groups, as they do for the own-price elasticities. They are not negligible, however, so it is not wise to ignore them, as was often done in the past.

Variables other than prices will affect the marketed surplus of a commodity. In this model, two sets of factors stand out. First are household characteristics such as size and age composition. These factors are modeled explicitly in the demand equations. They do not affect output directly, because of the separability of the model, but they might affect it indirectly through their general equilibrium effect on wages. The second set of factors are fixed inputs and the production technology. They will affect both consumption and production directly, the former through the profit effect.

The household characteristics used in this study are children younger than 10, children 11–15 years, males older than 15, and females older than 15. The latter three characteristics affect demand in two ways: they affect the commodity composition (including leisure) of demand given a level of full income; and they change the level of full income, since persons of those ages can work or take leisure. Children younger than 10 in our sample do not work; hence they do not affect full income, but they do change the commodity composition of goods and leisure demanded.

The first four columns of table 4-5 report elasticities of marketed surplus with respect to the four age-group variables. These elasticities are reported at the sample mean only. For the higher age groups, the signs of the elasticities for goods are predominantly negative (that is consumption increases). This is not surprising; any negative composition impact on consumption of a good is outweighed by the effect from increased full income. Exceptions exist for miscellaneous foods and root crops and other cereals for children aged 11–15 and females older than 15, though the magnitudes are quite small. Children younger than 10 change the household commodity composition by lowering consumption of oils and fats, fish and animal products, and leisure, but they raise consumption of everything else. Marketed surplus of labor responds positively to changes in persons in the older age groups, as might be expected since total time available to the household varies when the number of persons older than 10 changes. It does indicate that if adult household size decreases, say, because of migration, that the remaining members do not work hard

Table 4-5 *Elasticities of Marketed Surplus with Respect to Nonprice Variables, Sierra Leone*

Commodity/variable	Younger than 11 years	11–15 years	Males older than 15 years	Females older than 15 years	Technical change parameter, α
Rice	−0.12	−0.03	−0.21	−0.11	0.32
Root crops and other cereals	−0.05	0.01	−0.04	0.01	1.82
Oils and fats	0.11	−0.06	−0.52	−0.24	−0.16
Fish and animal products	0.31	−0.13	−4.35	−1.99	7.50
Miscellaneous foods	−0.23	0.02	−0.07	0.03	1.40
Nonfoods	−0.09	−0.02	−0.39	−0.13	−0.27
Labor	3.78	1.00	14.36	5.15	−13.62

Note: Evaluated at the sample mean.

enough to compensate, as Sen (1966) postulated. That the elasticity of marketed surplus with respect to female adults is less than that for male adults is partly due to the fact that household activities such as child-rearing and food preparation are classified with leisure.

Exogenous production factors will also change marketed surplus. Consider a factor neutral technological change: in the production function (equation [4-3]), an increase in α will be equivalent to an input neutral technological change. However, the equation still needs to be normalized to identify the δ_i parameters. This is done by dividing both sides by α. Consequently δ_i is replaced on the left-hand side of (4-3) by δ_i/α^ρ. Elasticities of marketed surplus with respect to α can then be computed (see the fifth column of table 4-5). Marketed surplus elasticities with respect to capital and labor are not shown, but they may be calculated directly from table 4-5. Given the production function, the elasticity with respect to capital will be β_K (0.36) times the elasticity with respect to α; and with respect to land it will be β_A (0.069) times the same.

Except for labor, most of the elasticities are positive; that is, production increases by more than consumption. The exceptions—for oils and fats and for nonfoods—are interesting. For oils and fats, the output elasticity with respect to α is small (0.11), but the elasticity of consumption is much larger (0.56). Nonfoods are primarily purchased, so that the weight $Q_i/|MS_i|$ on the output elasticity is small, whereas the weight $X_i/|MS_i|$ on the consumption elasticity is much larger. Labor's marketed surplus elasticity with respect to α is negative and large. In this case, the supply-and-demand responses reinforce each other. More labor is demanded as α increases, but less labor is supplied since leisure is a normal good.

Price and Income Effects for Caloric Availability

This study is concerned ultimately with the determinants of food consumption. This can be further translated into the effects of prices and other variables on the availability to the household of different nutrients, particularly calories. The effect of price on calories is

$$\frac{\partial cal}{\partial p_j} = \sum_{i=1}^{5} \frac{\partial cal}{\partial X_i} \frac{\partial X_i}{\partial p_j},$$

where $cal \equiv$ calories and 1–5 are the food groups. In elasticity form

$$\frac{p_j}{cal} \frac{\partial cal}{\partial p_j} = \frac{p_j}{cal} \sum_{i=1}^{5} \frac{\partial cal \partial X_i}{\partial X_i \partial p_j}.$$

Effects of price changes on calories are calculated both when profits are constant and when they are variable. The difference will clearly point out the effect on caloric availability of families producing the foods they consume.

Elasticities of caloric availability with respect to total expenditure are given below. The elasticities were calculated as $(TEXP/Cal) \sum_{i}^{5} (\partial Cal/\partial X_i)(\partial E(X_i)/\partial TEXP)$ (see table 4-1 for $\partial E(p_i X_i)/\partial TEXP$). Total expenditure, as opposed to full income, is endogenous in the model, but the results will still be of interest. The magnitudes are around 0.85, and they vary little among expenditure groups.

Low	Middle	High	Mean
0.85	0.83	0.93	0.86

The elasticity for the high-expenditure group is slightly higher than for the low-expenditure group because the marginal total expenditure share of oils and fats, an important contributor of calories, rises with the expenditure group. This apparently offsets the declining total expenditure share on rice.

As mentioned earlier, these elasticity estimates are high compared with other results. One reason may be the relatively high level of aggregation of the food groups. As full income rises, expenditures undoubtedly shift within these groups, not just between them. If foods with high costs per calorie are substituted for foods with low cost per calorie, then expenditures on a group can rise much more than calorie consumption from the group. A word of caution is in order here, however. First, the elasticities hold only for small movements of total expenditure where intragroup substitution may be small. Second, the calorie conversions from kilograms were calculated separately for the low-, middle-, and high-expenditure households, and some of the intragroup composition effect is accounted for by these separate conversion ratios.[7]

Table 4-6 reports caloric elasticities with respect to prices with profits held constant and allowed to vary. When profits are held constant, commodity prices increase, and caloric availability decreases, except with re-

Table 4-6. *Elasticities of Calorie Availability with Respect to Price, Sierra Leone*

Price	Expenditure group	Profits constant[a]	Profits variable[b]
Rice	Low	−0.58	0.19
	Middle	−0.38	−0.24
	High	−0.28	−0.20
	Mean	−0.38	−0.26
Root crops and other cereals	Low	−0.03	0.43
	Middle	−0.04	0.13
	High	−0.06	0.11
	Mean	−0.05	0.15
Oils and fats	Low	−0.07	0.27
	Middle	−0.12	−0.03
	High	−0.25	−0.21
	Mean	−0.15	−0.06
Fish and animal products	Low	−0.19	0.48
	Middle	−0.08	0.23
	High	−0.08	0.05
	Mean	−0.08	0.18
Miscellaneous foods	Low	−0.07	0.14
	Middle	−0.09	0.01
	High	−0.08	−0.01
	Mean	−0.08	0.007
Nonfoods	Low	0.008	0.12
	Middle	−0.02	0.03
	High	−0.02	0.01
	Mean	−0.02	0.04
Labor	Low	1.20	0.59
	Middle	0.57	0.40
	High	0.45	0.33
	Mean	0.56	0.41

a. Calculated as $\dfrac{p_j}{\text{cal}} \sum_i \dfrac{\partial \text{cal}}{\partial X_i} \dfrac{\partial E(X_i)}{\partial p_j} \bigg|_{d\pi=0}$ at expenditure group means.

b. Calculated as $\dfrac{p_j}{\text{cal}} \sum_i \dfrac{\partial \text{cal}}{\partial X_i} \dfrac{\partial E(X_i)}{\partial p_j}$ at expenditure group means.

spect to the nonfoods price for the low-expenditure group. There is no general pattern of elasticities across expenditure group, but the absolute change in caloric availability often increases with expenditure group. For commodity prices, the largest response of caloric availability is to changes in the price of rice, the principal staple. These range from −0.58 to −0.28.

When profits can vary, the situation changes substantially. Now most of the commodity price elasticities of calories are positive. If the price of a good increases, consumption of that good may decrease, but the increase in full income is distributed over the consumption of other foods, and the increase is large enough to increase total caloric availability. The price of rice and of oils and fats in all but the low-expenditure group is an exception, as is the price of miscellaneous foods in the high-expenditure group. The magnitudes of the positive elasticities are not high for the sample mean, but some are sizable for the low-expenditure group.

For all commodities, the positive effect of a change in price, with profits variable, is greatest for low-expenditure households because of the fact that, for every commodity, own-price profit effects are greatest among such households. For rice and for oils and fats, it is only among low-expenditure households that the profit effect is large enough to dominate the negative own-price effects upon calorie availability with profits constant. This is partly because in the middle- and high-expenditure households the negative own-price effects—with profits constant—are stronger for rice and for oils and fats than for other commodities.

Although caloric availability increases for low-expenditure households, with an increase in the price of rice or of oils and fats, it decreases for middle- and high-expenditure households, and at the sample mean. For rice price, the elasticities for the two higher expenditure groups are still quite negative, between −0.2 and −0.25. Hence, when profit effects are accounted for, increases in the price of rice seem to lessen the discrepancy in calories available to the rural expenditure groups. They increase availability for very low expenditure households and decrease availability for middle- and higher-expenditure households. The mean daily caloric availability per capita for high-expenditure households is quite high (2,600 calories), and for the middle-expenditure households it is more modest (2,130 calories). Although caloric availability will be lower than the group mean for some households in the high-expenditure group, lower availability may still allow these households to have sufficient calories available for weight maintenance under normal activity levels. Whether this would be true of middle-expenditure households is more questionable.

Policy Implications

These results have significant implications for the development process in Sierra Leone. The estimates of the calorie elasticity with respect to total expenditure suggest that promoting higher incomes may be an efficient way to reduce undernutrition. The present income levels for poor rural households are so low, however, that this process is likely to take a long time. Before the representative low-expenditure household could have caloric availability even at the level of 1,900 calories per capita per day (actual daily availability is 1,188 calories per capita for such a household), income would have to increase considerably. With prices and household characteristics constant, an average low-expenditure household would need an increase in annual full income of about 270 Leones to reach the availability level of 1,900 calories per capita per day. This new level of full income would result in total expenditures of roughly 445 Leones. That figure is 88 percent higher than the existing expenditure level (237 Leones) of the representative low-expenditure household. If we assume, optimistically, an annual growth rate in real total expenditures of 3 percent, it would take almost twenty-two years for an average low-expenditure family to reach this point. Of course, if family size grew along with total expenditure, as is likely, it would take even longer.

The usual caution is needed here. Caloric availability at the household level says little about the intake of individuals. The intrahousehold distribution of food depends on household choices, which in turn may depend on household income, prices, and tastes. This discussion abstracts from that admittedly important issue.

In general, increased food prices in this model lead to increased caloric availability owing to the profit effect for producers. Response by the household in its role as a farm-firm does make a difference to consumption patterns. Despite the profit effect, however, caloric availability responds negatively to rice price changes for middle- and high-expenditure households. This may indicate a tradeoff between long-run output growth and short-run nutritional goals if output growth is pursued solely by a policy of high producer prices. Policies that induce household investments leading to higher full income would mitigate or reverse this tradeoff.

In the longer run, rice price may be lower than otherwise if production growth has been stimulated. The distributional impacts of technical change have long been debated, but questions of access to technology are beyond the scope of this study. The results do have something to say, however, about the differential price effects of technical change.

The effect of a price change on household welfare can be shown to be proportional to net marketed surplus of the commodity. Indeed, the elasticity of real full income with respect to rice price can be quantified. It is positive, but small, for all three expenditure groups; ranging from 0.13 for the lowest group to 0.06 for the highest, being 0.09 at the sample mean. This result occurs because on the one hand marketed surplus of rice is highest for the low expenditure group (table 4A-4), and on the other hand full income (based on a sixteen-hour day) is lowest for this group. These magnitudes imply a small welfare loss because of potentially decreased rice prices in rural Sierra Leone, with the largest losses being for the lowest expenditure households. At the same time, the nutritional status of households, at least for the middle and higher expenditure groups, would be raised by such a price decrease, although it would be lowered for low-income households. Of course, to the extent that there is an autonomous increase in nominal full income caused by the technical change, welfare and nutritional status might both increase. However, the points remain that changes in nutritional status and changes in welfare may be in opposite directions, and that price increases are both a welfare and nutrition status equalizer in rural Sierra Leone, whereas price decreases worsen distributional consequences.

Another question that has bearing on calorie availability is to what extent a country should promote exports of cash crops such as palm oil, coffee, and cocoa. Some have argued that increasing the production of cash crops at the expense of subsistence crops will have an adverse impact on nutritional status. According to the results of this study, an increase in own-price of oils and fats—of which palm products are the lion's share in value—results in decreased calorie availability for high- and middle-expenditure groups but increased availability for the low-expenditure group. Marketed surplus increases for all groups. Hence, increased reliance on the market for oils and fats as a consequence of a rise in the price of oils and fats results in higher caloric availability for a typical low-expenditure household, but lower caloric availability for typical middle- and high-expenditure households.

Alternatively, an increase in the price of rice decreases the marketed surplus of oils and fats for the low- and middle-expenditure groups. Such a price increase will lead to increased calorie availability for the low-expenditure group and decreased availability for the middle-expenditure group. This is contrary to the relationship often hypothesized. For low expenditure households, however, decreased market reliance is associated with higher calorie availability when the source of the change is an increase in the price of rice. Note that, for low- and middle-expenditure households, the relationships between the direction of change of marketed surplus of oils and fats and of calorie availability differ when they are a result of changes in the price of rice compared with changes in the price of oils and fats. Since both calorie availability and marketed surplus are endogenous variables, this situation is not surprising.

When greater market reliance does coincide with reduced caloric availability, the causative factors underlying this relationship turn out to be opposite to the ones just suggested. More, not less, of the rice and root crops and other cereals is consumed when the price of oils and fats increases. This is primarily due to the profit effect in increasing full income. As a result, less of these foods is marketed, and less, not more, of the oils and fats is consumed. That reduction in consumption is the source of lowered caloric availability.

When the price of rice increases, the consumption of oils and fats goes up and rice consumption decreases. For the low-expenditure group, a reduction in reliance on the market for oils and fats due to rice-price changes results in the expected increases in caloric availability, but again for different reasons than commonly assumed. In this case, calorie availability increases because enough additional oils and fats, as well as other commodities, are consumed to offset the reduced consumption of rice.

The foregoing partial-equilibrium implications are examples of the wider variety of policy questions that may be addressed by a farm-household model having more commodity detail than the three-commodity models commonly used in the past. This research has shown that such multicommodity farm-household models can be estimated econometrically using cross-sectional household data if the functional forms allow for a wide variety of behavior. The results can then be fitted into a general equilibrium analysis (see chapter 7).

Appendix: Data Sources

Estimates of quantities apparently consumed out of home production were derived by subtracting sales and wages in kind paid out (and seed use for rice, the major crop) from production, and by adding wages in kind received. These were adjusted for processing (to avoid double-counting) and for storage losses. (Net changes in storage were assumed to be zero.) Quantities consumed out of own-production were multiplied by regional farm-gate sales prices to transform into values. Values of foods purchased were then added to calculate the total value of foods consumed. These were aggregated into five groups, which, with nonfoods and labor, constitute the seven commodities used in the study (see table 4A-1).

Values of production were derived by multiplying quantities produced by farm-gate sales price, and then added into the appropriate groups. Production of raw products was used; processed food production was not added in order to avoid double-counting. For example, only estimates of fresh and not dried fish production were used.

Household labor-supplied data were formed by summing hours worked for agricultural and nonagricultural enterprises and for labor sold out. Labor supply includes such activities as work by women and children on vegetable production, for which women generally take responsibility, as well as the cleaning of rice. Excluded are household production activities such as food preparation, child care, and ceremonies. Units are in terms of male equivalents with weights 1 for males older than 15, 0.75 for females older than 15, and 0.5 for children aged 10–15. The weights are derived from an analysis of variance of wage rates as reported by Spencer and Byerlee (1977). Household labor demand, also measured in male equivalents, includes work on all agricultural and nonagricultural activities in the household exclusive of processing agricultural products. Both family and hired labor are included.

Prices used in estimating the demand system were formed on the basis of the eight geographical regions. Annual sales prices were formed using the larger sample of 328 households for which reliable production and labor use data were available. The value of regional sales was divided by sales quantity for each of 195 commodities. Likewise, regional purchase prices were formed for 113 commodities. A concordance between commodities purchased and sold was established and a commodity price for each region was then formed by taking a weighted average of sales and purchase prices, with region-specific weights being the share of total expenditure for a commodity coming from either purchases or home production. Commodities were then aggregated into six groups, and regional values consumed were used as weights to form arithmetically weighted prices.[8] Wage is expressed in male equivalents.

Farm sales prices for the 128 foods were aggregated into the same groups as were the weighted sales and purchase prices. In this case, the weights were the proportion of value of regional sales for the group represented by each of its component foods. These were the prices used in estimating the system of output supplies and labor demands.

Data on household characteristics were available for total size and age composition by 0–5 years, 5–10 years, 11–15 years, 16–65 years, and older than 65 years. In addition, data on number of wives, years of English and Arabic education by the household head, age of household head, ethnic

Table 4A-1. *Components of Commodities, Sierra Leone*

Commodity subgroup	Number	Components
Rice	1	
Root crops and other cereals	2	
Root crops		Cassava (including gari, foofoo and cassava bread), yam, water yam, Chinese yam, cocoyam, sweet potato, ginger, unspecified
Other cereals		Benniseed, fundi, millet, maize (shelled), sorghum, agidi,[a] biscuits (natco)[a]
Oils and fats	3	Palm oil, palm kernel oil, palm kernels,[b] groundnut oil,[a] coconut oil, cocoa butter, margarine,[a] cooking oil,[a] unspecified[a]
Fish and animal products	4	
Fish		Bonga (fresh), bonga (dried),[a] other saltwater (fresh), other saltwater (dried),[a] frozen fish,[a] freshwater (fresh),[a] tinned fish[a]
Animal products		Beef, pork,[a] goats and sheep (dressed), poultry (dressed), deer (dressed), wild bird (dressed), bush meat (dressed), cow milk, milk (tinned), eggs, honey bee output, unspecified[a]
Miscellaneous foods	5	
Legumes		Groundnuts (shelled), blackeyed bean (shelled), broadbean (shelled), pigeon pea (shelled), soybean (shelled), green bean (in shell), unspecified (shelled)
Vegetables		Onions, okra, peppers and chillies, cabbage, eggplant, greens, jakato, pumpkin, tomato, tomato paste,[a] watermelon, cucumber, egusi, other
Fruits		Orange, lemon, pineapple, banana, plantain, avocado, pawpaw, mango, guava, breadfruit, coconut, unspecified
Salt and other condiments		Salt,[a] sugar,[a] maggicubes,[a] unspecified[a]
Kolanut		
Nonalcoholic beverages		Coffee, tea,[a] soft drinks (bottled),[a] ginger beer (local)[a]
Alcoholic beverages		Palm wine, raffia wine, beer,[a] omole,[a] gin (local), liquor (rum, etc.)[a]
Nonfoods	6	Clothing, cloth, fuel and light, metal work, woodwork, other household and personal goods, transport, services and ceremonial, education, local saving, tobacco products, miscellaneous
Household labor	7	All farm and nonfarm production and marketing activities (for labor demand work on processed agricultural products excluded); labor sold out;[a] excludes household activities such as food preparation, child care, and ceremonies

a. Commodity is not included in production figures for use in estimating system of output supplies and labor demand either because it is only purchased or because it is a more processed form of a commodity already counted.

b. Not included in consumption data but included in production data.

group (there are three principal ones in our sample), and region of residence are available. Since ethnic groups tend to live in contiguous areas, this information is also regional in character (though not identical to the eight survey regions).

Land is measured as total land area cropped, in acres. It includes land in perennial as well as annual crops. It is a simple sum of acres. No weighting to reflect different qualities (for example, of swamp and of upland lands) was made because such data were unavailable. The rental markets are very thin and rental prices reflect a household's standing in the community as much as the economic value of the land (Spencer and Byerlee 1977, pp. 21–24). For a very few households, data on the land variable were missing. Since these households had usable data for all other variables, they were not dropped. Spencer and Byerlee had classified households into many different farm types. From the production sample of 328 households, average land-labor use ratios were computed for each farm type. Knowing the farm type and the labor used for these households enabled us to estimate total land cropped.

Capital is measured as the value of its flow. For variable capital, this represents no problem. For our sample, however, variable capital is minuscule, mostly rice seed. Only a little fertilizer is used and a little machinery hired, and these were added into the total. Since there are some values for variable capital, which is a flow, it was necessary to convert the stock of fixed capital into the equivalent flow in order to add the two.[9]

Sample characteristics of the variables that enter into the demand system are shown in table 4A-2. The sample is divided into three expenditure groups, and for each group simple averages are computed for each characteristic. These groups are total expenditure under 350 Leones, between 350 and 750 Leones, and greater than 750 Leones. Just how poor these households are can be seen from the annual per capita expenditures in 1974–75, which in U.S. dollars amount to $54, $88, and $136 for the low-, middle-, and high-expenditure groups, respectively. When the capital city, Freetown, was divided into three groups for a migration component of this study, the average income of the middle group was found to be $153. Hence, even the "high" expenditure households are quite poor compared with both urban Sierra Leone and other countries.

As can be seen from the expenditures reported in table 4A-2, rice is the principal staple and cassava (included in "root crops and other cereals") the main substitute. Rice tends to be eaten with a sauce and boiled cassava with a stew, both cooked with palm oil. Both sauce and stew are made with vegetables (onions, peppers, tomatoes, and leafy greens) and some meats. Sauces tend to include dried fish and stews fresh fish.

Table 4A-2. *Mean Values of Data, Sierra Leone*

| | Expenditure group | | | |
Variable	Low	Middle	High	Mean
Expenditures[a]				
Rice	58.2	125.2	262.9	146.7
Root crops and other cereals	10.7	32.4	147.4	61.3
Oils and fats	19.2	37.2	122.8	58.1
Fish and animal products	30.6	61.9	118.3	69.5
Miscellaneous foods	28.0	65.8	99.0	64.1
Nonfoods	90.0	190.1	324.0	199.9
Value of Household Labor	306.4	361.8	530.1	396.5
Prices[b]				
Rice	0.25	0.23	0.27	0.25
Root crops and other cereals	0.36	0.66	0.63	0.55
Oils and fats	0.73	0.62	0.66	0.67
Fish and animal products	0.62	0.60	0.39	0.54
Miscellaneous foods	0.56	0.58	0.60	0.58
Nonfoods	0.62	0.64	0.75	0.66
Household labor	0.08	0.08	0.09	0.08
Household characteristics[c]				
Total size	4.8	6.4	8.7	6.7
Members under 10 years	1.2	2.1	2.7	2.0
Members 11–15 years	0.5	0.7	1.1	0.8
Males over 15 years	1.7	1.8	2.6	2.1
Females over 15 years	1.4	1.8	2.3	1.8
Proportion Limba or Temne	0.45	0.29	0.44	0.39
Proportion northern	0.43	0.25	0.40	0.36
Number of households	44	51	43	138

Note: Households in the low-expenditure group are those with total expenditure less than 350 Leones. Households in the middle-expenditure group are those with total expenditure between 350 and 750 Leones. Households in the high-expenditure group are those with total expenditure greater than 750 Leones.

a. In Leones. One Leone = US$1.1 in 1974–75.

b. Weighted average of sales and purchase prices. In Leones per kilogram for foods and per hour of male equivalent for labor.

c. In numbers.

Production characteristics of the sample of 138 households are shown in table 4A-3. So that average values can be reported, the sample is divided into the ten households in Enumeration Area 13 (EA 13) and the remainder. Most in the ten households are commercial fishermen who also grow and sell a large quantity of vegetables to the Freetown market. In their production characteristics, they are quite different from the rest of the households (but their consumption characteristics are somewhat

Table 4A-3. *Mean Values of Production-Related Data,*
EA 13 and Other Households in Sierra Leone

Variable	EA 13	Non-EA 13	Entire sample
Value of production[a]			
Rice	62.7	283.5	267.5
Root crops and other cereals	27.9	64.4	61.8
Oils and fats	20.6	104.2	98.1
Fish and animal products	733.5	23.0	74.5
Miscellaneous foods	331.8	53.3	73.5
Nonfoods	82.8	25.0	29.2
Value of Labor Demand	954.7	367.5	410.0
Prices[b]			
Rice	0.19	0.22	0.22
Root crops and other cereals	0.25	0.14	0.15
Oils and fats	0.37	0.41	0.41
Fish and animal products	0.17	0.52	0.49
Miscellaneous foods	0.15	0.29	0.28
Nonfoods	2.23	1.25	1.32
Labor	0.15	0.08	0.08
Household characteristics			
Cultivated land[c]	1.6	6.8	6.4
Capital[d]	214.3	35.1	48.1
Proportion of households in EA 13	1.00	0.00	0.07
Number of households	10	128	138

a. In Leones (one Leone = US$1.1 in 1974–75). Valued by weighted sales prices.

b. Weighted sales prices. In Leones per kilogram for foods and per hour of male equivalent for labor.

c. In acres.

d. Annual flow in Leones.

similar). The fishing households cultivate much less land than the other households (an average of 1.6 rather than 6.8 acres), but they have considerably more capital in the form of boats and the like. Prices are also different, with the price of fish and animal products being considerably lower in EA 13.

Quantities produced and consumed and net marketed surplus are shown in table 4A-4. Notice that the low-expenditure group was a larger marketed surplus than the other two groups for rice (though not for other commodities). This is significant since the combined income effect—the profit effect plus the real income effect—is proportional to the net marketed surplus (see Technical Appendix, equation A-8), which means that

Table 4A-4. *Quantities Produced, Consumed, and Marketed in Sierra Leone*

Commodity	Expenditure group	Produced	Consumed	Marketed
Rice	Low	902.8	232.8	670.0
	Middle	1,164.3	544.3	620.0
	High	1,622.2	973.7	648.5
	Mean	1,227.5	586.8	640.7
Root crops and other	Low	69.0	29.7	39.3
cereals	Middle	335.8	49.1	286.7
	High	744.6	194.9	549.7
	Mean	422.1	111.5	310.6
Oils and fats	Low	85.5	26.3	59.2
	Middle	242.0	60.0	182.0
	High	447.2	186.1	261.1
	Mean	242.2	86.7	155.5
Fish and animal products	Low	18.0	49.4	−31.4
	Middle	48.3	103.2	−54.9
	High	508.7	303.3	205.4
	Mean	151.5	128.7	22.8
Miscellaneous foods	Low	93.0	50.0	43.0
	Middle	191.3	113.4	77.9
	High	515.3	165.0	350.3
	Mean	262.3	110.5	151.8
Nonfoods	Low	10.8	145.2	−134.4
	Middle	19.4	297.0	−277.6
	High	33.9	432.0	−398.1
	Mean	22.1	302.9	−280.8
Labor[a]	Low	3,963.8	3,800.3	163.5
	Middle	4,286.7	4,425.1	−138.4
	High	5,687.8	6,141.4	−453.6
	Mean	4,670.2	4,829.7	−159.5

Note: In kilograms for foods, hours for labor.

a. Produced and consumed correspond to supply and demand.

the low-expenditure group will have a relatively large combined income effect when rice price is varied.

Notes

1. There was little use of other variable inputs, for example, fertilizer. The few nonlabor variable inputs that are used are grouped with capital flows.

2. The original specification by Howe, Pollak, and Wales (1979) added a parameter, λ, multiplying the second term in equation 4-2. In that formulation, the QES becomes an LES if either $\lambda = 0$ or $a_i = d_i$, $\forall$. In this chapter, λ is set to unity since the important property (allowing

quadratic Engel curves) of the QES is not affected, and since the number of parameters needing estimation is reduced by one.

3. See Pollak and Wales (1980, 1981) for a much more complete discussion. The method is called translation since, in the direct utility function, the commodity specific translation parameters, b_i, are subtracted from quantities consumed $U(X_1 - b_1, \ldots, X_N - b_N)$. Thus the origin in utility space is "translated." One possible interpretation of $\Sigma_{k=1}^{N} p_k b_k$ is as the fixed cost (or committed) component of expenditures. However, it is empirically possible for the b_k to be negative, in which case the fixed cost interpretation does not make much sense.

4. When translation is used for the household characteristics, the variables are multiplied by prices as they enter the QES. An identification problem arises from the choice of demographic variables because wage times household size equals wage times persons 10 or older plus wage times persons younger than 10. Hence one of these variables must be dropped to avoid perfect multicollinearity. Thus the household size variable was dropped and the expenditure equation became

$$
p_i X_i^c = p_i c_i + p_i \sum_{r=1}^{3} \sigma_{ir} z_r + a_i \{ p_7 m_1 (\gamma_1 - \sigma_{71}) + p_7 \sum_{r=2}^{3} \gamma_r m_r + \pi
$$

$$
+ E - \sum_{k=1}^{6} p_k \left(c_k + \sum_{r=1}^{3} \sigma_{kr} z_r \right) - p_7 [c_7 + (\sigma_{72} + \sigma_{71}) z_2 + \sigma_{73} z_3] \}
$$

$$
- (a_i - d_i) \sum_{k=1}^{7} p_k^{-d_k} \{ p_7 m_1 (\gamma_1 - \sigma_{71}) + p_7 \sum_{r=2}^{3} \gamma_r m_r + \pi + E
$$

$$
- \sum_{k=1}^{6} p_k \left(c_k + \sum_{r=1}^{3} \sigma_{kr} z_r \right) - p_7 [c_7 + (\sigma_{72} + \sigma_{71}) z_2 + \sigma_{73} z_3] \}^2
$$

$z_1 \equiv$ household size,
$z_2 \equiv$ children younger than 10 years,
$z_3 \equiv$ region dummy (1 if northern),
$m_1 \equiv$ persons older than 10 years,
$m_2 \equiv$ children 11–15 years,
$m_3 \equiv$ females older than 15 years.

The commodity numbers (i and k) are from table 4A-1; for example, $1 \equiv$ rice, $7 \equiv$ labor. It is apparent from this equation that the coefficient of wage times persons older than 10 ($\gamma_1 - \sigma_{71}$) is identified, but not its components. This is also the case for the coefficient of wage times children younger than 10 ($\sigma_{72} + \sigma_{71}$). Therefore total time, $T = \Sigma_{r=1}^{3} \gamma_r m_r$, is not identified. This is not troublesome for the main questions addressed here. Since leisure is not directly observed, the value of time available to the household is subtracted from both sides of the leisure expenditure equation. The left-hand side becomes the negative of the value of household labor, which is observed. That is, for the leisure equation, take the basic equation, where i now equals 7 and subtract from both sides $p_7 T$. The first two terms on the right-hand side become

$$
p_7 c_7 + p_7 m_1 (\sigma_{71} - \gamma_1) + p_7 \sum_{r=2}^{3} \sigma_{7r} z_r - p_7 \sum_{r=2}^{3} \gamma_r m_r.
$$

5. In a single equation Tobit model, a latent variable Y_i^*, is defined where $Y_i^* = g_i(\beta) + \epsilon_i$. This latent variable may or may not have an economic interpretation. Y_i^* is not observed (it is latent), but $Y_i = \max(0, Y_i^*)$ is. If the ϵ_i are normally distributed, the Y_i have their probability distributions piled up, or censored, at zero. This is the source of the inconsistency of OLS, or nonlinear least squares.

Since, from equation (4-4), $g_i(\beta)$ is necessarily positive, the probability that $y_i^* > 0$ is ≥ 0.5. Although this is different from the usual Tobit model, it might not be detrimental to the results reported here; when evaluated at the sample average for independent variables, the probability of having positive production is an estimator of the sample proportion with positive production, which is always greater than half for these data.

Because the output-supply and input-demand equations are a system, a multivariate Tobit model is applicable. In this case, ϵ is an N vector with covariance matrix Σ, which is constrained to be diagonal in order to keep estimation from being prohibitively expensive. Cross-equation parameter restrictions are still imposed, however. Had Σ not been constrained to be diagonal, the probability density for each household would have involved evaluating multiple integrals, one for each good not produced. In this study, there are many households not producing one or two goods and a few households not producing as many as four goods. For these households, the corresponding density involves evaluating a quadruple integral. This is not only awkward to program, but also expensive to compute. When independence is assumed between each of the error terms, the household density is the product of 7-K normal densities and K standard normal distribution functions. If K outputs are not produced, only a single integral would have to be evaluated, but one for each of the normal distribution functions corresponding to the K outputs not produced. Evaluating a single integral K times is a much less costly and less difficult procedure than evaluating a K-dimensional integral once.

It should be noted that for a demand system Σ cannot be diagonal since expenditures on goods plus the value of household leisure equal full income. Thus error terms add up to zero, resulting in a singular covariance matrix, which it could not be if it were diagonal. However, this is not true for the values of output supply less the value of input demand, which sums to profits, because profits contain an error term.

Moreover, ignoring cross-equation restrictions, maximum likelihood estimates assuming independence retain their consistency even if the assumption is violated. Hence, the assumption remains attractive statistically. All that would be sacrificed is asymptotic efficiency.

Although there is a problem in using the CET output aggregator in representing this behavior, the alternatives create even greater problems. The trouble with the CET is that the marginal rate of transformation is infinite between a good not being produced and one that is. Hence a profit maximizing firm would always produce an infinitesimal amount of every output. This characteristic is shared by other output aggregators that rely on few parameters, for instance, the transcendental (Mundlak 1963). An alternative might be to use a flexible form. For instance, one might assume a translog profit function. Then, however, one would estimate share equations, which must add to unity. Hence the error terms must add to zero so they cannot be assumed to be independent, as already mentioned. Another alternative might be a general quadratic production function, but in this case, the number of parameters to be estimated is a multiple of the square of the number of specified outputs. In this case, the Tobit estimation might be prohibitively expensive.

6. Write

$$\partial p_i X_i / \partial(p_N T + \pi + E) = \left[\partial p_i X_i / \partial\left(\sum_{j=1}^{N-1} p_j X_j\right)\right]\left[\partial\left(\sum_{j=1}^{N-1} p_j X_j\right) / \partial(p_N T + \pi + E)\right]$$

from which $\partial p_i X_i / \partial(\Sigma_{j=1}^{N-1} p_j X_j)$, the marginal total expenditure for good i, can be solved for.

7. The calorie conversion ratios were virtually identical for rice and for oils and fats (almost all palm oil), both very homogeneous groups. The conversion factors differed substantially for the other three food groups, which are fairly heterogeneous. For example, the conversion factor for miscellaneous foods was twice as high for the representative high-expenditure household as for the representative low-expenditure household (4,750 calories per kilogram to 2,430). Conversion factors from kilograms to calories are available from the author.

8. In principle, separate prices could have been calculated for each household, but that would have created serious statistical problems. Assume that every household in a region faced the same set of sales and purchase prices (or the same set of prices for different qualities of goods). Even with a common utility function, different households would buy and sell foods at different times during the year (or buy different qualities), because of differences in household characteris-

tics and in full income. Since prices have a seasonal movement (quality differential), if an average price was calculated for each household, those averages would be different for each household even though the households actually faced the same set of prices. Not only would there be spurious variation in such prices, but these prices would be endogenous to the farm-household model we use to explain household behavior. This is so since purchase and sales decisions are endogenous to the model. Hence, if these prices were used to estimate a system of demand- or output-supply equations, the parameter estimates would be inconsistent. The same problem would occur if we used sales prices for net sellers and purchase prices for net purchasers. One way to avoid the problems of spurious variation and endogeneity of prices is to average prices across households. One interpretation of these prices is thus as a proxy for the constellation of true prices faced by a household. For this purpose, it is desirable to define the proxy prices over a market area. Region was chosen instead of enumeration area as the definition of market area because it was feared that the latter might be too small. Also, region is the area used by Spencer and Byerlee (1977) in computing their prices.

9. Let $K = rV/[1 - (1 + r)^{-n}]$, where $K \equiv$ annual service user cost, $V \equiv$ acquisition cost of capital, and $n \equiv$ expected life of capital in years. In a perfect market, the acquisition cost of the asset equals the discounted sum of its annual flows. If we assume the annual flows to be constant in real value and to start in year 1, the equation for K is obtained. Spencer and Byerlee (1977) use a discount rate of 0.1 and expected lives that were different for different types of capital (1977, pp. 47–48). The types of capital included are farm tools, animal equipment (including fishing equipment), nonfarm equipment, livestock, and tree crops.

References

Bardhan, Kalpana. 1970. "Price and Output Response of Marketed Surplus of Food-grains: A Cross-Sectional Study of Some North Indian Villages." *American Journal of Agricultural Economics*, vol. 52, pp. 51–61.

Barnum, Howard, and Lyn Squire. 1979. *A Model of An Agricultural Household*, Washington, D.C.: World Bank.

Behrman, Jere, and Barbara Wolfe. 1984. "More Evidence on Nutrition Demand: Still Income Seems Overrated and Women's Schooling Underemphasized." *Journal of Development Economics*, vol. 14, pp. 105–28.

Howe, Howard, Robert Pollak, and Terence Wales. 1979. "Theory and Time Series Estimation of the Quadratic Expenditure System." *Econometrica*, vol. 47, pp. 1231–47.

Jones, W. O. 1972. *Marketing Staple Food Crops in Tropical Africa*. 1972. Ithaca, N.Y.: Cornell University Press.

Krishna, Raj. 1962. "A Note on the Elasticity of the Marketable Surplus of a Subsistence Crop." *Indian Journal of Agricultural Economics*, vol. 17, pp. 79–84.

Lau, Lawrence, Wuu-Long Lin, and Pan Yotopoulos. 1978. "The Linear Logarithmic Expenditure System: An Application to Consumption Leisure Choice." *Econometrica*, vol. 46, pp. 843–68.

Mundlak, Yair. 1963. "Specification and Estimation of Multiproduct Production Functions." *Journal of Farm Economics*, vol. 45, pp. 433–43.

Mutti, R., D. Atere-Roberts, and D. Spencer. 1968. *Marketing Staple Food Crops in Sierra Leone*. Department of Agricultural Economics, University of Illinois, Urbana.

Pinstrup-Andersen, P., and E. Caicedo. 1978. "The Potential Impact of Changes in Income Distribution on Food Demand and Human Nutrition." *American Journal of Agricultural Economics*, vol. 60, pp. 402–15.

Pitt, Mark. 1983. "Food Preferences and Nutrition in Rural Bangladesh." *Review of Economics and Statistics*, vol. 65, pp. 105–14.

Pollak, Robert, and Terence Wales. 1981. "Demographic Variables in Demand Analysis." *Econometrica*, vol. 49, pp. 1533–51.

_____. 1980. "Comparison of the Quadratic Expenditure System and Translog Demand Systems with Alternative Specifications of Demographic Effects." *Econometrica*, vol. 48, pp. 595–612.

Powell, Alan, and F. H. G. Gruen. 1968. "The Constant Elasticity of Transformation Production Frontier and Linear Supply System." *International Economic Review*, vol. 9, pp. 315–28.

Reutlinger, Shlomo, and Marcelo Selowsky. 1976. *Malnutrition and Poverty, Magnitude and Policy Options*. Washington, D.C.: World Bank.

Rosenzweig, Mark. 1980. "Neoclassical Theory and the Optimizing Peasant: An Econometric Analysis of Market Family Labor Supply in a Developing Country." *Quarterly Journal of Economics*, vol. 94, pp. 31–55.

Sen, A. K. 1966. "Peasant and Dualism with or without Surplus Labor." *Journal of Political Economy*, vol. 74, pp. 425–50.

Spencer, Dunstan, and Derek Byerlee. 1977. "Small Farms in West Africa: A Descriptive Analysis of Employment, Incomes and Productivity in Sierra Leone." African Rural Economy Program Working Paper no. 19. East Lansing. Michigan State University.

Strauss, John. 1982. "Determinants of Food Consumption in Rural Sierra Leone: Application of the Quadratic Expenditure System to the Consumption-Leisure Component of a Household-Firm Model." *Journal of Development Economics*, vol. 11, pp. 327–53.

_____. 1984a. "Joint Determination of Food Consumption and Production in Rural Sierra Leone: Estimates of a Household-Firm Model." *Journal of Development Economics*, vol. 14, pp. 77–103.

_____. 1984b. "Market Surpluses of Agricultural Households in Sierra Leone." *American Journal of Agricultural Economics*, vol. 66, pp. 321–31.

Sukhatme, P. V. 1970. "Incidence of Protein Deficiency in Relation to Different Diets in India." *British Journal of Nutrition*, vol. 24, pp. 447–87.

Timmer, C. Peter, and Harold Alderman. 1979. "Estimating Consumption Parameters for Food Policy Analysis." *American Journal of Agricultural Economics*, vol. 61, pp. 982–87.

University of California at Los Angeles, Nutrition Assessment Unit, School of Public Health. 1978. *Sierra Leone National Nutrition Survey*. Washington, D.C.: Agency for International Development.

Ward, John, and John Sanders. 1980. "Nutritional Determinants and Migration in the Brazilian Northeast: A Case Study of Rural and Urban Ceará." *Economic Development and Cultural Change*, vol. 29, pp. 141–63.

5

Agricultural Prices, Food Consumption, and the Health and Productivity of Indonesian Farmers

Mark M. Pitt and Mark R. Rosenzweig

THIS CHAPTER EXAMINES existing household survey data from Indonesia to determine how food price changes and health program interventions affect the health, nutritional status, and profits of farm households. Many policies adopted by developing and developed countries serve to alter the price structure faced by consumers and food producers. Such macro price-intervention strategies as tariffs, support prices, ceilings, export taxes, and exchange-rate policies directly alter relative prices and thus alter the distribution of income and dietary patterns of the population. Food aid programs, depending on the manner in which they are implemented, also may affect the price structure of foods. In addition, agricultural development policies that are crop specific, either by design or by consequence, and all projects that enhance employment opportunities affect the relative prices of not only foods, but also nonfood resources supplied by family members to children—parental time and breastmilk.

Despite the well-recognized potential importance of the nutritional consequences of most programs and policies, there is little empirical evidence on the linkages between price changes, food intake, and nutritional well-being. A great impediment to the acquisition of this knowledge has been the lack of data. Although a number of localized case studies have emerged, the small size of the samples, the lack of price variability, and the noncomparability of sample designs and the analyses have made it difficult to draw defensible inferences or generalities from such information (Martin 1983). Recently, however, sets of household data have been collected in developing countries that have enabled analysts to compute estimates of the relationship between relative food prices and household food consumption patterns (Pitt 1983; Strauss 1982). Although such studies provide the first theoretically based estimates of aggregate household food consumption by disaggregated food groups from national probability samples, they do not provide any insight into the health consequences of the observed alterations in nutritional intake for individuals. Nor do they provide any information on the income or productivity changes arising from alterations in food consumption and in health status.

To the extent that food consumption is only one direct determinant of health and the rules by which households distribute their resources among their members is unknown, estimates of the effects on household-level consumption of food price and programmatic interventions do not necessarily provide sufficient information on the health consequences of such initiatives. The health of the population may also depend on the cost or availability of medical services, on the sanitation conditions of the environment, and, in the case of children, on the availability of parental care. To the extent that programs designed to alter the health status of populations may compete for donor funds with food-oriented projects and aid programs, it is useful to assess from comparable data both the relative effects of food price changes and of health program interventions on health or nutritional status. In this chapter, we extend the now conventional model of the producer-cum-consumer farm-household model by incorporating a household health production sector in which the household-produced good, health, can both affect the production of farm output and provide direct additional utility to the household. We use farm household data from an Indonesian national probability sample to estimate the effects of the short-term illness of farmers and their spouses on farm profits and labor supply; the effects of changes in eleven food-group prices, health programs, and farm profits on the probability and severity of illness of farmers and farmer spouses; and the effects of alterations in food consumption on the level of household health.

Determinants and Consequences of Changes in Health in Farm Households

Consumption, Farm Production, and Health Production

To understand health determination and the consequences of changes in health or nutritional levels in the farm sector, it is necessary to specify the processes (technology) by which health is produced, the way in which health is valued by the producer household, the effects of changes in health on household constraints, the mechanisms by which changes in health directly affect farm production, and the efficiency of input and output markets.

To illustrate how these relationships involving the market environment, health, production, and consumption influence the appropriate methods of estimating health determinants and health effects as well as policy conclusions, we consider first the simplest model of the farm household, in which the farm commodity is produced with one input, labor; there is one adult member, the farmer; and the farmer's health is also produced. The farmer derives utility from his or her level of health, H, from the consumption of the produced food commodity X (at level X^c) and purchased food commodity Y, and from leisure l, such that

$$(5\text{-}1) \qquad\qquad U = U(H, X^c, Y, l).$$

The level of health is assumed to be influenced by the levels of X^c and Y consumed, a health input Z (which yields no direct utility), the farmer's work time l_f and by environmental factors and the individual's health endowment, summarized by μ, beyond the control of the household; that is,

$$(5\text{-}2) \qquad H = h(X^c, Y, Z, l_f) + \mu \qquad h_1, h_2, h_3, > 0; \qquad h_4 < 0.$$

Expression (5-2) is the health production function, which depicts how changes in food consumption, work, time, health goods (such as medical services), and the environment affect the farmer's health. Just as with conventional firm or farm production functions, the technology embodied in (5-2) may change over time and may be known more or less precisely by different households.

The farm output production function is conventional, except that it also describes how the farmer's health may affect production; that is,

$$(5\text{-}3) \qquad\qquad X = \Gamma(L; H)$$

where L = farm labor input, defined below. The level of health may affect the productivity of farm inputs ($\partial^2 X/\partial L \partial H > 0$) but may have no direct productivity effect. That is, the health of the farmer may affect his or her ability to utilize (supervise, allocate) resources. The level of health might also directly affect the quality of the labor input supplied by the farmer. In other words, the "effective" labor units L_f the farmer supplies might be both a function of health and time worked; that is,

$$(5\text{-}4) \qquad\qquad L_f = \Theta(l_f, H) \qquad\qquad \Theta_1 > 0, \qquad \Theta_2 > 0.$$

If labor time can be hired in the market at a wage rate per unit of time W and each unit of *hired* labor time provides σ efficiency units of labor, then the labor input L in efficiency units is $L_f + \sigma L_H$, where L_H is hired labor time. The price of an efficiency unit is thus $\omega = W/\sigma$ and labor costs of production on the farm are $L\omega$. We note that W (or ω) may be determined according to the "efficiency" wage models of Leibenstein (1957), Mirrlees (1975) or Stiglitz (1976), or may be the result of standard supply-demand equilibrium. The critical assumption, discussed below, is that hired and farmer labor are perfect substitutes in farm production and the supply of hired labor to an individual farm is perfectly elastic at the market (efficiency) wage.

As noted in Grossman's (1972) original work on health production, an increase in the farmer's health may also increase the number of healthy days available for leisure l or work l_f; that is,

$$(5\text{-}5) \qquad\qquad l_f + l = \Omega(H), \qquad\qquad \Omega' > 0.$$

The income constraint of the household is thus

$$(5\text{-}6) \quad p_xX^c + p_yY + p_zZ = \pi + \omega L_f = \pi + \omega\Theta(\Omega(H) - l, H) = I$$

where p_x, p_y, p_z are the market prices of X, Y, and Z; ω is the market wage rate, I is income, and $\pi = p_xX - \omega L = $ profits.

Separability and the Effects of Farmer's Health on Farm Profits and Farm Income

As we have just seen, changes in the health status of the farmer can affect income by altering the farmer's available time Ω, managerial abilities, or the productivity of work time. We now discuss more precisely the effects of changes in the farmer's health on potential output or income, farm profits, and actual family income, given that the world consists of households that maximize the utility function described by (5-1), subject to the constraints and structural relations (5-2) through (5-6). Note that, since health is an endogenous choice variable in the model, it is necessary to distinguish the exogenous component of health (μ) from that part influenced by behavior (consumption choice and thus tastes) in order to draw causal conclusions from relationships between observed health and other variables. We thus examine how changes in μ—the health environment or endowment—which is exogenous to the farmer but possibly manipulable by policy, affect these various components and concepts of incomes. To further simplify, for the time being we ignore the managerial effect of health. The utility-maximizing (necessary) first-order conditions for the optimal quantities of the consumption and household production inputs X^c, Y, Z and l and the farm production input L are

$$(5\text{-}7) \qquad\qquad U_{x^c} + U_H h_{x^c} = \lambda[p_x - \omega h_{x^c}(\Theta, \Omega' + \Theta_2)]$$

(5-8) $$U_Y + U_H h_Y = \lambda[p_y - \omega h_y(\Theta, \Omega' + \Theta_2)]$$

(5-9) $$U_H h_z = \lambda[p_z - \omega h_z(\Theta, \Omega' + \Theta_2)]$$

(5-10) $$U_1 + U_1 h_1 = \lambda\omega[\Theta_1 - h_2(\Theta_1\Omega' + \Theta_2)]$$

(5-11) $$P_x\Gamma_L = \omega$$

where λ = Lagrangian multiplier.

Conditions (5-7), (5-8), and (5-10) indicate how changes in the consumption of the food items as well as in leisure time augment utility both directly and indirectly, by changing the level of health, and also influence income indirectly by altering the efficiency of the farmer's labor time and the time available for leisure or work. Despite the interdependence between the farmer's consumption and his labor productivity, however, the level of the farm (labor) input L is independent of the farmer's consumption and leisure choices. Expression (5-11) is the profit maximization condition for the use of the farm labor input; farm production and consumption allocations are thus separable. The reason is that, whatever the endogenously determined efficiency per unit of time supplied by the farmer to farm production and whatever the quantity of time supplied, labor time (and efficiency units) can be hired at constant cost per unit to perfectly substitute for changes in the farmer's labor supply. Thus, farm profits will be independent of the farmer's health status when market substitutes are easily available for labor input, measured in efficiency units or time. Conversely, only if such substitution is imperfect will consumption decisions and health affect production decisions and farm productivity. If, for example, the farmer's health affects management performance and the market for management is absent or imperfect, then the separability between production and health will be broken.

The independence of farm profits and farmer's health in the perfect (input and output) market case does not imply that potential income or household income is unaffected by changes in the health environment. We can define the household's potential, or full, income $F(H^*)$ in the perfect market (separable) case, for a given health level H^*, as the sum of the profit-maximizing level of profits π (independent of H^*) and labor income when the farmer works full time (all available time = $\Omega(H^*)$); that is,

(5-12) $$F(H^*) = \pi + \omega\Theta(\Omega(H^*), H^*).$$

The effect of a small change, $d\mu$, in the health environment on full income is thus

(5-13) $$\frac{dF(H^*)}{d\mu} = \omega(\Theta_1\Omega' + \Theta_2)\frac{dH}{d\mu} > 0.$$

Since second-order conditions constrain $dH/d\mu > 0$, increases in health always increase full income by altering the (potential) time available for work and by augmenting efficiency per unit of labor time. Even though the farmer's profits are unaffected by the healthiness of the environment, potential output to society is affected (hired labor time can be released for use in other productive pursuits).

Although full or potential income rises when the farmer's health environment improves, even in the separable case no prediction can be made from the model with respect to how actual or realized income will change in response to changes in μ, since realized income depends on labor time supplied:

$$(5\text{-}14) \qquad\qquad \frac{dI(H^*)}{d\mu} = \omega\left(\theta_1 \frac{dl_f}{d\mu} + \theta_2 \frac{dH}{d\mu}\right).$$

The effect of μ on the level of the farmer's work time cannot be predicted because it depends on the properties of the unknown utility function as well as on the characteristics of the health production and efficiency labor functions. Thus, changes in farm profits, actual or realized income, and potential income in response to changes in health will generally not be identical. Indeed, if health was purely a consumption good and had no effects on time availability or on labor efficiency, farmer's income (via labor supply) would be likely to change when the healthiness of the environment changes, but output and full or potential income would not.

It is clear that the effect of health on farm profits (which depends on the nature of input and output markets), or on income (which depends in part on the labor-leisure choices of the household), is not an appropriate measure of the total costs to society (or benefits) from changes in the health environment. In the absence of direct measures of efficiency units of labor, measures of health, labor time, and all farm inputs could be used in a production-function analysis to discern how farm output changes, given labor time, in response to changes in health. (Of course, this approach—that is, holding all inputs constant—would not capture any effects of health on the allocative ability of the farmer.) Additionally, if illness fully prevents any work effort, then the cost of illness is simply lost earnings. The value of marginal changes in lost work days from severe (fully constraining) illness, however, although relatively easy to measure, will understate the total returns from investments in health when health also affects worker efficiency.

Finally, it can be easily demonstrated that the absence of markets for any of the consumed commodities or inputs in health production, which lead to own-production of those factors, also breaks down the separability of farm production and consumption, as hired resources are diverted from the cash crop to produce nonmarketable commodities. Farm profits will thus be affected by the farmer's health even if input markets are perfect, although in the latter case, production of the cash crop will be efficient.

Food Prices and Health Programs: The Exogenous Determinants of Health

The reduced-form consumption-demand equations for the foods, other health inputs, and leisure, conditional on farm profits, derived from the model incorporating health production are

$$(5\text{-}15) \qquad X^c, Y, Z, l = D^i(P_x, P_y, P_z, \omega, \Pi, \mu) \qquad\qquad i = X^c, Y, Z, l.$$

These conditional-demand equations have all the usual properties of demand equations derived from models without household (health) production. Thus, own-compensated price effects are negative, cross-compensated price effects are symmetric, and so on. However, the functional form of these demand equations depends on (or implies) the characteristics of both the household utility function (5-1) and the household production technology embodied in (5-2). Thus, the assumption that the utility function is Stone-Geary, Extended Linear Expenditure System (ELES), or Cobb-Douglas, for example, does not, under most circumstances, result in the usual demand-system parameterizations derived from these specific functional forms, since the system will depend as well on the household technology. In most cases, no exact closed-form solutions for the demand equations in (5-15) can be obtained from explicit parameterizations of the preference orderings and technology of the household. One special case where this is possible, considered in Rosenzweig and Schultz (1983), occurs when the Cobb-Douglas form characterizes both the utility and household production sector. Conversely, ad hoc specification of the reduced-form consumption-demand equations does not generally allow retrieval of either the underlying technological or utility parameters. Household health production and consumption are never separable, unlike consumption and farm production with perfect input and output markets, because there is no market for the produced good, in this case, health.

Although the consumption-demand equations derived from the household production model, as noted, do contain all the predictions of conventional utility maximizing models, the parallel reduced-form demand equation for health, in (5-16), does not have any predictive content:

$$(5\text{-}16) \qquad\qquad H = D^H(P_x, P_y, P_z, \omega, \Pi, \mu).$$

To see why, consider the effects of a change in the price of the food good X, P_x, on the household's health:

$$(5\text{-}17) \qquad \frac{dH}{dP_x} = h_{x^c} \frac{dX^c}{dP_x} + h_y \frac{dY}{dP_x} + h_z \frac{dZ}{dP_x} + h_{l_f} \frac{dl}{dP_x}.$$

Even if all inputs including the food good X in the health production function have positive marginal products and contribute to improving health, it can be seen from (5-17) that a rise in the price of X or of any food good may increase or decrease health. The reason is that a change in any one price of food also (generally) affects the consumption of other foods and leisure (cross-price effects are nonzero) in directions that cannot be predicted. In (5-17) for example, although dX^c/dP_x is likely to be negative, consumption of the Y good and the Z-input may increase (if Y and health are gross substitutes for X in consumption) and health may improve. For example, governmentally subsidized technological improvements in cash crops, such as wheat, which result in higher relative prices for noninternationally traded items such as some vegetables, could lower or raise health levels even if farm profits are unaltered and vegetables are healthier than bread (consumption of butter, rich in vitamin A and a likely complement to bread, might increase).

The net effect of a food price change on health will thus depend on the magnitudes and signs of the own- and cross-price effects in consumption and on the relative magnitudes of the marginal productivities of the inputs in the health production function. That is, food price effects on health depend on both the properties of the health production technology and the underlying preference ordering of the household for foods and other health-related goods. As a consequence, conclusions about the health impact of various food policies, which alter the relative prices of foods and other goods, cannot be known a priori without estimates of the health reduced-form equation (5-16) or estimates of both the consumption (food and other health inputs) demand system (5-15) and the health technology, from (5-2).

Finally, the composition and nutrient level of the household diet reflects not only relative food costs and the constraints of income, but also the cost or availability of health services P_Z and the healthiness of the environment μ. Moreover, just as a change in one food price may reduce or increase health levels because of theoretically ambiguous substitution among foods of different health marginal productivities (nutritiousness), the health effects of interventions that alter the cost of pure health inputs will be augmented or diminished by substitutions in health production and consumption. Thus, reductions in health service costs may induce a change in diet toward less nutritious (but more tasty?) foods, if nutritious foods and health services are substitutes in health production and such foods and health are substitutes in consumption. Similarly, programs aimed at improving the health environment (cleaner sources of water) will alter the composition of demand and the demand for health services in ways that may reinforce or attenuate the health effects of such interventions. Estimates of the health reduced-form equation provide information about the joint health effects of food policies and health programs that reflect these household allocations of resources.

The Multiperson Household, Consumption Aggregation, and Intrafamily Resource Allocation

An important element of unrealism in the model discussed so far is the assumption that the farm household consists of one person. Although one-person household models are extensively used in the development literature (for example, Barnum and Squire 1979; Iqbal, chapter 6), analyses of labor supply in developed countries (Ashenfelter and Heckman 1974; Schultz 1980) have demonstrated the importance of the interaction between heterogeneous members residing in the same household (husband and wife) as well as the differential intrahousehold responsiveness of spouses' labor supply to price and wage changes. Since almost all households in all developing societies consist of at least one adult female and one adult male, and wage rates for males and females are not always in fixed proportion (see Rosenzweig 1984, for evidence from India; Hansen 1969, for evidence from Egypt), treatment of family members as one aggregate person or as a collection of identical individuals (Sen 1966) facing a "unisex" wage would appear to be overly simplistic, at best. Moreover, in the area of health and nutrition, the well-documented differentials and variation in male and female infant survival rates across countries suggest that changes in income and prices may have significant distributional effects on the health of individuals within families, given that most households contain children and adults of both sexes.

The question of how a household distributes its available resources among its members is particularly important in the study of food price, food consumption, and nutrition relationships, because most available household data sets are likely to provide information only on household consumption aggregates, given the expense of collecting individual-specific consumption data. To the extent that interest in aggregate (family-level) consumption or overall nutritional availability in low-income households is derived mainly from concern about the nutrition, health status, or productivity of members of such households, understanding how household aggregates map into the well-being and health of individuals is critical.

In this section we consider three related questions: How does a change in a particular food or other price faced by a household affect the consumption and health of individual household members? What inferences regarding the health of individual members of a household can be drawn from information on total household food consumption or nutritional availability? Given data on the health of individual family members and the total household intake of food, what inferences can be made about the relationship between food intake and health; that is, when can the health technology be retrieved, given data on the health of individuals and household-level input information?

We first generalize the model discussed in the previous section by adding $n - 1$ family members, whose individual-specific vectors of consumption goods, leisure, and health enter the household utility function such that:

$$(5\text{-}18) \qquad\qquad U = U(H^i, X^i, Y^i, l^i) \qquad\qquad i = 1 \cdots n$$

$$(5\text{-}19) \qquad\qquad H^i = h^i(X^{ci}, Y^i, Z^i, l^i) + \mu^i$$

$$(5\text{-}20) \qquad\qquad L^i_f = \Theta^i(l^i_f, H^i)$$

$$(5\text{-}21) \qquad\qquad X = \Gamma(L^i)$$

$$(5\text{-}22) \qquad\qquad P_z Z + P_x X^c + P_y Y = \pi + \sum_{i=1}^{n} \omega^i L^i_f$$

where $Z = \Sigma z^i$, $X^c = \Sigma X^{ci}$, $Y = \Sigma Y^i$, $L^i = L^i_f + L^i_H$, and superscripts denote individuals. Note that the μ^i term includes both household-specific factors—the health environment—and individual-specific factors—the health endowment. As constructed, the model allows each person to have unique health and efficiency unit production functions and assumes that each type of person has an equivalent market substitute, at wage rate ω^i, in farm production. Thus the model retains its separability between the profit and consumption sections.

The first-order condition, derived from maximization of (5-18) subject to (5-19) through (5-22) for the intrahousehold allocation of, say, good X between person j and person k, is

$$(5\text{-}23) \qquad\qquad \frac{U_{xj} + U_{Hj}\, h_{xj}}{U_{xk} + U_{Hk}\, h_{xk}} = \frac{P_x - \omega^j h_{xj}\theta^j_2}{P_x - \omega^k h_{xk}\theta^k_2}.$$

As can be seen from (5-23), the allocation of resources between members of the household will depend on how the household values the health and consumption of each member (U_{Hi}, U_{xi}); how the relationships between health and consumption (the health technology) and between productivity and health (Θ^i) differ among members; and how the pecuniary returns to investments in the health of individual family members (the ω^i) differ.

The reduced-form demand equations for the multiperson model are

$$(5\text{-}24) \quad \begin{bmatrix} X^{ci} \\ Y^i \\ Z^i \\ l^i \\ H^i \end{bmatrix} = R^{ji}(P_x, P_y, P_z, \pi, \omega, \mu) \ j = X, Y, Z, l, H; \ i = 1 \cdots n$$

where ω, μ are the household vectors of individual-specific wages and endowments containing the elements ω^i, μ^i, $i = 1 \cdots n$.

Comparing the single-person model to its multiple-person counterpart, we see that each has the same number of exogenous food and input prices, but the number of endogenous consumption variables to be determined (solved for) in the multiperson model is greater by $n - 1$ times the number of choice variables. As a consequence, no additional predictions can be made from the multiperson model regarding the effects of changes in the food and health input prices beyond those for foods and health inputs aggregated over individuals; that is, own-compensated price effects for X^c, Z, Y are negative. Thus, no predictions can be derived from the multiperson model as to how changes in food prices alter the distribution of food consumption across members of the household without the imposition of a great deal of additional structure.

Because, however, there is a unique price of time ω_i corresponding to each individual in the model, the compensated effects of person-specific wage changes on the consumption of individual household members and thus on the intrahousehold allocation of foods can be discerned with little additional structure imposed. For example, a compensated increase in the wage of person type j can be shown to increase the allocation of food to person j and decrease the allocation of food to person k, if the health, food consumption, and leisure of j and k are Hicksian substitutes. Thus, the household will tend to distribute more resources to persons with higher earnings capacities, as given by the market wage per labor efficiency unit, when the individual-specific goods in the household welfare function are substitutes. This feature of the multiperson household is exploited in Rosenzweig and Schultz (1982) to show how differences in economic opportunities for women could account for the variation in male-female infant survival ratios across India.

To examine the relationships between the aggregate quantity of household consumption and the consumption and health of individual family members, we employ a simpler multiperson model in which there are only two persons. For simplicity, we also ignore labor/leisure decisions and farm production. The household's utility thus depends on the health status H

and consumption of food good X of each individual as well as on a jointly consumed good Y. The health of each individual depends in turn on own-consumption of the X good.

Thus,

(5-25) $$U = U(H^1, H^2, X^1, X - X^1, Y)$$

(5-26) $$H^1 = h^1(X^1) \qquad h^i_{x^i} > 0, \qquad h^i_{x^i x^i} < 0$$

(5-27) $$H^2 = h^2(X - X^1)$$

(5-28) $$p_x X + p_x Y = I$$

where $X^2 = X - X^1$ and I is total income, assumed exogenous.

To facilitate the comparison between aggregate household consumption X and person-specific consumption, we treat the aggregate food X and the consumption of X by individual one, X^1, as control variables. Determination of X and X^1 obviously determines the consumption of X by person 2, X^2, in this two-person case. The necessary first-order condition for the allocation of X between household members 1 and 2, the intrafamily allocation "rule," given the optimal aggregate consumption of X, is

(5-29) $$U_{H^1} h^1_{X^1} + U_{X^1} = U_{H^2} h^2_{X^2} + U_{X^2}$$

that is, allocate resources across family members to equate their marginal contributions to household welfare. These marginal values will depend on both the unique utility-generating traits of each individual and on individual-specific differences in the health technology.

The relevant first-order conditions for the aggregate household consumption of X^2 and Y are given by:

(5-30) $$U_{H^2} h^2_{x^2} + U_{x^2} = \lambda p_x$$

(5-31) $$U_y = \lambda p_y$$

where λ is the Lagrangian multiplier.

We now consider how member one's health status, H^1 changes when there is an exogenous change in the total amount of X, the commodity affecting health, consumed by the household. That is, we wish to know how a change in the availability of total or per capita X, $x = X/2$, alters X^1 (and X^2) and thus the individual health levels of 1 and 2. Using rationing theory (Tobin and Houthakker 1950–51) and assuming that the exogenous change in the aggregate consumption of X occurs at the optimal level, as given by expressions (5-30) and (5-31), we know that dX^1/dx is just $(dX^1/dp_x)/dx/dp_x)$, the ratio of the compensated effects of a change in the price of the X commodity on individual one's consumption of X and the compensated effect of a change in the price of X on the total or per capita consumption of X in the household. In the two-person model, when the utility function is strongly separable, the relationships between a change in per-capita X, x, and the consumption of X by person one is thus:

$$(5\text{-}32) \qquad \frac{dX^1}{dx} = 2\left\{ \frac{U_{H^1H^1}(h_{x^1}^1)^2 + U_{H^1}h_{xx}^1 + U_{x^1x^1}}{U_{H^1H^2}(h_{x^2}^2)^2 + U_{H^2}h_{xx}^2 + U_{x^1x^1}} + 1 \right\}^{-1}.$$

Only if the numerator and denominator of the first parenthetical term in (5-32) are equal will changes in per capita X consumption and changes in the consumption of all individuals in the household be equal; a sufficient condition is that the health production functions among individuals be identical and the family consider all persons perfect substitutes for each other. In the absence of blindness to individual traits by households and perfect biological homogeneity across family members, however, little can be said a priori about how alterations in the per capita (or adult-equivalent) availability of food in the household affect any individual's health status in that household, unless the intrafamily distributional rules are also known.

Lack of information on intrafamily allocations also means that little can be said about the magnitude of the change in average family health status when average family consumption changes, so long as individual food or nutrient consumption is not in fixed proportion to health. The effect of per capita X on average health ($\Lambda = H/2$) in the model is

$$(5\text{-}33) \qquad \frac{d\Lambda}{dx} = \left[h_{x^1}^1 \frac{dX^1}{dx} + h_{x^2}^2 \frac{dX^2}{dX} \right] \frac{1}{2}$$

which will depend on both the allocative rule dX^1/dx and on the properties of the health production functions. Expression (5-33) above shows that even if the individual-specific health functions are identical, as long as health production functions exhibit diminishing returns in food and allocations of X across individuals are not equal, then

1. If the *relationship* between individual food consumption and health is known, knowledge of per capita family food consumption will not yield the level of per capita household health, since $d\Lambda/dx \neq 1/n \, \Sigma_i^n h_{x^i}^i$

2. If the *relationship* between individual food consumption and health (the health production function) is *not* known, it cannot be inferred from information on the health status of individuals and family per capita food consumption, since $dH^1/dx = h_{x^1}dX^1/dx \neq h_{x^1}$.

Conversely, only if the relationship between individual consumption and health is in fixed proportions, that is, if $h_{x^1} = h_{x^2} = a$, then, independent of how the household distributes its resources:

1. If the consumption-health coefficients are known, the average health of the household can be inferred from knowledge only of per capita household consumption, although individual-specific levels of health or nutritional status cannot be known
2. If the health production coefficients are unknown, they can be inferred from information on the individual health levels of all family members and total family consumption, since, from (5-33), $\Sigma_i^2 dH^i / dX = a \Sigma_i^2 dX^i / dX = a.$

Given the difficulty of directly estimating the health production function owing to the need for individual-specific consumption (intake) information, it may be preferable to estimate individual-specific reduced-form health-demand equations (such as [5-24]). Although such reduced-form estimates do not provide information on how the consumption of food items directly affect health, they do yield information on how changes in the prices of foods, medical services, and other goods result in changes in health or nutritional status. Since it is relatively more difficult for policy-makers to alter directly (dictate) how households allocate their resources than to manipulate prices or provide services, the health-reduced forms may provide more policy-relevant information than will estimation of the health technology, as long as technology (and tastes) remain unchanged. The reduced-form equations for health and other consumption items, including leisure, also can provide information on how changes in measurable aspects of the health environment alter health, health practices (inputs) and the supply of labor.

Finally, reduced-form health estimates obtained for different members of the same family also allow a test of whether family members can be (or are) considered to be identical, since, under the null hypothesis of perfect intra-family substitution and biological homogeneity, all coefficients in the person-specific reduced forms will be equal across household members. Rejection of the null hypothesis, of course, does not reveal the underlying cause (biological or behavioral) of the observed differences in health responses to commonly experienced price and income effects across members of the same family in the absence of direct estimates of the health technology.

Estimation of the Relationships between Health, Food Prices, Farm Profits, and Aggregate Food Consumption: Indonesia

Heterogeneity, Separability, and Estimation Procedures

We estimate the relationships between health and food prices, consumption and production using household-level data from an Indonesian national probability sample. These data provide information on short-term illness, labor supply, and earnings for all household members, detailed food and other consumption data and farm profits at the household level, and food and other price data at the village level. The data thus enable the estimation of

1. The effects of changes in farmer's and spouse's health on farm profits and on labor supply.
2. The effects of changes in food prices and health infrastructure on the health of the farmer and spouse, on the demand for household-level health inputs, and on differences in the illness incidence between farmer and spouse.
3. The effects of changes in the level and composition of individual food consumption on individual health levels, under the fixed coefficient and homogeneity assumptions for the individual health production function.

The estimation procedures used to obtain these estimates as well as the appropriate specifications of the profit function and health reduced forms depend not only on whether the farm production and consumption (household production) sectors are separable, as noted, but also on the existence of variations among individuals or households in exogenous characteristics that are unobserved or unrecorded in the data, that is, heterogeneity. It is now well recognized (Mundlak 1961) that heterogeneity in farmer's managerial capacities may lead to bias in least squares estimates of farm production functions, as farmers of different abilities may choose different input combinations and will obtain higher output from a given input mix. Accordingly, in estimating the effects of farmer's health on farm profits, a correlation between those unobserved farmer characteristics that (conditional on prices) augment profits and unobserved characteristics that increase health status (the μ) will also lead to bias in estimating the effects of health on profits, even if changes in profit levels do not influence the household's demand for health. Thus it is possible to find that health and profits are correlated, even if health does not structurally affect farm profits, solely because of heterogeneity bias. Since price changes are likely to be uncorrelated with farmer characteristics, health input prices (P_x in the model) are suitable instruments for estimating the direct, structural effect of farmer health on farm profits.

Estimation of the reduced-form equations that include farm profit by ordinary least squares will provide consistent estimates of food price and profit effects on health and other goods (as long as unmeasured aspects of μ are independent of prices or farm profits). If exogenous changes in the farmer's health or in μ affect profits (nonseparability), however, profits and unobserved components of μ will be correlated and all reduced-form equations that include farm profits will be subject to bias. It is thus important to test for separability before estimation or specification of the profit-inclusive reduced-form equations.

Heterogeneity bias also potentially plagues estimates of household (or health) production functions. Households reside in different health environments and may have different, genetically endowed propensities for ill health, as embodied in the μ or μ^i terms in the model. Some of these exogenous environmental conditions (for example, water facilities) can be measured relatively easily; others, related to genetic endowments, almost never. Yet, the model suggests that food-consumption choices and labor supply will respond to environmental conditions (the μ) that also affect health, and thus that bias will be present when the health production function is estimated by least squares. Because prices of *all* consumed goods—whether or not all of the goods strictly affect health—as well as prices of production inputs (labor) influence the choice of those commodities affecting health, however, such prices can serve as instruments to obtain consistent estimates of the parameters describing the production of health.

Households are also heterogeneous with respect to tastes, which jointly influence the level of health demanded and produced by a household, as well as household consumption patterns and labor or leisure choices. Accordingly, least squares associations between measures of health (as a regressor) and such household choices as labor supply and food consumption are contaminated by heterogeneity bias even when all markets are perfect. As noted above, the reduced-form effects of health changes (even stripped

Table 5-1. *Observed Associations between Farmer's Health, Farm Profits, and Labor Supply, Indonesia*

Dependent variable and type of association with health	Perfect labor substitution			Imperfect labor substitution		
	No productivity effect	Labor efficiency effect	Mana-gerial[a] effect	No productivity effect	Labor efficiency effect	Mana-gerial[a] effect
Profits						
Structural	None	None	Positive	Positive[b]	Positive[b]	Unknown
Heterogeneity	Possible	Possible	Possible	Possible	Possible	Possible
Labor supply						
Structural	Positive[b]	Positive[b]	Unknown	Positive[b]	Positive[b]	Unknown
Heterogeneity	Possible	Possible	Possible	Possible	Possible	Possible

a. Assumes no perfect complements for own-management.
b. If health and leisure are gross substitutes.

of heterogeneity bias) on behavioral outcomes, controlling for prices, combine (and confound) the underlying utility and technological or biological parameters. Given the stability of those parameters, they do, however, yield information on the consequences of (if not the social returns to) improvements in health.

Table 5-1 summarizes the expected types of relationships, and their signs, between health and farm profits and labor supply, when structural health estimates are obtained using proxies for health input prices as identifying instruments. Although in some cases structural effects are signed, or known to be absent, heterogeneity leads to a theoretically unknown relationship between health, profits, and labor supply in all cases.

Results

Data. The household-level sample used to estimate the relationships between health and food prices, food consumption and production are from the April–June 1978 subround of the National Socio-Economic Survey of Indonesia (SUSENAS 1978) carried out by the Central Bureau of Statistics (Biro Pusat Statistik). This survey provides information on farm profits, itemized household consumption and expenditures, water sources, drinking water treatment, land ownership, cultivation, income and, for each household member, information on the incidence and severity of illness in the previous seven days as well as age, education, labor supply, and wages. These data were augmented with information on the availability of health programs in local areas, irrigation quality and attributes of the nonfarm labor market. In this analysis, the sample size for households cultivating land and having both a head and spouse present is 2,347. Irrigation information, however, was only available for 2,175 households. Data sources for all the areal variables as well as sample characteristics and definitions of all variables used in obtaining the estimates below are in the appendix.

Wages for the head (male in all sample households) and spouse were computed by means of wage equations estimated from a sample of all household members aged 10 years and older, stratified by sex, and corrected for selectivity bias. The least squares correction for selectivity bias was applied (Olsen 1980). Variables measuring land ownership and marital status were used to identify the selectivity correction in the wage equations. To achieve identification of the health and profit equations using predicted wages, kabupaten (district)–specific measures of industrial capital and manufacturing workers per capita, derived from the raw data tapes of a 1978 survey of manufacturing establishments (Survey Tahunan Perusahaan Industri 1978), were included as regressors in the individual wage equations.

To maintain tractability, the 112 separate expenditure items in the SUSENAS were aggregated into thirteen commodity groups, eleven foods plus tobacco-betel and fuel. Consumption of the commodity aggregate tobacco-betel—which includes the use of sirih, an intoxicating quid consisting of betel leaf, areca nut, gambier, and lime—may influence a respondent's perception of illness in addition to any actual effect. Therefore caution is required in interpreting its estimated effects on the respondent's reported health.

The principal shortcoming of the SUSENAS data is that they provide information only on short-term farm profits, labor supply, and illness. The health status of family members is indicated by the occurrence of (self-reported) illness during the previous week; illness intensity is captured by information as to whether the illness required bed rest.

The Effects of Illness on Farm Profit and Farmer Labor Supply. We first determine whether the allocation of resources in farm production can be treated as separable from household health and consumption decisions by estimating a farm-profit equation including the illness of the head of household and his wife. First we tested whether the illness variables were independent of the profit function residuals. The Wu statistic (3.00) was less than the critical value for (2,2500) degrees of freedom. Thus the profit function can be appropriately estimated by ordinary least squares (OLS). The parameter estimates are presented in the first two columns of table 5-2. The results of our tests of the structural effects of illness and heterogeneity bias appear in table 5-3. The hypothesis that the illness of the farmer or the farmer's spouse do not structurally influence farm profits cannot be rejected ($F[2,2144] = 1.62$). Thus, we cannot reject the separability of farm production and consumption sectors.

The hypothesis that health is exogenous in the labor-supply equation for the male head of household is, however, rejected ($F[2,2144] = 7.16$); leisure and the household production of health are not separable. Consistent with farm production-consumption sector separability, however, farm profits are exogenous to labor-supply decisions by the farmer ($F[1,2170] = 0.92$). Instrumental variable estimates of the male labor-supply equation are reported in the second column of table 5-2, with health program variables used as instruments. As predicted in table 5-1, we find that illness experienced by the farmer does significantly reduce his labor supply, even though his illness does not reduce farm profits. The hypothesis that illness has no structural effects on the amount of work performed by the male head is rejected at the 0.01 level of significance ($X^2[2] = 9.40$). Thus, rural labor markets in Indonesia appear to be operating smoothly enough so that market substitutes can be found for significant illness-induced reductions in the

Table 5-2. *Estimates of the Effects of Illness on Farm Profits and Farmer Labor Supply, Indonesia*

Variable/estimation method	Farm profits (×10⁻³) OLS	Male labor supply IV	Household boils water probit
Illness, head[a]	3.24	−68.0	—
	(0.37)[b]	(1.80)[c]	
Illness, wife[a]	−16.7	−69.7	—
	(1.71)	(1.72)	
Profits (×10⁻³)	—	−0.0455	0.00211
		(6.34)	(2.24)
Owned land	0.0115	0.00102	0.000106
	(9.32)	(2.55)	(2.36)
Age, head	0.615	−0.346	0.00231
	(2.01)	(3.24)	(0.26)
Age, wife	−0.535	0.222	−0.00267
	(1.59)	(2.12)	(0.03)
Education, head	1.31	0.150	−0.00489
	(1.64)	(0.44)	(0.19)
Education, wife	−3.52	−0.489	0.0861
	(0.37)	(1.56)	(2.60)
Wage, head	−1.93	−0.205	0.0901
	(1.61)	(0.47)	(1.67)
Wage, wife	3.24	−1.90	0.325
	(0.18)	(−0.30)	(0.41)
Price of grain	4.01	−7.29	1.16
	(0.39)	(−1.94)	(3.85)
Price of tubers	16.6	3.37	0.262
	(2.83)	(1.73)	(1.34)
Price of fish	3.21	0.0335	−0.0439
	(2.24)	(0.06)	(0.98)
Price of meat	0.385	0.230	0.0975
	(0.44)	(0.80)	(3.69)
Price of milk	−0.445	0.169	−0.0374
	(0.71)	(0.85)	(2.11)
Price of vegetables	−8.55	0.597	−0.00725
	(2.98)	(0.58)	(0.07)
Price of legumes	3.43	0.101	−0.0360
	(1.44)	(0.12)	(0.44)
Price of fruit	1.09	1.07	−0.0416
	(0.36)	(1.10)	(0.42)
Price of other foods	−0.871	0.483	−0.158
	(0.91)	(1.59)	(0.13)
Price of vegetable oil	0.668	0.424	0.0873
	(0.48)	(0.88)	(1.85)
Price of sugar	−6.79	−3.04	−0.231
	(1.03)	(1.30)	(1.01)
Price of tobacco-betel	−2.47	1.21	0.393
	(0.51)	(0.78)	(2.49)

(*Table continues on the following page.*)

Table 5-2. (continued)

Variable/estimation method	Farm profits ($\times 10^{-3}$) OLS	Male labor supply IV	Household boils water probit
Price of fuel	−0.136 (0.63)	−0.0127 (0.19)	−0.0152 (2.50)
Irrigation-1	25.6 (3.06)	—	—
Irrigation-2	−16.0 (2.01)	—	—
Irrigation-3	−21.5 (1.72)	—	—
Well	—	—	0.207 (1.67)
River	—	—	0.0149 (0.97)
Hospital	—	—	0.261 (0.45)
Clinic	—	—	4.09 (3.25)
Maternity hospitals	—	—	0.826 (0.98)
Family planning	—	—	1.35 (4.28)
Public lavatories	—	—	0.375 (1.36)
Households in kabupaten	—	—	−0.000687 (3.34)
Intercept	−3.91 (0.18)	55.2 (8.40)	−1.44 (1.81)
d.f.	2,171	2,171	2,347

a. Endogenous variable in labor-supply equation. See text.

b. Absolute values of t-ratios in parentheses.

c. Absolute values of asymptotic t-ratios in parentheses.

farmer's cultivation time that leave levels of production unaffected, at least in the short term.

The labor-supply parameter estimates indicate that the illness of the husband and wife jointly and significantly reduce the head's labor supply, reflecting both the expected complementarity between health and leisure and intrafamily substitution of time in household production. The illness reported in the sample appears to reduce labor supply strongly, by almost seventy hours a week. The low incidence of illness (2.6 to 3.4 percent) combined with this result suggests that only severely debilitating illness is re-

Table 5-3. *Test Statistics: Profit and Farmer Labor-Supply Equations, Indonesia*

Variable	Test statistic (d.f.)	Profit equation	Labor supply equation
Illness			
Structural effect (Wald)	χ^2 (2)	3.00	9.40
Exogeneity (Wu)	F (2,2144)	1.56	7.16
Profits			
Structural effect (Wald)	t (2319)	—	6.34
Exogeneity (Wu)	t (2319)	—	0.958

ported by the respondents; thus the illness variable may not be a sensitive indicator of actual health status. Of the other coefficients, in accord with prior studies of labor supply, increases in farm profits (which are exogenous to consumption decisions) reduce the farmer's total labor supply, and thus indicate the normality of leisure. Of the food price variables, only the price of grain significantly affects labor-supply decisions—for given farm profits, an increase in grain prices reduces the farmer's labor supply (grain consumption and the head's leisure are substitutes).

Determinants of Drinking Water Treatment and the Illness of Farm Heads and Farm Wives: Reduced Forms. The last column of table 5-2 provides the reduced-form probit maximum likelihood estimates of the determinants of whether the household boils its drinking water. The estimates indicate that higher farm profits, larger land holdings, and higher educational attainment of farm wives tend to increase the propensity of households to take the precautionary step of boiling water before it is consumed. Commodity prices are also important determinants of boiling behavior—t-values for five of the price parameters (those for grains, meat, milk, tobacco, and fuel) exceed 2.0 in absolute value. Although we cannot, as noted, sign a priori the reduced-form price effects without knowledge of the fundamental technological and utility parameters, it is probably not surprising that higher fuel prices are significantly associated with unboiled drinking water in our sample, given that fuel is an important input in the production of this intermediate health input.

All the health program variables are positively associated with water boiling, although only public health and family planning clinics have highly significant coefficients. These results suggest that such programs may provide information on health practices in addition to providing remedial services. The estimates also indicate that poorer qualities of water—

that from wells and rivers rather than from springs and piped water systems—tend to increase the propensity to boil water.

In Pitt and Rosenzweig (1985), we estimated sex-specific illness reduced forms for heads and their wives. A likelihood-ratio test indicated, however, that all the slope parameters in the equation for heads and wives were jointly different from zero at the 0.05 and 0.10 levels of significance, respectively. The patterns of signs for commodity prices were quite different in the farm-head- and farm-wife-illness reduced forms. As noted, of course, it is not possible to infer to what extent these apparent differences represent differences in sex-specific health technologies or the nature of intrahousehold allocation rules.

Among the more precisely estimated parameters for heads of households, the prices of grains and sugar were negatively related to illness, whereas the prices of vegetables and vegetable oil were positively related to illness. Although the popular notions that sugar is bad for health and vegetables are good for health conform to these results, we reiterate that such conclusions cannot be drawn from the reduced form. The estimates do imply that reductions in the relative prices of vegetables will increase health levels, whereas subsidies to sugar, for given farm profits, will increase the incidence of illness. At the sample means, the estimates indicated that a 10 percent reduction in the prices of vegetables and vegetable oil will decrease the probability of illness by 4.2 and 9.3 percent, respectively. Similar proportional decreases in the prices of grains and sugars will increase the incidence of illness by 15 and 25 percent, respectively.

A rigorous test of the joint hypotheses that there is both perfect intrafamily substitution and identical health production functions across the farm head and his wife is carried out by estimating a model obtained by subtracting the wife's illness reduced form from that of her husband using fixed-effect logit (Chamberlain 1980). A likelihood-ratio test failed to reject (at the 0.05 level) the hypothesis that the set of slope parameters of the head's illness reduced form is different from that of the wife's reduced form. Among the individual food prices, however, the prices of fish and vegetables had statistically different impacts on the differential incidence of illness of heads and wives. Higher fish prices tend to make wives relatively more ill and higher vegetable prices tend to make heads relatively more ill.

The Illness Production Function. As noted, we are unable to estimate directly individual-specific health production functions because individual-specific consumption data are not available. If we assume that the relationship between individual consumption and health is in fixed proportions and is the same for all individuals, however, we can estimate the person-specific health production function, formed by summing the linear health production functions for all the individuals residing in the household, even if household resources are allocated differentially across individuals. Food- and tobacco-consumption levels in this aggregated, linear, household-ill- ness production function are now household totals; the intercept is repre- sented by the total number of household members and the age variable is the sum of the ages of all household members. Possible differences in the individual male and female health production functions are permitted by including an intercept dummy variable for sex (male $= 1$, female $= 0$), which, in summing to an aggregated function, becomes the total number of male household members.

Also included in the production-function specification are household public good inputs, that is, household-level variables that are assumed to affect the health of all individual family members net of their own con- sumption of foods. These are the (endogenous) boil variable, which affects the drinking water of all household members, the water sources, and the schooling attainment of the head and wife. The latter are included to test if schooling improves health net of input levels, that is, to test for schooling effects in household production that are analogous to worker or efficiency effects in farm production.

All variables are divided by the size of the family in order to eliminate the heteroscedasticity caused by differences in household size. As a conse- quence, the illness-dependent variable, average illness incidence in the household, has a large concentration of observations at zero but also obser- vations that may range up to a value of one (when there are no observa- tions). The Tobit estimation procedure is therefore employed. Because of possible heterogeneity in health endowments and environmental factors, which would bias these single-equation estimates, the health production function is also estimated using two-stage Tobit, where the endogenous food and other inputs are first regressed on the prices and programs. Al- though the two-stage Tobit estimates are consistent estimates of the (linear) production coefficients, the standard errors are not unbiased, so that cau- tion should be exercised in interpreting the two-stage results.

Table 5-4 presents both Tobit and two-stage Tobit estimates of the linear household production function. As we have noted, heterogeneity bias aris- ing from differences in health environments and endowments, and tastes, potentially contaminate the single-stage estimates. The difference between the Tobit and two-stage Tobit estimates is indeed quite striking. For exam- ple, the Tobit estimates indicate that fruit consumption is implausibly posi- tively and significantly associated with household illness, whereas the two- stage estimates suggest that the reverse pattern is more likely the case.

The consistent two-stage Tobit estimates indicate that six of eleven food commodities have negative production coefficients in the production of ill-

Table 5-4. *Linear Household Illness Production Function, Indonesia*

Variable/estimation technique	Two-stage tobit	Tobit
Grain consumption[a,b]	0.193	−0.0135
	(0.53)	(0.10)
Tuber consumption[b]	−0.453	−0.129
	(0.28)	(1.13)
Fish consumption[b]	−3.92	−0.678
	(2.96)	(1.58)
Meat consumption[b]	4.82	0.133
	(1.01)	(0.14)
Milk consumption[b]	19.5	2.63
	(0.30)	(0.89)
Vegetable consumption[b]	−2.74	0.199
	(2.21)	(0.70)
Legume consumption[b]	2.21	.144
	(0.20)	(0.21)
Fruit consumption[b]	−1.98	0.408
	(1.77)	(2.27)
Other food consumption[b]	−1.40	−2.20
	(0.19)	(1.90)
Vegetable oil consumption[b]	−4.78	−0.958
	(0.18)	(0.39)
Sugar consumption[b]	14.5	0.807
	(2.16)	(0.79)
Tobacco-betel consumption[b]	−1.78	−0.355
	(1.72)	(1.75)
Hours of work[b]	−0.00711	−0.0059
	(1.14)	(3.54)
Male	−0.0213	−0.0396
	(0.99)	(0.47)
Age[b]	−0.0904	−0.0043
	(3.52)	(0.76)
Age squared[b]	0.00117	−0.000085
	(3.53)	(1.19)
Boil water[b]	−0.314	−0.0450
	(1.30)	(0.48)
Well × boil[b]	0.575	0.0387
	(1.82)	(0.32)
Well	−0.566	−0.0715
	(1.88)	(0.62)
River × boil[b]	1.11	0.167
	(2.86)	(1.07)
River	−1.08	−0.217
	(2.93)	(1.44)
Education, head	0.0165	0.0138
	(2.44)	(2.45)
Education, wife	−0.00431	0.0013
	(0.53)	(0.19)
Intercept	1.22	−0.240
	(2.63)	(1.99)

a. All consumption variables divided by 100 ($\times 10^{-3}$).
b. Endogenous variables.

ness. Of these, three are statistically significant at least at the 10 percent level of significance (fish, fruit, vegetables). The negative coefficient for to-bacco-betel suggests that consumption of this commodity reduces reported illness. As noted earlier, however, the sirih (betel) component of this con-sumption aggregate is intoxicating and may distort perceptions of health status. Sugar consumption, on the other hand, appears to increase signifi-cantly the production of illness. (It should be remembered, that the stan-dard errors of the two-stage Tobit model are not unbiased.) The (consistent) point estimates indicate that a 10 percent increase in vegetable, fruit, and fish consumption reduces the probability of illness by 9.1, 3.4, and 5.6 per-cent, respectively, and that a similar proportional increase in sugar intake increases this probability by 11.5 percent. The results also suggest that for any level of the specified health inputs, males are no less likely to become ill than are females, and that illness incidence declines with age up to age 38 and then increases.

Of the household-level variables, the set of water-source and water-treat-ment variables are statistically significant. The educational level of the household head, but not the wife, is also statistically significant. As in the health reduced forms, however, higher male educational attainment is asso-ciated with higher levels of reported illness incidence, perhaps because of a greater propensity among educated respondents to report illness in re-sponse to given illness symptoms. Although individual differences in ill-ness-reporting propensities may be uncorrelated with (village-level) prices and programs, personal characteristics may influence both objectively mea-sured health conditions and reporting errors.

Conclusions

A number of recent studies have focused on the allocation of food nutri-ents across households and the response of household nutrient intake to changes in food prices and income. Since nutrient intake itself cannot be considered an argument in the utility function or even a good indicator of welfare, it seems likely that implicit in this focus on nutrient intake is the view that food nutrients are an important set of inputs into the production of health. In addressing the direct relationships between food (and other health inputs) prices, income, and health, we demonstrate that policy im-plications derived from studying how the level and distribution of a subset of health inputs (foods) changes with price subsidies or other interventions may be seriously flawed if the ultimate policy goal is to improve the levels or distribution of health in the population.

The traditional model of the producer-cum-consumer farm household incorporating a household health production sector is used to demonstrate the difficulty in predicting the effects of policies on health or of the consequences of changes in health status. We show that theory offers no predictions for the signs of the effects of food price changes on health without complete knowledge of preferences and of the health technology. Moreover, we show that the change in farm profits resulting from changes in health status is not a measure of the output loss resulting from illness, but rather an indicator of the imperfection of markets and the substitutability of inputs in farm production. Indeed, no prediction can be made from the model with respect to how household income will change in response to changes in health status.

Although in principle the health technology is estimable, estimation requires individual-specific information on health inputs consumed and instruments such as prices. Available household data sets are likely to provide information only on household consumption aggregates. Thus, we consider how household aggregates map into the well-being and health of individuals. In general, no predictions can be derived as to how changes in prices or per capita consumption affect the distribution of consumption across individuals, the health of individuals, or even the average health of the household. If the health technology is linear and homogeneous across individuals, however, it is possible to estimate the relationship between household consumption and an individual's health.

From a sample survey of farm households in Indonesia, we estimated farm profit and labor supply equations and reduced-form equations for one household health input (the boiling of drinking water) and for the illness of the (male) head of household and his wife. Exogenous regressors included the prices of eleven food groups, tobacco and fuel, wage rates for the head and his wife, education, and measures of the availability of water and the health infrastructure.

Our estimates of the profit and labor supply equations suggested that although the illness of either spouse decreased significantly the amount of labor supplied by the farmer, there was little or no effect on farm profits exclusive of family opportunity costs. Further tests were consistent with the hypothesis that the substitution of hired labor for illness-induced lost family labor time was fully compensating, as the production and consumption sectors of the farm household were found to be separable owing to evidently well-functioning input and output markets.

With respect to the determinants of health, the estimates also suggest that both the health environment and costs of inputs affect a household's choice of precautionary health measures and that certain foods play particularly important roles in determining the short-term illness propensities of adult farm-family members. In particular, households residing in areas where sanitary sources of water are limited and where fuel costs are low are more likely to boil their drinking water. Furthermore, the consumption of vegetables, fruit, and fish are significantly and negatively associated with the incidence of adult illness, and increased sugar consumption appears to significantly increase the probability of illness. Alterations in the prices of foods also appear to have a significant effect on the illness probabilities of adult males—reductions in the prices of vegetables and vegetable oil improve health and reductions in the price of sugar increase the incidence of illness.

Although our theoretical framework implies that changes in actual or realized income or farm profits associated with changes in health status are not good measures of either the output loss due to illness or of changes in the welfare of individuals, with appropriate data it may be possible to obtain at least boundary measures of health effects on output. One approach would be to estimate a farm production function that includes the health status of family workers as an additional input and to control for their labor input in units of time as well as other production factors. A second approach would be to estimate the relationship between (time) wages and health status, as implied by efficiency wage theories. Measurement of the productivity gains associated with investments in health is a neglected but important area of research that may be useful in assessing the full consequences of both agricultural and "basic needs" policies.

Appendix: Data Sources

The basic data used in this study have already been described. A few other details should be mentioned, however. First, a village is assumed to represent a distinct market and the average village price of every item is calculated as the average price of the commodity consumed by the sampled households in the village. All food prices are measured in rupiahs per kilogram and fuel prices in rupiah per British thermal unit. Price indices are formed by geometrically weighting component prices with the average budget shares of the relevant district (kabupaten) of residence. A quantity index for each commodity group is formed by dividing expenditure by this price index.

The household-level information was augmented with data on the proportion of rural villages in each kabupaten in which there was at least one hospital, public health clinic, maternity hospital, family planning clinic, health personnel, or public lavatory (Biro Pusat Statistik 1979, 1980).

Table 5A-1. *Sample Characteristics, Indonesia*

Endogenous variables	Mean	Standard deviation
Farm profits in past 3 months (rupiahs)	13,860.0	75,041.0
Illness in past week (farmer)	0.0336	0.180
Illness in past week (farmer's spouse)	0.0267	0.161
Hours employed in past week (farmer)	37.3	17.81
Household boils drinking water	0.932	0.252
Family size	5.16	3.95
Grains[a]	1,420.0	749.0
Tubers[a]	373.0	744.0
Fish[a]	166.0	199.0
Meat[a]	34.3	81.6
Milk[a]	6.64	22.0
Vegetables[a]	379.0	290.0
Legumes[a]	67.0	116.0
Fruit[a]	196.0	347.0
Other Foods[a]	96.1	83.4
Vegetable Oil[a]	31.3	34.1
Sugar[a]	93.8	88.0
Tobacco-betel[b]	237.0	382.0
Fuel[b]	282.0	383.0
Exogenous variables—household characteristics		
Age of farmer	42.6	12.2
Age of farmer's spouse	36.0	11.0
Years of schooling (farmer)	3.71	3.10
Years of schooling (farmer's spouse)	2.58	2.79
Predicted hourly wage (farmer, rupiah/hour)	103.0	59.1
Predicted hourly wage (farmer's spouse)	4.30	3.04
Land owned	1,047.0	1,401.0
Exogenous variables—village or kabupaten characteristics		
Grain[c]	1.28	0.213
Tubers[c]	0.493	0.315
Fish[c]	3.41	1.22
Meat[c]	8.80	2.20
Milk[c]	7.65	2.72
Vegetables[c]	1.15	0.652
Legumes[c]	2.24	0.807
Fruit[c]	1.07	0.582
Other foods[c]	4.57	1.82
Vegetable oil[c]	5.18	1.17
Sugar[c]	2.33	0.288
Tobacco-betel[d]	1.22	0.378
Fuel[d]	6.20	8.10
Water sources		
Well or pump	0.575	0.494
River	0.203	0.402
Other (rainfall, spring)	0.778	

Table 5A-1. (*continued*)

Endogenous variables	Mean	Standard deviation
Proportion of rural villages in kabupaten with		
Hospitals	0.237	0.169
Public health clinics	0.111	0.0930
Maternity hospitals	0.147	0.133
Family planning clinics	0.503	0.378
Public lavatories	0.486	0.271
Health personnel services	0.568	0.225
Number of households in village	611.0	553.0
Proportion of cultivated acres in kabupaten (district) irrigated		
Controlled and partly controlled	0.200	0.214
Simple, with bunds	0.261	0.227
Runoff	0.0380	0.145
Dry land	0.499	

a. Quantity index, all components measured in 100 grams.

b. Quantity index.

c. Price index, all components in price per 10 grams.

d. Price index.

Data on the quality of irrigation by kabupaten, a determinant of farm profits, were also merged in from a separate survey (Direktorat Jenderal Pertanian 1973). Table 5A-1 lists the sample characteristics and definitions of all variables used in obtaining the econometric estimates.

References

Ashenfelter, O., and J. Heckman. 1974. "The Estimation of Income and Substitution Effects in a Model of Family Labor Supply." *Econometrica*, vol. 42 (January), pp. 73–86.

Barnum, H., and L. Squire. 1979. "An Econometric Application of the Theory of the Farm Household." *Journal of Development Economics*, vol. 6 (June), pp. 79–102.

Biro Pusat Statistik. 1979, 1980. *Fasilitas Sosial Desa.* 2 vols., Jakarta.

Chamberlain, G. 1980. "Analysis of Covariance with Qualitative Data." *Review of Economic Studies*, vol. 47, pp. 225–38.

Direktorat Jenderal Pertanian. 1973. *Statistik Bahan Makanan Utama Di-Indonesia.* Jakarta.

Grossman, M. 1972. "On the Concept of Health Capital and the Demand for Health." *Journal of Political Economy*, vol. 80 (March–April), pp. 223–55.

Hansen, B. 1969. "Employment and Wages in Rural Egypt." *American Economic Review*, vol. 59 (June), pp. 298–313.

Leibenstein, H. 1957. *Economic Backwardness and Economic Growth.* New York: John Wiley & Sons.

Martin, Terence H. 1983. "Nutritional Consequences of Agricultural Development Projects: A Survey of the Evidence." Washington, D.C.: World Bank. Processed.

Mirrlees, J. A. 1975. "A Pure Theory of Underdeveloped Economies." In *Agriculture in Development Theory.* Edited by L. G. Reynolds. New Haven, Conn.: Yale University Press.

Mundlak, Y. 1961. "Empirical Production Functions Free of Management Bias." *Journal of Farm Economics,* vol. 43, pp. 44–56.

Olsen, R. J. 1980. "A Least Squares Correction for Selection Bias." *Econometrica,* vol. 48, no. 7, pp. 1815–20.

Pitt, M. M. 1983. "Food Preferences and Nutrition in Rural Bangladesh." *Review of Economics and Statistics,* vol. 65 (February), pp. 105–14.

Pitt, M. M., and M. R. Rosenzweig. 1985. "Health and Nutrient Consumption across and within Farm Households." *Review of Economics and Statistics,* vol. 67 (May), pp. 212–23.

Rosenzweig, M. R. 1984. "Determinants of Wage Rates and Labor Supply Behavior in the Rural Sector of a Developing Country." In *Contractual Arrangements, Employment and Wages in Rural Labor Markets in Asia.* Edited by H. P. Binswanger and M. R. Rosenzweig. New Haven, Conn.: Yale University Press.

Rosenzweig, M. R., and T. P. Schultz. 1982. "Market Opportunities, Genetic Endowments and Intra-Family Resource Distribution: Child Survival in Rural India." *American Economic Review,* vol. 72 (September), pp. 803–15.

————. 1983. "Estimating a Household Production Function: Heterogeneity, the Demand for Health Inputs and Their Effects on Birthweight." *Journal of Political Economy,* vol. 91 (October), pp. 723–46.

Sen, A. K. 1966. "Peasants and Dualism with or without Surplus Labor." *Journal of Political Economy,* vol. 74, pp. 425–50.

Schultz, T. P. 1980. "Estimating Labor Supply Functions for Married Women." In *Female Labor Supply.* Edited by J. P. Smith. Princeton, N.J.: Princeton University Press.

Stiglitz, J. E. 1976. "The Efficiency Wage Hypothesis, Surplus Labour, and the Distribution of Income in L.D.C.'s." *Oxford Economic Papers.* New Series, vol. 28, pp. 185–207.

Strauss, J. 1982. "Determinants of Food Consumption in Rural Sierra Leone: Application of the Quadratic Expenditure System to the Consumption-Leisure Component of a Household-Firm Model." *Journal of Development Economics,* vol. 11, no. 3, pp. 327–54.

Survai Sosial Ekonomi Nasional (Susenas) Data Tapes. 1978. Biro Pusat Statistik, Jakarta.

Tobin, J., and H. S. Houthakker. 1950–51. "The Effects of Rationing on Demand Elasticities." *Review of Economic Studies,* vol. 18, pp. 140–53.

6

The Demand and Supply of Funds among Agricultural Households in India

Farrukh Iqbal

AGRICULTURAL CREDIT PROGRAMS have become important components of development strategy in most developing countries. More than US$30 billion in rural credit is now disbursed annually by the governments in these countries and more than US$5 billion has been spent on such programs by international aid agencies over the past several decades (Adams and Graham 1981). Since such programs have staked out substantial claims upon national development budgets, it is important that their costs and benefits be assessed. Such an assessment will not be possible, however, without a theoretical and empirical understanding of the determinants of the demand and supply for funds among agricultural households. This study attempts to contribute toward that understanding.

Several dimensions of the demand for credit are important for development policy. For example, there has been considerable technical change in agriculture in the developing countries (especially in populous South Asia) in recent decades and it is believed that the pace and spread of such change is dependent on the availability of funds and terms of financing. If the momentum of agricultural innovation is to be maintained, its link with the borrowing, saving, and investment behavior of agricultural households needs to be better understood. Similarly, interest rate policy

Note: This is a considerably revised version of a paper put out originally as Rand Note N-1631-AID by the Rand Corporation. My research at Rand was supported by Grant no. AID/Otr-1822 from the Agency for International Development. I would like to record my gratitude for the comments and suggestions of Kenneth Wolpin, Robert Evenson, Surjit Bhalla, Dennis De Tray, and John Strauss. The views contained herein are to be attributed to me alone and not to any of the individuals or agencies with whom I have been affiliated.

could be another important determinant of this behavior and it has certainly been accorded pride of place among relevant policy instruments by policymakers in the developing countries. The existing literature (reviewed in David and Myer 1979) has little to offer in this area, however. A systematic statistical investigation of the interest elasticity of borrowing would shed light on many policy debates that have hitherto been conducted largely on the basis of conjecture.

This study departs from previous ones in that it analyzes the borrowing behavior of farmers in the context of an agricultural household model. As noted elsewhere in this volume, the main reason for investigating such models is that agricultural households combine in themselves the characteristics of both producers and consumers. Their production decisions and outcomes affect their consumption decisions and outcomes, and vice versa. Up to now, attention has been focused on two activities of farm households where such interactions are important: the production-consumption of food and of labor. Among others, Barnum and Squire (1979) have demonstrated that the magnitudes of market food and labor supply and the relevant elasticities with respect to important policy variables depend substantially on whether or not we take an agricultural household approach to theoretical and empirical analysis. The objective of this study is to extend this framework to cover the borrowing and saving behavior of farm households. Such an extension is both realistic and important. It is realistic because farmers make borrowing decisions not just on the basis of market conditions defining their production, but also on the basis of their own savings or self-financing capacity (and vice versa). Just as such households supply part of the food and labor that they demand, so also do they supply part of the funds needed to make investments and intertemporal adjustments in consumption. The extension is important because it leads to some empirical results and implications that are quite different from those available in the literature.

The data for the empirical analysis were obtained from a comprehensive national (panel) survey of approximately 3,000 farm households in India carried out from 1968 to 1971. This survey was conducted by the National Council for Applied Economic Research (NCAER). Relevant details appear in the text and a general description is provided in the appendix.

Structure and Selected Features of the Model

Basic Structure

The basic structure of a farm-household model (see chapter 2 for details) is as follows: the household is supposed to act as if it were maximizing a utility function subject to a budget and a time constraint. The utility function is assumed to have properties that ensure tractability and the constraints are simply accounting identities that link amounts (by sources) to uses of income and of time. The exact specification of the utility function and of the constraints depends on the focus of the particular inquiry concerned. Thus Sen (1966), in seeking to establish the preconditions for surplus labor in peasant households, focuses on the labor-leisure choice implicit in a utility function of the general form $U = U(C, L)$, where C denotes the consumption of (undifferentiated) goods and L that of leisure. Barnum and Squire (1979) are interested in exploring the marketable surplus of output and labor and therefore expand the utility function to $U = U[C, L, F]$, where F denotes the consumption of market-purchased goods and C that of home-produced goods. Their budget constraint is correspondingly specified to take into account expenditures on F and income from the sale of C.

The above approach is quite general and may also be applied to a study of the borrowing and lending behavior of farm households. Since borrowing is a means of adjusting consumption over time, we need to attach time subscripts to the arguments of the utility function as a first step toward an intertemporal specification. As far as the choice of arguments is concerned, we can restrict our attention to the consumption of (undifferentiated) goods and of leisure since we are not specifically interested in the composition of consumption. This results in a general utility function of the form: $U = U[C_1, \ldots C_n; L_1, \ldots L_n]$. For analytical convenience a simple two-period utility function is used:

$$(6\text{-}1) \qquad U = U[C_1, C_2, L_1, L_2]$$

where the time subscripts refer to the "current" and "future" periods and are meant to capture essentially the duration of an entire borrowing-investment-repayment cycle.

Intertemporal specification also requires that a budget and time constraint be specified for each period. How does borrowing affect these? Borrowing expands income directly in the period in which it is undertaken and reduces it in subsequent periods through repayment obligations. However, it also expands income indirectly in the subsequent periods by making possible investment that pays off in those years. All of these basic notions can be captured by a two-period constraint system as in

$$(6\text{-}2) \qquad p_1 f[K_1, H_1] + w_1 M_1 + B = C_1 + I$$

$$(6\text{-}3) \qquad p_2 \alpha f(K_2, H_2) + w_2 M_2 = C_2 + B(1 + r)$$

$$(6\text{-}4) \qquad M_1 = T - L_1 - H_1$$

$$(6\text{-}5) \qquad\qquad M_2 = T - L_2 - H_2$$

where the subscripts refer to the two periods being considered, and

C = consumption expenditure
L = leisure or nonmarket time
M = net market labor supply
H = on-farm labor (family + hired)
K_1 = initial endowment of productive capital
I = on-farm investment such that $K_2 = K_1 + I$
p = price of output
w = market wage rate
r = interest rate or cost of funds
B = amount borrowed or lent
α = technical improvement parameter
T = total available time.

Selected Features of the Model

Two special features of this model deserve attention because of their relevance to present-day agriculture in developing countries: the incorporation of a labor-leisure choice in the utility function and labor market participation in the budget constraint; and the use of an index of technological change or investment opportunity on the production side. The first feature broadens the range of economic activities hitherto considered to be important in the borrowing and saving decisions of farmers in developing countries, and the second allows for explicit analysis of the link between these decisions and the opportunity to invest, a connection whose importance became acutely obvious during the Green Revolution of the late 1960s.

The connection between labor-leisure choices and the demand for borrowing has typically been ignored in previous studies. Thus the models implicit in the studies of Pani (1966) and Long (1968) assume a production function defined·on only one input, capital, so that the borrowing decision is viewed simply as a one-period rental of capital presumably for investment. Hesser and Schuh (1962) take a firm-theoretic view in which labor enters the budget constraint but not the utility function. Both formulations are inadequate to the extent that borrowing takes place in order to consume and invest, labor-leisure choices are important to agricultural households, and borrowing can affect such choices, and vice versa. There is growing evidence to suggest that rural labor market developments have an important effect on rural production and incomes. Consequently, the effects of developments in the labor market (captured, for example, through movements in wage rates), on the demand and supply of credit should be of interest.

The role of technical change in influencing the demand for credit has also been largely ignored in most previous studies in this area. Although it is generally agreed that credit availability affects the decision to adopt new technology (Feder, Just, and Zilberman 1982), it is not known how agricultural technical change affects the demand for credit. One way to approach this matter is to consider the effects of technical change on farm incomes and productivity. By and large, the technical change experienced by agriculture in the developing countries since the early 1960s has raised average farm incomes and productivity. In particular, the seed-fertilizer-irrigation package of Green Revolution fame has tended to be scale-neutral and income-augmenting in its effects. Now, the greater the value of expected future income, the greater the tendency to borrow in anticipation of it. Similarly, the higher the rate of return to capital, the greater the tendency to borrow and thereby employ more capital. Both of these effects can be captured by the use of a measure of investment opportunity or the opportunity to shift from one possible income stream to another.

In the case of farm households, an improvement in investment opportunities could be thought of as an outward shift of the production-possibility frontier. This effect is captured in our model by a parameter, α, which shifts the production function in a manner analogous to Hicks-neutral technical change. Empirically, α is meant to be interpreted as a vector containing all the factors that bring about differences in the investment opportunities open to farmers. As such, it should include managerial ability, together with soil quality and differences in the availability of government extension services, irrigation services, and the like. The actual empirical implementation of this hypothesis is discussed later.

The Truncation Issue

Perhaps the most important feature of our model is that it yields a flow-of-funds measure of the demand for credit that is theoretically superior to the one used in previous studies. This measure is based on the first-period constraint (equation 6-2), which can be rewritten as

$$(6\text{-}6) \qquad [p_1 f(K_1, H_1) + w_1 M_1 - C_1] + B = I$$

and, by condensing the income terms on the left-hand side into an overall income term Y_1, as

$$(6\text{-}7) \qquad (Y_1 - C_1) + B = I.$$

Our definition of borrowing is now seen to be simply the difference between on-farm investment and current savings:

$$(6\text{-}8) \qquad\qquad B = I - (Y_1 - C_1) \quad \text{or} \quad B = I - S.$$

The difference between this measure and the conventional one can best be understood by examining the components of B. From the definition of savings, S, as the change in net worth from one period to the next, we can write

$$(6\text{-}9) \qquad\qquad S = I + CD + FA + EL - EB,$$

where I is on-farm investment, CD is the net change in consumer durables, FA is the net change in financial assets, and EL and EB refer to external lending and external borrowing. Substituting for S in (6-8) gives us

$$(6\text{-}10) \qquad\qquad B = EB - EL - FA - CD.$$

This indicates that the demand for funds is simply the algebraic sum of changes in liabilities ($EB - EL$), changes in internal borrowing ($-FA$), and changes in the stock of consumer durables ($-CD$).

Previous studies have used EB rather than B as their measure of the demand for credit. This leads to truncation bias, a problem formally akin to that arising in the case of female market labor supply, where nonmarket hours and wages (for housewives) are unobserved. In the borrowing case, because the conventional definition is restricted to EB and does not take into account borrowing from internal sources (for example, savings accounts) or lending, the dependent variable is effectively truncated at zero.

Truncation produces biased coefficient estimates for one or both of two reasons. Suppose we assume that separating the sample into borrowers and lenders is correct because there are essentially two distinct populations with different behaviors that should be estimated separately. It is then important that the discrimination between the two populations be quite accurate; otherwise, biases are likely to be produced. In the case of rural borrowing, it does not seem appropriate to use the level of current borrowing to distinguish between populations of borrowers and nonborrowers, because current borrowing behavior is likely to vary for reasons that do not reflect the permanent status of a household. The second, more important, problem is that the assumption that two separate populations exist may not be tenable. There may, in fact, be only one population, and it may contain some households that choose to borrow and others that choose to lend in the face of a common set of exogenous determinants. Consider the relationship between the interest rate and the amount borrowed. This relationship is a stochastic and not a deterministic one—that is, some individuals will borrow more and others will borrow less, even when faced with the same interest rate. By focusing only on those who borrow, we increase the likelihood of observing a positive, rather than the expected negative, relationship between these two variables, partly because those who reduce their borrowings by a large amount (in response to an increase in the interest rate) are more likely to switch from borrower to nonborrower status and therefore to be excluded from the sample; those who reduce their borrowings by a small amount are more likely to remain in the sample. The bias produced by stratifying along the dependent variable has been most commonly observed and discussed in the literature on the human-capital earnings function. In particular, it has been shown that looking at a subsample of relatively poor households alone tends to underestimate the true effect of schooling on earning power.

Interest Rate Endogeneity

Thus far, the model has been developed as if the agricultural household faces a capital market in which it can borrow (or lend) all it wants at a constant, exogenously given, interest rate. This is a convenient assumption because it allows us to invoke separability between production and consumption-related determinants of borrowing—the household first chooses a production level determined by the point of tangency between its production possibility frontier and the market opportunity line; having fixed a production level, it then borrows or lends to make up the difference between production income and consumption expenditure. In most agricultural household models (for example, Barnum and Squire 1979), a similar assumption is typically invoked with respect to the hiring in or out of labor.

The constant exogenous interest rate assumption, however, may not be realistic in the case of rural capital markets in developing countries. It might be more realistic to assume that in the informal lending arrangements that prevail in such markets, interest rates are household-specific and vary in accordance with household characteristics such as wealth and education. In fact, it can even be argued that the "effective" interest rate charged in the formal rural capital market (that is, cooperative credit societies and agricultural development banks) is also household-specific— whereas all borrowers are charged the same nominal rate by law, poorer clients may be subject to higher bribe demands. The possible endogeneity of the interest rate can also be depicted by considering its relationship to the amount borrowed. There are several reasons why interest rates may vary directly with loan exposure. It is possible, for example, that individual lenders may attach higher risk to larger loans and hence charge higher interest rates as the loan amount demanded increases. It is also possible that households may have to draw funds away from more and more rewarding uses in order to lend more and more; if so, they will have to be compensated by higher and higher returns to lending. This would certainly be a reasonable possibility in informal markets where households often lend and compete, as it were, with professional moneylenders. In the case of borrowing from moneylenders, it is quite likely that different moneylenders have to be approached as borrowing needs increase, each being more expensive than the previous one. In each of these cases an upward-sloping supply curve would be generated. This possibility has to be set against the possibility that there may be economies of scale in lending—the larger the loan, the lower the unit costs of administering it and hence the lower the interest charge. Whether an upward or downward sloping cost of funds schedule is faced is ultimately an empirical matter. What is being asserted here is that agricultural households may face interest rates that are a function of household characteristics and loan demand and that may not, therefore, be exogenous.

Some Theoretical Results

The incorporation of an endogenous interest rate into the model is straightforward. It requires replacing r by $r(B)$ in equation (6-3), the second-period budget constraint. Assume also that $r_B > 0$ and $r_{BB} < 0$, that is, that the supply-of-funds schedule slopes upward but at a declining rate—these assumptions keep the model theoretically tractable.

The optimizing problem can now be stated as

(6-1′) maximize $$U = U[C_1, C_2, L_1, L_2]$$

(6-2′) subject to $$p_1 f(K_1, H_1) + w_1 M_1 + B = C_1 + I$$

(6-3′) $$p_2 \alpha f(K_2, H_2) + w_2 M_2 = C_1 + B[1 + r(B)]$$

(6-4′) $$M_1 = T - L_1 - H_1$$

(6-5′) $$M_2 = T - L_2 - H_2.$$

The optimal amount of borrowing and its variation with respect to changes in exogenous variables can be derived from the model depicted by (6-1′)–(6-5′) in standard fashion by specifying the appropriate Lagrangian and solving the differentials of the first-order conditions via Cramer's Rule. Readers interested in the algebraic exercises may turn to Iqbal (1981a). For the purposes of this paper, only the consequences of interest rate endogeneity and the coefficient signs derived from the model are elaborated.

One consequence of interest rate endogeneity is that the optimizing condition for borrowing changes: that the marginal product of capital no longer be equal to the interest rate but that it be equal to the term $r(B) + Br_B$. The demand function for borrowing takes the form $B = B[E, x_i, r(B)]$, where E denotes all farm specific endowments, x_i denotes prices of different inputs and outputs except capital, and $r(B)$ denotes the endogenous price of capital. A typical coefficient in the borrowing function could be written as

$$dB/dx_i = dB/dx_i|\bar{r} + \partial B/\partial r \cdot \partial \bar{r}/\partial \bar{x_i}.$$

It has been the practice to estimate agricultural household models by first estimating the production-profit function, next estimating a system of consumption-demand equations, and then integrating the results of the two to obtain full coefficient and elasticity values. This practice cannot be followed if the interest rate is considered endogenous because the production and consumption parts of the model are not theoretically separable—the interest rate affects both decisions and is jointly determined by these decisions. An alternative way to estimate this model is to adopt a two-stage simultaneous-equations procedure involving a borrowing function and an interest rate function as the structural equations. The exact procedure followed and the reasons for it are discussed in a later section.

The following coefficient signs are derived from the model: $dB/dr < 0$ for $B > 0$; $dB/dp_1 < 0$; $dB/dp_2 > 0$; $dB/d\alpha > 0$. The signs for dB/dw_1, dB/dw_2, and dB/dK_1 remain ambiguous. These results depend essentially on what may be called period-specific income effects. Thus, when variations in an exogenous factor cause income to rise in period 1, the household transfers some of this increase to consumption in period 2 by reducing its borrowings; increases in period-2 income similarly lead to an increase in borrowing as the household attempts to raise period-1 consumption. Thus $dB/d\alpha$ and dB/dp_2 are positive in sign because increases in α and p_2 amount to increases in second-period income, whereas dB/dp_1 is negative because an increase in p_1 amounts to an increase in current-period income.

The results for dB/dw_1 and dB/dw_2 involve, in addition, what could be called leisure substitution effects. An increase in w_1, for example, increases the cost of L_1, and if we assume L_1 and L_2 are substitutes, the consequence is a decrease in L_1 and an increase in L_2. This intertemporal transfer of leisure is accomplished by a decrease in borrowing, which reduces repayment claims in period 2 and thereby permits greater consumption of goods and leisure. The case of an increase in w_2—which, other things being equal, leads to an increase in borrowing—is similar. It should be noted that the signs of dB/dw_1 and dB/dw_2 also depend on whether the household is a net labor importer or exporter and also on the relationship of on-farm labor (H_1, H_2) to leisure. Thus, in the case of an employed but landless household, where M_1 and M_2 are always positive and $H_1 = H_2 = 0$, it can be shown that $dB/dw_1 < 0$ and $dB/dw_2 > 0$.

The expression for dB/dK_1 contains both income effects and is therefore ambiguous. An increase in K_1 causes first-period income to rise (through the production-function relationship) and thereby induces a decrease in borrowings. It also causes second-period income to rise (since K_1 is included in K_2) and thereby induces an increase in borrowings. The two effects oppose each other. Alternative models, by failing to take into account future-period effects, conclude that an increase in assets must have a negative effect on borrowing. Also, the expression dB/dK_1 contains terms pertaining to the cross-partial relationship of the arguments of the production function, and hence the sign will depend on the specifics of these relationships as well.

Data, Estimation Issues, and Empirical Results

Discussion of the Variables

The theoretical analysis calls for the following regressors in the borrowing function: initial endowment, current and expected wage, current and expected output prices, investment opportunity measures, and the marginal cost of borrowing. Since the model is specified intertemporally, we should also include measures of life cycle stage as independent determinants. In the empirical analysis that follows, output prices are not included under the assumption that prices for identical outputs ought to be invariant in the cross section. The same argument could have been applied to remove input costs from consideration. There is, however, considerable geographical immobility in factor markets in India so that variations in both wages and interest rates are observed in the cross section. The variables actually used in the empirical analysis (table 6-1) are discussed below.

Borrowing

The data collected by NCAER provide information on each of the components of B, that is, external borrowing and lending, changes in financial assets, and changes in consumer durable stocks. The measure of

Table 6-1. *Selected Sample Means and Standard Deviations for Farm Households in India*

Variable and units	All households	Large landholders[a] only	Small landholders only
Amount borrowed per year	420	453	318
(rupees per household)	(2,207)	(2,467)	(1,050)
Wage rate	3.23	3.21	3.26
(rupees per day)	(1.25)	(1.31)	(1.08)
Land owned	11.25	14.33	1.73
(hectares per household)	(12.95)	(13.52)	(0.87)
Proportion irrigated land	33.15	33.32	32.65
(percent of gross cropped area)	(23.92)	(24.30)	(22.71)
Research expenditures	25.60	27.58	19.46
(thousand rupees per block)	(15.65)	(16.48)	(10.61)
Transitory income	371.90	470.30	67.30
(rupees per household)	(1,872)	(2,111)	(660)
Age of head	48.80	50.90	45.20
(years)	(12.90)	(13.20)	(11.40)
Education of head	1.07	1.09	0.98
(years)	(1.44)	(1.43)	(1.48)
Family size	7.51	9.00	5.96
(number of live-in members)	(3.74)	(3.93)	(2.51)
Interest rate[b]	155.40	153.40	161.70
	(39.6)	(37.7)	(44.74)
Number of observations	1,602	1,211	391

Note: Standard deviations in parentheses.

a. Large landholders are defined as those owning more than 3 hectares of land.

b. An interest rate of y percent is recorded in the data as the number $10y$.

B reported here, however, differs from that shown in equation (6-10) in that it does not include CD. Two measures of B were calculated, one including and the other excluding CD. The results for the two measures were broadly similar, so only those for the latter definition are reported on the judgment that such stocks are not normally used by Indian farmers to make liquidity adjustments. It is worth noting here that B differs substantially from EB in our sample—the mean level of B is one-third of the mean level of EB and its coefficient of variation is two and a half times that of EB.

Borrowing was also calculated as the difference between investment and saving. However, reported savings are adjusted for repayment of loans such that if a loan was taken and completely repaid within the reference period, the calculation of B would not reflect the taking of the loan at all. Direct information on repayments is not available for many in the sample. Hence the component approach is preferred. It should also be noted that the data do not allow for a complete account of a household's flow of funds. For example, no data are available on changes in the stocks of gold and jewelry. This could be an important item in the balance sheets of rural households in a country such as India and its omission could result in a significant measurement error. To the extent, however, that there is no reason to expect the error to be nonrandomly distributed, the coefficient estimates need not be biased.

Wage Rates

Because the NCAER data do not contain individual wage information, the average district agricultural wage per day for males (for 1970–71) is used as the measure of the opportunity cost of leisure. The theoretical analysis calls for an expected future wage in addition to the current wage; it is assumed that the future wage rate is simply a multiple of the current one. This eliminates the separate role of the unobservable variable, but the coefficient of w_1 must now be interpreted as the sum of the effects of both current and expected wages.

Initial Endowment

It is common to use a monetary measure of wealth or assets owned (for example, land, livestock, implements) as a proxy for endowments (see Pani 1966; Long 1968). If, however, we take the point of view that the asset accumulation and borrowing decisions are jointly made over the course of a household's life cycle, such a measure of current wealth becomes inappropriate in the framework of an ordinary least squares equation. The proxy that comes closest to measuring initial endowment and is also less likely to introduce simultaneous bias is probably a physical measure of the total land owned by the farm household. Owing to differences in soil quality and terrain, however, the physical measure alone will not reflect the differences in endowment value across Indian farms.

It is also possible that the use of a physical measure of initial endowment rather than a monetary one may introduce some error. The quality of land varies so much in India that a 10-hectare plot in, say, the Punjab area may reflect a different endowment position than a plot of the same size in, say, remote Madhya Pradesh. A monetary measure would capture differences in land quality, whereas a physical one does not. To the extent that the value of land is affected by choices regarding irrigation and fertilizer use among other such endogenous land improvement measures, however, a monetary measure might introduce simultaneity bias in the sort of life cycle framework we are using here. For this reason, we have retained the physical measure in spite of its possible disadvantages.

To account for such differences a district-level index of soil quality as measured by the proportion of irrigated area to total area is included as an additional regressor. Because this variable is not measured at the individual farm level, it is not as likely to involve simultaneity bias as a more direct measure.

Investment Opportunity Measures

The investment opportunity index is supposed to capture differences in expected future income. These differences could arise from two sources: environment-specific characteristics and farm-specific characteristics. Among the former one could list differences in soil quality and the availability of credit, extension services, and fertilizer across regions. A broader measure might be the magnitude of exogenous government expenditures on rural development (by region) in general and on agricultural technical change in particular. An approximation to such a measure is the level of annual expenditures on research on principal crops by each state and the federal govenment. The underlying assumption is that crop research expenditures in a region produce new investment opportunities within a few years and also signify a commitment by the government to continued technical improvements in that region.

The research expenditure figures used here pertain to 1968 and are taken from Evenson and Kislev (1975). Total research expenditures are divided by the number of community development blocks in each state to obtain a measure of research intensity on a per farm basis. Community development blocks are so demarcated as to contain an equal number of farms and they form the basic extension and village development units in India.

Among farm-specific characteristics that denote differences in investment opportunities and expected future income, one could list many things, including natural ability considerations and some investments made by the farmer, such as the adoption of modern inputs. The problem with measures such as modern inputs is that the adoption decision and the borrowing decision may be jointly determined and thus a simultaneity bias issue would arise. One measure that is not likely to involve a simultaneity bias and, at the same time, might even capture differences in natural ability, is the education (investment in human capital) of the farmer. Better-educated farmers might be expected to face brighter futures and be better able to exploit technical opportunities when they arise. Education can be treated as exogenous because the original decision to invest is most likely to have been taken by a person other than the recipient of the education (for example, by the farmer's father)—most farmers in India do not acquire much education (sample mean is 1.07 years) and the little they do obtain is acquired in early years rather than in adulthood. Two measures are therefore used to capture differences in expected future incomes across farms: crop research expenditures (by state) and farmer's education.

Life Cycle Variables

Age of the head of household is included as a measure of the farm household's life cycle stage. In case age alone is not sufficient, we have added another variable, family size, which, in rural contexts, displays a regular pattern over the household's life cycle and can therefore serve as a proxy for it. Family size could also serve as a proxy for expected future income: a large family size would denote a family that expects a larger flow of income in the future as the children grow up and begin to work. Since family size is clearly a determinant of current income also, its effect on borrowing cannot be theoretically predicted.

Transitory Income

We have included a measure of transitory income in our analysis to account for variation in the demand for funds that arise simply from transient and unanticipated variations in income. This variable is calculated as the difference between current income and permanent income, where the latter is calculated as a weighted average of the incomes of the past three years. The technique used to derive the weights is employed by Bhalla (1980) in an analysis of the savings behavior of Indian farmers based on the same data set that is used here. The equation for permanent income, Yp, is: $Yp = 0.43Y3 + 0.32Y2 + 0.25Y1$, where $Y3$ refers to current income and the others to past incomes. Bhalla reports that the role of Yp in savings behavior is not greatly affected by the choice of discount rates.

Special characteristics of our data set affect the manner in which we introduce the marginal cost of borrowing into the demand for funds regression. This issue is discussed in the next section.

The Interest Rate Function

Information on interest rates paid is available only for those households in our sample that report positive levels of external borrowing—this amounts to 1,080 households out of a total of 1,602 for which the non-truncated flow-of-funds measure of borrowing can be calculated. The resulting problem of missing interest rates for a large fraction of the sample is similar to the missing-wage (for housewives) problem in the labor-supply literature, and the solution adopted here is one that has been widely used in that literature. For nonreporters, interest rates are imputed from an interest rate function regressed over a set of personal characteristics and a set of locality-specific characteristics that denote differences in transaction costs of supply across districts and villages. An advantage of this procedure is that it accommodates interest rate endogeneity since the interest rate enters as a predicted variable rather than a directly reported variable. Since this "conventional" regression is based only on information from the subsample that did report positive levels of external borrowing, the estimates could be subject to selection bias resulting from the confounding of the behavioral function relating the interest rate to its determinants with the sample-selection function relating the probability of borrowing to its determinants. This possibility is ignored in the present analysis.

Table 6-2 presents the interest rate equation. Since the purpose is mainly to obtain an instrumental variable and since a fuller discussion of such an equation is available elsewhere (Iqbal 1981b), the discussion here is brief. The dependent variable in table 6-2 is the highest nominal interest rate reported by a household from among all its current loans. This should come closest to being a measure of the current marginal cost of borrowing for the relevant household. It is an inexact measure of the latter, however, to the extent that significant "other" costs of borrowing exist that are not captured by the nominal rate. Some evidence in the literature, for example, suggests that small farmers in particular face fairly high unobserved extra costs of borrowing in the form of bribes, fees to intermediaries, and the like, when applying for formal sector loans (Adams and Nehman 1979).

As far as the independent variables are concerned, all included variables, except transitory income, can be justified in terms of their affecting the costs of lending in an uncertain environment. Transitory income is used as an identifying variable since it affects borrowing but not the interest rate. Similarly, the following four variables are used as identifiers on the assumption that they affect the interest rate but not the individual

Table 6-2. *Interest Rate Equation for Farm Households in India*

Variable	Coefficient	t-statistic (absolute value)
Intercept	183	(17.1)
Land owned	−0.19	(1.96)
Proportion irrigated land	−0.19	(2.10)
Research expenditures	−1.00	(2.42)
Wage rate	16.31	(1.78)
Education of head	−10.22	(4.40)
Age of head	−0.0004	(0.52)
Family size	3.12	(1.18)
Source of loan[a]	−58.21	(10.82)
Existence of bank[b]	−14.10	(1.94)
Distance to market	0.39	(2.40)
Village population	−0.008	(4.80)
Transitory income	0.0005	(0.66)
R^2	0.18	
Number of observations	1,080	

Note: A y percent interest rate is recorded in the data as the number 10y.

a. Dummy variable, 1 is borrowed from official sources, 0 otherwise.

b. Dummy variable, 1 if bank present in village, 0 otherwise.

amounts borrowed: source of loan, existence of bank, distance to market, and village population. The rationale for including the source-of-loan variable is that official lending agencies (for example, banks or cooperative credit societies) are constrained to give subsidized loans and therefore those who can borrow from such agencies pay lower interest rates. Because the selection of clients by such agencies is based on certain creditworthiness indicators, this variable could also be a proxy for some of the costs of lending pertaining to risk. The mere presence of such agencies in a village can reduce average interest rates partly by reducing possible monopoly power margins of moneylenders. Residents of a village can benefit from the mere existence of a bank or cooperative even if they do not themselves borrow from such agencies. This effect is captured by the dummy variable, which registers the existence or absence of banks in the respondent's village.

Distance of village from markets and towns can be thought of as affecting the riskiness of farming in the village or even the opportunity costs incurred by moneylenders in lending in such villages. Village size can be thought of as affecting the administrative cost of lending. The larger the village, the greater the demand for funds and the easier for the money-lender to spread his overhead costs across loans.

The remaining variables can be thought of as affecting the costs of lending pertaining to risk and are also determinants of how much is borrowed. From a lender's point of view, such variables as quantity and quality of land owned, age and education, wage faced, and the prospect of income growth through technical change all ought to be indicators of how risky it is to lend to a particular farmer.

The interest rate function regression results are broadly consistent with the arguments made above. All included variables save transitory income, age, and family size turn out to be significant in their effects. Interest rates imputed from the results shown in table 6-2 are used in estimating the borrowing functions reported in table 6-3.

Table 6-3. *Borrowing Functions for Farm Households in India*

Variable	All households	Large farmers	Small farmers
Intercept	625.80	972.10	−521.32
	(1.91)	(2.29)	(1.34)
Land owned	−14.84	−16.65	24.32
	(3.24)	(3.05)	(0.39)
Wage rate	−158.20	−171.41	−114.50
	(2.56)	(1.90)	(2.08)
Proportion irrigated land	−4.98	−6.82	2.24
	(1.86)	(2.00)	(0.82)
Research expenditures	26.44	29.46	12.61
	(5.60)	(4.41)	(2.38)
Education of head	68.33	60.98	83.24
	(1.48)	(1.00)	(1.89)
Age of head	0.84	1.31	0.30
	(1.10)	(1.11)	(0.88)
Family size	62.63	62.35	74.47
	(4.25)	(3.52)	(3.57)
Interest rate	−3.23	−5.11	2.14
	(2.02)	(2.32)	(1.52)
Transitory income	−0.23	−0.23	−0.27
	(7.77)	(6.72)	(3.36)
R^2	0.08	0.08	0.09
Number of observations	1,602	1,211	391
F Ratio	16.70	13.17	5.00

Note: Absolute values of asymptotic *t*-statistics are in parentheses. Large landholders are defined as those owning more than 3 hectares of land. The rest are considered small farmers. The interest rate is predicted (as an instrumental variable) from the regression reported in table 6-2. A y percent rate is recorded in the data as the number 10y.

Borrowing Function Results

Table 6-3 presents results for identical borrowing functions estimated for three different sample groups. The results in the first column are for all households for which a measure of B could be calculated as shown by equation (6-10). The second and third column results pertain to subsamples from this group obtained by separating the large landholders from the small ones. The purpose of this segmentation is to check the robustness of the results reported in column 1 and see if any nonlinearities might be present.

Land owned, the proxy for initial endowment, is negatively related to the demand for funds. This is also the case for proportion of irrigated land, the proxy for the quality component of initial endowment. Although the theoretical analysis offered no unambiguous predictions for this effect, the general presumption in the literature (Pani 1966; Long 1968) is that of a negative relationship. None of the relevant empirical studies in this area have demonstrated such a relationship however; indeed, most studies have tended to find a positive sign for this effect, a finding typically explained by an appeal to the effects of multicollinearity or scale. The results from this analysis suggest the incorrect definition of the dependent variable may have been responsible for the anomalous results reported in previous studies.

The very different results obtained for small farmers—the coefficient on land owned is positive but quite insignificant—could indicate the presence of a nonlinearity. It is possible that land ownership does not affect the demand for credit noticeably until a sort of threshold farm size is reached, after which self-financing capability is strengthened and external borrowing needs lessen. An alternative explanation of the difference in statistical significance of the coefficient on "land owned" is that it arises from the segmentation procedure that sharply reduces the range over which this variable can move for small farmers while allowing a larger range in the case of large farmers. If the first explanation is valid, we could draw an implication for land reform policy to the effect that redistribution would lead initially to an increased demand for funds that would have to be accommodated by an increased inflow of funds from outside the rural sector. If such an inflow is not forthcoming from the private sector, say, because of the high risks involved in lending to small farmers, it is possible that there will occur both a rise in informal rural interest rates and a drop in rural investment. A reformist government might therefore need to link its redistribution strategy with an expansion of official lending in the rural sector.

The wage rate effect is negative and, with an elasticity of 1.22, quite strong. This effect does not change when the sample is separated into small and large farmers. It is hard to offer a clear explanation for this result. The theoretical model contains no unambiguous prediction for this effect and, at the empirical level, it has not been possible to distinguish either between current and expected wages or between labor-importing and labor-exporting households. Perhaps the most that can be said for the moment is that interactions between the labor market and the credit market appear to be empirically detectable in the latter: both interest rates and the demand for credit are affected by the district-level daily agricultural wage rate. The results support the view that factor market interactions are important, a view also stressed in the slightly different context of the landlord-tenant relationship by Bardhan (1980) and Braverman and Srinivasan (1980). Policy implications cannot be drawn, however, because it has not been possible to trace the exact linkages involved.

Both research expenditures and the education variable are positively related to the demand for funds, although the latter is not uniformly significant. This may be interpreted as confirming that increases in expected income owing to the prospect of technical change in agriculture lead farmers to increase their demand for credit. It might also be noted that the proxies used here reduce the interest rates faced by farmers (see table 6-2). Thus, there is evidence that the rural credit market is affected by agricultural technical change (and the ability to profit from such change) on both the demand and the supply sides. These findings are consistent with the view that the sort of technical change that has been associated with the Green Revolution (which was based on fertilizer and new seed varieties for wheat and rice) is risk-reducing in nature. Borrowers apparently see the prospect of higher future earnings on the average and hence increase their demand for funds. Lenders apparently see a similar prospect for those of their clients who are in a position to benefit from such technical change because of their location in an area receiving high levels of government funds for agricultural research and also because of their ability to cope with the new opportunities being offered.

It might be noted that even small farmers raise their demand for funds if they happen to be located in a state with higher levels of crop research expenditures, although, in elasticity terms, their response is less strong (1.8 versus 0.8). This could suggest an interaction between land size and the ability to benefit from agricultural research and technical change. When an interaction term was specified directly, however, it turned out not to have a significant coefficient (results not shown here). Finally, we note that education appears to play a stronger role for small farmers than it does for large farmers with respect to stimulating demand for funds.

Of the two life cycle variables included, only family size is consistently significant. The larger the family size, the greater the household's demand for funds. One could interpret this as indicating that relatively larger households have relatively higher present consumption requirements or relatively higher levels of expected future income—both of these factors would raise the household's desire to borrow now and pay later. This interpretation is also consistent with the results of a related study (Iqbal 1981c) in which family size is shown to be negatively related to household savings. The results are consistent across farm size groups. Both large and small farmers display similar behavior as far as the borrowing–family size connection is concerned, and thus it appears that the results are robust. For small farmers, in fact, this connection seems especially important: the demand for funds rises by 1.4 percent for every 1 percent increase in family size. (Age was also entered in squared form so as to pick up the hump pattern expected from life cycle savings theory; neither age nor age squared was significant in any regression.)

The interest rate effect is quite revealing. It is significantly and strongly negative for all households taken together and for large farmers taken separately. It is positive, although not significant, for small farmers. Several comments are in order. First, it should be noted that the high level of significance obtained for this variable in the full sample regression stands in contrast to the generally inconclusive results obtained in other studies. Neither Pani (1966) nor Long (1968), for example, find uniformly significant or strong interest rate effects on borrowing. Second, the strength of this effect, as measured by an elasticity of 1.2, suggests that interest rates can be an important policy instrument in influencing the level of debt held by farmers. Third, the pattern of response across size groups suggests that large farmers are more sensitive to interest rate changes; hence, increases in the interest rate are more likely to drive large farmers out of the credit market. This has implications for official credit policy: by raising the official or formal interest rate, the government can improve efficiency (by coming closer to the market rate of interest) and equity (since the relative participation of small farmers in the concessional credit schemes will increase as large farmers drop out disproportionately).

It is worth noting briefly the differences between the results reported here and those obtained from an alternative regression (see Iqbal 1983) in which the interest rate is entered exogenously and the dependent variable is defined conventionally as EB rather than B. In this case, all coefficients are biased toward zero (relative to the coefficient values reported in column 1 of table 6-3), as is to be generally expected in regressions involving truncated dependent variables. Two results are especially damaging to the conventional case. The interest rate coefficient is positive (though not significant) in contradiction of theoretical prediction. The coefficient on land owned (proxy for initial endowment) is also positive (and significant), in contradiction of general expectation if not of theoretical prediction.

The R^2 coefficients obtained in the regressions reported in table 6-3 are all uniformly low. Alternative specifications were tried to improve the fit: these consisted mainly of employing alternative proxies for investment opportunity and regional dummies. The latter improve the R^2 to about 0.16 but pose new problems. It is difficult to interpret the economic meaning of a regional dummy in the absence of specific information about each region. In some cases the regional dummies appear to be conveying the same information that our other aggregate variables, wage levels, and agricultural research expenditures, convey. Alternative functional forms were not particularly helpful, either. Reasons for the low R^2 compared with levels obtained in previous studies include the fact that the present study is based on household-level observations, whereas previous ones have been based on aggregate observations and the fact that the redefined dependent variable, B, turns out to have a coefficient of variation about two and a half times that of the conventional dependent variable, EB.

Summary

In this study the borrowing behavior of farmers in rural India was investigated within the context of the agricultural household modeling framework. It is shown here that this framework suggests two departures from previous analyses that are both realistic and empirically important. The first consists of a redefinition of the demand for funds so as to take into account the possibility of self-financing and the second involves consideration of the cost of borrowing as an endogenous variable. Both changes lead to empirical results more in accord with theory than obtained in earlier studies. Generally speaking, the following factors appear to influence developments in the rural finance market as far as both the demand for funds and the determination of interest rates are concerned: labor market developments as captured by the agricultural wage rate, agricultural technical change as indicated by the level of crop research expenditures, life cycle stage of the household as measured by current family size, and farm-specific characteristics such as quantity and quality of land owned. It is also shown that interest rates have an important effect on amount borrowed and that this effect varies across farm size in a manner that suggests that raising formal interest rates may succeed in increasing the relative participation of small landowners in the official concessional loan market.

Appendix: Data and Sample

In 1968–69, the National Council of Applied Economics Research (NCAER) undertook a national survey, known as the Additional Rural Incomes Survey, of approximately 5,000 agricultural households in India. This survey was repeated in 1969–70 and 1970–71 on the same households, but in the final year a core group of approximately 3,000 cultivating households were asked additional questions regarding borrowing, lending, interest rates, and interaction with formal lending agencies. The sampling design of the survey resulted in oversampling of rich households.

The present analysis is based on the core sample of households that comprised cultivators in 1970–71. Some exclusionary restrictions were applied to this group. Households with savings rates greater than 75 percent were excluded to eliminate some cases of logical inconsistency (savings greater than income, which implies negative consumption) and also to eliminate some cases where transcription errors appeared to be highly probable. These restrictions reduced the working sample to 2,912 observations.

Three categories can be distinguished within this group: the first and second comprising those households reporting positive (1,080) and zero (522) levels of external borrowing and the third those for which the relevant information is missing (1,310). The present analysis is based on a sample size consisting of only the first two categories. Since the exclusion of the third category could have involved censoring problems, we also ran regressions over a larger sample by assuming that the third category also consisted of zero-level borrowers. The results obtained were roughly similar in terms of signs and t-statistics to those reported here. Some elasticities change considerably, however. In particular, the interest elasticity of borrowing was found to be much greater in the larger sample.

References

Adams, D., and D. Graham. 1981. "A Critique of Traditional Agricultural Projects and Policies." *Journal of Development Economics*, vol. 8, pp. 347–66.

Adams, D. W., and G. I. Nehman. 1979. "Borrowing Costs and the Demand for Rural Credit." *The Journal of Development Studies*, vol. 15, no. 1 (January), pp. 165–76.

Bardhan, P. K. 1980. "Interlocking Factor Markets and Agrarian Development: A Review of Issues." *Oxford Economic Papers*, vol. 32, no. 1, pp. 82–98.

Barnum, H., and L. Squire. 1979. *A Model of An Agricultural Household*. Washington, D.C.: World Bank.

Bhalla, S. S. 1980. "The Measurement of Permanent Income and Its Applications to Savings Behavior." *Journal of Political Economy*, vol. 88, no. 4, pp. 722–44.

Braverman, A., and T. N. Srinivasan. 1980. "Credit and Sharecropping in Agrarian Societies." *Journal of Development Economics*, vol. 9, no. 3, pp. 289–312.

David, C. C., and R. L. Myer. 1979. *A Review of Empirical Studies of the Demand for Agricultural Loans*. Economics and Sociology Occasional Paper no. 603. Ohio State University, Columbus.

Evenson, R. E., and Y. Kislev. 1975. *Agricultural Research and Productivity*. New Haven, Conn.: Yale University Press.

Feder, G., R. Just, and D. Zilberman. 1982. *Adoption of Agricultural Innovations in Developing Countries: A Survey*. World Bank Staff Working Paper no. 542. Washington, D.C.

Hesser, L. F., and G. C. Schuh. 1962. "The Demand for Agricultural Mortgage Credit." *Journal of Farm Economics*, vol. 44, no. 5, pp. 1583–88.

Iqbal, F. 1981a. "The Demand and Supply of Funds among Agricultural Households." Ph.D. dissertation, Yale University, New Haven. Processed.

——. 1981b. "Dualism, Technical Change, and Rural Finance Markets in Developing Countries." Rand Note N-1723-AID. Santa Monica, Calif.: Rand Corporation.

——. 1981c. "Rural Savings, Investment and Interest Rates in Developing Countries: Evidence from India." Rand Note N-1763-AID. Santa Monica, Calif.: Rand Corporation.

——. 1983. "The Demand for Funds among Agricultural Households: Evidence from Rural India." *Journal of Development Studies* (October), vol. 20, no. 1, pp. 68–86.

Long, M. G. 1968. "Why Peasant Farmers Borrow." *American Journal of Agricultural Economics*, vol. 50, no. 4, pp. 991–1008.

Pani, P. K. 1966. "Cultivator's Demand for Credit: A Cross-Section Analysis." *International Economic Review*, vol. 7, no. 2, pp. 176–203.

Sen, A. K. 1966. "Peasants and Dualism with or without Surplus Labor." *Journal of Political Economy*, vol. 74, pp. 425–50.

7

Simulating the Rural Economy in a Subsistence Environment: Sierra Leone

Victor E. Smith and John Strauss

FOR POLICY PURPOSES, we often estimate the effects on household behavior of exogenous changes in prices and other economic variables by using point elasticities for a representative household (see chapter 4). Microsimulation offers an alternative approach that may be preferred for several reasons. First, this method takes full account of nonlinearities in the model and of the fact that each household faces a different set of independent variables and that therefore response elasticities vary among households. It also allows us to see how outcomes vary when elasticities change as price and other parameters go outside the range of the point estimates. Second, several prices can be varied at once, even though a change in only one price may alter elasticities for several commodities—this is an important advantage when examining general equilibrium effects. And finally, microsimulation is ideally suited for analyzing the distribution of the effects of economic policies, especially when the simulation is at the level of individual households.[1]

If effects upon the poor are particularly important, microsimulation allows us to classify the households so as to bring out those effects. Furthermore, effects that depend upon the distribution of households within the class are not lost because we look only at a representative household. (Those effects can be important. The distribution of low-expenditure households about their mean differs greatly from that for the high-expenditure households.) These advantages of microsimulation are illustrated in this chapter by an analysis of household data from Sierra Leone.

Note: The research on which this paper is based was funded under USAID Contract No. AID/DSAN-C-0008.

A Comparison of Microsimulation
and Direct Population Estimates

Rural households in Sierra Leone are poor. In 1974–75, the mean annual expenditure per capita in our sample was 90 Leones (one Leone equaled U.S.$1.10 at that time), of which 24 percent was spent for rice and 67 percent on all food (table 7-1). But some households are much poorer than others. Average per capita expenditure among the 32 percent of the sample households that had total annual expenditures below 350 Leones was only 49 Leones. Calories available per capita in that group were at an extremely low level—1,190 per day.

Under these circumstances, it is vitally important to know how the energy content of rural diets would change if Sierra Leone should decide to raise producer prices for rice in order to reduce the use of foreign exchange for rice imports. We begin by establishing a benchmark—simulation estimates of per capita production and consumption at 1974–75 prices.

The model is a separable agricultural household model (see part 1, appendix). The commodity-demand and household labor-supply equations

Table 7-1. *Characteristics of Households by Expenditure Classes, Sierra Leone*

Expenditure class	Low	Medium	High	Whole sample
Range of annual expenditures (Leones)	<350	350 to 750	>750	—
Mean annual expenditure (Leones)	237	513	1,074	600
Mean value of labor supplied (Leones)	306	362	530	397
Number of households	44	51	43	138
Household size	4.8	6.4	8.7	6.7
Percentage 10 years old or less	25	33	31	30
Percentage 11–15 years old	10	11	13	12
Percentage 15 and older	65	56	56	58
Percentage of males among those older than 15	55	50	53	54
Per capita expenditure (Leones)	49	80	123	90
Percentage spent on rice	25	24	24	24
Percentage spent on all food	62	63	70	67
Calories available per capita	1,188	2,132	2,608	2,109

— Not applicable.
Note: These data are for the sample, not the population.
Source: Strauss (chapter 4 herein) and Strauss and others (1981, table B.1).

Table 7-2. *Per Capita Estimates of Annual Production, Consumption, and Net Marketed Surplus, Rural Sierra Leone, 1974-75 Prices and Other Variables*

Commodity group	Expenditure group	Production Simulation estimate	Production Percentage deviation from estimate based on observed values	Consumption Simulation estimate	Consumption Percentage deviation from estimate based on observed values	Net marketed surplus Simulation estimate	Net marketed surplus Percentage deviation from estimate based on observed values
Rice	**Mean**	**212.7**	**+3**	**69.8**	**−20**	**142.9**[a]	**+19**
	Low	290.4	+52	55.7	+24	234.7[c]	+60
	Middle	195.6	−23	76.4	−15	119.2[c]	−27
	High	164.3	−7	75.4	−37	88.9[c]	+52
Root crops and other cereals	**Mean**	**240.8**	**+511**	**18.6**	**+72**	**222.2**	**+677**
	Low	322.6	+2,008	8.1	+62	314.5	+2,953
	Middle	221.0	+541	8.9	+6	212.1	+713
	High	191.3	+201	35.8	+103	155.5	+238
Oils and fats	**Mean**	**51.8**	**+25**	**16.4**	**+5**	**35.4**	**+37**
	Low	72.8	+355	3.9	−54	68.9	+807
	Middle	47.0	−13	12.3	+15	34.7	−20
	High	38.8	−24	30.4	+17	8.4	−67
Fish and animal products	**Mean**	**139.7**	**+154**	**27.4**	**−8**	**112.3**	**+347**
	Low	127.5	+5,000	23.2	+40	104.3	+840
	Middle	90.8	+501	22.2	−20	68.6	+649
	High	193.6	+44	35.4	−18	158.2	+74

Miscellaneous foods	**Mean**	**71.5**	**+44**	**14.1**	**−9**	**57.4**	**+69**
	Low	74.5	+1,420	10.3	+66	64.2	+655
	Middle	52.1	+107	14.0	−1	38.1	+246
	High	86.4	−13	17.2	−29	69.2	−8
Nonfoods	**Mean**	**7.1**	**+34**	**51.6**	**−2**	**−44.5**	**+6**
	Low	9.5	+150	42.5	+15	−33.0	0
	Middle	6.3	+21	46.1	−13	−39.8	+17
	High	5.7	−12	63.8	−2	−58.1	+1
Labor[b]	**Mean**	**585.8**	**−27**	**687.1**	**−12**	**101.3**	**+692**
	Low	754.1	−8	963.3	+9	209.2	+231
	Middle	526.8	−36	645.3	−13	118.5	+294
	High	500.5	−34	497.6	−31	−2.9	+93
Calories	**Mean**	—	—	**1,917.3**	**−12**	—	—
	Low	—	—	1,297.1	+17	—	—
	Middle	—	—	1,797.6	−7	—	—
	High	—	—	2,556.0	−6	—	—

— Not applicable.

Note: Commodities in kilograms, labor in adult man-hour equivalents, and calories in calories per day.

a. Including the quantity retained by rural households for use as seed; for other products, any quantities retained for use as seed are treated as consumption.

b. Production entry is labor demanded; consumption entry labor supplied.

209

are specified by a quadratic expenditure system with variables for household characteristics (see chapter 4). This permits the Engel curves to be quadratic if the data so determine. This is a potentially important consideration when commodities are disaggregated. Nonlinear Engel curves also prove to be important when the interest is in the differential responses of expenditure class groups. The multiple output-supply and input-demand equations are derived by assuming that the production function is separable between all outputs and all inputs. A constant elasticity of transformation function is used for the outputs and a Cobb-Douglas function for the inputs.

Using this model, as estimated from the 1974–75 data, we predict production and consumption values for each of the 138 sample households, taking the exogenous variables at their 1974–75 levels. From the predicted values for the dependent variables, we derive per capita population estimates—by expenditure class and for rural Sierra Leone as a whole (except for the Northern Plateau)—for each of the quantities with which we are concerned: consumption and production, labor use and supply, and marketed surpluses of goods and labor (table 7-2).[2]

The simulation estimates of aggregate consumption capture the observed behavior for 1974–75 very well for the region as a whole. Except for one food group (root crops and other cereals), the percentage deviations between the simulated mean per capita figures and the estimates based directly on the observed data are modest. Predicted mean caloric availability—the figure most important for policy—is within 12 percent of the estimate from the observed data. (For those estimates see appendix table 7A-1.)

The simulations of mean per capita production do not accord as well with the figures from the observed data—except for rice, the most important food. For root crops and other cereals, as for fish and animal products, the simulations are poor, yet that for rice is excellent (within 3 percent of the estimate based upon observed data). Our model, although incapable of handling every commodity as well as we would have liked, did perform well for rice, the commodity in which we were primarily interested—the estimate of rice production is the crucial one for the policy issues we discuss.

The mean marketed surplus estimates, which depend heavily on production simulations, also show some large deviations from the estimates based on observed data. Again, however, the overall estimate most important for policy—that for rice—is quite good.

The simulation estimates are more successful in capturing the observed behavior of the whole population than that of the different expenditure groups. To be sure, one usually expects better predictions for the average of all households than for households restricted to the upper or lower third of the expenditure distribution. Yet our policy interest in the distribution of the effects of price changes requires us to look at each segment of the population distribution, particularly at low-expenditure households. Unfortunately, production estimates for the latter group are consistently high in comparison with estimates from observed data (as are most of the marketed surplus estimates).

In part this is because measuring deviations as percentages of the estimates obtained from observed data exaggerates deviations in the low-expenditure group; almost without exception, those percentages are measured from smaller bases than the others. But some of the production estimates from simulation, particularly those for root crops and other cereals and for fish and animal products, are simply unreliable.

But the estimates for rice produced by low-expenditure households are much better than for other commodities, and the estimate for total calories available, although 17 percent higher than the estimate derived from observed data, is still quite good. Thus we can proceed with a measure of confidence when examining the effects of rice-price policy on low-expenditure households.

Point Elasticities versus Microsimulation

The standard approach to policy analysis is to apply point elasticities to a representative household (or households). This method may be reasonable when just one variable changes and the range of variation is small, but if we want to predict outcomes from a larger change, point elasticities, if they are not constant, will yield poor predictions. Simulation demands no restrictive assumption about the behavior of elasticities.

To determine whether the two methods lead to different results in the Sierra Leone situation, we simulate production and consumption responses to several independent price changes: a 10 percent increase in the price of rice, a 10 percent increase in the price of oils and fats, a 10 percent decrease in the price of fish and animal products, and a 5 percent increase in the price of labor. The results for a representative sample household are shown in arc elasticity form in the second column of table 7-3. Arc and point elasticities are virtually identical for outputs, but differ somewhat for consumption and labor supplied and demanded.

Given that there are potential advantages from simulation a further question arises: whether to simulate for a representative household or for each household in the sample, combining the results later as desired. The conditions under which using a representative household generates the true aggregate demand are exacting, however, and are not satisfied by the quadratic expenditure system used here (see chapter 4). [3]

The effect of using average prices, full income, and household characteristics can be seen in the third column of table 7-3. The second column gives arc elasticities for a representative household. The third gives the arc elasticities when consumption and production are predicted for each of the 138 households in the sample using the values of the variables that apply to that household. These predictions are then added to obtain aggregate values for consumption and production. There are obviously considerable differences in the output price elasticities: most notably, they are larger when all household responses are used. The differences in the consumption elasticities are smaller, but not negligible. If such differences between outcomes for a supposedly representative household and those based upon simulations for individual households can exist for the whole sample, it is particularly important to use the simulation approach for any study concerned with the effects on a specified group of households or a particular segment of the income distribution.

Table 7-3. *Comparison of Own-Price Elasticities, Sierra Leone*

	For representative sample household		Aggregating over all households[a]	
Activity	Point	Arc[b]	Sample[b]	Rural Sierra Leone[b,c]
Outputs				
Rice	0.11[d]	0.11	0.34	0.33
Oils and fats	0.02[d]	0.02	0.12	0.11
Fish and animal products	0.09[d]	0.09	0.24	0.21
Labor demanded	−0.75[d]	−0.70	−1.17	−1.12
Consumption				
Rice	−0.71[e]	−0.65	−0.49	−0.53
Oils and fats	−0.85[e]	−0.76	−0.76	−0.72
Fish and animal products	−0.67[e]	−0.74	−0.67	−0.62
Labor supplied	0.30[e]	0.28	0.44	0.34

a. Arc elasticities.

b. Rice price increase of 10 percent, oils and fats price increase of 10 percent, fish and animal product price decrease of 10 percent, and wage increase of 5 percent.

c. Excludes Northern Plateau region.

d. Strauss and others (1981, table V.1).

e. Differs from the entry in table 4-3 because here we use predicted, not actual, consumption in the denominator.

For the sake of completeness, arc elasticities are also reported when a projection to the national level is made from the sample households (column 4). Although some differences exist between arc elasticities for the sample observations and for rural Sierra Leone, they are not large. (The differences occur because the weights for each household differ in the two cases and because the five households in the Northern Plateau region are not included when projecting to the national level.)

In summary, for the representative household, there are small differences between arc and point elasticities for consumption and for labor supplied and demanded; for production, the differences are negligible. Using a representative household instead of aggregating the results for individual households likewise affects consumption estimates; for the estimates of production and labor use, the differences are quite large.

Using simulation instead of point elasticities has another advantage, not dealt with in table 7-3. When several variables are allowed to change simultaneously, looking at individual elasticities makes it considerably more difficult to make projections, especially when the elasticities are not constant or when interactions between changes in different variables can be important. By allowing several variables to change simultaneously we can also allow for some general equilibrium effects. If, for instance, the rural labor supply curve is upward sloping, as it seems to be, then an increase in an output price for the entire country raises labor demand and puts upward pressure on wages. As the effect of a wage increase on output is to counteract the output price increase, one should take account of it. In our results, allowing wages to adjust makes a large difference in the predictions.

Microsimulation and Partial Equilibrium

Since 1961, Sierra Leone has sought self-sufficiency in rice production. The government establishes official producers' prices through the Sierra Leone Produce Marketing Board. Since the late 1970s, government prices have usually been above the prices of imported rice, but the price the trader actually pays the farmer is normally 20 to 40 percent below the official price (see Snodgrass and others 1980, pp. 44, 97–98, 100). Yet rice imports still remain a problem. How effective would an increase in the price actually received by the producer be in expanding the marketed surplus of rice? And what effects would a change in rice prices have on the nutritional status of rural households?

Suppose that government decree or an autonomous shift in the urban demand for rice causes a 10 percent increase in the producer's price, and

Table 7-4. *Per Capita Estimates of Annual Production, Consumption, and Net Marketed Surplus, Rural Sierra Leone (7 Zones)*
(rice prices rise 10 percent)

Commodity group	Expenditure group	Production		Consumption		Net marketed surplus	
		Level	Percentage change from base	Level	Percentage change from base	Level	Percentage change from base
Rice	**Mean**	**219.7**	**3.3**	**66.0**	**−5.4**	**153.7**	**7.6**
	Low	299.8	3.2	53.1	−4.7	246.7	5.1
	Middle	202.0	3.3	72.6	−5.0	129.4	8.6
	High	169.7	3.3	70.8	−6.1	98.9	11.2
Root crops	**Mean**	**241.4**	**0.2**	**19.1**	**2.7**	**222.3**	**0.0**
and other	Low	323.3	0.2	8.9	9.9	314.4	−0.0
cereals	Middle	221.6	0.3	9.2	3.4	212.4	0.1
	High	191.8	0.3	36.4	1.7	155.4	−0.1
Oils and	**Mean**	**52.0**	**0.4**	**17.1**	**4.3**	**34.8**	**−1.7**
fats	Low	73.0	0.3	4.7	20.5	68.3	−0.9
	Middle	47.1	0.2	12.9	4.9	34.2	−1.4
	High	39.0	0.5	31.1	2.3	7.9	−6.0
Fish and	**Mean**	**139.9**	**0.1**	**28.4**	**3.6**	**111.5**	**−0.7**
animal	Low	127.8	0.2	24.8	6.9	103.0	−1.2
products	Middle	90.9	0.1	23.1	4.1	67.8	−1.2
	High	193.8	0.1	36.1	2.0	157.7	−0.3
Miscella-	**Mean**	**71.7**	**0.3**	**14.5**	**2.8**	**57.2**	**−0.3**
neous	Low	74.7	0.3	10.9	5.8	63.8	−0.6
foods	Middle	52.3	0.4	14.4	2.9	37.9	−0.5
	High	86.6	0.2	17.5	1.7	69.1	−0.1
Nonfoods	**Mean**	**7.1**	**0.0**	**53.8**	**4.3**	**−46.7**	**−4.9**
	Low	9.5	0.1	46.1	8.5	−36.6	−10.9
	Middle	6.4	1.6	47.9	3.9	−41.5	−4.3
	High	5.7	0.0	65.3	2.4	−59.6	−2.6
Labor[a]	**Mean**	**616.0**	**5.2**	**666.8**	**−3.0**	**50.8**	**−49.9**
	Low	794.1	5.3	932.7	−3.2	138.6	−33.7
	Middle	554.8	5.3	627.7	−2.7	72.9	−38.5
	High	524.6	4.8	483.4	−2.9	−41.2	−1,320.7
Calories	**Mean**	−	−	**1,922.7**	**0.3**	−	−
	Low	−	−	1,341.1	3.4	−	−
	Middle	−	−	1,794.0	−0.2	−	−
	High	−	−	2,547.2	−0.3	−	−

— Not applicable.

Note: Commodities in kilograms, labor in adult man-hour equivalents, and calories in calories per day.

a. Production entry is labor demanded; consumption entry labor supplied.

that consumer prices for rice consumed within the rural sector change in the same proportion, but that neither wage rates nor other prices change at all. Given that other exogenous variables are at the levels prevailing in 1974–75, we see in table 7-4 that overall per capita rice production will rise 3.3 percent, consumption will fall 5.4 percent, and the marketed surplus of rice will rise 7.6 percent (by 16,700 metric tons, or 30 percent of 1980 imports for all of Sierra Leone, estimated at 55,000 tons by Snodgrass et al. 1980, p. 100). The net effect on per capita calorie availability is negligible for the rural population as a whole, as households counteract the reductions in rice consumption by consuming more of the foods for which prices have not risen.

The higher prices of rice cause a significant reduction in rice imports, but do not appreciably affect the availability of food energy in rural Sierra Leone as a whole. Sierra Leone now needs less foreign exchange for imported rice, but spends more on imported palm oil, dried fish, and other items of which the rural sector now provides smaller marketed surpluses. Of course, maintaining higher producers' prices puts a strain on the government budget unless urban rice prices are allowed to rise.

Although the nutritional effects of the higher rice prices are negligible for the rural population as a whole, they are positively beneficial for low-expenditure households (the L households), which contain 30 percent of that population (Smith and others 1981, p. 38). These households increase their per capita calorie intake (availability) by 3.4 percent. As only 1,300 calories per capita are being consumed daily (table 7-2), even a 3.4 percent increase constitutes significant nutritional gain. The remaining 70 percent of the population reduces its per capita calorie intake, but the amounts are small (0.3 percent or less), and the high-expenditure (H) group, at least, appears able to support them. About the M group we must be less complacent. There is a serious need for more calories among perhaps half of those households as in the benchmark simulation the average per capita caloric intake of all M-households was only 1,800 per day.

Both in absolute and percentage terms, L households reduce rice consumption less and increase their consumption of other foods more than other households. The net effect is that, on balance, L households consume more calories when rice prices rise, whereas others consume slightly fewer.

Why should this be so? Differences in the consumption responses of different expenditure groups are partly the result of differences among the groups in income-consumption elasticities and in income-compensated price elasticities (see Strauss, Smith, and Schmidt 1981, pp. 23–28). But, in the present case, these differences are relatively inconsequential compared with the differences in the magnitude of the effective income change that occurs for a semisubsistence household when both producer and consumer prices change. If we hold profits constant for the moment, a rise in the consumption price has a negative income effect on rice consumption. But if the household produces all the rice it consumes and sells none, a rise of the same amount in the producer's price creates an opposite income effect exactly equal in size. If both producer and consumer prices are equal, and if a household has a positive net marketed surplus, there will be a net positive income effect when both prices rise.[4] The magnitude of the effect will depend upon the size of the net marketed surplus.[5]

The primary reason that low-expenditure households in Sierra Leone gain nutritionally when rice prices rise is that they have large marketed surpluses of rice. The mean marketed surplus among L households (235 kilograms per capita, table 7-2) is approximately twice as great as in either of the other expenditure groups, so the net effect on household expenditure is about twice as great. This large net income effect is important not only for rice consumption, but also for the consumption of all commodities. When the effect of a higher rice-production price is taken into account, the cross elasticities of consumption for other foods, with respect to a joint increase in the producer and consumer prices of rice, become very large for L households (see table 4-3). As a result, L households have a positive elasticity of 0.19 for calorie availability with respect to the price of rice; for other expenditure groups, these calorie elasticities are negative (see table 4-6). In Sierra Leone, at least, it is useful to assert as a rule of thumb that the amount of gain (or loss) in calorie availability depends upon the size of a household's marketed surplus of rice. Although L households in general benefit nutritionally when rice prices rise, individual L households may be harmed, for it is not the level of household expenditure, but the size of the marketed surplus that appears to be crucial in predicting the effect upon caloric intake.

The observed data make it clear that L households produce large per capita marketed surpluses of rice, but they do not support the simulation estimate of a marketed surplus as large as 235 kilograms per capita (table 7-2).[6] According to the direct population estimates (table 7A-1) rice marketed surpluses are 147 and 164 kilograms per capita for the average L and M households, respectively. The simulation estimate exceeds the direct population estimate for the L households by about 100 kilograms per capita, both for production and for the marketed surplus. Actually, the observed data for upland rice production may have been somewhat low in comparison with a normal year. In 1974–75, the rains came late and thus upland rice yields were reduced significantly (Spencer and Byerlee 1977, p. 54). We may assume that the direct population estimate for the marketed surplus figure imposes a lower bound for the true effect of a 10 percent rise in rice prices on calorie availability. If the simulation estimates are correct, calorie availability rises 3.4 percent for L households; if they significantly overstate the benefit to L households, it is still likely that the L households do no worse than the M households, so at least Sierra Leone needs fear no significant reduction in calorie availability as the result of a decision to increase the government's producer price for rice.

Microsimulation and General Equilibrium

When there is a change in the price of a staple product such as rice, other prices are also likely to change as factor and product markets move to new equilibria. We do not have a full general equilibrium model, so we cannot predict those changes, but microsimulation makes it easy to examine the consequences of induced price changes for any set of changes one may wish to consider.

An Induced Increase in Wages

We examine an induced wage change, asking how such a change would alter the effects of a 10 percent increase in rice prices on rice production and calorie availability. At 1974–75 wage levels, a 10 percent change in rice prices would raise the use of rural labor by 5 percent and reduce labor supply by 3 percent (table 7-4). This would put upward pressure on agricultural wages and reduce the marketed surplus of labor (the labor supply to nonrural enterprises in the region) by 50 percent. If the nonrural demand function for this marketed surplus is given, the rural wage rate must rise unless that demand function is infinitely elastic. We put an upper bound on this induced rise by assuming zero elasticity of nonrural demand; in this case, the wage must rise until the marketed surplus of rural labor equals its amount before rice prices rose. According to our data, the upper bound is approximately 5 percent, which we established by experimental simulation runs. A 5 percent wage increase raises the marketed surplus of labor by 44 percent, substantially offsetting the negative effect of a 10 percent increase in rice prices.

When a 5 percent induced wage increase occurs along with a 10 percent increase in rice prices, the gain in the marketed surplus of rice is cut by more than one-half, but there are nutritional gains for each expenditure class, the largest being among L households. For them, calories available rise twice as much as they do when wages do not rise. (Table 7-5 shows the new levels of output and consumption.)

Table 7-5. *Per Capita Estimates of Annual Production, Consumption, and Net Marketed Surplus, Rural Sierra Leone (7 Zones)*
(rice prices rise 10 percent, wages 5 percent)

Commodity group	Expenditure group	Production		Consumption		Net marketed surplus	
		Level	Percentage change from base	Level	Percentage change from base	Level	Percentage change from base
Rice	**Mean**	**215.0**	**1.1**	**67.5**	**−3.3**	**147.5**	**3.2**
	Low	293.5	1.1	54.9	−1.4	238.6	1.7
	Middle	197.7	1.1	74.0	−3.1	123.7	3.8
	High	166.0	1.0	71.9	−4.6	94.1	5.8
Root crops	**Mean**	**239.8**	**−0.4**	**19.6**	**5.4**	**220.2**	**−0.9**
and other	Low	321.5	−0.3	9.2	13.6	312.3	−0.7
cereals	Middle	220.1	−0.4	9.3	4.5	210.8	−0.6
	High	190.3	−0.5	37.2	3.9	153.1	−1.5
Oils and	**Mean**	**51.5**	**−0.6**	**17.6**	**7.3**	**33.9**	**−4.2**
fats	Low	72.4	−0.5	5.0	28.2	67.4	−2.2
	Middle	46.7	−0.6	13.3	8.1	33.4	−3.7
	High	38.6	−0.5	31.7	4.3	6.9	−17.9
Fish and	**Mean**	**138.1**	**−1.1**	**29.0**	**5.8**	**109.1**	**−2.8**
animal	Low	127.1	−0.3	25.4	9.5	101.7	−2.5
products	Middle	90.3	−0.6	23.6	6.3	66.7	−2.8
	High	190.0	−1.9	36.8	4.0	153.2	−3.2
Miscella-	**Mean**	**70.6**	**−1.3**	**14.8**	**5.0**	**55.9**	**−2.6**
neous	Low	74.0	−0.7	11.2	8.7	62.8	−2.2
food	Middle	51.7	−0.8	14.6	4.3	37.1	−2.6
	High	84.8	−1.9	17.8	3.5	67.0	−3.2
Nonfoods	**Mean**	**7.0**	**−0.2**	**54.9**	**6.4**	**−47.9**	**−7.6**
	Low	9.5	−0.2	47.4	11.5	−37.9	−14.8
	Middle	6.3	−0.2	48.9	6.1	−42.6	−7.0
	High	5.6	−0.5	66.5	4.2	−60.9	−4.8
Labor[a]	**Mean**	**580.5**	**−0.9**	**679.7**	**−1.1**	**99.2**	**−2.1**
	Low	749.8	−0.6	942.5	−2.2	192.7	−7.9
	Middle	523.3	−0.7	637.0	−1.3	113.7	−4.1
	High	492.7	−1.6	502.1	0.9	9.4	+424.1
Calories	**Mean**	−	−	**1,969.8**	**2.7**	−	−
	Low	−	−	1,387.5	7.0	−	−
	Middle	−	−	1,829.8	1.8	−	−
	High	−	−	2,592.8	1.4	−	−

− Not applicable.

Note: Commodities in kilograms, labor in adult man-hour equivalents, and calories in calories per day.

a. Production entry is labor demanded; consumption entry labor supplied.

The marketed surplus of rice (7,100 metric tons, or 13 percent of estimated 1980 imports) is still well above benchmark levels, even though rice production is now only 1 percent above benchmark. (Rice consumption is 3 percent below the benchmark.) In general, the effect of the induced change in wages has been to reduce production, increase the consumption of goods, and reduce the consumption of leisure. As the new wage rate keeps the marketed surplus of labor essentially constant, the expansion of rice production is limited to what is possible by diverting rural labor from nonrice production and reducing the consumption of leisure.

How does it happen that higher rice prices increase the calorie content of the diet for the rural sector as a whole when they induce an increase in wages, even though they have little effect, or a negative one, when they do not induce such an increase? When prices alone increase, net calorie effects are small because the profit effects, if all households are taken together, hardly more than offset the adverse effects on calorie intake that higher rice prices would have if profit effects were ignored. (Compare the calorie-price elasticities in table 4-6.) With an induced increase in wage rates, a large part of the aggregate increase in profit is converted into larger labor incomes. But for the rural sector as a whole, labor incomes rise more than profits fall. That sector is a net seller of labor. As wages rise, profit shares fall on all production within the rural sector if labor supply is held constant. For that part of production carried out by the household's own labor, net income is not affected, but where there is hired labor, part of the profit formerly received by the producing household is transferred (as wages) to another household—the seller of labor. A household gains or loses in accordance with the size (and sign) of its net marketed surplus of labor. (By net income, we mean profits plus the value of labor supply; this equals the value of consumption excluding leisure and differs from full income by the value of leisure.) Where rural households in the aggregate sell 7.6 percent of the labor they supply (as in table 7-4, at rice prices 10 percent above 1974–75 levels), increases in labor incomes for this part of the labor supplied are net gains for the sector. The profit shares from which these gains come lie outside the rural sector.

In addition, when wages rise there is a labor supply response that increases the consumption of all foods. At any given level of full income, households reduce their consumption of leisure and increase their consumption of goods by using for consumption the proceeds (in money or in goods) of the extra labor they supply.

Since we are dealing with discrete price and wage changes, we must also remember that for such changes the use of outputs and labor is affected (adversely) by the rise in wages. The effect of these adjustments to a new equilibrium position is to moderate the adverse effect of the wage increase upon profits, so their effect upon food consumption and calorie intake can only be positive. As employment falls and labor supply rises, the net result is to shift some labor from less productive uses within the rural sector to more productive activities outside.

In sum, for the rural sector as a whole, each of the mechanisms discussed leads to greater food consumption and a larger calorie intake. Aggregate calorie availability, in response to these factors, rises nearly 2.5 percent above its level when only the 10 percent change in rice prices occurs.

The induced wage increase brings calorie availability among L households to 3.5 percent above its level when only rice prices rise; M and H households gain by only 2 percent. (In absolute terms gains are essentially equal for the M and the H households.) The L-household gains reflect their relatively large net marketed surpluses of labor (table 7-4). Adverse effects upon food consumption are possible only for net purchasers of labor. Some of those exist within the H group, but there is an offsetting factor: the positive labor supply response is much stronger among H households. (The 5 percent induced wage increase raises labor supplied among the L, M, and H households by 1.1 percent, 1.5 percent, and 3.9 percent, respectively, as compared with the quantities supplied when rice prices rise but the wage remains constant.) The relatively strong supply response among H households is enough to cause a gain in calorie availability for the group as a whole.

The simulation analysis predicts that an induced wage increase will bring a net gain in calorie availability for the rural sector as a whole. This results in part from its prediction of a positive marketed surplus of labor (101 man-hours per capita per year for the 1974–75 situation). Yet the direct estimates from observed data (see table 7A-1) do not confirm that such a surplus exists for the rural sector as a whole. Instead, they show a small net marketed deficit (of 17 man-hours). The L households, however, do have a net marketed surplus (63 man-hours per capita). Consequently, a conservative interpretation of our results would be that food energy consumption among L households would rise if induced wage increases occurred, whereas gains are possible, but not assured, among M and H households.

The policy significance of all this, in a semisubsistence economy where most labor is used by the household that provides it, is that high product prices may or may not improve the energy content of the diet, but that rural wage increases induced by high product prices do—except possibly for households that are net purchasers of labor. Moreover, benefits from higher product prices accrue only to households with net marketed surpluses of those products, unless they lead to higher wages. In that case, producers of all products benefit, in amounts that depend partly upon their net marketed surpluses of labor and the elasticities of household labor-supply responses to higher wages.

As wages rise, there will be complaints about high wages and shortages of labor, but, for the rural sector as a whole, induced wage increases are a beneficial mechanism, spreading the benefits of higher prices for particular products throughout the economy. To be sure, some households may lose. Wage increases cause some reallocation of benefits—in the present case, away from all rice producers (as they cut back somewhat on rice output), particularly from those who are net buyers of labor. (In an economy with landless laborers, they benefit from higher product prices only if more employment or higher wages occur.) In Sierra Leone, we expect at least the L households to gain because they have relatively high marketed surpluses of both rice and of labor.

Where calorie consumption rises although rice consumption declines in response to a higher relative price for rice, it is because the consumption of other foods expands enough to more than offset the loss of calories from rice. This can occur because the prices of other foods remain constant, or at least lag behind rice prices and wage rates. If all prices and wage rates rose 10 percent, neither consumption nor output patterns would change from benchmark levels except for such minor effects as might arise because the autonomous component of income remained unchanged. (In this model, both demand and production systems are homogeneous of zero degree; see Smith and others 1981.)

In fact, however, the prices of many foods (including such important items as palm oil and fish) are determined partly in world markets, or at least outside the rural sector of Sierra Leone, so some net change in the relative price of rice is likely to persist even after all induced effects on other prices have been fully felt. Thus, even in the long run, general equilibrium effects on prices of other foods are unlikely to nullify completely any gains that a rise in the government buying price might bring.

Improved Productivity

What of measures to improve general agricultural productivity? With a 5 percent improvement in overall productivity[7] at benchmark prices and wages, calorie consumption increases 4.3, labor use 6.1 percent, rice output 6.4 percent, and the outputs of other foods 2.0–4.3 percent (table 7-6). The quantity of labor supplied falls 2.3 percent, and thus the marketed surplus of labor falls. Consumption increases (more for oils and fats and for root crops and other cereals than for anything else), but rice

Table 7-6. *Per Capita Estimates of Annual Production, Consumption, and Net Marketed Surplus, Rural Sierra Leone (7 Zones)*
(production function shifts upward 5 percent)

Commodity group	Expenditure group	Production		Consumption		Net marketed surplus	
		Level	Percentage change from base	Level	Percentage change from base	Level	Percentage change from base
Rice	Mean	226.3	6.4	71.2	2.0	155.1	8.5
	Low	308.8	6.3	58.5	5.0	250.3	6.6
	Middle	208.0	6.3	78.1	2.2	129.9	9.0
	High	174.8	6.4	75.4	0.0	99.4	11.8
Root crops	Mean	245.5	2.0	19.7	5.9	225.9	1.6
and other	Low	328.0	1.7	8.8	8.6	319.2	1.5
cereals	Middle	225.4	2.0	9.3	4.5	216.1	1.9
	High	195.8	2.4	37.9	5.9	157.9	1.5
Oils and	Mean	53.2	2.7	17.5	6.7	35.7	0.8
fats	Low	74.8	2.7	4.5	15.4	70.3	2.0
	Middle	48.2	2.6	13.0	5.7	35.2	1.4
	High	39.9	2.8	32.1	5.6	7.8	−0.7
Fish and	Mean	145.2	3.9	28.2	2.9	117.0	4.2
animal	Low	129.4	1.5	24.2	4.3	105.2	0.9
products	Middle	92.7	2.1	22.9	3.2	69.8	1.7
	High	205.2	6.0	36.2	2.3	169.0	6.8
Miscella-	Mean	74.6	4.3	14.4	2.1	60.2	4.9
neous	Low	76.7	3.0	10.7	3.9	66.0	2.8
foods	Middle	53.9	1.0	14.3	2.1	39.6	3.9
	High	91.5	5.9	17.5	1.7	74.0	6.9
Nonfoods	Mean	7.1	1.0	53.4	3.5	−46.2	−3.8
	Low	9.6	0.7	44.9	5.6	−35.3	−7.0
	Middle	6.4	0.9	47.6	3.3	−41.2	−3.5
	High	5.7	1.4	65.5	2.7	−59.8	−2.9
Labor[a]	Mean	621.8	6.1	671.1	−2.3	49.3	−51.3
	Low	798.8	5.9	943.2	−2.1	144.4	−31.0
	Middle	558.5	6.0	631.0	−2.2	72.5	−38.8
	High	533.1	6.5	483.4	−2.9	−49.7	−1,613.8
Calories	Mean	−	−	2,000.6	4.3	−	−
	Low	−	−	1,379.6	6.4	−	−
	Middle	−	−	1,854.0	3.1	−	−
	High	−	−	2,641.2	3.3	−	−

− Not applicable.

Note: Commodities in kilograms, labor in adult man-hour equivalents, and calories in calories per day.

a. Production entry is labor demanded; consumption entry labor supplied.

consumption rises only 2.0 percent. The marketed surplus of rice rises 8.5 percent (more than for any other commodity); it now amounts to 18,900 metric tons, 34 percent of estimated 1980 imports.

The effect on the nutritional status of L households is especially important. A 5 percent increase in general productivity increases calorie availability among L household by 6.4 percent. Their rice consumption rises by 5 percent and their intake of oils and fats by 15.4 percent. If low-expenditure households share equally in productivity improvement, they gain more than proportionally in nutritional well-being—presumably because the largest percentage gains in output occur for rice, a relatively more important product for L households than for others.

Higher agricultural productivity of course means greater demand for labor and upward pressure on wages. Again, if we assume zero nonrural elasticity of demand for the marketed surplus of labor, we can define an upper bound for the wage increase (slightly more than 5 percent in the present case). A 5 percent increase restores labor use to the benchmark level, but does not quite return the marketed surplus to the benchmark state because the quantity of labor supplied remains slightly below that level (table 7-7).

Transforming some of the gains in productivity into a 5 percent increase in wages reduces goods production and marketed surpluses, but still leaves outputs above benchmark levels. Rice production, consumption, and marketed surplus remain 4 percent above the base situation. This gives a total seven-zone marketed surplus of 9,000 metric tons, 16 percent of the country's estimated 1980 imports. On the average, calorie availability improves, rising to 6.3 percent above the benchmark and 10.2 percent for L households. (For those households, the elasticity of calorie availability with respect to productivity is 2.0 when the effects of the wage increase are included.)

This 10 percent increase in calorie availability among L households is nearly 50 percent more than was achieved by a 10 percent increase in rice prices plus the induced wage increase. For M and H households, the 5 percent nutritional gains from productivity improvement with wage increase were some 200 percent greater than those from the change in rice prices with a wage increase.

The assumption that output prices do not change when productivity increases is realistic where commodity prices are set in world markets, or perhaps by government policy. For at least two of the most important foods (rice and palm oil), this is the case. Of course, whatever happens to prices, the fundamental fact is that an increase in productivity reduces the price of food in terms of labor. Thus, food consumption in general should increase. Yet if money prices decrease more for some foods than

Table 7-7. *Per Capita Estimates of Annual Production, Consumption, and Net Marketed Surplus, Rural Sierra Leone (7 Zones)*
(production function shifts upward 5 percent, wages rise 5 percent)

| Commodity group | Expenditure group | Production | | Consumption | | Net marketed surplus | |
		Level	Percentage change from base	Level	Percentage change from base	Level	Percentage change from base
Rice	**Mean**	**221.4**	**4.1**	**72.7**	**4.2**	**148.7**	**4.1**
	Low	302.1	4.0	60.5	8.6	241.6	2.9
	Middle	203.5	4.0	79.7	4.3	123.8	3.9
	High	171.0	4.1	76.5	1.5	94.5	6.3
Root crops	**Mean**	**243.8**	**1.2**	**20.1**	**8.1**	**223.7**	**0.6**
and other	Low	326.0	1.1	9.1	12.3	316.9	0.8
cereals	Middle	223.8	1.3	9.4	5.6	214.4	1.1
	High	194.2	1.5	38.7	8.1	155.5	0.0
Oils and	**Mean**	**52.7**	**1.7**	**17.9**	**9.1**	**34.7**	**−2.0**
fats	Low	74.0	1.6	4.9	25.6	69.1	0.3
	Middle	47.7	1.5	13.4	8.9	34.3	−1.2
	High	39.5	1.8	32.7	7.6	6.8	−19.0
Fish and	**Mean**	**143.2**	**2.5**	**28.8**	**5.1**	**114.4**	**1.9**
animal	Low	128.7	0.9	24.8	6.9	103.9	−0.4
products	Middle	92.0	1.3	23.3	5.0	68.7	0.1
	High	201.0	3.8	36.9	4.2	164.1	3.7
Miscella-	**Mean**	**73.5**	**2.8**	**14.7**	**4.3**	**58.8**	**2.4**
neous	Low	75.9	1.9	11.0	6.8	64.9	1.1
foods	Middle	53.2	2.1	14.6	4.3	38.6	1.3
	High	89.7	3.8	17.8	3.5	71.9	3.9
Nonfoods	**Mean**	**7.1**	**0.6**	**54.5**	**5.6**	**−47.4**	**−6.5**
	Low	9.6	0.4	46.3	8.9	−36.7	−11.2
	Middle	6.4	0.6	48.6	5.4	−42.2	−6.0
	High	5.7	0.9	66.6	4.4	−60.9	−4.8
Labor[a]	**Mean**	**585.8**	**0.0**	**683.8**	**−0.5**	**98.0**	**−3.5**
	Low	754.1	0.0	952.5	−1.1	198.4	−5.2
	Middle	526.8	0.0	640.1	−0.8	113.3	−4.4
	High	500.5	0.0	502.2	0.9	1.7	58.6
Calories	**Mean**	−	−	**2,038.0**	**6.3**	−	−
	Low	−	−	1,429.4	10.2	−	−
	Middle	−	−	1,802.2	5.3	−	−
	High	−	−	2,688.8	5.2	−	−

− Not applicable.

Note: Commodities in kilograms, labor in adult man-hour equivalents, and calories in calories per day.

a. Production entry is labor demanded; consumption entry labor supplied.

for others, it is at least conceivable that the new consumption pattern might contain fewer calories than the old.

Either higher rice prices or higher agricultural productivity (along with the associated changes in rural wages) increases calorie availability, especially for the L households. But the magnitudes of these effects promise no easy solution for the 30 percent of the rural population whose per capita caloric intake needs to be increased by some 50 percent to approach conventional nutritional standards. Even if rates of induced wage change and elasticities of caloric intake do not change as rice prices or productivity increase, it would take a 70 percent rise in rice prices or a 25 percent increase in productivity to raise caloric intake by 50 percent for the L household group. One hesitates to assume that these predictions would remain valid for such large changes.

Microsimulation and the Interhousehold Distribution of Calories

Once microsimulation estimates have been made, one can classify the households in as many ways as one likes and examine the distributional effects of policy measures in detail. Grouping by household expenditures, as we have done so far, has shown that low-expenditure households reap the largest percentage gains in calorie intake from each of the policy alternatives discussed. Such households are typically poor and undernourished. Those in our sample had mean per capita expenditures of 49 Leones per year and daily calorie availability per capita of only 1,188 calories. But not all L households are poor and not all H households well-to-do. A two-person household with a per capita expenditure of 174 Leones per year would be classified as an L household, and an H household with ten members could be spending little more than 75 Leones per capita.

To reduce the effect of family size and to look at nutritional situations in individual households, we array the households by predicted caloric availability per capita at 1974–75 values of the independent variables (figure 7-1). (Even calories per capita is not an ideal measure of nutritional adequacy, however; the energy needs of a child of three months differ from those of a fourteen-year-old boy.) We restrict ourselves to the 138 households in the sample. For 100 households (72 percent of the sample) per capita availability lies between 800 and 2,800 calories per day, with no strong concentration around any point in that range. As the distribution appears to be approximately flat over a wide range, more than one-third of which extends below 1,500 calories per day, we anticipate many nutritional problems. There are 48 households, comprising 370 persons, with an estimated per capita caloric intake of less than 1,500 per day. Yet the

Figure 7.1. *Distribution of Sample Households by Calories Available per Capita (Benchmark Simulation)*

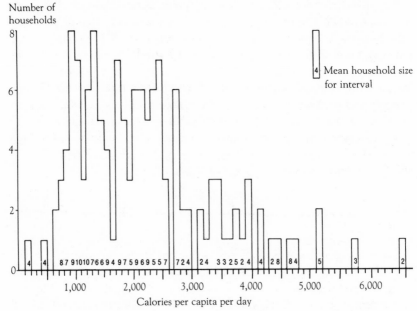

Number of households

Calories per capita per day

4 Mean household size for interval

low per capita figures are not quite as serious as we might think in that they tend to be associated with large households. (See the household-size data, given to the nearest integer, at the bottoms of the bars in figure 7-1.) Large households are likely to include small children, who have lower energy needs than teenagers or adults.

In the aggregate, the 48 households with daily per capita intakes below 1,500 calories fall 161,000 calories short of the 1,500 calorie level in the base simulation (a per capita deficit of 435 calories). A 10 percent increase in rice prices reduces that deficit by 7 percent—by 11,400 calories, or 31 calories per person. Although a rise in rice prices would improve the nutrition of these households, at this rate it would take more than a 140 percent increase in relative rice prices just to wipe out the average deficit (measured from a 1,500-calorie standard). We hesitate to predict from our data the results of such a large change. Households with daily per capita calorie availability between 1,500 and 1,900 calories experience slight calorie losses when rice prices rise 10 percent.

A 10 percent increase in rice prices accompanied by a 5 percent rise in rural wages is more beneficial. It reduces the deficit by 12 percent among households below 1,500 calories—by 20,000 calories or 54 calories per person. Eliminating the deficit below 1,500 calories would still require very large changes in prices and wages. When both wages and prices rise, there is some gain in calorie availability for households between the 1,500 and 1,900 levels.

To know how individual households (or at least very small groups of households) are affected by a change in rice prices, see figure 7-2. The solid lines show percentage changes in per capita calorie availability when rice prices rise 10 percent; the dashed lines apply when the wage rate also rises (by 5 percent). Note that at each extreme there is a single wide class interval. Because outlying observations may be unreliable, we present averages for households at the extremes rather than more detailed results.

Households below the 1,500 level for daily per capita calorie availability gain when prices rise 10 percent. The lower the initial level of availability, the greater the percentage gain. For all households below 1,000 calories per day, the average gain is 8.3 percent. Between 1,500 and 2,700 calories,

Figure 7.2. *Percentage Changes in Calories per Capita, with Households Classified by Calories Available per Capita in the Benchmark Simulation*

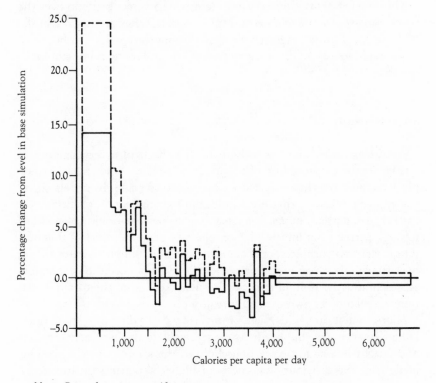

Note:—Price of rice increases 10 percent

---Price of rice increases 10 percent, and wage rate increases 5 percent

average caloric intake is little affected; beyond 2,700 calories, almost all households reduce their calorie intake.

Practically all households benefit if the higher prices of rice induce a 5 percent wage increase. Except at the highest and lowest ends of the distribution, the increments in percentage gain from the wage increases are about the same at all calorie levels. At the lowest levels, the increments are greater; at the highest, less. The pattern of total gain is still a falling one—the largest percentage gains accrue to the households most disadvantaged in the benchmark simulation. In this case, the average gain in calorie availability is 12 percent for households with less than 1,000 calories per capita before the price and wage changes.

Whether we look at households with low total expenditures or households with low per capita calorie availability, an increase in rice prices increases availability for approximately the lowest one-third of the households. (Total household expenditures and per capita caloric intake are highly correlated.) The percentage gains are largest for the households at the lowest caloric levels. On balance, households above the 1,500 calorie level lose slightly when rice prices rise.

The benefits of an induced wage increase of 5 percent extend over the whole range of calorie and expenditure levels, but they are smallest at the higher ends of those ranges. (Although it is conceivable that net buyers of labor might lose from the wage increase, we found no such households in the sample.)

Conclusion

Point elasticities allow us to estimate the effects of a very small price change on the consumption of a representative household and, in principle, by combining those effects for all foods, to estimate the net effects on calorie availability for that household. But to cumulate those effects over the range of a price change as large as 5 or 10 percent would be awkward (though perhaps not impossible), particularly in view of the fact that outputs, marketed surpluses, and quantities of labor supplied are changing over the whole range of the price change. Furthermore the presumably representative household may not be characteristic of the total population, or even of its own expenditure group.

Microsimulation avoids these problems by going directly to the underlying demand and supply functions to calculate the new consumption and output levels—for every household in the sample, if we wish. Our analysis of the distributional effects of higher rice prices on individual households would not have been feasible without microsimulation. Nor would our examination of the consequences of combining an induced wage increase with higher rice prices or greater productivity. Indeed, it was only by the use of microsimulation that we were able to determine what wage increase would occur if the nonrural demand for labor were perfectly inelastic.

Microsimulation proved effective as a means of proceeding directly to the policy issue of most interest to us—how a rice policy or improvements in agricultural productivity would affect the caloric content of rural diets. Our analysis shows that a government policy of guaranteeing producers high rice prices can increase the marketed surplus of rice without serious adverse effects on the calorie content of rural diets, and with beneficial effects for those households most at nutritional risk (those whose daily per capita calorie intake is 1,500 or less). If induced wage increases follow, calorie availability increases for all households.

A 5 percent gain in general agricultural productivity raises calorie intake among all rural households, but the largest percentage gains occur among low-expenditure households. An induced wage increase again benefits all households, especially those in the lowest-expenditure group. Any increase in the demand for rural labor benefits households in all expenditure classes, whether it comes from outside the agricultural sector, from gains in the physical productivity of agriculture, or from an increase in the relative price of rice—or of other outputs. (Labor income is more important than profits to most households.) In each case, the percentage of calorie availability rises most for the L households.

Unfortunately, neither higher rice prices nor greater productivity provides an easy solution to undernutrition. Before the per capita caloric intake of the low-expenditure group could go up to 1,950 calories per day, the relative prices of rice would have to rise by 70 percent or more, or agricultural productivity would have to rise by at least 25 percent, even if induced wage increases that are near their upper bound were taken into account. These policies help, but do not of themselves promise early success in the fight against malnutrition.

Appendix: Estimates of Rural per Capita Aggregates from Observed Data

Table 7A-1. *Per Capita Annual Production, Consumption, and Net Marketed Surplus, Rural Sierra Leone (7 Zones), 1974–75*

Commodity group	Expenditure group	Production	Consumption	Net marketed surplus
Rice	Mean	206.9	86.9	119.9
	Low	191.6	45.0	146.6
	Middle	254.1	89.9	164.2
	High	177.1	118.8	58.3
Root crops and	Mean	39.4	10.8	28.6
other cereals	Low	15.3	5.0	10.3
	Middle	34.5	8.4	26.1
	High	63.6	17.6	46.0
Oils and fats	Mean	41.6	15.6	25.9
	Low	16.0	8.4	7.6
	Middle	54.2	10.7	43.5
	High	51.3	26.0	25.3
Fish and animal	Mean	55.1	29.9	25.1
products	Low	2.5	16.6	−14.1
	Middle	15.1	27.6	−12.5
	High	134.1	43.1	91.0
Miscellaneous	Mean	49.5	15.5	34.0
foods	Low	14.7	6.2	8.5
	Middle	25.2	14.2	11.0
	High	99.8	24.2	75.6
Nonfoods	Mean	5.3	52.5	−47.2
	Low	3.8	36.8	−33.0
	Middle	5.2	53.0	−47.8
	High	6.5	64.9	58.4
Labor[a]	Mean	797.6	780.4	−17.1
	Low	817.5	880.7	63.2
	Middle	816.9	755.8	−61.1
	High	763.9	720.1	−43.8
Calories	Mean	—	2,178.7	—
	Low	—	1,108.5	—
	Middle	—	1,942.0	—
	High	—	2,729.4	—

— Not applicable.

Note: Commodities in kilograms, labor in adult man-hour equivalents, and calories in calories per day.

a. Production entry is labor demanded; consumption entry labor supplied.

Notes

1. Lau and others (1981) used microsimulation applied to average households taken as representative of each of some forty region-size classes.

2. The underlying data were collected by Spencer and Byerlee (1977) in a survey of rural households in Sierra Leone. They used a stratified sample with equal numbers of households in each of eight ecological zones (agroclimatic resource regions). To make estimates for the population, we estimated per capita consumption or production levels in each zone, weighted each zonal estimate by the proportion of the total rural population found in that zone, and combined these weighted consumption ratios into a single ratio for the whole rural population (see Smith and others 1981, pp. 3–7, 15–18). Because of problems in data collection, in one zone the sample contained only five usable households. Thus the estimates presented here apply only to the remaining seven zones, which have an estimated rural population of 1,546,600. The estimated population of the omitted zone (the Northern Plateau) was 495,500 in 1974–75 (Spencer and Byerlee 1977, Table 3.1).

3. When a representative household is used, it is implicitly assumed that demand and output-supply functions aggregate perfectly over households in the sense that we can model aggregate demand (or supply) as a function of prices and of aggregate, or average, income (fixed factors). Further, we might want the aggregate demand function to be consistent with some utility function (of a representative household). For instance, the ith household's demand function for rice might be $R_i = f(y_i, p)$, where y_i is full income and p is a price vector. Averaging rice demands over N households we obtain

$$\bar{R} = \frac{1}{N} \sum_{i=1}^{N} f(y_i, p),$$

assuming all households face the same prices. The question is whether there exists a demand function $g(\cdot)$ such that $g(\bar{y}, p) = \bar{R}$, where $\bar{y}$ is average full income and $g(\cdot)$ is consistent with some utility function. The well-known answer is yes, provided each household has the same marginal propensity to consume rice, which implies linear Engel curves (see Deaton and Muellbauer 1980).

A weaker alternative (Muellbauer 1976; Deaton and Muellbauer 1980) is to let the average rice budget share depend on prices and on some representative (not necessarily average) full income. This representative full income might even be a function of the distribution of incomes as well as of prices. In this case, we can still talk about average demand being generated by a representative consumer. Muellbauer derives conditions on the household cost (or expenditure) functions that are required if the representative consumer is to exist. Although the Quadratic Expenditure System does not satisfy these restrictions, the Almost Ideal Demand System (see chapter 8) does. When prices or wages vary over households, as they do in our data, however, the conditions under which the representative household exists are even more strict (Deaton and Muellbauer 1980).

4. Inasmuch as the average household in Sierra Leone produces 74 percent of the rice it consumes (Smith and others 1980, table 3.1) and this portion of its consumption is valued at the producer price, the consumer price for all rice consumed does not normally differ greatly from the producer price.

5. If we were dealing only with point elasticities, we could leave the discussion at this point, but over the range defined by a finite price change, as in table 7-4, marketed surpluses change because the consumption elasticities just mentioned reduce rice consumption and because outputs also respond to change in price. But the percentage of output changes differs little by expenditure group, so that such changes have little effect on consumption-response differences among expenditure classes.

6. Apparently L households have such high marketed surpluses of rice because, having low incomes, they consume much less rice per capita than others, and they concentrate their resources heavily on rice production. Snodgrass and others (1980, pp. 155–56) found that most rice production yielded negative returns in 1980 (see also Spencer, Byerlee, and Franzel 1979, p. 43). The L households produce relatively little of the more profitable crops, such as palm products, fish, and vegetables.

7. In the production function,

$$(\Sigma_i \delta_i Q_i^\rho)^{1/\rho} = \alpha L_T^{B_L} A^{B_A} K^{B_K}$$

the constant α is changed from 1.00 to 1.05. As this is a Hicks neutral production function, such a shift does not of itself change the proportions among outputs. It does, however, affect both labor demand and the overall output level.

References

Deaton, Angus, and John Muellbauer. 1980. *Economics and Consumer Behavior*. Cambridge: Cambridge University Press.

Lau, Lawrence J., and others. 1981. "The Microeconomics of Distribution: A Simulation of the Farm Economy." *Journal of Policy Modeling* 3(2):175–206.

Muellbauer, John. 1976. "Community Preferences and the Representative Consumer." *Econometrica* 44(5):979–99.

Smith, Victor E., and others. 1980. "Non-Price Factors Affecting Household Food Consumption in Sierra Leone." Rural Development Working Paper no. 12. East Lansing: Michigan State University.

———. 1981. "Food Flows and Simulations: Rural Sierra Leone." Rural Development Working Paper no. 19. East Lansing: Michigan State University.

Snodgrass, Milton M., and others. 1980. *Agricultural Sector Assessment Report for Sierra Leone*. Logan, Utah: Consortium for International Development.

Spencer, Dunstan S.C., and Derek Byerlee. 1977. "Small Farms in West Africa: A Descriptive Analysis of Employment, Incomes and Productivity in Sierra Leone." African Rural Economy Working Paper no. 19. East Lansing: Michigan State University.

Spencer, Dunstan S.C., Derek Byerlee, and Steven Franzel. 1979. "Annual Costs, Returns, and Seasonal Labor Requirements for Selected Farm and Nonfarm Enterprises in Sierra Leone." African Rural Economy Working Paper no. 27. East Lansing: Michigan State University.

Strauss, John, Victor E. Smith, and Peter Schmidt. 1981. "Determinants of Food Consumption in Rural Sierra Leone: Application of the Quadratic Expenditure System to the Consumption-Leisure Component of a Household Firm Model." Rural Development Working Paper no. 14. East Lansing: Michigan State University.

Strauss, John, and others. 1981. "Joint Determination of Food Consumption and Production in Rural Sierra Leone: Estimates of a Household-Firm Model." Rural Development Working Paper no. 17. East Lansing: Michigan State University.

8

Multimarket Analysis of Agricultural Pricing Policies in Senegal

Avishay Braverman and Jeffrey S. Hammer

THIS CHAPTER PRESENTS an approach to analyzing the effects of agricultural pricing in less developed countries. The same general method under different institutional constraints has been used in Korea, Sierra Leone, Cyprus, and Malawi (see Braverman, Ahn, and Hammer 1983; Braverman, Hammer, and Jorgensen 1983, 1984; and Singh, Squire, and Kirchner 1984). Here we are concerned with the pricing policies of Senegal. The method presented is only a deterministic one; for an attempt at introducing uncertainty into such a framework see Braverman, Hammer, and Levinsohn (1983, chapter 5) and Hammer (forthcoming).

Our general method takes as a starting point the theory of the farm household (Yotopoulos and Lau 1974; Barnum and Squire 1979) and incorporates it into a simulation model that traces the short- to medium-run effects of pricing policies on a variety of outcomes of interest to policymakers. These outcomes have to do with the distribution of income (between income groups or between regions), agricultural production and consumption, and foreign trade. In many cases, pricing policies generate large deficits in the agricultural sector and the reduction of these deficits is often a high-priority concern.

We are living in a quantitative era in which political debate necessitates some quantitative assessments of evaluated policies for the sake of public

Note: For a detailed description of the study on Senegal see Braverman, Hammer, and Levinsohn (1983). We thank Jim Levinsohn and Erika Jorgensen for excellent research assistance. Many persons at the World Bank and in Senegal contributed to this study through discussions and suggestions. In particular, we would like to thank Joseph Baah-Dwomoh and Christopher Redfern. Special thanks are due to Sangone Amar, who joined our mission in Senegal and who provided us with invaluable support. We alone are responsible for all views expressed.

accountability. Many economists use two standard operational tools in their quantitative assessment of agricultural pricing policies. The most commonly used class of measures includes the domestic resource cost (DRC) and the effective protection rate (EPR), which are modified ratios of domestic prices to international prices. (For agricultural pricing studies using EPR, see, for example, Scandizzo and Bruce 1980.) This type of measure does not address the income distribution and public revenue issues, nor can it address the quantitative impact of taxes and subsidies on production and consumption. The second method, single-market calculation of consumers' and producers' surplus, does not address the interaction among markets (that is, the substitution effects in consumption and production), and does not devote sufficient attention to income distribution beyond classifying agents into consumers and producers. It also ignores the impact on and feedback from the rural labor market. In addition, agricultural price reforms often include simultaneous changes in several prices, where interaction among the different commodities is critical, and where the effects of policies may not be additive across commodities.

The methodology presented here extends the single-market surplus method to include income distribution and some general equilibrium considerations. Balancing the need for more complete information on the consequences of policy is the need for simplicity in operational work and the need to maintain intuitive understanding of the system under investigation. For this reason, our method stops short of the computable general equilibrium models, which often become cumbersome tools, especially when institutional details are important in the structure of the economy. As with any model of economic activity, the appropriate boundaries of the analysis are a matter of judgment. The agricultural sector is considered the proper unit of study and the urban sector (except for agrobusiness concerns) is taken to be exogenous. Market equilibrium includes the urban sector, however. Previous work that used the farm-household model in a policy simulation study (Lau and others 1981) limited the analysis to the agricultural sector alone. In the case of Senegal, this division is artificial and would ignore most of the important policy questions, such as government deficits arising from urban consumption. Therefore, the boundaries of the problem were set to include urban consumption and the cost of living, with nominal urban wages left exogenous.

The Senegalese Problem

The performance of the agricultural sector in Senegal is extremely important to the national economy. Agriculture employs 77 percent of the labor force and contributes 26 percent of GDP. Agricultural products generate 70 percent of export earnings. At the same time, government intervention in the agricultural sector has become costly. In 1982–83 deficits related to agricultural pricing funds amounted to 23 percent of government expenditure and 2.6 percent of GDP.

A policy initiative discussed recently would promote the production, consumption, and marketing of millet, the main subsistence crop. The advantages envisioned for this approach were the saving of foreign exchange (from reduced rice imports) and the creation of new income-generating activities for farmers. The policy would be implemented by increasing the consumer price of rice, which is currently controlled. This might be accompanied by a reduction in the price of groundnuts, millet's main competitor for cultivated land; such a measure would help to reduce the deficit in groundnut-marketing operations.

The policies selected for analysis are concerned with reducing government deficits and with addressing the millet problem. The market interventions that are analyzed are reductions of 15 and 35 percent in the price of groundnuts paid to farmers; increases of 10 and 50 percent in the price of rice; increases of 50 and 118 percent in the price of cotton (the latter representing world prices in 1981); and increases of 100, 200, and 300 percent in the price of fertilizer (the last representing factory prices).

Since the agricultural sector is treated as a whole, integrated policy packages can also be analyzed. The multiple price changes to be examined are reducing the price of fertilizer from 25 to 5 CFAF per kilogram and lowering the price of groundnuts to farmers by 5 CFAF (such a scheme under consideration within Senegal would provide virtually free fertilizer through an added tax on groundnuts); reducing groundnut prices while increasing the price of rice to encourage millet production and pursue deficit reductions; and simulating a devaluation by raising the prices of traded commodities.

Structure of the Model

The model was constructed with two concerns in mind: it had to be complex enough to capture the essential tradeoffs between competing government goals, but it also had to be simple enough to highlight the most important features of the rural sector and not overtax the limited information available. The model is quite straightforward. We model the demand for four *consumer goods*: rice and groundnut oil (which are generally taxed and subsidized, respectively) and millet and maize (which are modeled as if in a free market). On the *supply side*, we model the production of five commodities: groundnuts, rice and cotton (which are subject to government-controlled prices), and millet and maize (which, as already mentioned, are traded freely in domestic markets).

The official marketing channels for millet and maize in Senegal have controlled prices. Very little of the millet and maize produced passes through these channels, however. Most is used for on-farm consumption, is traded in local village markets, or finds its way to urban areas through private traders. An issue of critical concern at-present is the development of better marketing facilities for millet. Although they do not directly contribute to government deficits, these crops are included in the model because they are important substitutes for the other three crops in both production and consumption. Policy changes will affect the production of these crops and their market prices. In consequence, farm incomes and the cost of living will also be affected.

The country is divided into *four regions* according to the crops grown in each. The Groundnut Basin, which is the largest region (it holds almost half the population), consists of the administrative districts of Sine-Saloum, Diorbel, Louga, and Thies. For the purposes of the model, it is assumed that the basin produces only groundnuts and millet. Land devoted to other crops constitutes less than 1 percent of the total in the region and is ignored. The southern region, which is made up of the administrative divisions of Casamance and Senegal Oriental, has the most varied agricultural system. Crops grown there are groundnuts, millet, rice, maize, and cotton (in the order of acreage in the base year). The Flueve is assumed to grow millet, rice, and groundnuts. The final region to be considered is Dakar, which is entirely a consuming area for agricultural products.

Each producing region is endowed with a fixed supply of land and labor that may be allocated to the crops produced within it. Because we are using a short-run model, we exclude interregional migration as well as the expansion of total land farmed within a region. Various assumptions will be made concerning the degree of substitution possibilities for land in the short run. Labor is assumed to move freely between crops within a region according to its marginal productivity in each use. Variable factors are fertilizer and a residual category consisting of other factors. These are chosen by profit maximization decisions and are not limited to any specific amount.

Supply responses are derived from underlying production functions. The demand functions are derived from their underlying utility functions, which characterize preferences for consumer goods. The use of production and utility functions was preferred to the direct use of supply and demand elasticities for a variety of reasons, even at the expense of computational simplicity. In the tradition of the farm-household model that integrates production and consumption decisions (Barnum and Squire 1979; Yotopoulos and Lau 1974), aspects of the production structure influence the consumption pattern of the household. Profits from farm production yield income that influences demand and marketed surplus of food crops. Information on supply response alone cannot easily be used to generate this income gain. In addition, factor demand is an essential feature of the current model. Fertilizer is distributed directly by the government and is a substantial contributor to the deficit. Also, the government is currently discussing the possibility of increasing the subsidies to fertilizer and financing them in part with lowered prices for crops, particularly for groundnuts. A full production structure is necessary to ensure consistency between factor demands and crop supply. This policy option could not be adequately analyzed without a consistent framework.

On the consumption side, demand curves are linked to their underlying utility functions in order to assess the welfare implications of consumer price changes involving a number of goods simultaneously. By using a well-specified utility function, we can calculate the compensating variation of policy changes, giving a CFAF amount for the gain or loss of each person. This allows us to incorporate some of the insight provided by the new public economics literature (see, for example, Atkinson and Stiglitz 1980).

Agricultural Production

The four regions of the model constitute the basic units of the analysis. Since data on income distribution and the size distribution of farms are scanty, we are unable to model the intraregional distribution effects of policies. Within each of the three producing regions (that is, excluding Dakar), the production structure of crops is characterized by use of the translog restricted profit function (Lau 1976). This functional form is quite flexible and can represent a wide variety of substitution possibilities between factors. Again, because data are scarce, the function is specialized to correspond to the Cobb-Douglas form. The restricted profit function is composed of two parts: one for variable factors of production and one for factors that are fixed to the region. Rents accruing to the fixed factors (land and labor) become part of the income of the region.

All allocation decisions assume profit-maximizing behavior on the part of farmers. The profit function yields the appropriate amount of the variable factors (fertilizer and "other") as functions of their prices and the quantities of the fixed factors used. Although land and labor are fixed to the region, they can be shifted between crops within the region. Land and labor are allocated so that the value of their marginal products are equated between uses. Since most production takes place on family farms and the markets for both land and wage labor are quite thin in Senegal, this seemed the most appropriate way of modeling the allocation decision. The alternative, which would be to discuss explicitly the determination of wages and rental rates on land, does not seem to fit the general picture of Senegalese agriculture and would make it difficult to collect relevant information.

Conventionally, production functions are assumed to be subject to constant returns to scale. For the Groundnut Basin and the Flueve, this poses no problem and the above structure is completely straightforward. Because so many crops are produced in the south, however, one added difficulty is that three of the crops—cotton, groundnuts, and rice—are subject to fixed prices. Since there are only two fixed factors of production and constant returns to scale, the production possibility frontier for these three goods contains "flats" or linear areas. This would imply that only two of these crops would ever be produced at the same time. If one crop was more profitable than another, both land and labor would flow to it. With constant returns and fixed prices, the former crop would remain more profitable even after this factor movement and would drive out the other crop. The fact remains, however, that all three crops are produced in this region (as well as maize and millet, the price flexibility of which avoids this problem). Therefore, one of the assumptions must be abandoned. We have decided to replace constant returns to scale with decreasing returns. This can be justified in one of two ways. First, an explanation of the multiplicity of crops may be that the assumption of homogeneous land is incorrect. Some land is simply more suitable for one crop than another. Irrigated paddy land could conceivably be used for crops other than rice but (in the short run, at least) is far more profitable in its present use. This type of land cannot be easily expanded in the short run. Therefore some of the land may be fixed not only to the region as a whole but also to its present use. More generally, the suitability of land for different crops varies greatly and the substitution between crops cannot take place with equal ease at all levels of output. The decline in quality of land as a crop acreage expands is precisely the justification given for the assumption of decreasing returns in classical economic theory.

The second possible explanation for the variety of crops is that it is a way of reducing riskiness of yields. Rainfall is erratic in Senegal and although little rain will hurt all crops, diversification is still advantageous as long as yields are not perfectly correlated. A complete model of farmer behavior under uncertainty is beyond the scope of this chapter, but such a model would balance the additional gain of expanding the production of a more profitable crop (in expected value) against the additional cost (in terms of increased variability in yields) of overspecialization. This decision can also be modeled on an as-if basis by assuming decreasing returns to scale in any one crop. The increased costs to scale are not technological in this case but are psychic costs resulting from a decline in the diversity of a farmer's portfolio of crops. For either of the above reasons, then, the model adopts decreasing returns to scale in the underlying production function as a means of ensuring the observed diversity of crops in production.

Incomes and Demand

Incomes in the three producing regions come from two sources, the more important being the profit generated by agricultural production. Profit is the joint return to the two fixed factors, labor and land, and is the value of production minus payments to the two variable factors. This value is determined endogenously via the production system described above. The second source of income covers all nonagricultural receipts and is held exogenous in the exercise. The value is determined by the difference between computed agricultural income and actual income in the base period. Since the three producing areas include some urban areas without agricultural activities, this term is not trivial. Income in Dakar is entirely nonagricultural and is held constant, in nominal terms, throughout.

The demand system used is based on a flexible functional form for the utility function similar to the translog form for the production function. It was devised by Deaton and Muellbauer (1980) and called the Almost Ideal Demand System (AIDS). Certain features of this model make it attractive for the Senegal model. First, this functional form allows a greater variety of price elasticities to be incorporated than most common demand systems (such as the Linear Expenditure System [LES]). Second, it is also flexible with respect to income elasticities. Since we are concerned with substitution between basic grains, there is a good possibility that the Engel curve for some of these commodities will have an inverse U shape. Purchases increase rapidly with income at low levels of income. As incomes rise, preferred foods substitute for the necessity items, and demand for the latter begins to fall off. If the commodities are sufficiently disaggregated (as in this case), it is quite likely that demand will decline absolutely for the subsistence commodity. The AIDS system allows for this possibility, whereas many alternative systems (LES, in particular) impose positive income elasticities. Since consumption of rice is an important variable in this analysis for balance of payment purposes, the effect of income changes on consumption will be of central concern.

Market-Clearing Conditions

Having defined the behavioral relations assumed to characterize producers and consumers, we can construct the market-clearing conditions that incorporate the institutional details of the Senegalese economy. For the crops directly controlled by government, the conditions that ensure materials will balance are quite simple. For the cash crops groundnuts and cotton, the entire crop is purchased from the farmers at the government set price. This accords with the arrangement that SONACOS and SEIB (for groundnuts) and SODIFITEX (cotton) have with the government of Senegal. These companies then process the materials into oil and fiber and export their total production. Demand from world markets is then perfectly elastic and absorbs the domestic supply.

In principle, the government also buys rice from producers at a fixed price. The price of rice consumption is also set by the government; these prices are usually lower than the (milled equivalent) producer price. Since domestic production is always short of consumption, the remaining rice is imported from Thailand. Again, international trade clears the market. In most years, however, the amount of marketed surplus is very small. Almost the entire crop is consumed on the farm and the government handles very little domestic rice. Nonetheless, the opportunity to sell at the government price is assumed to be present for the farmers, and that price is assumed to be used by the farmers in their allocation decisions. The problem of arbitrage between high producer and relatively low consumer prices is removed by the fact that farmers sell paddy rice and the government sells milled grain.

Millet and maize are modeled as being traded on free markets isolated from world markets. The prices of these goods vary endogenously to equate supply and demand. There are official government channels and government prices for these crops. However, most of the production is for on-farm use and whatever is traded usually goes through unofficial channels at prices above the government levels. Although the absence of a distribution system is frequently cited as a problem for farmers in disposing of their crops, the fact remains that millet and (to some extent) maize find their way to Dakar and other urban areas. The imperfection of the distribution system is modeled by inserting a wedge between the prices in Dakar and the producing regions to represent transport costs.

Deficits

The calculation of the deficits is not expected to match the actual accounting procedures of the CPSP (the government agricultural pricing board). Simplifications are made for each of the six funds that have been of interest in recent years. Three of these funds relate to groundnuts. The main component in the groundnut deficit corresponds to the subsidies to SONACOS and SEIB. It is calculated as the difference between the producer price of groundnuts and the implicit price paid by the companies (which includes transportation and handling costs), all multiplied by the total marketed surplus of the grain. The implicit price is derived from total deficit figures for the 1981–82 crop year. The actual subsidy for the operation of the groundnut companies is a matter of negotiation and usually depends on the world price of oil, among other variables. For a given set of world prices and an agreed cost structure for marketing, however, the above formula should reflect the fund costs adequately.

The second component of the deficit is associated with the distribution of seeds. The government currently sells seeds to the farmers by exacting a 10 CFAF per kilogram tax on groundnut production. The deficit is the difference between the (fixed) total cost of seed distribution and the revenue from the tax. The last of the groundnut costs is the consumption subsidy for oil. This is the difference between the cost of the oil distributed (a blend of groundnut and imported soybean oils) and the price charged the consumer, multiplied by total consumer demand.

The rice deficit is, in principle, composed of two parts. The first is the gap between relatively high producer prices and the consumer prices, multiplied by the marketed surplus. This is offset by the difference between world prices of Thai 100 percent broken rice and (usually higher) consumer prices, multiplied by the level of imports derived in the model. The level of marketed surplus is usually negligible in reality, however, and, because of the regional aggregations, is always zero in the model. Therefore, the rice fund will generally be in surplus and be equal to the implicit tariff revenue earned on imports.

The cotton fund is modeled the same way as the groundnut fund. The deficit per ton in 1981–82 is attributed to the difference between marketing costs plus the implicit payment to SODIFITEX and the producer price of cotton. In the simulation exercises, the producer prices and the total production will change, but the deficit will be computed the same way.

Finally, the fertilizer deficit is calculated as the difference in the cost of production of the principal fertilizers and the price charged to the farmer, multiplied by total fertilizer use.

Calibration of the Model

Rainfall, and consequently yields, fluctuate substantially from year to year in Senegal. Therefore, picking a particular year from which to calibrate the model runs the risk of generalizing results from a special case. To avoid this problem, we calibrated the model to match outputs, input usage, and consumption patterns for a three-year period in which all the information needed was available. Thus, fluctuations can be smoothed out to obtain an average year on which to base comparisons. The three crop years were 1976–77, 1977–78, and 1978–79. The years 1976–77 and 1977–78 were slightly below average in rainfall, whereas 1978–79 was a year with relatively high rainfall.

Basic data concerning prices, output, and acreage came from an Arthur Anderson study. Information concerning the production functions of the various crops was based on the study by SONED (1981). In this study, technical input-output coefficients and expenditure data are derived for labor, fertilizer, and other inputs. When used in combination with price data, the share information required for the Cobb-Douglas profit function can be recovered. Total production and acreage of each crop by region are readily available from the Ministry of Agriculture, as is fertilizer use.

Data concerning the demand side of the model were somewhat more elusive. The main source of this information is a study by the Center for Research in Economic Development (CRED 1982) at the University of Michigan. Income and price elasticities, per capita consumption for the principal grains in the model, and some estimates of per capita income were obtained from that study. This information was then incorporated into the Almost Ideal Demand System framework. Although flawed in a number of ways, this remains the only source of information available on consumption patterns.

For some of the policy runs, especially the rice price increase used to spur millet consumption, this type of information is potentially important. In such cases, it is essential to use sensitivity analysis to see how far off the conclusions can be with deficient data. Aggregate figures for the market-clearing equations are fairly precise. Imports of rice, exports of groundnut oil and cotton fiber, and total production levels are measured with reasonable accuracy.

The method used to ensure consistency between these disparate sources of information and the structure of the model are discussed in detail in Braverman, Ahn, and Hammer (1983) and Braverman, Hammer, and Jorgensen (1984). Briefly, a nonlinear programming model is constructed that minimizes deviations of variables and behavioral parameters from known values, subject to various constraints. This yields all the parameter values needed for the base period of the model. Included are all the variables for which information is available, such as levels of production, consumption, imports, and the like. Also included are behavioral parameters such as price and income elasticities of demand, which are functions of parameters in the AIDS demand system. The known values come from various sources. Actual levels come from national statistics or the CPSP accounts. Elasticities come from the CRED (1982) study for demand; supply elasticities from simple Nerlove-style econometric exercises for farmer responses.

The constraints that the programming model must satisfy are of two kinds. First, all of the model equations must be satisfied for the base period. Second, the theory of demand imposes a number of constraints on the AIDS system. As with all flexible functional forms, the AIDS system does not ensure the concavity of the underlying expenditure function. This requirement was imposed on the calibration exercise and took the form of restricting parameters such that the Slutsky matrix is negative semidefinite.

Results

The analysis takes the model as derived in the calibration described above, changes prices as would be done in the proposed policies, and records percentage changes in the supply of all five crops, in real incomes in the four regions, in total export earnings, in government deficits (from 1981 base), and in rice imports. Changes in real income are defined as the (negative of) compensating variation of the price change. The compensating variation is the amount of money that must be paid to a person after a policy change in order to make him or her as well off as before the policy. (The basic results of the model are presented in table 8-1.)

Groundnut Prices

The price of groundnuts is, rightfully, a sensitive topic. Since it represents so large a share of agricultural production, we cannot tamper with the price without making substantial changes in output and farm incomes. Further, since prices are announced before the growing season and world prices of groundnut oil are fairly volatile, it is not easy to assess an appropriate border price that can be used as a base for efficiency comparisons.

A 15 percent decline in the producer price of groundnuts has the following consequences.

- Government deficits fall by 18.1 percent. This is composed of a 22 percent fall in the three groundnut funds combined with a counter-

Table 8-1. *Basic Results of Agriculture Pricing Analysis, Senegal*
(percentage changes)

Policy	Supply				
	Ground-nuts	Rice	Cotton	Millet	Maize
Groundnut prices decline 15 percent	−6.9	10.8	13.1	4.9	4.1
Groundnut prices decline 35 percent	−19.3	27.3	33.2	12.7	9.4
Rice producer prices are raised 10 percent	−0.8	10.2	−3.3	−0.2	−1.2
Rice producer prices are raised 50 percent	−4.2	46.6	−17.3	−1.2	−6.5
Cotton prices are raised 50 percent	−2.5	−8.6	84.7	−0.7	−3.9
Cotton prices are raised to world prices (118 percent)	−7.0	−23.3	191.2	−2.1	−11.8
Fertilizer price rises 100 percent	−2.3	−2.3	−16.3	−0.6	0.6
Fertilizer price rises 200 percent	−3.6	−3.7	−24.6	−1.0	0.8
Fertilizer price rises 300 percent	−4.5	−4.7	−30.1	−1.2	1.0
Free trade at 1982 prices	0.03	−29.0	152.2	−14.8	−23.8
10 percent devaluation from base prices	2.5	1.8	2.2	−3.3	−4.1
50 percent devaluation from base prices	9.9	7.2	8.7	−13.7	−17.4
Cotton raised 118 percent fertilizer 300 percent	−10.1	−22.9	119.6	−3.0	−8.2
Consumer price of rice raised 25 percent	−8.4	−5.6	−6.9	11.3	0.9
Rice consumer and producer raised 10 percent	−4.4	7.6	−6.0	4.8	−0.7
Fertilizer price = 5CFAF per kilogram groundnut price reduced by 5 CFAF per kilogram	−0.4	13.4	64.8	5.4	1.5

Real income				Demand				Agricultural export earnings	Government deficit in agriculture	Rice imports
Groundnut Basin	South	Flueve	Dakar	Rice	Maize	Groundnut	Millet			
−5.7	−4.7	1.2	0.6	−9.1	2.6	−3.9	5.3	−1.9	−18.1	−13.9
−13.1	−10.0	3.0	1.5	−21.2	6.0	−9.2	13.9	−7.9	−36.4	−33.0
0.03	1.5	0.7	−0.03	0.6	−0.7	0.3	−0.2	−0.7	−0.02	−1.7
0.2	9.3	3.5	−0.2	3.3	−4.2	1.8	−1.3	−4.5	−0.1	−7.2
0.1	5.4	−0.3	−0.1	1.8	−2.5	0.9	−0.8	5.0	22.2	4.4
0.3	18.0	−0.9	−0.3	5.4	−7.5	2.9	−2.2	8.6	72.3	12.4
−1.1	−1.1	−0.4	−0.1	0.3	0.4	−0.3	−0.7	−5.2	−10.4	1.0
−1.7	−1.7	−0.6	−0.1	0.5	0.5	−0.5	−1.1	−8.1	−14.1	1.6
−2.1	−2.2	−0.8	−0.1	0.7	0.7	−0.7	−1.4	−10.1	−16.0	2.0
14.9	40.0	−2.4	−2.0	35.2	−15.2	14.7	−16.2	−1.9	133.6	50.8
3.7	5.3	−0.1	−0.4	6.9	−2.6	3.0	−3.6	13.3	24.8	8.1
18.9	26.6	0.4	−1.8	33.3	−11.2	14.3	−15.0	68.0	145.3	39.6
−1.9	11.1	−1.5	−0.4	5.2	−5.2	1.6	−3.2	−3.5	34.1	12.0
−1.6	−5.1	−7.8	−5.1	−6.7	0.6	−1.5	12.3	−8.8	−24.6	−7.0
−0.6	−0.7	−2.6	−2.2	−2.1	−0.4	−0.3	5.3	−4.6	−10.2	−4.4
−2.3	−0.7	1.9	0.6	−8.1	1.0	−2.4	5.9	12.3	61.0	−13.3

vailing increase in costs in the cotton fund and reduced tariff revenue from rice.

- The burden of lower groundnut prices is not shared equally. The real incomes of farmers in the important producing regions of the Groundnut Basin and the south decline by 5.7 and 4.7 percent, respectively. In the Flueve and Dakar, the decline in prices of millet and maize leads to gains in real incomes of 1.2 and 0.6 percent, respectively.
- Export earnings drop by 1.9 percent. This is composed of a 7 percent drop in groundnut earnings, on the one hand, and increases in earnings from cotton and saved foreign exchange from reduced rice imports, on the other.

Comparison of Methods

To illustrate the value of the multimarket approach, we calculate the predicted effects of the same policy change by using the same supply elasticity for groundnuts in a single-market analysis (see table 8-2). The main

Table 8-2. *Effect of a 15 Percent Decline in Groundnut Prices, Senegal: Comparison of Analytical Methods*
(percentage change)

Variable	Multimarket analysis	Isolated market analysis
Supply		
Groundnut	−6.9	−6.9
Rice	10.8	n.a.
Cotton	13.1	n.a.
Millet	4.9	n.a.
Maize	4.1	n.a.
Real incomes		
Groundnut Basin	−5.7	−4.2
South	−4.7	−3.7
Flueve	1.2	−0.1
Dakar	0.6	n.a.
Demand		
Rice	−9.1	n.a.
Maize	2.6	n.a.
Groundnut oil	−3.9	n.a.
Millet	5.3	n.a.
Agricultural export earnings	−1.9	−7.9
Government deficit in agriculture	−18.1	−17.9
Rice imports	−13.9	n.a.

n.a. Not applicable.

advantage of the multimarket approach, of course, is that more issues can be addressed and side effects examined in the more complete version. Supply responses of other crops, cost of living in Dakar, and demand for all consumption goods are simply beyond the scope of an analysis of the groundnut market in isolation.

Although both methods provide answers, some differences remain. The multimarket analysis shows a larger fall in income in the Groundnut Basin and the south. This is due to the fall in prices of millet (in both regions) and maize (in the south). With substitution possibilities available, the reduction in groundnut prices induces substitution to other crops. Prices for millet and maize fall as a result of the extra supply. Since these prices are inelastically demanded, net income from these crops falls. This reinforces the income loss. In the Flueve, there is a small decline in income from groundnuts. When consumption effects of cheaper millet and maize are taken into account in the multimarket analysis, the real incomes actually increase.

The fact that the deficit figures are similar between the two versions is coincidental. In the multimarket framework, the side effects of a groundnut price reduction on other deficits operate in opposite directions. Fertilizer costs are reduced, some extra seed costs are not recovered, cotton deficits rise, and rice imports fall. These add up to be within a percentage point of the direct effect captured in an isolated market analysis (this may not be true in every case).

The principal difference between the two methods lies in the appraisal of the effect on foreign exchange earnings. The multimarket approach indicates that the fall in export earnings from groundnuts (the isolated market figure) is mitigated substantially by the increase in cotton exports and the decline in rice imports.

Cotton Prices

Cotton represents an important opportunity for the generation of export earnings and provides an alternative source of income in rural areas. In general, producer prices have been kept lower than international prices. A 50 percent increase in cotton prices has the following effects: export earnings rise 5 percent; cotton output increases greatly but groundnut production falls and rice imports increase; incomes increase appreciably only in the south; reduced millet supplies raise the cost of living in Dakar and the Flueve.

Fertilizer Price

Fertilizer has traditionally been provided at a substantial discount. Prices are approximately one-fourth of the cost of production. Doubling

Table 8-3. *Sensitivity Analysis of Rice Policies, Senegal*
(percentage change)

Variable	Millet production and consumption	Real income			Net foreign exchange earnings from agriculture	Government deficit in agriculture	Rice imports
		Groundnut Basin	South	Dakar			
Consumer price of rice increase 50 percent							
Cross-elasticity assumptions: Low	0.5	−8.6	−14.2	−11.1	13.6	−31.5	−36.7
Best estimate	11.6	−4.7	−10.7	−8.2	0.2	−34.8	−31.1
High	22.1	−3.9	−9.5	−8.8	−15.9	−41.7	−19.4
Consumer price of rice increases 50 percent and producer price of groundnuts falls 35 percent:							
Low	8.7	−17.4	−18.6	−4.3	4.05	−55.3	−58.4
Best estimate	21.0	−16.9	−20.7	−6.1	−8.0	−49.8	−61.3
High	32.3	−15.7	−20.3	−6.8	−22.3	−47.9	−58.2

the price would reduce the total agricultural deficit by 10 percent, reduce net agricultural export earnings by 5 percent, and reduce rural incomes in the main producing areas by 1 percent.

Rice Prices

Producer prices of rice are generally maintained above world prices. This may be to encourage self-sufficiency and to save foreign exchange from rice imports. The former goal is essentially noneconomic in nature but its cost can be evaluated quantitatively. The latter must be evaluated according to the substitution possibilities in production. Increasing the producer price of rice will increase the income of farmers in the south at the expense of urban dwellers (because of higher millet prices), and reduce the net foreign exchange earnings (because of the substitution of rice production for the production of important export crops such as groundnut and cotton).

Raising the consumer price of rice has recently been proposed to stimulate millet consumption and, hence, production. The strength of this argument rests on the cross-price elasticity of demand between rice and millet. Since this parameter is known only roughly, it is important to see how sensitive the results are with regard to this variable. Table 8-3 presents selected results for two policies: raising the consumer price of rice by 50 percent, and raising the price of rice in conjunction with a 35 percent decline in groundnut prices. Rice prices stimulate millet output from the demand side, but groundnut prices influence the supply side. Three formulations of the demand system are tried for each policy. The elasticity of demand for millet with respect to the price of rice is assumed to be unity (follow the results of the CRED 1982 demand study), zero, and two. Further, in order to show the effects of the policy proposal in its best light, we changed some other assumptions of the model. Since the drawback of these policies is likely to be losses in foreign exchange due to substitution away from the export crops, the model was changed to lower the substitution possibilities. In this version, land allocated to each crop is fixed. Increases in output can be achieved only by increasing the intensity of cultivation using the other factors of production. The basic results can be summarized as follows:

- Although sensitive to the assumption concerning cross elasticities, millet production can be stimulated by means of an increase in rice prices.
- The public deficit is reduced substantially by this policy, although this is mostly due to the gain in tariff revenue from rice imports. This result is relatively insensitive to the elasticity assumption.

- These benefits come at a cost. Net foreign exchange earnings, very sensitive to the elasticity assumption, can be expected to fall with higher elasticities because extra millet production comes at the expense of groundnuts, the main export earner. Real incomes nationwide fall substantially; this result is insensitive to the demand structure. When combined with a reduction in groundnut prices, the above remarks hold; the effects are merely strengthened.

Although some of the results are quite sensitive to the underlying demand system, proponents of raising the rice price are faced with a serious problem. There is no unambiguously good scenario. Real incomes and deficits are reduced together and are not greatly affected by the uncertainty surrounding the cross-price parameter. However, the cases in which millet production is successfully stimulated by higher rice prices are precisely the cases in which foreign exchange earnings are hurt most. Thus, even though the degree of substitution between rice and millet is unknown, the tradeoff between the goals of millet production and foreign exchange earnings is known quite well. The costs with respect to a loss in foreign exchange go up with the degree of success in increasing millet production through the use of prices alone with a given technology.

Conclusions

This chapter has presented an analysis of agricultural pricing policies in a multimarket framework for a data-scarce country. Even with limited data, a consistent framework of analysis brings into focus the short-run economic issues for an intelligent debate in the political arena. Most policymakers would like to clarify the issues and probable outcomes. Without an assessment of the short-run impact of changes in taxes and subsidies, the credibility of any position on a policy may be questioned. Numbers can also be used out of context and models abused by political advocates. Nonetheless, we believe that the advantage of simple modeling of tax changes providing a consistent framework and quantitative structure for discussion greatly outweighs this cost.

The method presented here will remain valid despite the scarcity of data if sensitivity analysis is properly used, as demonstrated here in the analysis of rice price policies. It is important to know when gaps in one's knowledge affect policy conclusions and when conclusions are relatively robust.

This method was designed to be an operational tool for economists. The elaborateness of the calibration technique requires sophisticated technical skills, however, and diminishes the replicability of such exercises. Therefore we have modified this approach to make it more accessible to operational economists. The cost of accessibility is that the analysis is restricted to small changes in policy. Such a model has already been installed on personal computers for the case of Cyprus (see Braverman, Hammer, and Gron 1985 for a discussion and comparison of the two multimarket approaches).

Appendix: Mathematical Formulation

Production

By region, indexed $r = 1$ to 3 for Groundnut Basin, South, and Flueve. Profit functions:

$$\log \Pi_n^r = \alpha_{on} + \sum_{i=1}^{2} \alpha_{in} \log \frac{w_i}{P_n} + \gamma_n \beta_n^r \log L_n^r + \gamma_n (1 - \beta_n^r) \log A_n^r$$

$$n = \text{crop index (by region).}$$

$$i = \text{variable factor index: fertilizer, other}$$

	Groundnut Basin	Flueve	South
(G)	Groundnuts	Groundnuts	Groundnuts
(Ml)	Millet	Millet	Millet
(R)		Rice	Rice
(Mz)			Maize
(C)			Cotton

Supply functions:

$$Q_n^r = \Pi_n^r \left(1 - \sum_{i=1}^{2} \alpha_{in}\right)$$

Market supply:

$$Q_n = \sum_{r=1}^{3} Q_n^r$$

Factor demand functions (variable factors):

$$X_{in}^r = -\frac{\Pi_n^r \alpha_{in} P_n}{w_i}$$

$$\text{Total demand} = \sum_{r=1}^{3} \sum_{n=1}^{5} X_{in}^r.$$

Consumption

By region, indexed $r = 1$ to 4 as in production plus Dakar.
Income (Dakar income has no profit component)

$$Y^r = \sum_n P_n \cdot \Pi_n^r + \Theta^r.$$

Demand:

$$D_j^r = \left(a_j^r + b_j \log \frac{Y^r}{P_r N_r} + \Sigma g_{jk} \log P_k \right) \frac{Y^r}{P_j}$$

$$\log P_r = a_o^r + \Sigma a_j^r \log P_j^r + \frac{1}{2} \sum_j \sum_k g_{jk} \log P_j \log P_k$$

$$D_j = \sum_{r=1}^{4} D_j^r.$$

Market-Clearing Conditions

Land allocation:

I.
$$\frac{P_n \Pi_n (1 - \beta)\, \gamma_n}{A_n} = \frac{P_m \Pi_m (1 - \beta_m)\, \gamma_m}{A_m}$$

for all pairs of crops within a region.

II. As in I with the exclusion of rice. Rice area is fixed at base level.

III. All areas are fixed at base level.

Labor allocation:

$$\frac{P_n \Pi_n \beta_n \gamma_n}{L_n} = \frac{P_m \Pi_m \beta_m \gamma_m}{L_m}$$

for all pairs of crops within a region.

Groundnuts: $a_1 Q_G = E_o + b D_o$

Rice: $a_2 Q_R + M_R = D_R$

Cotton: $a_3 Q_c = E_c$

Millet: $a_4 Q_{ml} = D_{ml}$

Maize: $a_5 Q_{mz} = D_{mz}$

Variables

Production:

Π_n^r Profit from crop n in region r (in units of output)
W_i Price of factor i (fertilizer, other)
P_n Price of crop n
L_n^r Labor used for crop n in region r
A_n^r Land used for crop n in region r
Q_n^r Supply of crop n in region r
Q_n Total supply of crop n
X_{in}^r Demand for factor i by crop n in region r
X_i Total demand for factor i

Consumption:

Y^r Total income in region r
Θ^r Nonfarm income in region r
P_r Price index in region r
N_r Population of region r
D_j^r Demand for commodity j in region r

Market clearing conditions:

E_j Exports of good j
M_R Imports of rice
a_j Waste factor (ensures the equation of supply and demand in the base period)
b Conversion factor of groundnuts to oil

References

Atkinson, A. B., and Joseph E. Stiglitz. 1980. *Lectures in Public Economics.* New York: McGraw-Hill.

Barnum, Howard N., and Lyn Squire. 1979. *A Model of an Agricultural Household: Theory and Evidence.* Washington, D.C.: World Bank.

Braverman, Avishay, Choong Yong Ahn, and Jeffrey S. Hammer. 1983. *Alternative Agricultural Pricing Policies in Korea: Their Implications for Government Deficits, Income Distribution, and Balance of Payments.* World Bank Staff Working Paper no. 621. Washington, D.C.

Braverman, Avishay, Jeffrey S. Hammer, and James Levinsohn. 1983. "Agricultural Pricing Policies in Senegal: Their Implications for Government Budget, Foreign Exchange, and Regional Income Distribution." Country Policy Department Draft. Washington, D.C.: World Bank.

Braverman, Avishay, Jeffrey S. Hammer, and Erika Jorgensen. 1983. "Agricultural Taxation and Trade Policies in Sierra Leone." Country Policy Department Draft. Washington, D.C.: World Bank.

———. Forthcoming. *An Economic Analysis of Reducing Input Subsidies to the Livestock Sector in Cyprus.* World Bank Staff Working Paper no. 782. Washington, D.C.

Braverman, Avishay, Jeffrey S. Hammer, and Anne Gron. 1985. "Multi-Market Analysis of Agricultural Pricing in an Operational Context: the Case of Cyprus." World Bank Agricultural and Rural Development Department Discussion Paper. Washington, D.C.

Braverman, Avishay, Jeffrey Hammer, and Choong Yong Ahn. Forthcoming. "Multimarket Analysis of Agricultural Pricing Policies in Korea." In *Modern Tax Theory for Developing Countries.* Edited by David Newbery and Nicholas Stern. Washington, D.C.: World Bank.

Center for Research on Economic Development (CRED). 1982. "Consumption Effects of Agricultural Policies: Cameroon and Senegal." Ann Arbor, Mich.: University of Michigan.

Deaton, Angus, and John Muellbauer. 1980. "An Almost Ideal Demand System." *American Economic Review,* vol. 70, no. 3 (June), pp. 312–26.

Hammer, Jeffrey S. Forthcoming. "Subsistence First: Farm Allocation Decisions in Senegal." *Journal of Development Economics.*

Lau, Lawrence. 1976. "A Characterization of the Normalized Restricted Profit Function." *Journal of Economic Theory,* vol. 12, no. 1 (February), pp. 131–63.

Lau, Lawrence, P. A. Yotopoulos, E. C. Chou, and W. L. Lin. 1981. "The Microeconomics of Distribution: A Simulation of the Farm Economy." *Journal of Policy Modeling,* vol. 3, pp. 175–206.

Scandizzo, P., and C. Bruce. 1980. *Methodologies for Measuring Agricultural Price Intervention Effects.* World Bank Staff Working Paper no. 394. Washington, D.C.

Singh, I., L. Squire, and J. Kirchner. 1984. "Agricultural Pricing Policies in Malawi." Country Policy Department Paper, preliminary draft. Washington, D.C.: World Bank.

SONED. 1981. "Modelisation des Prix Agricoles." Processed.

Yotopoulos, P.A., and L. J. Lau. 1974. "On Modelling the Agricultural Sector in Developing Countries: An Integrated Approach of Micro and Macro-economics." *Journal of Development Economics,* vol. 1, pp. 105–27.

9

Yield Risk in a Dynamic Model of the Agricultural Household

Terry Roe and Theodore Graham-Tomasi

NUMEROUS STUDIES HAVE FOUND that farmers in developing countries prefer lower but certain levels of income to marginally higher uncertain income levels (Moscardi and de Janvry 1977; Dillon and Scandizzo 1978; and Binswanger 1980). Estimates of farmers' aversion to risk in these studies range from a measurement of 0.9 for absolute risk aversion in Northeastern Brazil to 0.316–1.74 for partial risk aversion among farmers in India. Since contingency markets are surely imperfect in developing economies, risk averse farmers tend, in an effort to reduce income uncertainty, to allocate resources to activities with lower expected marginal value products than they would in the absence of uncertainty.[1]

The relationship between depressed income due to risk and household consumption has not been studied in models of the agricultural household. An implication of assuming the absence of risk when risk is present is that inferences drawn from such models may be misleading. The problem is to determine the nature of the misleading inferences that might otherwise be drawn. Moreover, failure to consider the effect of risk on household choices limits the insight that can be gained into the welfare effects of market imperfections, such as those that inhibit households from allocating resources to off-farm activities, crop insurance, or imperfections that provide limited access to production technologies and other risk-reducing inputs.

In this chapter, we seek to incorporate production risk into a dynamic version of the agricultural household model. We investigate a fairly simple

Note: The authors thank John Strauss, Cliff Hildreth, Bob Myers, and participants in the Consumption Economics Workshop at the University of Minnesota for helpful comments on an earlier draft of this chapter.

model in an effort to determine the impact of yield risk and the household's risk preferences on its production and consumption decisions. Our model gives the familiar result that consumption and production occur along the locus of points formed by the tangency of marginal utilities and marginal products to their respective price ratios. An analogue of Roy's Identity is also found that relates consumption and input demands to the derivatives of a dynamic version of the household's indirect utility function. At this point, the results depart from those of the traditional model. In general, separability between production and consumption decisions does not hold, although a special case is demonstrated in which a type of separability exists. Even though relationships between the household's choices and increasing risk can be derived for this special case, parameters of the household's direct utility function and prices of the arguments appearing in this function are found to determine the "risk aversion parameter" appearing in the product-supply and input-demand functions. Also, for this special case, demand is found to be a function of certainty-equivalent income. Hence, our findings suggest that parameter restrictions on estimating equations derived from models of the agricultural household that assume an absence of risk may be inappropriate if risk and risk aversion are important.

Background

The theory of the individual consumer provides some insight into the effect of increasing income uncertainty on consumption levels. Results are not easy to obtain, however, and generally depend on third-derivative properties of the utility function. In the case of a single-good, two-period, utility function with uncertain income in the second period, the third-derivative property implies the convexity of the marginal utility of the good consumed in the second period; this is compatible with decreasing absolute risk aversion. In the models considered by Leland (1968), Mirman (1971), and others,[2] the third-derivative property implies a decrease in first-period consumption or an increase in savings as uncertainty increases. The problem faced by the agricultural household in our model is more complex than the problem studied in this literature in two ways.

First, income in these models is exogenous, and second, there is only one consumption good. Clearly, the essence of the agricultural household model as outlined in chapter 1 is endogenous income and the existence of both a staple and a market good. With respect to the first issue, Block and Heineke (1973) study a static model in which utility is a function of income and labor. They show that if $(-\partial^2 U/\partial Y^2)/(\partial U/\partial Y)$, where Y is income, is decreasing in income for a given quantity of labor supply, then an increase in risk increases labor supply when there is additive income risk ($Y = wL + \tilde{Y}$). Thus, the individual self-insures against income risk by working more. With wage rate uncertainty ($Y = Y + \tilde{w}L$), Block and Heineke show that an increase in risk has an ambiguous effect. A dynamic model takes into account savings as well as labor effort, and thus it is not clear that the Block and Heineke results will hold.

The definition and measurement of risk aversion in situations where there are several goods has been studied by Kihlstrom and Mirman (1974, 1981). In addition, Stiglitz (1969) and Hanoch (1977) have investigated the implications of risk aversion for demands for commodities. All of these analyses take place in static models, however. The most important results for our purposes are those of Kihlstrom and Mirman, which indicate that with homothetic preferences and income risk, the risk preferences of the consumer are reflected by the indirect utility function considered as a function of income alone. Similarly, the dynamic, single-good models show that the value function in a dynamic programming approach to solving the problem embodies the curvature properties of the direct utility function (Miller 1976).

Our efforts along these lines are complicated by the production activities of the agricultural household. If we consider production decisions alone, the most relevant study is one by Pope and Kramer (1979) that examines production uncertainty for a competitive firm.[3] They find that, if the production function is multiplicative in the random variable (a form we assume in this paper), then an increase in risk reduces output if absolute risk aversion is decreasing. Our research extends their model to a dynamic setting.

The introduction of risk into a dynamic model of the agricultural household has two significant implications: (1) in general, the model is no longer separable into independent consumption and production activities, although a type of separability exists in one special case, and (2) restrictions on estimating equations derived from certainty theory are not appropriate when production is risky. These results hold even for our relatively simple special case, in which utility is additively separable over time, input and output prices are known, risk enters the production function multiplicatively, and production shocks are distributed independently over time.

A basic reason for the lack of separability is that risk aversion in consumption induces risk aversion where profits are concerned.[4] Thus, the expected utility of profits must be maximized. The form of this function depends on the form of the consumption utility function and consumption decisions.

A more fundamental reason for the lack of separability is the absence of a market. As discussed in chapter 1, separability of the static household production model obtains if a complete set of markets exists. Iqbal (chapter 6) extends this to a two-period model by introducing a capital market. In this chapter, with risk, separability does not hold because contingent claims markets do not exist; if contingent claims markets were introduced, separability would be restored. We believe, however, that positing such perfect insurance markets is inappropriate.[5]

The Conceptual Framework

The household gains utility from a sequence of consumptions of goods X_t and leisure X_{lt} over its time horizon $t = 0, 1, \ldots, T$ and from a bequest. The household's utility is given by an additively separable, time-invariant utility function:

$$(9\text{-}1) \quad U\!\left(\{\, X_t,\, X_{lt},\, b_t \}^{\,t=T}_{\,t=0}\right) = \sum_{t=1}^{t=T} \alpha^t u(X_t,\, X_{lt}) + \alpha^{T+1}\delta(b_{T+1}).$$

Here, as in the basic model presented in chapter 1, there are two goods: an agricultural staple, X_{qt}, and a good purchased in a market, X_{mt}. The household is assumed to hold a single financial asset, b_t. The discount factor $\alpha = (1 + e)^{-1}$, where e is the rate of utility discount; we assume that $0 < e < 1$.

Farm production of the agricultural staple is given by the stochastic production function

$$(9\text{-}2) \qquad\qquad Q_{t+1} = Q(L_t,\, A_t;\, \bar{\epsilon}_{t+1})$$

where L_t and A_t are labor and land inputs at t, and $\bar{\epsilon}_t$ is a random variable. Note that both labor and land are variable here, and that there is a lag in production. L_t and A_t are the sum of allocations to production out of the household's endowments, plus net market purchases of labor and land.

In contrast to the basic model of chapter 1, the model studied here is dynamic. The household consumes goods and leisure in period t from income generated by allocations of land and labor made in the previous period, $t - 1$. We assume that Q_t is known when (X_{qt}, X_{mt}, X_{lt}) are chosen. In period t, the household also decides upon the resource allocation (L_t, A_t), which determines output in the next period, $t + 1$. As with goods and leisure, we assume that Q_t is known when choices of A_t and L_t are made. Another departure from the basic model is the existence of a financial asset with rate of return, r. As we shall see, this asset serves to smooth intertemporal household consumption by linking, over time periods, the household's marginal utility of income. Note that b_t represents beginning-of-period holdings of the asset.

Markets for commodities, land, and labor are assumed to exist. The market prices of X_{qt} and X_{mt} are P_{qt} and P_{mt}, respectively. The rental rate for land is a_t and the wage is w_t.

Full income in period t can be expressed as the value of the household's endowment of land and time plus interest income plus profits, that is,

$$(9\text{-}3) \quad I_t = a_t \bar{A} + w_t \bar{L} + P_{qt}Q(L_{t-1}, A_{t-1}; \bar{\epsilon}_t) - a_t A_t - w_t L_t + (1 + r)b_t$$
$$= \bar{W}_t + \pi_t + (1 + r)b_t$$

where $\bar{A}$ and $\bar{L}$ represent endowments of land and labor, respectively. Expenditure on goods and leisure in period t is

$$(9\text{-}4) \qquad\qquad C_t = P_{qt}X_{qt} + P_{mt}X_{mt} + w_t X_{lt}.$$

Then, the holdings of the financial asset evolve according to

$$(9\text{-}5) \qquad\qquad b_{t+1} = I_t - C_t.$$

In summary, we have the following statement of the household's maximization problem:

$$\lambda: \max_{[z_t]} E \sum_t^T \alpha^t u(X_t, X_{lt}) + \alpha^{T+1}\delta(b_{T+1})$$

$$\text{s.t. } Q_{t+1} = Q(L_t, A_t; \bar{\epsilon}_{t+1})$$
$$b_{t+1} = \bar{W}_t + \pi_t - C_t + (1 + r)b_t$$

where
$$z_t = (X_{qt}, X_{mt}, X_{lt}, A_t, L_t).$$

Under an assumption that the stochastic process $[\epsilon_t]$ is a stationary Markov process, the solution to λ can usefully be studied using a dynamic programming approach. A Markov process is such that the probability distribution on $\bar{\epsilon}_{t+1}$ is conditional only on ϵ_t and not on the entire history of the process. Thus, we write the conditional distribution on the next period's realization of the random event (called the transition probability) as $\phi(\bar{\epsilon}_{t+1}, \epsilon_t)$.

Let $V^t(Q_t, b_t, \epsilon_t)$ be the value function for the household's problem at date t. $V^t(\cdot)$ gives the maximal expected present value of utility from date t to $T + 1$, starting with "initial" condition (Q_t, b_t, ϵ_t). Thus, V^0 is the indirect objective function for the overall problem; it is the dynamic equivalent of the household's indirect utility function. The dynamic programming approach to characterizing a solution to the problem makes use of the recursive relationship

$$(9\text{-}6) \quad V^t(Q_t, b_t, \epsilon_t) =$$

$$\sup_{\{z_t\}} [U(X_{qt}, X_{mt}, X_{lt}) + \alpha \int V^{t+1}(Q_{t+1}, b_{t+1}, \bar{\epsilon}_{t+1}) \, d\phi(\bar{\epsilon}_{t+1}, \epsilon_t)$$

$$|Q_{t+1} = Q(L_t, A_t; \bar{\epsilon}_{t+1}); b_{t+1} = \bar{W}_t + (1 + r)b_t + \pi_t - C_t].$$

In the terminology of dynamic programming, the state of the system at t is the vector (Q_t, b_t, ϵ_t). A plan is a map at each date giving the current action z_t as a function of the history of the state until t, that is, $z_t = z_t([Q_\tau, b_\tau, \epsilon_\tau]_{\tau=0}^{\tau=t})$. An optimal plan is a solution to λ. An optimal plan, if one exists, solves the functional equation in (9-6) at each date.

Under some fairly mild assumptions, it is possible to show that an optimal plan for our problem exists, is continuous, and depends only on the current state and not on the history of states. Furthermore, if the functions $u(\cdot)$ and $Q(\cdot)$ are strictly concave and p-times continuously differentiable, then if solutions are interior, it may be shown that the value function $V^t(\cdot)$ is p-times differentiable, and that the optimal plan $z_t^*(Q_t, b_t, \epsilon_t)$ is $(p - 1)$-times differentiable. The optimal plan can be obtained by applying the Implicit Function Theorem to the first-order, necessary (and sufficient, owing to strict concavity) conditions for the problem

$$(9\text{-}7) \qquad \max_{[z_t]} u(X_{qt}, X_{mt}, X_{lt}) + \alpha EV^{t+1}(Q_{t+1}, b_{t+1}, \bar{\epsilon}_{t+1}).$$

The statements in the previous two paragraphs are asserted without proof in this chapter since the proofs involve technical details that are not particularly interesting per se. (For a more formal analysis of a problem similar to the one stated here and for formal proofs of assertions in this chapter, see Graham-Tomasi and Roe 1985).

Characterizing a Solution

We turn now to a special case of the problem λ in which the production function for the agricultural staple takes the form

$$(9\text{-}8) \qquad Q(L_t, A_t; \bar{\epsilon}_{t+1}) = f(L_t, A_t)\, \bar{\epsilon}_{t+1}$$

and where the process $\{\epsilon_t\}$ is a sequence of independently and identically distributed random variables. For this special case, ϵ_t does not condition the distribution of $\bar{\epsilon}_{t+1}$. Thus, ϵ_t does not enter the value function directly as part of the state at t.

Let the price of goods and inputs be summarized by the vector $P_t = (P_{qt}, P_{mt}, w_t, a_t)$ and define

$$\delta^t(z_t; Q_t, b_t, P_t) = u(X_{qt}, X_{mt}, X_{lt}) + \alpha EV^{t+1}(Q_{t+1}, b_{t+1})$$

$$= u(X_{qt}, X_{mt}, X_{lt}) + \alpha EV^{t+1}(f(L_t, A_t)\,\epsilon,\, \bar{W}_t + (1 + r)b_t$$

$$+ P_{qt}Q_t - w_t L_t - a_t A_t - P_{qt}X_{qt} - P_{mt}X_{mt} - w_t X_{lt}).$$

Our discussion above indicates that z_t can be characterized by studying the first-order necessary conditions

$$(9\text{-}9) \qquad 0 = \frac{\partial \delta^t}{\partial X_{qt}} = \frac{\partial u}{\partial X_{qt}} - \alpha P_{qt} E\left(\frac{\partial V^{t+1}}{\partial b_{t+1}}\right)$$

$$(9\text{-}10) \qquad 0 = \frac{\partial \delta^t}{\partial X_{mt}} = \frac{\partial u}{\partial X_{mt}} - \alpha P_{mt} E\left(\frac{\partial V^{t+1}}{\partial b_{t+1}}\right)$$

$$(9\text{-}11) \qquad 0 = \frac{\partial \delta^t}{\partial X_{lt}} = \frac{\partial u}{\partial X_{lt}} - \alpha w_t E\left(\frac{\partial V^{t+1}}{\partial b_{t+1}}\right)$$

$$(9\text{-}12) \qquad 0 = \frac{\partial \delta^t}{\partial L_t} = \alpha E\left(\frac{\partial V^{t+1}}{\partial Q_{t+1}} \frac{\partial f}{\partial L_t}\epsilon\right) - w_t \alpha E\left(\frac{\partial V^{t+1}}{\partial b_{t+1}}\right)$$

$$(9\text{-}13) \qquad 0 = \frac{\partial \delta^t}{\partial A_t} = \alpha E\left(\frac{\partial V^{t+1}}{\partial Q_{t+1}} \frac{\partial f}{\partial A_t}\epsilon\right) - a_t \alpha E\left(\frac{\partial V^{t+1}}{\partial b_{t+1}}\right).$$

We now offer some economic interpretations of these conditions. First, (9-9), (9-10), and (9-11) imply

$$(9\text{-}14) \qquad \frac{\partial u/\partial X_{qt}}{P_{qt}} = \frac{\partial u/\partial X_{mt}}{P_{mt}} = \frac{\partial u/\partial X_{lt}}{w_t}.$$

This, of course, is the familiar result from static certainty theory that goods and leisure are consumed so as to equate marginal rates of substitution to price ratios. Thus, the household allocates the amount it decides to spend on consumption in accordance with the usual efficiency principles.

Intertemporal allocations of goods can be characterized by considering $V^{t+1}(\cdot)$. By definition,

$$(9\text{-}15) \quad V^{t+1}(Q_{t+1}, b_{t+1}) \max_{z_{t+1}} \equiv \delta^{t+1}(\cdot) = u(X_{qt+1}, X_{mqt+1}, X_{lt+1})$$
$$+ \alpha E V^{t+2}(Q_{t+2}, b_{t+2}).$$

As with choices of z_t, we have the following necessary condition for X_{qt+1}:

$$(9\text{-}16) \qquad 0 = \frac{\partial \delta^{t+1}}{\partial X_{qt+1}} = \frac{\partial u}{\partial X_{qt+1}} - \alpha P_{qt+1} E\left(\frac{\partial V^{t+2}}{\partial b_{t+2}}\right).$$

From (9-15) we also have

$$(9\text{-}17) \qquad \frac{\partial V^{t+1}}{\partial b_{t+1}} = \alpha E\left(\frac{\partial V^{t+2}}{\partial b_{t+2}}\right)(1 + r).$$

Substituting (9-17) into (9-16) yields

$$(9\text{-}18) \qquad \frac{\partial u}{\partial X_{qt+1}} \frac{(1 + r)}{P_{qt+1}} = \frac{\partial V^{t+1}}{\partial b_{t+1}}.$$

When X_{qt+1} is chosen, b_{t+1} is known. To compare this with the choice of X_{qt} so as to depict how the household plans to allocate consumption

through time, we must take the expectation of (9-18), conditional on information available at date t, and substitute into (9-9). After rearrangement,
we obtain

$$\frac{\partial u/\partial X}{P_{qt}} = \frac{E(\partial u/\partial X_{qt+1})/(1 + e)}{P_{qt+1}/(1 + r)}.$$

Thus, as in (9-14), the household equates the marginal rate of substitution
between current consumption and the expected present value of future
consumption (discounting at the utility discount rate) of a good to the ratio
of current price to present value future price (discounting at the rate of
return on the financial asset) of that good.

On the production side, our model can be given familiar interpretations
as well. From (9-15), we have

(9-19) $$\frac{\partial V^{t+1}}{\partial Q_{t+1}} = \alpha P_{qt+1} E\left(\frac{\partial V^{t+2}}{\partial b_{t+2}}\right).$$

Substituting (9-17) into (9-19), taking expectations, and substituting the resulting expression into (9-13) yields

(9-20) $$E\left[\frac{\partial V^{t+1}}{\partial b_{t+1}}\left(\frac{P_{qt+1}}{(1 + r)}\ \frac{\partial f}{\partial A_t}(\cdot)\ \epsilon_{t+1} - a_t\right)\right] = 0.$$

This is a first-order condition for a firm with risk preferences represented by
the utility function $V^{t+1}(\cdot)$ if it were to maximize the expected utility of
profits. In our model, costs are incurred at date t and output sold at date
$t + 1$; hence, the output price is discounted.[6] Of course, a similar expression holds for the labor input.

It is possible to show that the usual static efficiency conditions concerning the choice of inputs holds in our framework. To see this, divide (9-12) by
(9-13) to get

$$\frac{E\left(\dfrac{\partial V^{t+1}}{\partial Q_{t+1}}\ \dfrac{\partial f}{\partial L_t}\ \epsilon\right)}{E\left(\dfrac{\partial V^{t+1}}{\partial Q_{t+1}}\ \dfrac{\partial f}{\partial A_t}\ \epsilon\right)} = \frac{w_t}{a_t}.$$

But, when evaluated at optimal choices L_t^* and A_t^*, the derivatives $\partial f/\partial L_t$
and $\partial f/\partial A_t$ are constants. Thus, they can be taken out of the expectations
operation to achieve

(9-21) $$\frac{\partial f/\partial L_t}{\partial f/\partial A_t} = \frac{w_t}{a_t}.$$

This is a direct consequence of using a multiplicative form for our production function, as stated in (9-8). A similar result was derived by Pope and Kramer (1979) in a static model.

Returning to equation (9-20), we see why the model is not separable into consumption and production aspects of the household's problem. The function $V^t(\cdot)$ is a value function and therefore depends on the maximized quantities of all choice variables, including consumption goods. The consumption goods enter $V^{t+1}(\cdot)$ through the transition equation on assets. The risk preferences for solving the problem of maximizing the expected utility of profit must be derived from the household's preferences for income risk and ultimately from their preferences concerning consumption variability. Moreover, the results available from the theory of the firm and the theory of the consumer under uncertainty do not, in general, carry over to our nonseparable model.

Increases in Risk

It is apparent from the first-order condition stated in (9-9)–(9-13) that general comparative statics results with regard to changes in prices of goods and inputs and changes in the interest rate can be obtained in the usual fashion. At the same time, obtaining these results will be tedious because many choice variables and parameters exist in our model. To see the issues more clearly, we focus on a specific functional form of the general model presented above. In this case, unambiguous results can be obtained and problems of empirical application are more apparent.

A Specific Model

This simplification enables us to derive functional forms of the household's output-supply and commodity- and factor-demand equations and a value function exhibiting constant absolute risk aversion (CARA); it is similar to the form of the indirect utility function derived by Stiglitz. This derivation also demonstrates a type of separability between the household's production and consumption decisions. An empirical example of the model is also presented. Although the model was initialized to household data from the Dominican Republic, the empirical results are only intended to illustrate and provide further insight into the relationship between yield variance, risk aversion, and the household's choices, and thus, by implication, to suggest some of the likely consequences of not accounting for this type of behavior in the more traditional nonstochastic model of the agricultural household.

The specific form of the household's additively separable, time-invariant utility function corresponding to (9-1) is

$$U\left(\{X_{qt}, X_{mt}, X_{lt}\}_{t=0}^{t=T}\right)$$

$$= \sum_{t=0}^{t=T} (-\alpha^t \exp\{-\pi_i X_{it}^{\alpha_i}\}) + \alpha^{T+1}(-\exp\{-K(b_{T+1})\}),$$

where $i = q, m, l$. As shown below, it is important that the coefficients for α_i are positive and sum to unity. Hence, the direct utility function is a negative exponential where the exponential is a Cobb-Douglas (C-D) function, homogeneous of degree 1.

No production is assumed to occur in the terminal period $T + 1$ so, with respect to dynamic programming, the household's problem is to choose $X_{qt}, X_{mt},$ and X_{lt} to maximize terminal period utility subject to a given level of assets b_{T+1}. In this case, it is easily shown that the terminal period utility is given by

(9-22) $$-\exp\{-kb_{T+1}\} = -\exp\{-\pi_i \alpha_i^{\alpha_i} P^{-\alpha_i}_{iT+1} b_{T+1}\}$$

$$= -\exp\{-k(b_{T+1})\}$$

for $i = q, m, l$. The exponent of b_{T+1} on the LHS of (9-22) is unity because of the assumption that the values of α_i sum to one.

To simplify the problem, we eliminate the production lag, and for convenience, let production be given by the C-D production function

$$Q_t = \bar{Q}_t \epsilon = cL^{\gamma_1} A^{1-\gamma_1} \epsilon, \qquad\qquad 0 < \gamma_1 < 1$$

where $\epsilon \sim i^{id} N(1, V[\epsilon])$.[7] The problem is further simplified by assuming that prices remain unchanged—hence no time subscript appears on k in (9-22)—and by focusing on only two periods. The two-period assumption reduces the number of arguments in the t-th period value function, but otherwise it does not alter the nature of the problem. The state variable b_{t+1} is given by

$$b_{t+1} = P_q Q_t - aA_t - wL_t + (1 + r)b_t + a\bar{A}$$

$$+ w\bar{L} - P_q X_{qt} - P_m X_{mt} - wX_{lt}.$$

Under the above assumptions, the two-period problem can be stated as

$$\max_{\{z_i\}} - \exp\{-\pi_i X_{it}^{\alpha_i}\} + \alpha E[-\alpha \exp\{-kb_{t+1}\}]$$

or, from the moment-generating function, it can be stated as

$$\max_{\{z_i\}} - \exp\{-\pi_i X_{it}^{\alpha_i}\} - \alpha \exp\{-k(\bar{b}_{t+1} - .5k(P_q \bar{Q}_t)^2 V(\epsilon))\}$$

where $\bar{b}_{t+1}$ is the mean of b_{t+1}.

From the first-order necessary conditions, (9-14) implies the result, familiar to C-D forms, $X_{it} = (\alpha_i P_j / \alpha_j P_i) X_{jt}$ in the case of consumption, and (9-21) implies the result $L_t = (\gamma_1 a / (1 - \gamma_1) w) A_t$ in production. Moreover, the equivalent of (9-20) in this case is simply

$$P_q (\partial \bar{Q}_t / \partial L_t) - w - k P_q^2 \bar{Q}_t (\partial \bar{Q}_t / L_t) V(\epsilon) = 0$$

and similarly for A_t. This result is obtained because of the restrictions placed on the α_i. This result suggests a type of separability in the sense that production choices can be made independently of consumption choices. Contrary to the traditional nonstochastic version of the household model, however, preferences over goods and leisure affect input choice through the parameters embodied in k. Furthermore, risk aversion, as determined by k, is also a function of prices P_q, P_m, and w. Hence, contrary to most treatments of decisionmaking under risk, the simple model illustrated here serves to reinforce the point made in the preceding section that production depends on the properties of the direct utility function. Moreover, risk aversion (even in the case of constant absolute risk aversion) is not constant, but varies with changes in prices of the arguments appearing in the direct utility function.

The demand and supply functions are derived from the first-order necessary conditions and the transversality condition. It can be verified that the household functions are

(9-23) $X_{it} = (\alpha_i / 2 P_i)(Y_t - (\log \alpha) / k)$, $i = q, m; l$

where Y_t is the utility certainty-equivalent income given by

$$Y_t = P_q \bar{Q}_t - a A_t - w L_t + (1 + r) b_t + a \bar{A} + w \bar{L} - .5k (P_t \bar{Q}_t)^2 V[\epsilon].$$

The last term in (9-23) accounts for the substitution relationship between the utility the household obtains from current (relative to future) consumption. Since the discount term (α) is a fraction, its log is negative and thus serves to augment certainty-equivalent income as preferences for current utility from current (relative to future) consumption increases. The "2" in the denominator "divides" certainty-equivalent income between the current and the next period. Otherwise, (9-23) bears a close resemblance to the familiar demand functions derived from a direct utility function of the C-D form.

These results show more explicitly the nature of the empirical biases that might arise when the influence of risk aversion on the household's consumption choices is omitted. The compensated price elasticity terms derived from the demand equations (if we assume that they can be identified) are likely to be unaffected by risk attitudes. This result is also suggested by (9-14). However, the profit effect on consumption (equation [1-7], chapter 1) from a change in the price of a good (staple) produced by the household

Table 9-1. *Selected Results Illustrating the Effects of Yield Risk on Choice Variables*

Item	Unit	Values used to initialize model	Base solution of model	Solutions obtained for two levels of yield risk measured relative to base solution[a]	
				Low risk	High risk
Household rice consumption[b]	Kilograms/ household[c]	48.9	42.2	55.6	34.2
Rice price	U.S. dollars/ kilogram	0.352		unchanged	
Consumption of other goods[b]	Index	91.2	173.4	228.4	140.4
Price of other goods	Index	1.5		unchanged	
Total expenditure[b]	U.S. dollars per household	154.0	275.0	362.1	222.7
Production, labor input[b]	Hours per hectare	1,072.0	1,066.6	1,066.6	1,066.6
Land in rice[b]	Hectare	5.2	4.8	6.4	3.9
Yield[b]	Kilograms per hectare	3,127.0	5,879.0	5,879.0	5,879.0
Land rental rate	U.S. dollars per hectare	448.0		unchanged	
Labor wage	U.S. dollars per hour	0.42		unchanged	
Sales[b]	Quintals per year	162.1	282.8	377.1	226.3
Net labor allocation[b]	Hours per year[d]	3,231.5	1,783.9	4,411.3	207.5
Net land allocation[b]	Hectares per year[d]	n.a.	−0.372	1.2	−1.3
State variable $b(t+1)$	100 U.S. dollars per year	n.a.	43.13	57.3	34.7

n.a. Not applicable.

a. Yield risk of the base solution was augmented by the multiples 0.75 and 1.25 for the respective low and high yield risk solutions.

b. Denotes choice variables.

c. Rice consumed is in terms of rough rice.

d. Positive (negative) values denote quantities of hired (off farm) labor and similarly for land.

will likely be overestimated if risk is present in the form considered here. That is to say, the income effect of a price change in a good the household produces is likely to be overestimated because the traditional model ignores the risk discount term, which will increase in value (and thus decrease income) since $\partial(.5k(P_qQ_t)^2V[\epsilon])/\partial P_q > 0$.

The factor-demand functions can be verified to be of the form:

$$L_t = (P_q - \gamma_1^{-\gamma_1}\gamma_2^{-\gamma_2} a^{\gamma_2}w^{\gamma_1}c^{-1})/kP_q^2 \, V[\epsilon]\gamma_1^{-\gamma_2}\gamma_2^{-\gamma_2}a^{-\gamma_2}w^{\gamma_2}c \quad \text{and}$$

(9-24)

$$A_t = (P_q - \gamma_1^{-\gamma_1}\gamma_2^{-\gamma_2} a^{\gamma_2}w^{\gamma_1}c^{-1})/kP_q^2 \, V[\epsilon]\gamma_1^{\gamma_1}\gamma_2^{-\gamma_1}a^{\gamma_1}w^{-\gamma_1}c$$

where $\gamma_2 = 1 - \gamma_1$. Hence, planned supply is

$$\bar{Q}_t = (P_qc - \gamma_1^{-\gamma_1}\gamma_2^{-\gamma_2}a^{\gamma_2}w^{\gamma_1})/ckP_q^2V[\epsilon].$$

As already pointed out, these production relationships include k, which contains the parameters and the prices of the arguments appearing in the direct utility function. This is an important departure from the literature, where k is related to the Arrow-Pratt coefficient and, in the case of CARA, simply treated as a constant. In this sense, the problem is not separable. Because of the restrictions placed on the parameters (α_i) of the direct utility function, however, the problem can be treated as though the household sought to maximize certainty-equivalent income (Y_t), and then as though it sought to choose the levels of goods and leisure to consume, subject to certainty-equivalent income adjusted for the discount factor $\log(\alpha)/k$.

The biases in empirical estimates of the household's production choices from ignoring risk when it is present in the context of the model developed here is to overestimate the quantity of output and the resources allocated to production, and to underestimate the resources allocated to off-farm activities.

An Empirical Example

To provide some insight into the possible magnitudinal implications of risk aversion and yield variance on the household's choices, we initialized the model to farm household data from the Dominican Republic for the crop year 1975–76. Only those agricultural households reporting rice as their sole cash crop were selected for this illustration.

The utility function parameters chosen were $(\alpha_q, \alpha_m, \alpha_l) = (0.01, 0.175, 0.815)$, and the production parameters were $(c, \gamma_1) = (180, 0.5)$. The other key data used to initialize the model appear in the third column of table 9-1. The base solution to which other solutions of the model are compared is reported in the fourth column. The values reported in the remaining two columns are the results obtained from parametrically ranging yield variance by ∓ 25 percent (denoted low- and high-risk, respectively) of the yield variance assumed in the base solution.

As implied by (9-23), an increase in yield variance results in a decrease in current period consumption; when yield variance increased by 25 percent, the quantity of rice consumed decreased by about 19 percent. Condition (9-14), together with the homothenticity of the direct utility function, requires that the ratio of rice consumed to other goods consumed and to leisure remain unchanged to variations in yield variance. Thus the consumption of these items decreased accordingly.

Figure 9.1. *Relation of Yield Variance to Commodity Expenditure Net Market Labor Supply, and Net Market Land Supply*

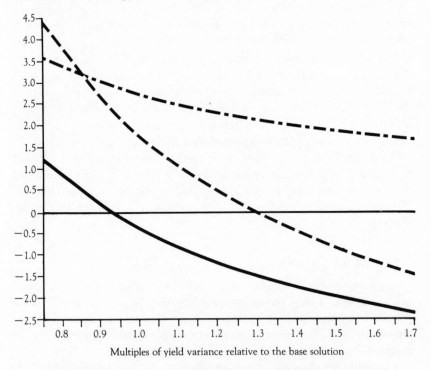

Multiples of yield variance relative to the base solution

Note: ▬ ▪ ▬ Expenditures on rice and other goods in hundreds of U.S. dollars
▬ ▬ ▬ Net labor market position; positive (negative) values denote hours of hired (off-farm) labor in thousands of hours.
▬▬▬ Net land market position; positive (negative) values denote hectares rented in (out).

An increase in yield variance also induces the household to decrease the quantity of rice produced by about 19 percent. Since the production function is homogeneous of degree 1, it follows from (9-21) that the labor-land ratio and rice yields remain unchanged. The increase in yield variance induces the household to increase the amount of land rented out and to decrease the amount of labor hired, and at the same time to reduce the amount of leisure consumed. In spite of the household's efforts to avoid the disutility of increases in the variance of yields (and hence income), assets transferred to the next period (b_{t+1}) decline.

It is clear from (9-23), (9-24), and the results reported in table 9-1 that declining consumption and the transfer of resources to other activities are not a linear function of changes in yield variance. The empirical nature of this nonlinearity for the example considered here can be gleaned from figure 9-1, where numerous solutions of the model are charted showing changes in the household's choices to various levels of yield risk. As yield variance increases, the welfare of the household becomes dependent on labor, land, and asset markets. It is possible for the household to reach a point where it withdraws all of its land and labor resources from rice production.

Asset holdings, certainty-equivalent income and the quantity of rice sold are charted in figure 9-2. Rice sales decline as resources are withdrawn from rice production, in spite of the decline in the quantity of rice consumed by the household. At a sufficiently high yield variance, the household will become a deficit producer of rice. The level of asset holdings will also depend on the "riskless" alternatives the household faces in the asset, land, and labor markets. Similarly, the level of certainty-equivalent income will tend to converge, though at diminishing rates, with the income earned from the resources that the household allocates to these markets.

Duality and Risk Aversion

Duality results are useful for providing restrictions on parameters in empirical investigations. For example, Hotelling's Lemma (Varian 1978) and the symmetry of cross second derivatives (Young's Theorem) establish the symmetry of derivatives of input demands with respect to factor prices.

The value function $V^t(.)$ is a dynamic indirect utility function. As such, one would expect that an analogue of Roy's Identity would emerge relating the demand for goods and the derivatives of the value function.

Let

$$z^*(P_t) \equiv (X_{qt}^* (P_t) - Q_t^*, X_{mt}^* (P_t), L_t^* (P_t) + X_{lt}^* (P_t) - \bar{L}, A_t^*(P_t) - \bar{A}).$$

Figure 9.2. *Relation of Yield Variance to Asset Holdings,*
Certainty-Equivalent Income, and Sales of Rice

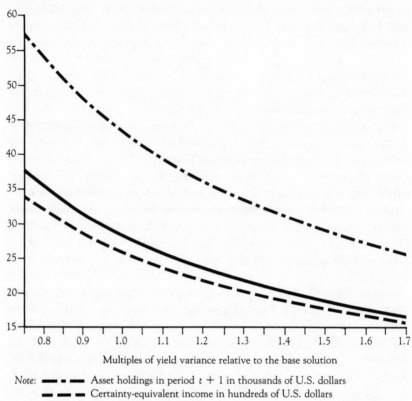

Multiples of yield variance relative to the base solution

Note: ▬ ▪ ▬ ▪ ▬ Asset holdings in period $t + 1$ in thousands of U.S. dollars
           ▬ ▬ ▬ Certainty-equivalent income in hundreds of U.S. dollars
           ▬▬▬▬ Sales of rice in tens of quintals

The first component of this optimal choice vector is the household's demand for the agricultural staple net of current supply. The third component is the household's net position in the labor market; that is, it is purchases of market labor minus the hours the household works off the farm.
Thus, it is net demand for labor. Of course, it may be negative, and the
household may be a net supplier of labor. Similarly, the last component is
the household's net position in the rental market for land.

Differentiation of the value function and use of the envelope theorem
constitutes a proof of the following analogy of Roy's Identity:

$$(9\text{-}25) \qquad z^*(P_t) = - \nabla_{p_t} V^t(Q_t, b_t) / \alpha \partial E(V^{t+1}(\cdot)/\partial b_{t+1})$$

where $\nabla_{p_t} V^t$ is the gradient vector of partial derivatives of V^t with respect to
prices. The denominator, the expected value of the marginal utility of

wealth, plays the role of the derivative of the indirect utility function with respect to income in Roy's Identity.

Two points are worth noting. First, the market surplus and demand for purchased goods correspond to similar results obtained from applying the equivalent of (9-25) to the static model. The component for labor reflects net positions in the market as well as leisure decisions and the household's endowment.

Second, the results indicating net factor demand correspond to the duality results obtained by Pope (1980, equation [8]) for the risk averse firm under price uncertainty. As Pope (1978) has shown, no simple and general comparative static results are obtainable from the static model under uncertainty without additional restrictions on the form of the utility function. Thus, it is clear from (9-25) that no simple and general results can be derived from the general model. The efficiency in production results (9-21) suggests that properties of the cost function and the corresponding conditional factor demand functions are, with one exception, identical to those obtained from static efficiency theory. The exception is that the output $(\bar{Q}_t)$ variable is planned (and hence not observable) rather than realized output.

For the type of separability that exists in the specific model discussed in the preceding section, note that the first-order conditions are identical to those obtained from maximizing certainty-equivalent income, Y_t. In this case, the term $E\{\partial V^{t+1}(Q_{t+1}, b_{t+1})/\partial b_{t+1}\}$ does not appear, so that L_t^* and A_t^* follow directly from the envelope theorem. However, Q_t^* does not follow from the theorem because P_{qt} appears in the risk-premium term of Y_t. From the Hessian of this problem, it can be shown that the sign of $\partial A_t^*/\partial a_t$ and $\partial L_t^*/\partial w_t$ cannot be established, although symmetry of the cross partial derivatives holds.

It is important to point out that equation (9-25) greatly depends on our assumptions that the production shocks are independently distributed and that the prices are fixed and known. Suppose, to the contrary, that production shocks form a Markov process and that they induce a Markov process on prices. Then, the current prices will condition the distribution of the future prices. In this circumstance, a derivative of $V^t(\cdot)$ with respect to price affects the choice variable both directly and indirectly through an alteration in the household's subjective probability estimate of future prices (Taylor 1984).

Discussion

In this brief chapter, we have attempted to introduce production risk into a model of the agricultural household in as simple a manner as possible.

Even then, the analysis of the model becomes difficult. The main problem is that, when risk is introduced, separability of the model into independent consumption and production "sides" no longer obtains in most cases. This lack of separability severely complicates both the analysis of the theoretical model and the empirical estimation of the model's parameters.

It is important to estimate these parameters, however, since many policy-relevant results are ambiguous on a theoretical level and need to be determined empirically. If risk and risk aversion are ignored, misleading inference may be made. The specific model described here suggests that the income effect of an increase in the price of a staple might significantly overestimate the level of resources employed in its production. The consideration of risk also clearly establishes the importance of markets that permit households to self-insure against increasing yield risk.

Our analysis raises several issues that suggest further research along these lines. We can mention only a few of these possibilities here. Obviously, it would be useful to know what alternative forms for utility and production functions, in combination with distributions on the random variable, imply for behavior toward risk and the effects of increases in risk. This type of information would clarify the results of our model under plausible representations of household activities and thus have some bearing on policy decisions. If increases in risk reduce consumption and production intensity, for example, institutions that allow more efficient risk sharing could increase output and consumption. Furthermore, findings establishing relationships between functional forms and comparative statics results (such as the type of separability found in the specific model) could guide researchers toward appropriate tests of the theory and away from imposing results by assumption.

The model could also be elaborated further with respect to the form of the production function. This should be generalized in two ways. First, work by Pope and Kramer (1979) demonstrates that the assumption of multiplicative risk is quite special. In particular, this assumption allows us to conclude that factors are used in accord with static efficiency principles (equation [9-21]). As well, the multiplicative form implies that all inputs increase risk. More general formulations that are tractable yet allow risk-reducing inputs have been proposed.[8] Second, we have assumed that all inputs must be chosen before the realization of the random variable is known. The literature on the firm under price uncertainty informs us that the *timing* of the resolution of uncertainty relative to the timing of input choices strongly influences what effect an increase in risk will have on production decisions.[9]

In this context, it would seem reasonable to allow the household some ex post flexibility. Although inputs associated with planting are fixed, for example, irrigation decisions can be altered in response to the current realization of rainfall. The substitution possibilities between these ex ante and ex post inputs will be important in establishing the response of factor use to increase in risk. This would also apply in a model with investment in durable capital.

A third possible generalization of the model would be to provide for the production of multiple goods. This permits us to understand a household's choice of crop portfolio. One would conjecture that covariances of yields across crops would prove to be important for policy decisions where some crops are grown for consumption and some for export.

It seems odd to construct a model with quantity risk but no price variability, especially when production shocks are correlated across large numbers of households. Price variability can be incorporated into the model by considering joint distributions on prices and production shocks. It is possible to define and study increases in risk in this situation as well (see Epstein 1978). As mentioned earlier, however, if prices are not independently distributed, then duality results become difficult to interpret. If all of the risk in prices is due to production risk, independence may be a reasonable assumption.

In considering the relationship between price risk and production risk, we encounter one of the many issues involved in moving from a single-agent to a market model. In particular, and as is well-known, we have to make some assessment of or assumption about how agents form expectations. This, in turn, raises some controversial economic issues that must squarely be faced in future research.

Notes

1. For a description of how farmers diversify crop production activities in order to lower the variation in their income associated with yield risk, see Walker and Jodha (1985).

2. Leland (1968) considers income uncertainty in a two-period model with a utility function that is not additively separable over time—that is, one of the form $U(C_1, C_2)$. He finds that if $(\partial^2 U/\partial C_2^2)/(\partial U/\partial C_2)$ is increasing in C_1 and decreasing in C_2, then savings increase with increasing uncertainty. Sandmo (1970) also obtained this result for small risks. Mirman (1971) studies an additively separable utility function $U(C_1, C_2) = U^1(C_1) + U^2(C_2)$ in a two-period model. He shows that with rate of return uncertainty, period-1 savings increase (decrease) with an increase in uncertainty if $C_2 dU^2(C_2)/dC_2$ is a convex (concave) function. Dreze and Modigliani (1972) provide a comprehensive exploration of the two-period model, including income and substitution effects of increasing uncertainty.

Phelps (1962) established, in an infinite horizon model with additively separable utility, that if the preperiod utility function exhibits decreasing absolute risk aversion, then an increase in income uncertainty increases savings. Miller (1976) generalizes the Phelps result somewhat. Miller demonstrates that, with an infinite horizon and additively separable utility function, consumption decreases when the sequence of incomes becomes more risky in the sense of Rothschild and

Stiglitz (1970) if the marginal utility of consumption is convex. A similar result is obtained by Sibley (1975) for a finite horizon model. A more complete review is provided by Lippman and McCall (1981).

3. There is a large literature on firms facing price uncertainty. A good summary and treatment can be found in Epstein (1978).

4. Many analyses of firms under price uncertainty posit some form of a utility function over profits without explaining where such a utility function comes from. A virtue of the household production model is that risk preferences concerning profit are deduced from risk preferences over consumption. That the introduction of risk may eliminate separability was pointed out by Barnum and Squire (1979, p. 39, n. 16).

5. Thus, general equilibrium models (with consumer incomes tied to firm profits), in which contingent claims markets do not exist and risk neutral behavior on the part of firms is posited, may be inconsistent. A set of securities that spans the states of nature may replace contingent claims markets (Arrow 1964).

6. To see this, consider the problem

$$\max_X EU(\pi); \ \pi = pf(X) - w \cdot x.$$

First-order conditions are

$$E\left[U'(\pi) \left(p \frac{\partial f}{\partial X_j} - w_j \right) \right] = 0 \quad \text{for all } j.$$

7. The normality assumption implies that a nonzero probability exists for negative and extremely high yield. The alternative is to apply the formulas for the moments of a truncated normal distribution (see Johnson and Kotz 1970, pp. 81–83) or to maintain that the variance of ϵ is sufficiently small that our treatment leads to a good approximation of the actual distribution of yields. Another alternative is to permit ϵ to be distributed log normal. Levy (1973) shows that mean variance analysis applied to a log normal distribution is a sufficient decision rule for all nondecreasing, strictly concave utility functions. In any case, the more rigorous approach of employing the formulas of a truncated normal distribution would seem to clutter unnecessarily the key purpose of the task at hand. Hence, we proceed with the normality assumption.

8. Pope and Kramer (1979) suggest the form

$$F(A, L; \epsilon) = f(A, L) + h(A, L)\epsilon,$$

which admits risk-reducing inputs, depending on the shape of the function $h(.)$. An input is risk-reducing (increasing) if risk averse producers use more (less) of it than a risk neutral producer. One of the basic implications of our analysis is that risk neutrality does not make sense once consumers are added to the model explicitly, except under stringent assumptions.

9. For a review of earlier work in this area, see, for example, Epstein (1978).

References

Arrow, K. 1964. "The Role of Securities in the Optimal Allocation of Risk-Bearing." *Review of Economic Studies*, vol. 31, pp. 91–96.

Barnum, H., and L. Squire. 1979. *A Model of an Agricultural Household: Theory and Evidence*. Washington, D.C.: World Bank.

Binswanger, H. 1980. "Attitudes toward Risk: Experimental Measurement in Rural India." *American Journal of Agricultural Economics*, vol. 62, pp. 395–407.

Block, M., and J. Heineke. 1973. "The Allocation of Effort under Uncertainty: The Case of Risk Averse Behavior." *Journal of Political Economy*, vol. 81, pp. 376–85.

Dillon, J., and P. Scandizzo. 1978. "Risk Attitudes of Subsistence Farmers in Northeast Brazil." *American Journal of Agricultural Economics*, vol. 60, pp. 425–35.

Dreze, J., and F. Modigliani. 1972. "Consumption Decisions under Uncertainty." *Journal of Economic Theory*, vol. 5, pp. 308–35.

Epstein, L. 1978. "Production Flexibility and the Behavior of the Competitive Firm under Price Uncertainty." *Review of Economic Studies*, vol. 45, pp. 251–61.

Graham-Tomasi, T., and T. Roe. 1985. "Production Uncertainty and the Behavior of the Agricultural Household." University of Minnesota, St. Paul. Processed.

Hanoch, G. 1977. "Risk Aversion and Consumer Preferences." *Econometrica*, vol. 45, pp. 413–26.

Johnson, N. L. and S. Kotz. 1970. *Distribution in Statistics: Continuous Univariate Distributions*. Vols. 1 and 2. Boston, Mass.: Houghton Mifflin.

Kihlstrom, R., and L. Mirman. 1974. "Risk Aversion with Many Commodities." *Journal of Economic Theory*, vol. 8, pp. 361–88.

———. 1981. "Constant, Increasing, and Decreasing Risk Aversion with Many Commodities." *Review of Economic Studies*, vol. 48, pp. 271–80.

Leland, H. 1968. "Saving and Uncertainty: The Precautionary Demand for Saving." *Quarterly Journal of Economics*, vol. 82, pp. 465–73.

Levy, H. 1973. "Stochastic Dominance among Log-Normal Prospects." *International Economic Review*, vol. 14, pp. 601–14.

Lippman, S., and J. McCall. 1981. "The Economics of Uncertainty: Selected Topics and Probabilistic Methods." In *Handbook of Mathematical Economics*, vol. 1. Edited by K. Arrow and M. Intriligator. Amsterdam: North-Holland.

Miller, B. 1976. "The Effect on Optimal Consumption of Increased Uncertainty in Labor Income in the Multiperiod Case." *Journal of Economic Theory*, vol. 13, pp. 154–67.

Mirman, L. 1971. "Uncertainty and Optimal Consumption Decisions." *Econometrica*, vol. 39, pp. 179–85.

Moscardi, E., and A. de Janvry. 1977. "Attitudes towards Risk among Peasants: An Econometric Approach." *American Journal of Agricultural Economics*, vol. 59, pp. 710–16.

Phelps, E. 1962. "The Accumulation of Risky Capital: A Sequential Utility Analysis." *Econometrica*, vol. 30, pp. 299–343.

Pope, Rulon D. 1978. "The Expected Utility Hypothesis and Supply Demand Restriction." *American Journal of Agricultural Economics*, vol. 62, pp. 619–27.

———. 1980. "The Generalized Envelope Theorem and Price Uncertainty." *International Economic Review*, vol. 21, pp. 75–86.

Pope, Rulon D., and R. Kramer. 1979. "Production Uncertainty and Factor Demands for the Competitive Firm." *Southern Economics Journal*, vol. 46, pp. 489–501.

Rothschild, M., and J. Stiglitz. 1970. "Increasing Risk I: A Definition." *Journal of Economic Theory*, vol. 2, pp. 225–43.

Sandmo, A. 1970. "The Effect of Uncertainty on Saving Decisions." *Review of Economic Studies*, vol. 37, pp. 353–60.

Sibley, D. 1975. "Permanent and Transitory Income Effects in a Model of Consumption with Wage Income Uncertainty." *Journal of Economic Theory*, vol. 11, pp. 68–82.

Stiglitz, J. 1969. "Behavior towards Risk with Many Commodities." *Econometrica*, vol. 3, pp. 660–67.

Taylor, C. 1984. "Stochastic Dynamic Duality: Theory and Empirical Applicability." *American Journal of Agricultural Economics*, vol. 66, pp. 351–57.

Varian, H. 1978. *Microeconomic Analysis*. New York: Norton.

Walker, T., and N. Jodha. 1985. "How Small Farm Households Adapt to Risk." In *Agricultural Risks and Insurance: Issues in Policy*. Edited by P. Hazell, C. Pomareda, and A. Valdes. Baltimore, Md.: Johns Hopkins University Press.

10

Using a Farm-Household Model to Analyze Labor Allocation on a Chinese Collective Farm

Terry Sicular

FARM-HOUSEHOLD MODELS are often used to analyze household labor allocation in agriculture in developing countries. Since these models incorporate both the consumption and production aspects of household decisionmaking, they capture the essential considerations underlying the allocation of family time between leisure and work. Moreover, they provide a framework for understanding household participation in labor markets as suppliers of family labor or as employers of hired labor.

The farm-household approach is equally useful for analyzing labor allocation within Chinese collective farms. In the People's Republic of China, the basic collective farm unit has been the production team. Production teams normally embraced the population and land surrounding a village. In 1979, the average number of households in a team was 34 and the population 157 (Chang and Luo 1980, p. 5). Although collective farms in China comprised a number of households, they were nonetheless farm units making dual production and consumption decisions. On the production side, collective farms chose the patterns and methods of cultivation on collective land and the mix between cultivation and other sideline activities. These production decisions implied certain derived demands for labor and a seasonal distribution of labor use. On the consumption side, collective farms planned for desired levels of collective income, both in kind and in cash, and for its distribution among members.

Note: This research was supported by a grant from the U.S.-China National Scholarly Exchange Program and by generous assistance from Yale University and the University of Wisconsin-Madison. I would like to thank N. R. Lardy, R. E. Evenson, J. M. Montias, W. P. Falcon, and J. Strauss for their helpful comments on earlier versions.

In these respects, Chinese collective farms have resembled farm house-holds elsewhere and so lend themselves to farm-household analysis.

In other respects, however, Chinese collective farms have differed from the usual farm household. First, although the collective performed many of the same functions as a farm household, it was not a household, but a collection of households. Member households supplied labor for collec-tive activities. Member households could also engage in private-produc-tion activities independently of the collective. Labor allocation within a collective farm therefore involved a choice among labor on the collective, labor in private household production, and leisure. Second, collective farms and their member households had no access to labor markets. Ac-cording to Marxist theory, employment of labor can lead to economic exploitation, class differentiation, and class conflict. Such socioeconomic processes were considered inappropriate under Chinese socialism. The government therefore did not permit exchange of labor. From the point of view of the collective farm, government suppression of labor markets forced self-sufficiency in labor: all labor employed in collective produc-tion had to be supplied by member households, and the only outside em-ployer for household labor was the collective. Third, the access of collec-tive farms to markets for nonlabor inputs, outputs, and consumer goods was restricted. Until the late 1970s, private exchange was discouraged, so collectives were more or less limited to trade with the state commercial system. In this trade, the state not only set prices (collectives were price-takers), but also fixed maximum quotas on collectives' purchases of cer-tain modern inputs and consumer goods, and minimum quotas on collec-tives' sales of farm products to the state. In general, collectives could sell as much output to the state as they desired at official prices. Fourth, col-lective farms faced certain production planning targets. These targets typ-ically specified minimum areas to be planted in crops such as grain and cotton. At times, they also specified yield levels or production methods, for example, chemical fertilizer applications per hectare. Together, mar-keting quotas and production targets formed a complex array of planning restrictions. Collective farms had to take such targets and quotas into account when deciding on a production plan. In the above respects, Chi-nese collective farms have differed from farm households observed in other countries. A farm-household analysis of Chinese collectives should pay attention to these specific characteristics of the Chinese case.

This chapter examines labor allocation within a Chinese collective farm by means of a modified farm-household model. First, it presents a theoretical model of the collective farm. This model is used to analyze the effects of planning targets, planning quotas, and the absence of a labor market on collective labor allocation. Next, it turns to an empirical linear programming model of a case-study collective farm, a production team in central China. The chapter concludes with a discussion of the implications of the theoretical and empirical results for Chinese agriculture and, more generally, for agriculture in developing countries.

Model of a Collective Farm

Consider, first, a household-type theoretical model of a production team. The model answers the question: how do restrictions on trade, whether in the form of marketing quotas or in the form of trade prohibitions, affect team labor allocation? I begin by examining team labor allocation in an unrestricted market environment. The effects of market restrictions on team labor allocation are revealed by comparing optimal labor allocation in the unrestricted environment with optimal labor allocation when marketing quotas or trade restrictions are imposed.

Like the usual farm household, the production team both consumes and produces. Thus its objective is to maximize the utility of its member households subject to a budget constraint, where income is the sum of its endowed wealth and that of its members plus net revenues from collective and individual production. Since the model is concerned with the effect of market restrictions and not group decisionmaking processes, I make the simplifying assumptions that all member households have identical preferences and that the team and all its members face the same prices. These assumptions imply that the collective utility function is a simple, monotonic transformation of the household utility function and rule out lack of consensus. In addition, I assume that team members are indifferent between participation in household and collective activities. Thus, in an unrestricted market environment, profitability considerations would determine the optimal amounts of resources devoted to private as opposed to collective endeavors. This latter assumption may appear to be at odds with the evidence. I would maintain, however, that the preference for private activities commonly observed in socialist agriculture is frequently no more than the desire to engage in activities that, because of government restrictions limiting their extent, are more profitable than collective activities. Such a desire is completely consistent with this model.[1]

Under these assumptions, in an unrestricted market environment a production team would behave in more or less the same way as the usual farm household. The team determines optimal levels of production, consumption, and marketing by maximizing collective utility $U(x_1, \ldots, x_n)$ subject to exogenous prices $p = (p_1, \ldots, p_n)$, its production function

(10-1) $$G(q_1, \ldots, q_n) = 0$$

and its budget constraint

(10-2) $$px' \le pq' + p\bar{w}'.$$

These utility and production functions are assumed to have the usual properties (see the appendix to this volume). Full income in the team's budget constraint is the sum value of profits from production pq' and team endowments $p\bar{w}'$, where endowments include collectively cultivated land, private plot land, the stock of available human time, and any other financial and physical assets belonging to the team and its members.[2] In this formulation, optimization causes consumption expenditures to exactly equal full income. Thus savings are not carried over between periods. In other words, this is essentially a one-period model.

Solution of the above maximization problem leads the team to produce at optimal production levels q^* and to consume the utility-maximizing consumption bundle x^*. As in the usual household model, production and consumption decisions are recursive but separable. Moreover, for all goods, the technical rates of substitution in production and marginal rates of substitution in consumption are equated to their respective price ratios. In other words,

(10-3) $$\frac{\partial G/\partial q_i}{\partial G/\partial q_j} = \frac{\partial U/\partial x_i}{\partial U/\partial x_j} = \frac{p_i}{p_j} \qquad \text{for all } i, j.$$

The usual profit function $\pi(p)$, net output supply functions $y_i(p) = \partial\pi(p)/\partial p_i$, Marshallian demand functions $x_i[p, \pi(p) + p\bar{w}']$, and net marketing (or sales) functions $s_i(p, \bar{w}) = y_i - x_i$ can be derived for the team. The derivation of these standard results can be found in the appendix to this volume.

Production teams differ from the usual farm household in that they cannot trade freely. In particular, they face two types of market restrictions: absolute quantity limits on team purchases and sales, and interlinked quantity limits on team purchases and sales, where those limits are tied to other variables. The former, which are referred to here as fixed quota restrictions, occur either when the state sets absolute quotas on procurement from and sales to production teams, or when the state prohibits trade. (Prohibition of trade effectively sets a fixed quota limit of zero on team sales and purchases.) The latter, which are referred to here as variable quota restrictions, occur either when the state requires that a certain percentage of team output be sold to the state, or when rations of consumer and producer goods sold to the team by the state are set on the basis of the team's production or marketing levels.

Fixed and variable quotas affect team labor allocation because they place additional constraints on the team's utility-maximization problem. A fixed quota can be represented as the restriction

$$(10\text{-}4) \qquad s_k = \bar{w}_k + q_k - x_k \geq \bar{s}_k.$$

Equation (10-4) states that team net sales of the kth good (net sales are defined as the team's initial endowment plus net output minus own consumption) must exceed a net sales quota $\bar{s}_k$. If $\bar{s}_k > 0$, then net sales must exceed the minimum quota level; if $\bar{s}_k < 0$, then net purchases (a negative number) must be smaller in absolute value than the quota level. If $\bar{s}_k = 0$, then either purchase or sale of the kth good is not permitted.

Variable quota restrictions can take three forms. If the marketing quota for the kth good is tied to its production, then

$$(10\text{-}5.1) \qquad s_k = \bar{w}_k + q_k - x_k \geq tq_k.$$

If the marketing quota for the kth good is tied to production of another good, then

$$(10\text{-}5.2) \qquad s_k = \bar{w}_k + q_k - x_k \geq tq_j.$$

If the marketing quota for the kth good is tied to team net sales of another good to the state, then

$$(10\text{-}5.3) \qquad s_k = \bar{w}_k + q_k - x_k \geq t(\bar{w}_j + q_j - x_j).$$

In each equation above, the constant t represents the terms of the linkage. For example, if $t = 0.50$, then (10-5.1) states that the team must sell to the state at least 50 percent of its output of good k.

The levels of fixed and variable quotas and the specific goods affected have varied between regions and over time. Both types of quotas can be and have been applied to production inputs, outputs, and manufactured consumer goods. For example, variable quotas of the type shown in equation (10-5.3) have been used to link team purchases of chemical fertilizers to the quantity of cotton sold to the state. Prohibitions on the trade of land and labor have constituted fixed quotas of the type shown in (10-4), with the quota level $\bar{s}_k$ set equal to zero. Note that regardless of whether the team can trade in a market, the model includes some external price p_i for each good (p_i can, of course, equal zero).

How do fixed and variable quota restrictions affect team allocation of labor? Suppose that the production team faces a fixed quota such as that shown in (10-4). The team's maximization problem becomes

(10-6)
$$\max_{x,q} L = U(x) + \lambda\{\textstyle\sum_i p_i(x_i - q_i - \bar{w}_i)\}$$
$$+ \gamma G(q) + \theta(\bar{s}_k + x_k - q_k - \bar{w}_k).$$

First-order conditions at an interior solution are now

(10-6.1a)
$$\frac{1}{\lambda}\frac{\partial L}{\partial x_i} = \frac{1}{\lambda}\frac{\partial U}{\partial x_i} + p_i = 0 \qquad\qquad \text{for } i \neq k$$

(10-6.1b)
$$\frac{1}{\lambda}\frac{\partial L}{\partial x_k} = \frac{1}{\lambda}\frac{\partial U}{\partial x_k} + p_k + \frac{\theta}{\lambda} = 0$$

(10-6.2)
$$\frac{\partial L}{\partial \lambda} = \textstyle\sum_i p_i(x_i - q_i - \bar{w}_i) = 0$$

(10-6.3a)
$$\frac{1}{\lambda}\frac{\partial L}{\partial q_i} = \frac{\gamma}{\lambda}\frac{\partial G}{\partial q_i} - p_i = 0 \qquad\qquad \text{for } i \neq k$$

(10-6.3b)
$$\frac{1}{\lambda}\frac{\partial L}{\partial q_k} = \frac{\gamma}{\lambda}\frac{\partial G}{\partial q_k} - p_k - \frac{\theta}{\lambda} = 0$$

(10-6.4)
$$\frac{\partial L}{\partial \gamma} = G(q) = 0$$

(10-6.5)
$$\frac{\partial L}{\partial \theta} = \bar{s}_k + x_k - q_k - \bar{w}_k = 0.$$

Earlier assumptions concerning $U(x)$ and $G(q)$ ensure that second-order conditions for maximization are satisfied. This set of equations can be solved for optimal consumption levels $\hat{x}$ and production levels $\hat{q}$.

Note that if optimal consumption levels $\hat{x}$ were known, the above problem could be rewritten as a profit-maximization problem solving for optimal production levels $\hat{q}$ subject to budget and quota constraints and conditional on team consumption at optimal levels $\hat{x}$. The empirical model of Liu Li Team no. 4 takes this form because of insufficient consumption data. For the purposes of exposition, however, the theoretical discussion continues within the utility-maximization framework.

When binding, a fixed quota can change a production team's economic behavior in two ways. First, when a fixed quota applies to a good both produced and consumed, it can eliminate the separability of production and consumption decisions. Examination of the bordered Hessian given by total differentiation of the new first-order conditions reveals this lack of separability:

$$(10\text{-}7) \quad
\begin{bmatrix}
\frac{1}{\lambda}U_{11} \cdots \frac{1}{\lambda}U_{1k} \cdots \frac{1}{\lambda}U_{1n} & U_1 & 0 & \cdots & 0 & \cdots & 0 & 0 & 0 \\
\vdots & & & & & & & & \\
\frac{1}{\lambda}U_{k1} \cdots \frac{1}{\lambda}U_{kk} \cdots \frac{1}{\lambda}U_{kn} & U_k & 0 & \cdots & 0 & \cdots & 0 & 0 & 1 \\
\vdots & & & & & & & & \\
\frac{1}{\lambda}U_{n1} \cdots \frac{1}{\lambda}U_{nk} \cdots \frac{1}{\lambda}U_{nn} & U_n & 0 & \cdots & 0 & \cdots & 0 & 0 & 0 \\
p_1 \cdots p_k \cdots p_n & 0 & 0 & \cdots & 0 & \cdots & 0 & 0 & 0 \\
0 \cdots 0 \cdots 0 & 0 & \frac{\gamma}{\lambda}G_{11}\cdots\frac{\gamma}{\lambda}G_{1k}\cdots\frac{\gamma}{\lambda}G_{1n} & G_1 & 0 \\
\vdots & & & & & & & & \\
0 \cdots 0 \cdots 0 & 0 & \frac{\gamma}{\lambda}G_{k1}\cdots\frac{\gamma}{\lambda}G_{kk}\cdots\frac{\gamma}{\lambda}G_{kn} & G_k & -1 \\
\vdots & & & & & & & & \\
0 \cdots 0 \cdots 0 & 0 & \frac{\gamma}{\lambda}G_{n1}\cdots\frac{\gamma}{\lambda}G_{nk}\cdots\frac{\gamma}{\lambda}G_{nn} & G_n & 0 \\
0 \cdots 0 \cdots 0 & 0 & G_1 \cdots G_k \cdots G_n & 0 & 0 \\
0 \cdots 1 \cdots 0 & 0 & 0 \cdots -1 \cdots 0 & 0 & 0
\end{bmatrix}
\begin{bmatrix}
dx_1 \\ \vdots \\ dx_k \\ \vdots \\ dx_n \\ d\left(\frac{1}{\lambda}\right) \\ dq_1 \\ \vdots \\ dq_k \\ \vdots \\ dq_n \\ d\left(\frac{\gamma}{\lambda}\right) \\ d\left(\frac{\theta}{\lambda}\right)
\end{bmatrix}
=
\begin{bmatrix}
-dp_1 \\ \vdots \\ -dp_k \\ \vdots \\ -dp_n \\ K^{-3} \\ dp_1 \\ \vdots \\ dp_k \\ \vdots \\ dp_n \\ 0 \\ 0
\end{bmatrix}$$

Because of the outer border associated with the quota constraint on good k, the system of equations (10-7) cannot be reduced into distinct, diagonal consumption and production partitions. The quota constraint therefore forces the team to decide consumption and production jointly.

Second, a fixed quota can alter optimal levels of consumption, production, and trade. First-order conditions (10-6.1a,b) state that at optimal consumption levels $\hat{x}$

$$(10\text{-}8.1) \qquad \frac{\partial U/\partial x_i}{\partial U/\partial x_j} = \frac{p_i}{p_j} \qquad \text{for } i, j \neq k$$

and

$$(10\text{-}8.2) \qquad \frac{\partial U/\partial x_k}{\partial U/\partial x_j} = \frac{p_k + \dfrac{\theta}{\lambda}}{p_j} \qquad \text{for } j \neq k.$$

First-order conditions (6.3a,b) state that at optimal production levels $\hat{q}$

$$(10\text{-}9.1) \qquad \frac{\partial G/\partial q_i}{\partial G/\partial q_j} = \frac{p_i}{p_j} \qquad \text{for } i, j \neq k$$

and

$$(10\text{-}9.2) \qquad \frac{\partial G/\partial q_k}{\partial G/\partial q_j} = \frac{p_k + \dfrac{\theta}{\lambda}}{p_j} \qquad \text{for } j \neq k.$$

Statements (10-8.1,2) and (10-9.1,2) are identical to statement (10-3) in the unrestricted market problem, except that $(p_k + \theta/\lambda)$ replaces p_k. In fact, if $\hat{p} = (p_1, \ldots, p_k + \theta/\lambda, \ldots, p_n)$ where θ and λ are at their solution values in the second problem, then maximizing the expression

$$(10\text{-}10) \quad \max_{x,q} L = U(x) + \lambda\{ \textstyle\sum_i \hat{p}_i(x_i - q_i - \bar{w}_i)\} + \gamma G(q)$$

will give exactly the same solution as the constrained trade problem (10-6) with price vector p. The solution value of θ/λ therefore serves as a key to understanding the quota's impact on team behavior.

Now λ can be interpreted as the incremental increase in collective welfare following a one-dollar increase in the team's income Y, and θ can be interpreted as the incremental change in welfare following a one-unit decrease in the quota restriction $\bar{s}_k$. In other words,

$$(10\text{-}11) \qquad \lambda = \frac{\partial L}{\partial[\pi(p) + p\bar{w}']} \text{ and } \theta = \frac{\partial L}{\partial \bar{s}_k}.$$

Thus

$$(10\text{-}12) \qquad \frac{\theta}{\lambda} = \frac{\dfrac{\partial L}{\partial \bar{s}_k}}{\dfrac{\partial L}{\partial[\pi(p) + p\bar{w}']}} = -\frac{\partial[\pi(p) + p\bar{w}']}{\partial \bar{s}_k}.$$

Since the endowment $\bar{w}$ and prices p are held fixed,

$$(10\text{-}13) \qquad \frac{\theta}{\lambda} = -\frac{\partial \pi(p)}{\partial \bar{s}_k}$$

that is, θ/λ equals the marginal change in team profits following a change in the quota level $\bar{s}_k$. If $\bar{s}_k > 0$ and sets a lower bound on team sales of good k, or if $\bar{s}_k < 0$ and sets an upper bound on team purchases of good k, then a decrease in $\bar{s}_k$ will increase team profits, and θ/λ will be nonnegative. In these cases where the team is forced to sell more than it wants or buy less than it wants, a binding quota will cause the implicit price of good k to exceed its external price p_k. If $\bar{s}_k > 0$ and sets an upper bound on team sales of good k, or if $\bar{s}_k < 0$ and sets a lower bound on team purchases of good k, then a decrease in $\bar{s}_k$ will reduce team profits, and θ/λ will be nonpositive. In these cases where the team is prevented from selling as much as it wants or is forced to buy more than it wants, a binding quota will cause the implicit price of good k to be lower than its external price p_k.

Consider the effect of a fixed quota on team labor allocation. Suppose a fixed quota of zero applies to labor, and that labor is the first good ($k = 1$). Moreover, suppose that in the absence of the quota, the team would be a net hirer of labor. At an interior solution, then, θ/λ is positive. Therefore

$$(10\text{-}14) \qquad \hat{p}_1 = p_1 + \frac{\theta}{\lambda} \geq p_1.$$

The amount of human time used in production is

$$(10\text{-}15) \qquad \hat{q}_1 = y_1(\hat{p}).$$

Since $\partial y_i/\partial p_i > 0$, the net output of human time will increase; that is, the team will reduce the amount of labor it employs in production: $\hat{q}_1 > q_1^*$. On the consumption side, optimal team leisure is now

$$(10\text{-}16) \qquad \hat{x}_1 = x_1[\hat{p},\ \pi(\hat{p}) + \hat{p}\bar{w}'].$$

Since $\partial x_i/\partial p_i < 0$, the team will substitute away from consumption of leisure now that it faces a higher implicit price for human time. In addition, team profits may change

$$(10\text{-}17) \qquad \pi(\hat{p}) = \sum_i \hat{p}_i \hat{q}_i \neq \pi^*(p)$$

and thus so may full team income Y. If income is reduced and leisure is a normal good, then the income effect will reinforce the decrease in team leisure consumption owing to the substitution effect. In sum, a fixed quota on labor or suppression of labor markets could force production teams that would hire labor in the absence of the constraint to decrease both their use of labor in production and the amount of leisure consumed. The pattern of production would then shift to less labor-intensive activities, and team members would increase the amount of time they spend working.

In contrast, suppose that, in the absence of the quota, the team would be a net exporter of labor. Then, at an interior solution, θ/λ is negative, and $\hat{p}_1$ will be less than p_1. At this lower implicit wage, the team will increase the amount of labor used in production, but substitute in consumption toward leisure.

If the fixed quota applies to a good other than human time, then the quota's effect on team labor allocation depends on the elasticities of human time with respect to the price of the other good. Suppose, for example, that the team faces a binding minimum quota on its grain sales to the state. The implicit price of grain to the team would then increase, and team grain production would expand. The quantity of labor employed in grain cultivation would therefore rise. If grain replaces a less labor-intensive crop, then total labor use would increase; if it replaces a more labor-intensive crop, then total labor use would decline. On the consumption side, there might be some small substitution toward or away from leisure, depending on whether it is a consumption complement or substitute for grain.

The effect of variable quotas on team labor allocation is similar to that for fixed quotas. First, variable quotas on goods both consumed and produced can eliminate the separability of production and consumption decisions. Thus team labor-leisure preferences can enter into the team's production decision. Second, variable quotas alter the implicit prices of goods consumed and produced and alter team profits. Thus, they cause substitution in production and consumption, as well as an income effect on consumption. The net effect on labor allocation will depend on the direction of the income effect and the complementarity or substitutability between labor and the goods affected by quotas. Table 10-1 summarizes the implicit prices associated with the various quota types.

Table 10-1. *Implicit Prices under Different Quota Restrictions*

Restriction	Implicit consumption prices	Implicit production prices
None	$(p_1, \ldots, p_n)$	$(p_1, \ldots, p_n)$
$q_k + \bar{w}_k - x_k \geq \bar{s}_k$	$(p_1, \ldots, p_k + \dfrac{\theta}{\lambda}, \ldots, p_n)$	$(p_1, \ldots, p_k + \dfrac{\theta}{\lambda}, \ldots, p_n)$
$q_k + \bar{w}_k - x_k \geq tq_k$	$(p_1, \ldots, p_k + \dfrac{\theta}{\lambda}, \ldots, p_n)$	$(p_1, \ldots, p_k + \dfrac{(1 - t)\,\theta}{\lambda}, \ldots, p_n)$
$q_k + \bar{w}_k - x_k \geq tq_j$	$(p_1, \ldots, p_j, p_k + \dfrac{\theta}{\lambda}, \ldots, p_n)$	$(p_1, \ldots, p_j - \dfrac{\theta t}{\lambda}, p_k + \dfrac{\theta}{\lambda}, \ldots, p_n)$
$q_k + \bar{w}_k - x_k \geq t(\bar{w}_j + q_j - x_j)$	$(p_1, \ldots, p_j - \dfrac{\theta t}{\lambda}, p_k + \dfrac{\theta}{\lambda}, \ldots, p_n)$	$(p_1, \ldots, p_j - \dfrac{\theta t}{\lambda}, p_k + \dfrac{\theta}{\lambda}, \ldots, p_n)$

Note: λ is the multiplier associated with the budget constraint, and θ is the multiplier associated with the quota constraint. The implicit prices are evaluated at the solution values of λ and θ.

Empirical Model of a Production Team

The theoretical model just described shows the effects of quota restrictions on team allocation of labor. In this section we look at a linear programming model used to illustrate empirically their effects on a case-study production team in Hubei Province—Liu Li Team no. 4. Solution of the programming model will show that state planning restrictions affect the level and seasonal distribution of labor employed by the team. Moreover, the model demonstrates the interrelated nature of team production and consumption decisions when markets are restricted.

Although the linear programming model incorporates the basic elements of the theoretical framework, it differs from the usual empirical household model in that it does not estimate both the production and consumption sides. Insufficient consumption data preclude estimation of team consumption. The model therefore estimates only the team's profits and production behavior, where profits and production are conditional on the optimal consumption bundle. Specifically, rather than solving for optimal consumption and production levels by maximizing collective utility subject to the team's technological, resource, and planning constraints, the empirical model solves for optimal production levels by maximizing collective profits subject not only to technological, resource, and planning constraints, but also subject to the restriction that consumption takes place at observed, and assumedly optimal, levels. The empirical model is presented in more detail below.

The case-study production team Liu Li Team no. 4 is located in Mianyang County, a commercial cotton and grain-growing county in Hubei Province. The climate in this central region of China is temperate, averaging 17° Centigrade. Frost-free days number about 235 annually. Rainfall is abundant, exceeding 1,000 millimeters a year.

Liu Li Team no. 4's pattern of cultivation is representative of the region. In 1979, the year of this study, the team planted 40 percent of collectively cultivated land in double-crop rice, 10 percent in single-crop rice, and 37 percent in cotton. The remaining collective land was usually planted in minor crops such as soybeans, sorghum, hemp, peanuts, and sesame. During the winter season, barley, naked barley, wheat, broadbeans, and green manure completed the annual rotations.

Production teams were permitted to devote a certain percentage of their land to private plots. In 1979, Liu Li Team no. 4 set aside 3 hectares or 6 percent of its total land area, the maximum allowed, for household private plots. On the average, each household privately cultivated 0.048 hectare. Vegetables and small amounts of cash crops were usually planted, as well as fodder for privately raised hogs. In 1979, team households raised an average of 2.5 hogs each.

The team population in 1979 was 365, and its labor force 135. Households numbered 63. With a total cultivatable land area of 49 hectares, the team's population density was 7.4 people per hectare (0.135 hectare per person), which was about equal to the county average. The dependency ratio was high, 1.70 dependents per working adult, as compared with 1.37 for the county as a whole.

In part because of the quality of its soil, Liu Li Team no. 4's yields were consistently higher than the county, provincial, and national averages. In 1979, the team's rice yields were 5.3 tons per hectare of sown area, which was 10 percent higher than the county average and 25 percent higher than the national average. Cotton yields were 995 kilograms per hectare of sown area, or 14 percent above the county average and more than double the national average (see State Statistical Bureau 1982, pp. 154–55).

As a result of these high yields, the team enjoyed high per capita output, which promoted high marketing rates and income. In 1979, the team sold 36 percent of its grain to the state, compared with the county average of 23 percent and national average of 20 percent. The team's cotton marketing rate was 98 percent, which was equal to the national but slightly higher than the county average (see Sicular 1983, pp. 18, 27). Team per capita distributed income from collective sources was 225 yuan, which was 57 percent higher than the county average of 143 yuan; the national average was 83.4 yuan (see Chang and Luo 1980, p. 41). These income figures include both cash and in-kind income distributed by collectives to their members, but do not include income earned privately by households or individuals.

Liu Li Team no. 4 was an above-average team by both county and national standards. It was not, however, a model team; that is, it did not receive preferential treatment in the form of superior access to markets, lower quota levels, special financial or technical support, and so on. Liu Li Team no. 4 was subject to the same types of institutional arrangements and planning restrictions as other teams in the county. Thus an empirical case study of this team can usefully illustrate the general effects of such restrictions.

Agricultural planning restrictions in China fall into two categories: direct restrictions on production, and marketing restrictions. Direct restrictions on production usually take the form of minimum crop area targets. In this part of China, area targets have applied to grain and cotton. Before 1979, teams in Mianyang County faced area targets for double-crop rice and cotton. After 1979, rice area targets were eliminated and only the cotton targets remained. In 1979, Liu Li Team no. 4's cotton area target was 18.067 hectares, or 41 percent of its collective land area.

As noted earlier, market restrictions can take the form of quotas or result from prohibition of trade. Trade prohibitions applied to land and labor. Cotton and cotton products could be traded through state channels, but not privately. Private trade of other items was tolerated to a varying degree. During the Cultural Revolution (1966–76), all private trade was discouraged. Since 1978, private exchange has been permitted and rural markets have gradually revived. As of 1979, Liu Li Team no. 4 did not engage in private trade as a collective, although team members probably did so individually.

The system of quotas was quite complex. As mentioned above, quotas can be fixed or variable in form, and can apply to sales as well as purchases. Fixed quotas were set on collective deliveries of grain and vegetable oil or oilseeds to the state. These quotas were set in weight and did not specify type of grain or oil. Variable quotas were set on deliveries of grain and cotton. With respect to grain, in addition to the fixed quota, a second, variable above-quota quota was set annually on the basis of the expected grain harvests of the teams. With respect to cotton, teams with yields exceeding 750 kilograms per hectare were required to deliver all their output except one kilogram ginned cotton per team member to the state; teams with lower yields had to deliver all but 0.75 kilogram per team member. In addition to these formal delivery quotas, an informal maximum delivery quota applied to hog sales to the state. After the state raised hog prices in 1979, households in Mianyang County increased their production beyond the state's capacity to procure. The state responded by informally limiting the number of hogs it would procure from any particular household or team. (The delivery quotas faced by Liu Li Team no. 4 in 1979 are summarized in table 10A-1 in the appendix.)

Fixed and variable quotas have at times also restricted collective and household opportunities to buy consumer and producer goods from the state. In general, the state does not supply grain or vegetable oils to the agricultural population. Effectively, then, teams faced a fixed import quota of zero on these items; that is, they had to be self-sufficient in these items and produce what they consumed. Cotton cloth ration coupons were allocated to teams on a fixed quota per capita basis. Occasionally, additional coupons were awarded on a variable-quota basis for deliveries of ginned cotton or hemp to the state. Supplies of producer goods were allocated to teams in some cases according to crop areas, in others on the basis of deliveries to the state. Diesel fuel was allocated on the basis of team-owned machine horsepower. The quantity of each item allocated per capita, per unit sown area, per ton delivery to the state, and so on, was set more or less uniformly across teams within a county, but varied from year to year depending on the county's total allocation from the state for that year. Since 1979, the county's total allocation of most producer goods has risen to the point where its quotas exceed team demand. Liu Li Team no. 4 reported that in 1979 it was able to buy as much of any modern input as it desired.

The empirical model of Liu Li Team no. 4 captures the specifics of this case-study team. The team's production function $G(q)$ takes the form of a linear, fixed-coefficient technology given by an input-output matrix A. Coefficients of the A matrix are calculated from 1979 field data. The A matrix includes columns representing Liu Li Team no. 4's observed collective cultivation activities; observed collective sideline, mechanization, and processing activities; a number of cultivation activities not observed (corner solution activities in which the team did not engage in 1979, but in which it had previously engaged or in which neighboring teams engaged); and private household hog-raising and manure-collecting activities. Because data on inputs used and outputs produced on private plots are insufficient, household private-plot cultivation activities do not appear in the model. (Activities included in the model are summarized in table 10A-2 in the appendix.) The A matrix includes alternate activity columns producing the same items, thus permitting some variation in relative factor proportions. For example, cotton can be produced using less chemical fertilizer per ton output in a cotton-broadbean rotation activity, or using more in a cotton-wheat rotation activity. (Broadbeans fix nitrogen in the soil, whereas wheat depletes it.)

The rows of the A matrix represent use of various inputs across production activities. Inputs include collectively cultivated land, human labor time, animal draft time, machine time, fuels, chemical fertilizers, organic fertilizers, and pesticides. Land is differentiated by quality. Labor is differentiated by time of year to capture the seasonality of labor use.

Associated with the A matrix is a right-hand side vector b giving the team's initial endowments of various inputs. The team has initial endowments of collective land, people, cows, and machinery. Since the endowments of these items cannot be augmented by production (the supplies of people, cows, and machinery are assumed to be fixed in the short run), or by purchase (market restrictions prevent exchange of land or labor), these initial endowments effectively set maximum limits on their availability.

Planning and market restrictions are represented by an additional set of rows R and its associated right-hand side vector k. Planning and market restrictions include a minimum acreage target of 18.07 hectares for cotton; a minimum cotton sales quota of all output minus 1 kilogram per team member; a minimum grain sales quota of 54.75 tons husked grain equivalents; and a minimum vegetable oil or oilseeds sales quota of 1.44 tons oil equivalents. Neither grain nor vegetable oils can be purchased by the team, only sold. Sales of hogs to the state are restricted to a maximum limit of 126 head, or two per household, the observed level of household hog sales in 1979. No formal maximum quota existed for hogs, but this constraint is necessary to capture the state's unwillingness to purchase as many hogs as team households wished to sell.

In the theoretical model, the production team maximizes utility subject to its income from production and its endowments and subject to planning and marketing restrictions. If no market restrictions constrained the team, then utility maximization would lead the team to select a profit-maximizing production plan. In this case, profits could be used as the objective function in an empirical model of team production. If, however, one or more restrictions on the purchase of a consumed good is binding, then preferences may enter directly into the production decision and must be specified as elements in either the objective function or body of the model. In view of the lack of data, I use the latter approach. The empirical model maximizes team profits conditional on consumption at optimal levels. Optimal consumption levels appear in R as a set of minimum consumption constraint rows for important consumer goods, specifically for grains, vegetable oils, and leisure. Consumption constraints do not specify type of grain or oil. In addition, leisure refers to all time not spent in collective work and private hog raising and manure collection. The labor-leisure choice depicted by the empirical model, therefore, is not strictly a choice between labor and leisure, but a choice between collective or hog-raising activities and leisure or labor in other household sidelines.

Consumption constraints are initially set equal to observed 1979 consumption levels, which I assume are the optimal consumption levels at 1979 prices, given 1979 planning and market restrictions. The leisure consumption constraint is set equal to the lowest level of leisure time observed during peak seasons in 1979. When binding, consumption constraints influence the model's optimal solution, and their associated shadow prices give the marginal value of team consumption in terms of foregone profit income.

The empirical model's objective function $Z = cy$ is defined as team short-run profits: the value of collectively produced output plus hogs minus the cost of purchased variable inputs. Outputs valued into the objective function include products marketed and retained for team consumption, but not products used as intermediate inputs in the production process. Inputs costed out of the objective function include only those that are purchased and variable in the short run, such as chemical fertilizers, fuels, and pesticides. Land, human labor time, animal draft time, and machinery—inputs of which the team has an endowment but that cannot be purchased or sold, or that are fixed in the short run—do not appear in the objective function. The scarcity values of these inputs to the team, however, enter the model's calculation through shadow prices.

Prices c used to value inputs and outputs in the objective function are, in theory, expected marginal prices. Since in 1979 rural free markets were still not fully developed in Mianyang County and since the production team did not participate in those markets, I use state prices. The state pricing system was multitiered; quota sales received a basic quota price, and above-quota sales received a price 30 to 50 percent higher than the quota price. Since the team had to fulfill the quota, the relevant price for an additional unit output was the above-quota price. Therefore, team output is valued at 1979 state above-quota prices. Commercial inputs such as chemical fertilizers and pesticides are valued at 1979 state retail sales prices.

The linear programming model of Liu Li Team no. 4 can be summarized in the following form:

(10-18)   maximize $Z = cy$
                         subject to $Ay \leq b$
                                       $Ry \leq k$
                                       $y \geq 0.$

Z is team net income, A represents the team's production technology, and b gives initial endowments. $Ry \leq k$ includes additional constraints due to planning and marketing restrictions and consumption constraints. (Table 10A-1 in the appendix gives a summary of the price and planning regime used in this basic version of the model.) Altogether, the model contains approximately 180 rows and 4,000 nonslack columns. Solution of the model will determine profit-maximizing production levels and the shadow prices for resource, planning, market, and consumption constraints.

Results

Solutions of the linear programming model described here show the effects of state planning restrictions on team income, cultivation patterns, and labor allocation. First, the solution of a basic model version that exactly replicates the team's price and planning environment in 1979 reveals which restrictions are binding and their respective shadow prices. The basic model solution can be compared with the team's observed behavior in 1979 to check the accuracy of the model. Second, solution of an unrestricted version of the model, where the team faces no state-imposed planning or market constraints, shows the level of team income and labor use in an unrestricted environment. Examination of both the basic and unrestricted model solutions demonstrates the interrelatedness of team consumption and production decisions.

When the basic model solution is compared with the team's observed behavior in 1979, the three major aspects of model-predicted and observed team behavior—patterns of land use, levels of production and input use, and the level of team profits—are consistent. In each of these three categories, the model predicts observed team behavior quite well.

Table 10-2 summarizes 1979 land use observed and predicted by the basic model. In both cases, cotton occupies 41.3 percent of the team's summer season land area, which is exactly equal to the planned area target. The balance between double-crop and single-crop rice differs between the predicted and observed cases; the model substitutes single-crop rice for some double-crop rice and for "other" minor crops (soybean-sorghum intercrop). In the winter season, observed and predicted cultivation patterns are also similar, except that the model eliminates naked barley and considerably reduces green manure cultivation, replacing them with barley. Barley cultivation expands from an observed 20.4 percent to a predicted 66.6 percent of team land.

Table 10-2. *Land Use Summary, Liu Li Team No. 4:*
Predicted and Observed
(percentages of collective land area)

Crop	Observed land use (1979)	Predicted land use (basic model)	Predicted land use (unrestricted model)
Summer			
Cotton	41.3	41.3	33.7
Double-crop rice	44.2	35.1	42.7
Single-crop rice	12.2	23.6	23.6
Other crops	2.3	0.0	0.0
Winter			
Broadbeans	13.7	15.4	12.9
Naked barley	13.0	0.0	0.0
Wheat	10.5	6.3	0.0
Barley	20.4	66.6	76.8
Green manure	42.4	11.6	10.3

The above differences in observed and predicted land use reflect substitutions in cropping rotations. The elimination of naked barley is the result of the model's substitution of a cotton-barley rotation for cotton–naked barley. The green manure area is reduced because the model replaces some of the double-crop rice-green manure rotation with double-crop rice-barley and single-crop rice-barley. Wheat, actually cultivated in rotation with cotton, is moved into rotation with single-crop rice. Broadbeans, actually cultivated in rotation with single-crop rice, are moved into rotation with cotton.

The above similarities and differences between observed and predicted land use are manifested in levels of production and input use. Table 10-3 gives 1979 production levels observed and predicted by the basic model. Despite the substitution of single-crop for double-crop rice cultivation, predicted total rice output is very close to the observed level. Increases in single-crop rice production balance the decrease in early and late double-cropped rices. The expansion of barley onto land actually planted in green manure, as well as barley's substitution for lower-yielding naked barley and wheat, however, cause predicted winter grain and total grain

Table 10-3. *Production, Liu Li Team No. 4: Basic and Unrestricted Models*
(tons)

Product	Observed (1979)	Predicted (basic model)	Predicted (unrestricted model)
Total grain	267.646	311.174	344.950
Total rice	214.591	218.450	243.700
Early rice	87.488	69.368	81.683
Late nonglutinous rice	75.785	66.202	79.137
Late glutinous rice	10.601	0.000	0.000
Single-crop rice	40.717	82.880	82.880
Total winter grains	50.784	92.724	101.250
Broadbeans	9.405	9.091	7.642
Naked barley	8.424	0.000	0.000
Wheat	10.042	4.786	0.000
Barley	22.913	78.847	93.608
Other grains	2.271	0.000	0.000
Cotton	17.977	19.602	18.028
Oilseed and oil			
Oilseed (not pressed)	25.65	27.8	27.7
Pressed oil[a]	0.912	0.912	0.000
Hogs[b] (head)	126.0	126.0	983.0

a. Cottonseed yields 12 percent its weight in oil.

b. Hogs are counted as the number of head raised and marketed. This number does not include the team breeding stock and immature hogs.

production to exceed their observed levels. Predicted cotton and oilseed (primarily cottonseed) production are slightly higher than observed. This difference is explained entirely by higher predicted yields caused by the model's substitution of nitrogen-fixing broadbeans for nitrogen-consuming wheat in the cotton rotation. Hog production, both predicted and observed, is equal to the maximum hog-marketing limit of 126 head.

Levels of input use appear in table 10-4. Despite changes in cropping patterns and production levels, predicted and observed input use are remarkably similar. The total labor used in collective production and hog raising as predicted by the basic model is only 2 percent different from the observed level. Predicted labor per capita adult laborer averages 302 work units per year, or about 3.98 hours per adult laborer per day. At peak seasons, the labor contribution reaches its maximum limit of 6.76 hours per adult laborer per day, which is equal to the observed maximum. The principal discrepancies between predicted and observed input levels oc-

Table 10-4. *Input Use, Liu Li Team No. 4: Predicted and Observed*

Input	Observed (1979)	Predicted (basic model)	Predicted (unrestricted model)	Basic model ÷ observed (percent)	Unrestricted ÷ basic (percent)
Labor					
Total[a]	40,000	40,818	58,041	102.0	142.2
Per adult laborer[a,b]	296	302	430		
Chemical fertilizers					
Urea	9,562	9,353	9,757	97.8	104.3
Ammonium nitrate	155	155	155	100.0	100.0
Ammonium bicarbonate	11,300	11,253	12,856	99.6	114.2
Calcium superphosphate	4,150	3,964	4,118	95.5	103.9
Compound fertilizer	1,350	1,350	1,067	100.0	79.0
Organic fertilizers					
Oilcake	12,301	11,794	12,180	95.9	103.3
Hog manure[a]	4,066	5,003	4,861	123.0	97.2
Cow manure[a]	804	1,190	1,267	148.0	106.5
Night soil[a]	451	414	417	91.8	100.7
Fuels					
Diesel oil	4,144[c]	3,028	3,427	73.1	113.2
Electricity (kilowatt-hours)	13,000[c]	11,977	13,233	92.1	110.5

Note: Kilograms, except where noted otherwise.

a. Measured in work units, each equivalent to approximately 4.8 hours of labor time.

b. The team had 135 adult laborers in 1979.

c. The data for observed fuel use include fuel used by team households for consumption purposes. These numbers therefore overstate fuel used as an input to production and so are not strictly comparable to the values predicted by the model.

cur for manure fertilizers: predicted applications of hog and cow manure are, respectively, 23 percent and 48 percent higher than observed. This increase is due to the higher manure requirements following substitution of barley for green manure on 9.4 hectares of the double-crop rice rotation.

What implications do the above differences between predicted and observed levels of production and input use hold for team profits? Predicted profits are 170,027 yuan, which is 3.8 percent greater than the observed 163,838 yuan. (Note that, in these calculations of predicted and observed profits, all output is valued at above-quota prices; profits would be lower if quota sales were valued at quota prices.) The model solution therefore gives profits very close to their observed level. Together with the basic consistency between predicted and observed land use, production levels, and input applications, the similarity between predicted and observed profits suggests that the linear programming model captures essential aspects of Liu Li Team no. 4's economic environment. The model can thus be usefully employed to analyze the effects of planning restrictions on the team.

The planning and market restrictions faced by Liu Li Team no. 4 appear in the linear programming model as row constraints on team production, sales, and consumption. A positive shadow price for one or more of these constraints in the basic model solution indicates that the corresponding restrictions are binding. Of the planning and market constraints in the basic model, four show positive shadow prices: the cotton area target, the hog-marketing limit, the vegetable oil self-sufficiency constraint, and the leisure consumption (labor availability) constraint for the period May 11–15. (Binding planning and market restrictions and their shadow prices are given in table 10-5.)

Table 10-5. *Binding Planning and Marketing Restrictions in the Basic Model Solution, Liu Li Team No. 4*

Constraint	Level	Shadow price (yuan)
Minimum cotton area target	18.067 hectares	1,385.26
Maximum hog-marketing limit	126 head	38.50
Minimum vegetable oil self-sufficient consumption constraint	0.912 tons	90.00
May 11–15 minimum leisure, maximum labor constraint	11,640 hours leisure, 4,560 hours (950 work units) labor	4.18 (per work unit)

A few points should be made concerning constraints that are not binding in the basic model solution. Neither the minimum grain sales quota nor the minimum grain consumption constraint is binding. The basic model predicts team grain production more than adequate to meet the team's livestock feed-grain requirements, grain sales quota, and desired consumption. The team's vegetable oil sales quota and cotton sales requirement are also nonbinding. The levels at which these quotas were set are also consistent with profit maximization. Leisure consumption constraints are not binding except during the period May 11–15. During all other periods, adult workers consume free time (time not spent raising hogs or working for the collective) greater than or equal to their minimum observed level of 17.28 hours per person per day. In other words, labor required for production is less than or equal to the 1.4 work units (6.72 hours) per laborer per day maximum implied by this level of leisure, and the shadow prices associated with the labor constraints are equal to zero.

Of the four binding constraints, two—the cotton area target and the hog-marketing limit—do not involve team consumption preferences. The minimum cotton area target of 18.067 hectares is binding with a shadow price of 1,385 yuan. The maximum hog sales limit of 126 head is binding with a shadow price of 38.50 yuan. Both these constraints reduce team profits and influence team behavior, but since they do not involve consumed items, they do not bring preferences directly into the production decision.

The binding vegetable oil consumption constraint and the May 11–15 labor-leisure constraint involve items consumed by team members and therefore make the team's production and consumption decisions interdependent. The minimum consumption constraint on vegetable oil is binding at 0.912 ton with a shadow price of 90.00 yuan. This constraint is binding even though the team produces enough cottonseed to more than fulfill the state quota, feed its livestock, and feed team members. This constraint is binding because at 1979 state prices it would cost the team less to sell raw cottonseed to the state and buy back pressed oil than to press the oil itself. If the team were permitted to buy pressed oil at state prices and eliminate its own oil-pressing activity, it would save 90.00 yuan per ton on oil consumed.

The May 11–15 labor-leisure constraint is binding at 950 work units (4,560 hours labor and 11,640 hours leisure) for the five-day period. This constraint is binding because at this time in the double-crop rice–barley rotation, barley must be harvested and early rice transplanted immediately thereafter to minimize delay in the early and late rice crops that follow. The binding May 11–15 labor constraint effectively limits team cultivation of this triple-grain rotation. An additional work unit of labor would enable the team to expand double-crop rice-barley cultivation and thus increase team profits by 4.18 yuan. Team members forego this income, however, in order to maintain free time for leisure or private sidelines.

Comparing the basic model solution with the solution of an unrestricted version of the model further clarifies the overall effect of the four binding constraints on team behavior and labor allocation. In the unrestricted version of the model, the team faces no quotas or area targets, can purchase desired amounts of grain and oil from the state at its above-quota procurement prices, and has an unlimited supply of free labor. This unrestricted version is, of course, a special case of an unrestricted economic environment. The unrestricted version of the model portrays a situation in which the team faces no area targets, is allowed to exchange unlimited quantities of commodities with the state at state prices, and has access to additional labor at zero cost. The unrestricted version of the model does not predict team behavior in a free market environment where prices can fluctuate in response to supply and demand or in an environment where prices reflect societywide scarcities.

The unrestricted model solution predicts a reduction in cotton area from the basic model level of 41.3 percent to 33.7 percent of team land (see table 10-2); this cotton is replaced by double-crop rice. Single-crop rice area remains unchanged at 23.6 percent of team land. In the winter, barley expands from 66.6 percent to 76.8 percent of team land, replacing broadbeans, wheat, and green manure. Part of this increase in barley cultivation reflects an expansion of the double-crop rice-barley rotation onto land formerly planted in cotton and onto some land formerly planted in the double-crop rice-green manure rotation in the basic model solution. These changes in cultivation are made possible by elimination of the cotton area target and the maximum labor constraints. In addition, barley replaces wheat on 2.761 hectares of the single-crop rice rotation. The substitution of barley for wheat in rotation with single-crop rice occurs because barley yields more tons of livestock feed than wheat, and that feed is now used to support expanded hog production. These shifts in land use are reflected in the output levels shown in table 10-3.

The most dramatic change from the basic to unrestricted model solution occurs for hog production. With the removal of the maximum hog-marketing limit, hog production soars from 126 head to 983 head, or 15.6 hogs per household (see table 10-3). All grain produced except 79.14 tons of late japonica rice, which is still sold to the state, now goes to feed livestock. It is more profitable for the team to use grain to raise hogs for sale to the state than to sell grain directly.

With the elimination of the minimum consumption constraint on vegetable oil, oil-pressing activities drop to zero. In the unrestricted model solution, all cottonseed is sold to the state in raw form. Any vegetable oil consumed would be purchased.

The above changes in team production have a substantial impact on its employment of labor. Since market restrictions limit the labor-intensive hog production and triple-cropped grain activities, once they are removed, the team's total and peak-season labor use increases. The unrestricted model solution requires 58,041 work units of labor, an increase of 17,223 work units, or 42.2 percent over the basic model solution of 40,818 work units. Work units per adult laborer jump from 302 to 430 per year, or from an average 3.98 hours to 5.66 hours per laborer per day (see table 10-4). The expansion of hog production accounts for most of this increase in total labor use. Not only does total labor employment increase, but so does peak-season employment. Use of labor during the May 11–15 period increases by 54 percent, from 950 to 1,463 work units. This growth in peak-season labor use reflects expansion of double-crop rice-barley cultivation. Growth in both total and peak-season employment is exaggerated, however, because additional labor is assumed to be available at zero wage. If additional labor were available at a positive wage, removal of marketing restrictions would probably cause less expansion in labor use than that predicted by the unrestricted model version.

The above changes in production and employment lead to a significant increase in the net income of the team. Profits in the unrestricted model rise to 187,061 yuan, which is a net increase of 16,989 yuan, or 10.0 percent more than the basic model solution. At prevailing prices, then, 1979 planning and marketing restrictions reduced Liu Li Team no. 4's ability to earn income.

The impact of planning and market restrictions on Liu Li Team no. 4 as illustrated by the basic and unrestricted linear programming model solutions is consistent with the theoretical conclusions discussed earlier. Binding restrictions lower team profits and alter levels of production and labor use. Although insufficient data on team preferences prevent the linear programming model from demonstrating the impact of binding restrictions on team consumption, theoretically one would expect different levels of consumption between the restricted and unrestricted cases. First, removal of restrictions would have a positive income effect on consumption. Since team profits are higher when planning restrictions are removed, team consumption of grain, oil, leisure, and other goods should increase. Second, since the implicit price of oil and peak-season leisure to the team declines, consumption of these two goods should experience an additional positive substitution effect. The planning restrictions imposed on Liu Li Team no. 4 therefore have a negative impact on team consumption, especially on the consumption of leisure and oil.

In addition to altering levels of team profits, production, and consumption, Liu Li Team no. 4's planning restrictions eliminate the separability of production and consumption concerns. Binding self-sufficiency constraints on oil and labor-leisure force the team to choose its production plan not just on the basis of profitability but also on the basis of its consumption preferences. Because of consumption preferences, the team maintains unprofitable oil-pressing activities and reduces cultivation of the profitable double-crop rice-barley rotation.

Conclusion

Theoretical and empirical analyses demonstrate that China's state policies restricting commercial exchange influence rural labor allocation as well as production, consumption, and income levels. Their effect is illustrated by the case of Liu Li Team no. 4. Commercial quotas and suppression of markets caused this team to reduce cultivation of labor-intensive crop rotations, maintain unprofitable oil-pressing activities, and raise fewer hogs. Total and peak-season labor use were reduced, as were team profits. Although the empirical model does not estimate team consumption, market restrictions should, in theory, also cause substitution among goods because the shadow prices of restricted goods differ from their external prices.

Furthermore, the analyses suggest that planning restrictions influence not only the levels of team production, consumption, and income, but also the mix between collective and household employment. In the case of Liu Li Team no. 4, restrictions on hog sales effectively suppressed a profitable household production activity, thus reducing the amount of labor devoted to private production. As a result, collective activities employed an artificially high proportion of team labor time. In the past, Chinese planning restrictions have proscribed not only hog raising, but also private-plot cultivation and a wide range of other household production and marketing activities. Recent reforms have lifted many of these restrictions. To the extent that household enterprise is more profitable than collective enterprise, these reforms should lead to a shift in labor allocation away from collective and toward household employment.

Finally, policies restricting trade undermine the separability of production and consumption decisions. When a collective farm is unable to trade items both produced and consumed, consumption preferences may enter directly into its production decisions. In the case of Liu Li Team no. 4, this is demonstrated by the reduction of peak-season labor activities in order to maintain desired leisure consumption, and by continued oil pressing in order to satisfy the team demand for vegetable oil. When consumption becomes a factor in production decisions, collective farms become less sensitive to external market signals; the price elasticities of both supply and demand may therefore be reduced. In such an environment, state pricing policy may be ineffective as a means of guiding resource allocation. Rural production and consumption may be responsive, however, to adjustments in quantity restrictions. Current research on Chinese agriculture supports this conclusion: in recent years agricultural production has apparently been more sensitive to quantity than price planning reforms. (See Sicular 1983 for a discussion of supply responses to price and planning reforms.)

Although Liu Li Team no. 4 provides a useful case study, the specific impact of market restrictions on levels of production, consumption, and income; on the mix between collective and private employment; and on the interrelation between consumption and production decisions could be quite different for a production team in another region, or even for another production team in the same region. For example, a team poorly endowed for grain production would be more severely affected by grain self-sufficiency constraints than a team such as Liu Li Team no. 4, which enjoyed a comparative advantage in grain and was able to produce large quantities of grain per team member. Thus, during the Cultural Revolution when teams were forced to be self-sufficient, regions of China traditionally known for their production of commercial crops such as cotton and sugar had no choice but to plant grain on land better suited to other crops, and so experienced reduced incomes and living standards (see Lardy 1983). Similarly, variations in population density and dependency ratios can influence the particular effect of labor market restrictions on the labor-leisure choice. A team with relatively abundant labor would have a low shadow value for human time, and so would consume more leisure and use more labor in production than a team in which labor was in short supply. The marginal product of labor therefore differs across teams. Variation in the impact of market restrictions among teams is caused by differences in the levels of restrictions relative to local resource endowments. Since China is a large and agriculturally diverse country, the effect of market restrictions has not been uniform.

The effect of market restrictions has varied not only across teams, but also over time with shifts in economic policy. In recent years, the Chinese government has instituted a number of reforms, including increased tolerance of private exchange in free markets, reformulation of quota policies, and implementation of the household responsibility system. Increased opportunities for private exchange and reformulation of quota policies have in general reduced restrictions on exchange and so have softened the impact of commercial quotas. Household responsibility system reforms have replaced collectives with households as the basic farm unit. Households continue to face market constraints similar to those that formerly applied to collectives, however. The analyses of the effects of market restrictions presented here should therefore apply equally well to a Chinese household farm unit.

What lessons does analysis of Chinese agriculture contain for other developing countries? First, it highlights some potential difficulties of state commercial planning in the agricultural sector. In countries where farms consume a significant portion of their output—for example, in areas characterized by small-scale household farming—the use of marketing quotas to promote national production objectives may have unanticipated effects. In such countries, marketing quotas will affect not only the quantity of farm output produced and marketed, but also consumption levels and the relationship between consumption and production decisions. Second, incomplete or fragmented rural markets affect microeconomic agents in more or less the same way as commercial quotas: they restrict opportunities for exchange, and so maintain the interrelation between production and consumption behavior, dampen price responsiveness, and reduce incomes (see Bardhan 1980; McKinnon 1973). Incomplete markets and market fragmentation are commonly observed in rural sectors of developing countries. Efforts to eliminate such obstacles to trade may promote rural employment, welfare, and the efficiency of agricultural production.

Appendix: Constraints and Activities of the Basic Model

Table 10A-1. *Price and Planning Regime, Liu Li Team No. 4:*
The Basic Model

	Level
Output prices	1979 state above-quota procurement prices
Input prices	1979 state retail sales prices
Marketing restrictions	
Minimum grain sales quota	54.75 tons husked grain equivalents
Minimum vegetable oil sales quota	1.44 tons oil equivalents
Maximum hog sales limit	126 head (2 head per household)
Minimum cotton sales requirement	All output produced except 365 kilograms
Self-sufficiency restrictions	Grain, vegetable oils, and cotton cannot be purchased by the team
Production planning restrictions	
Minimum cotton area target	18.067 hectares
Consumption constraints	
Grain	115.666 tons unhusked grain (317 kilograms per capita)
Vegetable oil	0.912 ton (2.5 kilograms per capita)
Ginned cotton	365 kilograms (1 kilogram per capita)
Labor-leisure constraints	
Maximum labor availability	1.4 work units per laborer per day (6.72 hours per laborer per day; labor cannot be hired in)
Minimum leisure consumption	17.28 hours per laborer per day

Table 10A-2. *Activities Included in the Linear Programming Model of Liu Li Team No. 4*

Cultivation activities: annual crop rotations
  Cotton: with broadbeans, wheat, barley, naked barley[a]
  Ambary hemp:[a] with barley,[a] naked barley[a]
  Jute:[a] with barley,[a] naked barley[a]
  Sesame:[a] with broadbeans,[a] wheat,[a] barley,[a] naked barley[a]
  Single-crop rice: with broadbeans, wheat,[a] barley, naked barley
  Double-crop rice (second crop japonica rice): with barley, naked barley,[a] green manure
  Double-crop rice (second crop glutinous rice): with barley, naked barley,[a] green manure
  Sorghum:[a] with broadbeans,[a] wheat,[a] barley,[a] naked barley[a]
  Soybeans:[a] with broadbeans,[a] wheat,[a] barley,[a] naked barley[a]
  Soybean-sorghum intercrop: with broadbeans,[a] wheat,[a] barley, naked barley[a]

Animal husbandry and manure production
  Collective cow raising, and cow labor and cow manure production
  Collective raising of breeding hogs, piglet production, and hog manure production
  Household hog and hog manure production
  Household human night soil manure production
  Household chicken manure production

Mechanical and processing activities
  Irrigation: using 10-horsepower diesel engine, 12-horsepower diesel engine, 12-horsepower diesel
    walking tractor, 10-kilowatt-hour electric engine, or 7.5-kilowatt-hour electric engine
  Ploughing: using 12-horsepower diesel engine or 12-horsepower diesel walking tractor
  Threshing: using 10-horsepower diesel engine, 12-horsepower diesel engine, 12-horsepower diesel
    walking tractor, 10-kilowatt-hour electric engine, 7.5-kilowatt-hour electric engine, or paying a
    fee for brigade threshing
  Transport: using 12-horsepower diesel walking tractor
  Cotton ginning: paying a fee for brigade ginning
  Oil pressing: paying a fee for brigade pressing

a. Crops and crop rotations not planted by Liu Li Team no. 4 in 1979 but included because they were planted in other years or by neighboring teams.

Notes

1. It is commonly observed that members of collective farms in socialist countries are not indifferent between collective and private activities, but prefer private activities. Preference for private activities can take two forms, one of which is economic preference, where the preference is due solely to differential returns in private and collective activities. In both the USSR and the People's Republic of China, restrictions on private enterprise have led to sustained profitability differentials between private and collective work. When private activities are more profitable, collective members will prefer them. Such economic preference due solely to differential returns among activities is allowed within the model. The second form of preference, pure preference, has nothing to do with relative profitabilities. If pure preference for private activities exists, collective members would prefer private to collective activities even if their returns were identical. The model assumes that this second type of preference does not exist. With the assumption of no pure preference for private activities, the model will predict that when private activities face no restrictions, they will expand to the point where their marginal profitability exactly equals that

of collective activities. If this assumption is incorrect, private activities could expand to a point where their profitability is lower than that of collective activities, in which case the model would understate the extent of private activities and overstate the extent of collective activities.

2. Note that the notation in this chapter differs slightly from that in the appendix to the volume. I do not use different letters to distinguish outputs, labor inputs, variable inputs, and fixed inputs in the production function. All inputs and outputs are referred to as q_i and distinguished only by the subscript. If $q_i < 0$, then the ith good is a net input; if $q_i > 0$, then it is a net output. This formulation allows the same good to be either an input or output. For example, grain could be either a final output or a net input used for livestock production. In the utility function n goods appear (including both the usual consumer goods and human time in the form of leisure). Finally, team endowments include the team's stock of human time valued at the price of labor, as well as other items valued at their respective prices.

3. $K = \sum_i (\bar{w}_i + q_i - x_i)dp_i.$

References

Bardhan, P. K. 1980. "Interlocking Factor Markets and Agrarian Development: A Review of Issues." *Oxford Economic Papers*.

Chang, Zi-zhong, and Han-xian Luo, eds. 1981. *Chinese Agricultural Yearbook, 1980* (Zhongguo Nongye Nianjian). Beijing: Agricultural Publishing House.

Gotsch, Carl H., B. Ahmed, W. P. Falcon, M. Naseem, and S. Yusuf. 1975. "Linear Programming and Agricultural Policy: Micro Studies of the Pakistan Punjab," *Food Research Institute Studies*, vol. 14, no. 1.

Heyer, Judith. 1971. "A Linear Programming Analysis of Constraints on Peasant Farms in Kenya," *Food Research Institute Studies*, vol. 10, no. 1, pp. 55–67.

Lardy, Nicholas R. 1983. *Agriculture in China's Modern Economic Development*. New York: Cambridge University Press.

McKinnon, R. I. 1973. *Money and Capital in Economic Development*. Washington, D.C.: Brookings Institution.

Perkins, Dwight H. 1966. *Market Control and Planning in Communist China*. Cambridge, Mass.: Harvard University Press.

Sicular, Terry. 1983. "Market Restrictions in Chinese Agriculture: A Microeconomic Analysis." Ph.D. dissertation. Yale University, New Haven, Conn.

State Statistical Bureau. 1982. *China Statistical Yearbook, 1981* (Zhongguo Tongji Nianjian). Beijing: China Statistical Publishing House.

11

Structural Models of the Farm Household That Allow for Interdependent Utility and Profit-Maximization Decisions

Ramon E. Lopez

THE EMPIRICAL LITERATURE on measuring the behavioral responses of farm households has typically used recursive models (see, for example, Lau, Lin, and Yotopoulos 1978; Barnum and Squire 1979; chapter 1). That is, it has been assumed that production conditions (farm technology, input, and output prices) affect consumption and labor-supply decisions exclusively via income levels and that production decisions are entirely independent of consumption and labor-supply decisions. Thus, these studies consider a one-way only effect (from the production to the consumption sector), and, moreover, this relation is restricted to the income effect. Changes in the production sector have no implications for the shadow prices of labor or consumption. This assumption has allowed researchers to estimate the consumption and production sectors of the model independently or, more frequently, recursively.

The purpose of this chapter is to show that there are several plausible situations for which the above procedure may not be appropriate. Furthermore, a relatively simple structural model is developed that allows for the measurement of interdependent utility- and profit-maximizing decisions, and a statistical test is proposed to discriminate between interdependent and recursive models. Finally, the working of the structural model is illustrated by applying it to farm-household cross-sectional data from Canada.

Note: I wish to thank A. D. Woodland and W. E. Diewert for their comments on an earlier version, and J. Strauss for helpful comments.

The main source of interdependence is the existence of endogenous shadow prices that would become a basic linkage between the production and consumption sectors of the model. In particular, if time allocations between on-farm and off-farm work have different utility connotations, then the shadow price of on-farm work is endogenously determined within the farm-household unit, even if the farm-household's members work off the farm. What is more important is that explicit consideration of commuting time associated with off-farm work leads to a model in which households behave as if they maximize a utility function with different preferences between on-farm and off-farm work *even* if preferences are defined in terms of total leisure only.[1]

Farm-Household Models

Two models of the farm household are presented here. One of them assumes that preferences for on-farm and off-farm work are different and ignores commuting time associated with off-farm work. The second model is more conventional in the sense that it assumes identical preferences for on-farm and off-farm time allocations, but it explicitly accounts for commuting time to off-farm work. Both models yield similar nonrecursive empirical specifications where utility- and profit-maximizing decisions are jointly determined.

A Model without Commuting Time and Different Preferences for On-Farm and Off-Farm Work

If we ignore commuting time and assume different preferences for on-farm and off-farm work, the utility-maximization model of the farm household can be represented as

(11-1) $$\max U(H - L_1, H - L_2, X)$$

s.t. (11-1.1) $$\sum_{n=1}^{N} p_n X_N \leq \pi(q; L_1) + w_2 L_2 + y$$

(11-1.2) $$L_1 + L_2 \leq H$$

(11-1.3) $$X_N \geq 0, L_1, L_2 \geq 0$$

where U is the household's utility function, X is the N dimensional vector of consumption goods, L_1 is the number of hours of work supplied to the family farm by household members, L_2 is the number of hours of off-farm work, p_n is the rental price of commodity n consumed by household members, y is net nonlabor income, q is the price vector of the s outputs and inputs used by the family farm, H is the total number of hours that household members have available for all activities including leisure, w_2 is the wage rate received by household members when they work off-farm, and $\pi(q; L_1)$ is the family farm's conditional profit function. The properties of $\pi(q; L_1)$ are those of the variable profit function discussed by Diewert (1974).

The utility function $U(\cdot)$ may also be represented by a more conventional preference structure such as $F(L_1, L_2, X)$. Moreover, if $F(\cdot)$ is continuous, quasi-concave, nondecreasing in X, and nonincreasing in L_1 and L_2, then $U(\cdot)$ will also have identical properties, except that it will be nondecreasing in $H - L_1$ and $H - L_2$ (Diewert 1974). The advantage of $U(\cdot)$ over $F(\cdot)$ is that the former is defined over the nonnegative orthant, and the corresponding budget constraint may be defined using nonnegative prices and positive full income.

The fact that the farm-profit function is dependent on L_1 and that preferences are allowed to be affected differently by on-farm and off-farm time allocations signifies that farm-household utility and profit maximization cannot in general be dichotomized. That is, labor-supply and production decisions are interdependent mainly because the shadow price of L_1 is endogenous (it is dependent on both the production and consumption sides of the model). This interdependence is reduced if one assumes either that the household's utility depends on total labor supply and not on the allocation of that supply between on-farm and off-farm employment, provided that households work off-farm and that commuting time is negligible; or that household labor and hired labor are perfect substitutes in production, provided that some hired labor is used.

Either of these assumptions makes it possible to consider the shadow price of on-farm household work to be exogenous, equal to the off-farm rate if the first assumption is used, or equal to the hired labor wage rate if the second assumption is used. In either case, the interdependence of utility- and profit-maximization decisions is reduced to the effects of farm profits on household income. That is, the model becomes recursive.

Both assumptions are likely to be unrealistic, however. It has long been recognized that the disutility associated with diverse working activities is different (see, for example, Benewitz and Zucker 1968; Diewert 1971; Fieldings and Hoseck 1973; Rottenberg 1956). Utility differences associated with different working activities are likely to be even greater when one of the activities involves self-employment with a large component of entrepreneurial work and the other is a wage-earning activity. The second assumption is also dubious if one considers differences in required supervision costs and in educational levels between farm operators and hired labor. Furthermore, the absence of perfect substitutability between hired and nonhired labor has been empirically established in studies applied to agriculture (see, for example, Barichello 1979).

Assume that constraint (11-1.2) is not binding. That is, assume that at all wage rates and commodity prices, households consume some leisure. Assume also that the production technology exhibits constant returns to scale. If this is the case and if there are no fixed factors of production, then the profit function is homogeneous of degree one in L_1 and can be decomposed as follows:[2]

$$(11\text{-}2) \qquad \pi(q; L_1) = L_1\bar{\pi}(q)$$

where $\bar{\pi}(q)$ is nonnegative, convex, continuous, and linear homogeneous in q.

Using (11-2), we may now write the utility maximization problem (11-1) as

$$(11\text{-}3) \qquad \max_{H-L_1,\, H-L_2,\, X} U(H - L_1, H - L_2, X)$$

s.t. (11-3.1)
$$pX + \bar{\pi}(q)(H - L_1) + w_2(H - L_2) \le H(\bar{\pi} + w_2) + y \equiv Z$$

$$(11\text{-}3.2) \qquad (H - L_1) \ge 0;\ (H - L_2) \ge 0;\ X \ge 0$$

$$(11\text{-}3.3) \qquad (H - L_1) \le H;\ (H - L_2) \le H.$$

The advantage of using (11-3) rather than (11-1), is that (11-3) is a standard maximization problem with a linear constraint, provided that $\bar{\pi}(q)$ is known, and that constraint (11-3.3) is not binding. Thus, standard duality theory (see, for example, Diewert 1974) can now be applied in order to derive the structural equations for household commodity demand and labor supply to the household farm, and off-farm labor supply. The wage rate for on-farm work, $\bar{\pi}(q)$, is determined by the farm production technology, output and input prices.

An indirect utility function, $G(p, \bar{\pi}, w_2; Z)$ can therefore be defined from (11-3) in the standard manner. The function $G(p, \bar{\pi}(q), w_2; Z)$ is continuous, quasi-convex in $p, \bar{\pi}, w_2$, and Z (Diewert 1974). From the function G, it is possible to derive the Marshallian demand functions for $H - L_1, H - L_2$, and X using Roy's identity:

$$(11\text{-}4.1) \qquad H - L_1 = -\frac{\partial G/\partial \bar{\pi}(q)}{\partial G/\partial Z} = \phi(p, \bar{\pi}, w_2, Z)$$

$$(11\text{-}4.2) \qquad H - L_2 = -\frac{\partial G/\partial w_2}{\partial G/\partial Z} = \psi(p, \bar{\pi}, w_2, Z)$$

(11-4.3) $X = -\dfrac{\partial G/\partial p}{\partial G/\partial Z} = \epsilon(p, \bar{\pi}, w_2, Z).$

Furthermore, the set of conditional output-supply and factor-demand functions can be derived from the conditional profit function using Hotelling's lemma (Hotelling 1932):

(11-5) $Q_i(q; L_1) = L_1 \cdot \dfrac{\partial \bar{\pi}(q)}{\partial q_i}$ $i = 1, \ldots, s$

where Q_i is the conditional supply or demand for commodity i. The unconditional output-supply and factor-demand functions are obtained by using (11-4.1) in (11-5):

(11-6) $Q_i(q; p, w_2, Z) = [H - \phi(p, \bar{\pi}(q), w_2, Z)]\dfrac{\partial \bar{\pi}(q)}{\partial q_i}$

$\qquad\qquad\quad = \Omega(p, \bar{\pi}, q, w_2, Z)$ $i = 1, \ldots, s.$

Equations (11-4) and (11-6) represent the set of supply-and-demand responses obtained from a model that considers consumption and production activities of the farm household within an integrated framework. Changes on the consumption side are transmitted to the net output-supply functions via the function $\phi(p, \bar{\pi}(q), w_2, Z)$ in (11-6). Similarly, changes on the production side affect utility maximization decisions not only via Z but also by changing the shadow price of L_1, that is, by changing $\bar{\pi}$ in (11-4). Thus if output prices increase, for example, then the household will reconsider its consumption and labor-supply allocations because the increased output prices imply a higher level for the shadow price of on-farm work $[\bar{\pi}(q)]$ as well as higher Z.

Modeling Commuting Time to Off-Farm Work

The model described above is nonrecursive because the assumption of identical preferences for time allocations between on-farm and off-farm work is removed. Relaxation of this assumption might seem appropriate for farm producers in developed countries but quite futile for developing countries. One might argue that farm households in developing countries face too many basic problems in procuring enough food, shelter, and health services to survive to be concerned about fine-tuning their preferences for on-farm or off-farm work. One might also argue that their principal concern is simply the total labor supply, regardless of the distribution of their work on and off the farm. This might seem a reasonable argument. It can be shown, however, that if off-farm work implies a time sacrifice in order to commute to work, then one can derive an interdependent model almost identical to the one presented earlier *even* if there are no time preferences for the distribution of work time among on-farm work, off-farm work, and commuting time.

The crucial observation is that although off-farm work usually implies that household members should commute long hours, on-farm work needs little or no additional commuting time cost. Each additional day of off-farm work implies further (commuting) time that is detrimental to productive activities and leisure. Commuting time costs can be considered important for rural families that usually live far away from urban and rural centers of employment. Moreover, the lack or insufficiency of modern transportation facilities in developing countries makes commuting to off-farm work even more time-costly than it is for rural families in developed countries.

Apart from the commuting time considerations, there are at least two other cases in which a nonrecursive model is required for the farm household in developing countries. The first case exists where institutional restrictions limit the off-farm work-time range of choice. When, for example, there are standard minimum weekly hours of work in off-farm activities, the shadow price of on-farm and off-farm work becomes endogenous and, in general, is different from the off-farm wage rate. This endogeneity of the shadow price of labor makes an interdependent model necessary. Second, in subsistence agriculture where farm households do not trade labor or produce certain goods to be entirely consumed by the farm household (the Z goods), then farm-household production and consumption activities are also interdependent. These latter two cases will not be considered here. (For an empirically feasible model of subsistence agriculture, see Lopez 1982.)

Consider the following model of the farm household where commuting time is explicitly accounted for:

(11-7) $$\max \bar{U}(H - L_1 - L_2 - t, X)$$

s.t. (11-7.1) $$px \le \pi(q, L_1) + w_2 L_2 + y$$

(11-7.2) $$t = g(L_2, M)$$

(11-7.3) $$H - L_1 - L_2 - t \ge 0, X \ge 0$$

where t is commuting time required for off-farm work, M is distance to off-farm work centers assumed to be an exogenous variable, $g(L_2, M)$ is a monotonic increasing function, and all other variables have been previously defined.

It should first be pointed out that preferences are expressed in the conventional manner, that is, in terms of leisure $(H - L_1 - L_2 - t)$ only.

Thus, it is assumed that households are indifferent with respect to their allocation of time among on-farm work, off-farm work, and commuting time. Furthermore, commuting time is assumed to be an increasing function of off-farm employment. Note that, in general, the function is nonlinear. Although commuting time may be seen as a linear function of the number of days worked, the fact that the number of hours of daily work can be changed implies that t is in general a nonlinear function of total hours of off-farm work. The total number of hours of off-farm work is

(11-8) $L_2 \equiv Nh$

where N is the number of days of off-farm work and h is the number of hours of work per day.

If we assume that commuting time is a linear function of days of off-farm work, t can be defined as

(11-9) $t = \eta N$

where η is a fixed coefficient. Using (11-8) and (11-9) we obtain

(11-10) $t = \dfrac{\eta}{h} L_2.$

In (11-10), commuting time is a nonlinear function, g, of L_2 because h is also likely to be affected by t. Substituting constraint (11-7.2) into the objective function yields the following equivalent problem:

(11-11) $\max \tilde{U}(H - L_1 - L_2 - g(L_2, M), X)$

s.t. $pX \leq \pi(q, L_1) + w_2 L_2 + y$

$$H - L_1 - L_2 - g(L_2) \geq 0, \ X \geq 0.$$

The first-order conditions for an interior solution (if we assume also that $L_1 > 0$ and $L_2 > 0$) are

(11-12) $(a) - \tilde{U}_l(1 + \dfrac{\partial g}{\partial L_2}) + \lambda w_2 = 0$

$(b) - \tilde{U}_l + \lambda \dfrac{\partial \pi}{\partial L_1} = 0$

where λ is the Lagrangian variable and

$$\tilde{U}_l \equiv \frac{\partial \tilde{U}}{\partial[H - L_1 - L_2 - g(L_2)]}$$

is the marginal utility of leisure.

The marginal utility of off-farm work $\partial \bar{U}/\partial L_2 = -U_l(1 + \partial g/\partial L_2)$ is different from the marginal utility of on-farm work, $\partial \bar{U}/\partial L_1 = -\bar{U}_l$. Therefore, in contrast with the models, the shadow price on on-farm work is not equal to the off-farm wage rate. In general, the shadow price of on-farm work is smaller than the off-farm wage rate. From (11-12) it is clear that

$$(11\text{-}13) \qquad \frac{\partial \pi}{\partial L_1} = \frac{w_2}{1 + \dfrac{\partial g(L_2)}{\partial L_2}}.$$

Thus, since $\partial g/\partial L_2 > 0$ it follows that $\partial \pi/\partial L_1 < w_2$. That is, in equilibrium the value of the marginal productivity of on-farm work is equal to the off-farm wage rate divided by an endogenous discount factor. The shadow price of labor is thus endogenous and different from w_2, and therefore the off-farm wage rate cannot be used as the unique exogenous shadow price of labor, as is usually assumed when recursive models are used.[3]

The utility-maximization model (11-11) can be expressed exactly as model (11-1). That is, one may postulate that households behave as if they maximize a utility function with different preferences for on-farm and off-farm work. Given the ordinality of $\bar{U}(\cdot)$ and the fact that H is fixed, the utility function $\bar{U}(\cdot)$ can be written as

$$(11\text{-}14) \quad \bar{U}(H - L_1 - L_2 - g(L_2, M), X)$$
$$\equiv f(L_1, L_2, X) = U(H - L_1, H - L_2, X; M)$$

where $U(\cdot)$ is another monotonically increasing function of X and decreasing function of L_1 and L_2.[4] Therefore, problem (11-13) can be written as

$(11\text{-}15) \qquad\qquad \max U(H - L_1, H - L_2, X; M)$

s.t. $(11\text{-}15.1) \qquad\qquad pX \le \pi(q, L_1) + w_2 L_2 + y$

$(11\text{-}15.2) \qquad\qquad\qquad L_1 + L_2 < H$

$(11\text{-}15.3) \qquad\qquad L_1 \ge 0, L_2 \ge 0, X \ge 0.$

Problem (11-15) is almost identical to problem (11-1) except that the inequality in (11-15.2) is now strict and that M is now a variable affecting UC-2. Hence, one can perform the same transformations that were made on model (11-1) to obtain an identical estimating model. Thus, nonrecursiveness is important in modeling farm-household behavior even if households do not have specific preferences for the allocation of time among different activities. Moreover, the model proposed in the previous section is more general than might be expected, and under a different interpretation is applicable to cases where commuting time is important even if households are indifferent to working on or off the household farm. A practical advantage of using the model represented in (11-15) is that there is no need for data on actual commuting time, which are usually difficult to obtain. However, data on distance to off-farm employment centers are refined. Finally, note that a model based on (11-15) or (11-1) can be estimated using linear regression if one is willing to assume homothetic preferences and constant returns to scale along with the actual rather than predicted $\tilde{\pi}(q)$.

Testing Recursive Models

Behavioral equations (11-4) and (11-6) represent a nonrecursive model of the farm household that can be compared with the conventional recursive model. A widely used recursive specification is the one proposed by Lau, Lin, and Yotopoulos 1978). This model avoids problems of interdependence by assuming that the off-farm wage rate is the unique exogenous price of leisure under the implicit assumption that households do off-farm work, as follows:

$$(11\text{-}16) \quad \bar{G}(p, w_2, \bar{Z}; E, F) \equiv \max_{H-L_1-L_2, X} [U(H - L_1 - L_2, X; E; F):$$

$$(11\text{-}16.1) \quad px + w_2(H - L_1, L_2) \leqq \pi(q, w_2; E) + w_2 H + y \equiv \bar{Z}$$

$$(11\text{-}16.2) \quad X \geqq 0; H - L_1 - L_2 \geqq 0; L_1 \geqq 0, L_2 \geqq 0],$$

where

$$\pi(q, w_2, E) \equiv [\max_{Q, L_1} q^T Q - w_2 L_1 : Q, L_1 \in \bar{T}(E)]$$

is the unconditional profit function, $\bar{G}(\cdot)$ is the indirect utility function, E is farm operator's education, F is a set of other demographic characteristics (which could include distance to off-farm employment centers), and all other variables are as previously defined.

Note that in this model the assumption of constant returns to scale needs to be relaxed in order to obtain a well-defined (unconditional) profit function, $\pi(q, w_2; E)$. Roy's identity can be used to derive the estimating utility-maximizing equations from $G(\cdot)$, and Hotelling's lemma can be used to obtain the unconditional net output-supply responses from $\pi(q, w_2; E)$. Thus, the estimating model is

$$(11\text{-}17.1) \qquad H - L_1 - L_2 = g^2(p, w_2, \bar{Z}; E, F)$$

(11-17.2) $Q_i = h^i(q, w_2; E)$ $(i = 1, \ldots, s)$

(11-17.3) $L_1 = h^6(q, w_2; E)$

(11-17.4) $X = g^3(p, w_2, \bar{Z}; E, F).$

We should briefly examine the structural differences between the model underlying equation (11-17) and the model represented by equations (11-4) and (11-6). The central difference is that although the labor-supply and consumption-demand equations (11-4) to (11-6) jointly reflect the household's preferences and the firm's production technology, in (11-17) they are determined solely by the household's preferences. Furthermore, in (11-4)–(11-6) the unconditional net output-supply responses are also jointly determined by the household's preferences and the firm's production technology. This situation is in contrast with (11-17) where the unconditional net output-supply equations are defined independently of the household's preferences.

The problem in formally testing the null hypothesis of independence—that is, in testing whether (11-17) holds—against the alternative hypothesis of no independence using models (11-4)–(11-6) is that neither model is nested in the other. That is, we are dealing with separate familes of hypotheses and thus the standard tests cannot be employed (Goldfeld and Quandt 1972). There are a number of alternative formal tests designed to discriminate between separate families of hypotheses. Here, the Hoel-Davidson-MacKinnon (HDM) test is used, which allows us to test the truth of a linear or nonlinear and multivariate regression model when a nonnested alternative hypothesis exists. (For a detailed description of the test and its asymptotic properties, see Davidson and MacKinnon 1981.)

The HDM procedure for testing the null hypothesis of independence represented by equations (11-17.1) to (11-17.3) against the alternative hypothesis embodied in equations (11-4)–(11-6) suggests the estimation of the following equation system:

(11-18.1) $L_1 = (1 - \beta_1)h^6(\cdot) + \beta_1[H - \hat{\phi}(p, \bar{\pi}, w_2, Z)] + \bar{\mu}_1$

(11-18.2)
$L_2 = (1 - \beta_2)[H - g^2(\cdot) - h^6(\cdot)] + \beta_2[H - \hat{\psi}(p, \bar{\pi}, w_2, Z)] + \bar{\mu}_2$

(11-18.3) $Q_i = (1 - \beta_{i+2})h^i(\cdot) + \beta_{i+2}[\hat{\Omega}(p, \bar{\pi}, q, w_2, Z] + \bar{\mu}_{2+i}$
$(i = 1, \ldots, s)$

where (ˆ) above the function indicates expected or predicted values.

Note that the second terms of the right-hand sides represent the predicted or expected values obtained from equations (11-4)–(11-6) for L_1, L_2 and Q_i. The null hypothesis that utility and profit-maximization decisions are independent (that is, that (11-17) is the true model) is tested against the alternative hypothesis of interdependence represented by models (11-4)–(11-6) by jointly testing whether $\beta_k = 0$ for ($k = 1, \ldots, 2+s$). It is clear that if H_O is true, then all β_k will vanish.

The first terms of the right-hand side correspond to (11-7) modified in order to obtain a specific equation for L_2 from (11-7.1) and (11-7.3). Note that the model based on independence does not provide two labor-supply equations. It only defines one aggregate labor-supply equation, and a demand equation for L_1 is determined at the firm level. Hence the equation for L_2 has been obtained from (11-7) as a residual reduced form, only for the purpose of making equations (11-7) comparable to (11-4)–(11-6).

If the true production technology does not approximately exhibit constant returns to scale, then it is possible that neither the null hypothesis nor the alternative hypotheses are true. In this case, the asymptotic properties of the test are generally unknown and hence it would be difficult to interpret the result of regression (11-8). Davidson and MacKinnon (1981) have shown, however, that if H_O is true, then the plim $\hat{\beta}_k = 0$ (for all k) and the variances of $\hat{\beta}_k$ are consistently estimated by (11-8). This implies that the confidence interval for $\hat{\beta}_k$ is correctly estimated if H_O is true, and hence the probability of a type I error is correctly given by the level of significance chosen. This makes intuitive sense; suppose that H_O is rejected against the H_A (which assumes constant returns to scale), but that the true technology does not indeed exhibit constant returns to scale. Had we used an H_A that did not employ this restrictive assumption, then the H_O would have been rejected by an even wider margin. The constant returns-to-scale assumption in H_A decreases the probability of rejecting H_O even if it is false. However, the probability of rejecting H_O, if it is indeed true, is not increased by the assumption of constant returns to scale in the alternative hypothesis. Therefore, a rejection of H_O would be a very strong indication that the hypothesis of independence is indeed false. (The roles of the alternative and null hypotheses were also reversed to test interdependence as the null hypothesis.)

Estimating a Nonrecursive Model

The applicability of the nonrecursive model (see Lopez 1984 for data regarding the details used) and the testing procedures proposed here is illustrated for farm-household cross-sectional data from Canada. To estimate the model represented by equations (11-2) and (11-4), it is necessary to postulate functional forms for the indirect utility function, G, and the conditional profit function, π.

Since the data used in the study are aggregated by census divisions, a Gorman Polar Form (GPF) consistent with the use of aggregate data is postulated:

$$G = \frac{Z - \left[\sum_{i=1}^{3} \sum_{j=1}^{3} \delta_{ij} p_i^{1/2} p_j^{1/2} + \sum_{i=1}^{3} l_i p_i E + \sum_{i=1}^{3} b_i p_i F \right]}{\left[\sum_{i=1}^{3} \alpha_i p_i^{\rho} \right]^{1/\rho}}$$

$$(i, j = 1, 2, 3)$$

where F is the number of family dependents, $\delta_{ij} = \delta_{ij}$, l_i, b_i, α_i, and ρ are parameters to be estimated, and $p_1 \equiv \bar{\pi}$; $p_2 \equiv w_2$, and $p_3 \equiv p$.

Note in (11-18) that demographic characteristics (that is, E and F) are assumed to affect only the subsistence requirements but not the marginal utility of the full income, Z. This preserves the desirable aggregation properties of the model even if households within a group exhibit different demographic characteristics.

Roy's identity can be used to derive the demand equations in expenditure form:

$$S_i = \frac{\alpha_i p_i^{\rho} \left[Z - \sum_{i=1}^{3} \sum_{j=1}^{3} \delta_{ij} p_i^{1/2} p_j^{1/2} - \sum_{i=1}^{3} l_i p_i E - \sum_{i=1}^{3} b_i p_i F \right]}{\sum_{i=1}^{3} \alpha_i p_i^{\rho}}$$

(11-19)
$$+ p_i \left[\sum_{j=1}^{3} \delta_{ij} \left(\frac{p_j}{p_i} \right)^{1/2} + \sum_{i=1}^{3} l_i E + \sum_{i=1}^{3} b_i F \right]$$

$$i = 1, 2, 3$$

where

$$S_1 \equiv p_1(H - L_1)$$
$$S_2 \equiv p_2(H - L_2)$$
$$S_3 \equiv p_3 X.$$

Note that it is possible to test for homotheticity to the origin by testing whether all $\delta_{ij} = 0$. If $\delta_{ij} = 0$ for $i \neq j$, then preferences would be homothetic to a fixed point in the positive orthant. Given that the total expenditures cannot exceed the after-tax income rather than the gross income, it is necessary to modify equation (11-19) in order to consider taxes. Here we follow the procedure used by Wales and Woodland (1977) and estimate (11-19) using the after-tax values of the wage rates as well as an after-tax measure of the full income Z.

The conditional profit function is dependent on one aggregate output price (q_1) and the following factor prices: rental price of land and structures (q_2), hired labor wage rate (q_3), rental price of livestock capital (q_4), and rental price of other forms of capital (q_5). In a cross-sectional framework, differences in the production technology among the observations might arise because differences in the educational levels of farm households may affect output supply and input demands in a nonneutral way; and there may be regional differences in climate and soil quality. Since the variable education is assumed to affect profits and net output supply, dummy variables were added to the conditional profit function for four regions.

If we assume constant returns to scale and specify a generalized Leontief function, the conditional profit function is thus defined by

$$(11\text{-}20) \qquad \pi(q; L_1) = L_1 \left[\sum_{i=1}^{5} \sum_{j=1}^{5} b_{ij} q_i^{1/2} q_j^{1/2} + \sum_{i=1}^{5} a_i q_i E + \sum_{i=1}^{5} \sum_{k=1}^{4} C_{ik} D_k q_i \right]$$

where $b_{ij} = b_{ji}$, a_i, and C_{ik} are parameters and D_k is the dummy corresponding to region k. Thus, $\bar{\pi}(q)$ is the expression in the bracket of the right-hand side of (11-20).

Given (11-20), the output-supply and factor-demand responses per unit of family labor can be obtained using Hotelling's lemma. Thus, the output-supply and factor-demand equations are

$$(11\text{-}21) \qquad \frac{Q_i}{L_1} = \sum_{j=1}^{5} b_{ij} \left(\frac{q_i}{q_i} \right)^{1/2} + a_i E + \sum_{k=1}^{4} C_{ik} D_k, \quad i = 1, \ldots, 5$$

where Q_1 is output supply and Q_2, Q_3, Q_4, and Q_5 are the demands for land, hired labor, animal stocks, and farm capital, respectively.

Equations (11-19) and (11-21) are estimated by appending additive disturbances that are assumed to be normally distributed with zero means and positive semidefinite variance-covariance matrix Σ. The system of equations (11-19) and (11-21) is jointly estimated after the consumption expenditure equation is dropped using a Full-Information Maximum Likelihood Method (FIML).

Given that the number of households varies across the different census divisions, the variances of the disturbance terms differ for the different observations even if the individual household's disturbances are assumed to be constant. Thus, one might expect to find that the disturbances of the grouped estimates are heteroscedastic. To correct this, equations (11-19) and (11-21) are multiplied through by the square root of the number of farms in each census division.

The data used were obtained from the 1971 agricultural and population census in Canada, which covered approximately 240 census divisions across the country. The data consisted of averages per farm household of number of days of off-farm work, number of days of on-farm work, the off-farm wage rate, the household's nonlabor income, output and input prices faced by the household's firm, output and input quantities, the farm operator's years of schooling, and the number of family dependents. An aggregated output price index and three input price indices—namely, the hired labor wage rate, an animal stocks rental price index, and a land rental price index—are needed. The price index of farm capital (machinery, implements, and other intermediate inputs) is not available and is assumed to be constant across the observations. Farm machinery, fertilizers, and spray materials, in contrast with other farm inputs (such as labor, land, and livestock), are traded by large firms that operate on a national scale. It is reasonable to assume that these firms charge approximately homogeneous prices for their products in the different regions of the country, and thus the above assumption may not be too unrealistic.

The most important empirical result is the testing of the null hypothesis that utility- and profit-maximizing decisions are independent. To test the null hypothesis, we must test whether $\beta_k = 0$ for $k = 1, \ldots, 7$. Asymptotic likelihood ratio tests were used for this purpose (Theil 1971). The calculated χ^2 value was 127.20, which is substantially higher than the critical χ^2 values for 7 degrees of freedom (14.07 and 18.48 at a 5 percent and 1 percent level of significance, respectively). Hence, the hypothesis of independent production and consumption decisions (that is, that a recursive model is appropriate) is categorically rejected. Furthermore, when the roles of the null and alternative hypotheses were reversed (that is, when the null hypothesis was interdependent), the calculated χ^2 was 9.89, which is not large enough to reject the hypothesis at a 1 percent or 5 percent level of significance. These results strongly suggest that the recursive model considered is restrictive and that the nonrecursive model used is superior.

The parameter estimates and asymptotic standard error obtained by the joint estimation of the consumption and production sides of the model are presented in table 11-1. Most coefficients in the consumption and production sectors are significant. There is one degree of freedom for the parameters of the CES function, which can be exhausted by any suitable normalization (see Blackorby, Boyce, and Russell 1981). The normalization chosen is that the share parameter, α_2, is equal to one. The goodness-of-fit measure used is the generalized R^2 originally proposed by Baxter and Cragg (1970).

Table 11-1. *Parameter Estimates of the Consumption and Production Equations* (equations 11-19 and 11-21)

Parameter	Parameter value	Asymptotic standard error
ρ	0.980	0.086
α_1	1.124	0.222
α_2	1	—
α_3	41.45	10.35
δ_{11}	612.5	4.591
δ_{12}	−9.111	3.746
δ_{13}	4.749	9.603
δ_{22}	829.3	15.94
δ_{23}	60.86	6.16
δ_{33}	−241.8	10.59
l_1	−14.83	3.205
l_2	−24.88	2.534
l_3	−2.812	1.055
b_1	160.5	7.149
b_2	166.3	5.835
b_3	42.76	1.078
b_{11}	113.6	7.044
b_{12}	147.4	2.562
b_{13}	−99.09	7.455
b_{14}	−39.61	2.755
b_{15}	−233.17	2.858
b_{22}	160.1	1.969
b_{23}	−68.71	4.562
b_{24}	2.584	1.683
b_{25}	−150.20	4.366
b_{33}	−102.6	22.21
b_{34}	37.01	4.702
b_{35}	88.86	9.743
b_{44}	−7.518	4.795
b_{45}	−2.359	3.499
b_{55}	−235.68	4.624
a_1	−38.77	2.276
a_2	−15.56	1.414
a_3	9.124	1.199
a_4	−1.011	0.346
a_5	32.48	1.783

Note: $\bar{R}^2 = 0.994$.

All the properties of an indirect utility function are satisfied by the estimated G(.), with the exception of quasi-convexity, which is not satisfied at 62 percent of the observations. The properties of a profit function are satisfied by the estimated $\pi(.)$, except for convexity, which is satisfied only at 40 percent of the observations. However, the diagonal elements of the Hessian matrix are positive for more than 80 percent of the observations. This implies that the price elasticities have the correct signs when evaluated at most of the observations.

Table 11-2 contains the on-farm and off-farm labor-supply elasticities with respect to on-farm returns to farm household labor, the off-farm wage rate received by household members, and the household's nonlabor income. The own-wage elasticities of labor supply are positive when evaluated at mean values, the off-farm labor-supply elasticity being substantially larger than the on-farm elasticity. The on-farm supply elasticity is negative at 8 percent of the observations, however, and the off-farm elasticity is negative at 19 percent. These estimates are not comparable to previous studies because they provide estimates for aggregate labor supply. The elasticity of total labor supply with respect to a simultaneous change in the on-farm labor returns and the off-farm wage rate is approximately 0.024, which is substantially lower than the labor-supply elasticities obtained in studies using recursive models, such as those by Lau, Lin, and Yotopoulos (1978), who used farm-household data from Taiwan (0.16), and by Barnum and Squire (1979), who used data from Malaysia (0.08). Moreover, the total labor-supply elasticity obtained by the recursive model (11-17) used in this study was 0.19, which is substantially larger than the elasticity estimate obtained using the nonrecursive model.

Table 11-2 also shows the cross-wage effects on labor supply. A 1 percent increase in the off-farm wage rate induces a 0.1 percent decrease in the number of days of on-farm work by the household members. The effect of on-farm labor returns on off-farm work is stronger. A 1 percent change in farm labor returns will induce a 0.25 percent decrease in the off-

Table 11-2. *Labor-Supply Elasticities with Respect to On-Farm Labor Returns, Off-Farm Wage, and Nonlabor Income*

Labor supply	On-farm labor returns	Off-farm wage rate	Nonlabor income
On-farm	0.119	−0.107	−0.612
Off-farm	−0.259	0.180	−0.539
Total	0.043	−0.049	−0.237

Note: Evaluated at mean values of the variables.

farm supply of labor. The effect of nonlabor income on total labor supply is approximately −0.23. This effect is also substantially biased upward by the estimate obtained using the recursive model, which was −0.492.

Table 11-3 presents the estimated labor-supply elasticities with respect to output and input price changes evaluated at mean values. As might be expected, changes in the output price have the largest effect (in terms of absolute values) on off-farm and on-farm labor supply. A 1 percent increase in output price increases the on-farm labor supply by 0.39 percent and decreases the off-farm supply of labor by approximately 0.85 percent.

Table 11-4 contains the unconditional supply-and-demand elasticities.[5] These elasticities measure the actual market net output-supply responses after the effects of output or factor-price changes on family and operator labor supply have been considered. The output-supply elasticity for agriculture is 0.73, which is somewhat lower than supply elasticities obtained in previous studies. For example, Tweeten and Quance (1969), who used different procedures, obtained estimates of 0.31, 1.79, and 1.52 for long-run aggregate output-supply elasticities in U.S. agriculture. The effects of factor-price changes on output supply are generally small, with the exception of the farm capital price. A 1 percent increase in the farm capital

Table 11-3. *Labor-Supply Elasticities with Respect to Net Output Prices*

Labor supply	Output price	Land price	Hired labor wage rate	Animal stock price	Farm capital price
On-farm	0.390	−0.046	−0.027	−0.015	−0.145
Off-farm	−0.849	0.101	0.059	0.033	0.315

Note: Evaluated at mean values of the variable.

Table 11-4. *Unconditional Net Output-Supply Elasticities with Respect to Net Output Prices*

	Prices of				
	Output	Land	Hired labor	Animal stocks	Farm capital
Output	0.732	0.066	−0.153	−0.064	−0.414
Land	−0.522	−0.464	0.430	−0.031	0.743
Hired labor	1.947	0.750	−0.447	−0.666	−1.479
Animal stocks	1.493	−0.999	−1.134	−0.021	−0.082
Farm capital	1.016	0.251	−0.287	−0.010	−0.835

price induces a 0.4 percent decrease in output supply. Changes in the land price index have a small effect on the demand for all inputs, with the exception of hired labor. Factor demands are not very responsive to changes in their own prices. Rather, all factors present inelastic demand schedules. These estimates can be compared with previous results for U.S. and Canadian agriculture. Binswanger's (1974) own-factor demand elasticity estimates for U.S. agriculture are -0.34 for land, -0.91 for labor, -1.089 for machinery, and -0.95 for fertilizers. Lopez's (1980) estimates for Canadian agriculture are -0.52 for labor, -0.35 for farm capital, -0.42 for land, and -0.41 for intermediate inputs. Thus, although the results are not entirely comparable—because the disaggregation of inputs is different and because these studies estimated compensated price elasticities (that is, for a constant level of output)—the general pattern of inelastic factor demands is consistent in the three studies.

Conclusions

This study has shown that under several circumstances the use of recursive models in estimating farm-household models may be quite restrictive. It is possible, however, to construct models that allow for interdependent production and consumption decisions and that are feasible to estimate. A statistical test to discriminate between an interdependent and a commonly used recursive model has been implemented using Canadian data. The hypothesis that production and consumption decisions are independent was categorically rejected, and it was shown that important gains in explanatory power result from estimating the consumption and production sectors jointly.

Some other important results emerge from the empirical estimation. First, the cross effects between the production equations and the labor-supply responses are quantitatively strong and thus suggest that interdependent models should be used for farm households. Second, the model estimated explains the behavior of farm households reasonably well and generates results that are generally consistent with economic theory. Third, the estimated labor-supply elasticities for on-farm and off-farm work are very different and thus suggest that the models for farm households should allow for different behavior toward on-farm and off-farm work. Finally, the total labor-supply elasticities obtained by using the nonrecursive and recursive models tend to be drastically different. The empirical findings thus imply that nonseparable models are both theoretically and empirically sounder than separable models.

Notes

1. There are several other sources of interdependent utility- and profit-maximizing decisions that are not dealt with in this study. For example, imperfections in capital markets (that is, credit rationing) lead to the specification of an intertemporal dynamic model, which ultimately implies that utility-maximizing and production decisions are not separable. See Chambers and Lopez (1984) for the comparative dynamics of such a model.

2. The assumption of constant returns to scale in agriculture has often not been rejected. See, for example, Chan (1981).

3. Note that if hours worked per day were not affected by commuting costs, then the shadow price of on-farm work would still be different from the off-farm wage rate. In this case, however, the discount factor would not be endogenous and, hence, the shadow price of on-farm work would be proportional to the off-farm wage rate.

4. Without loss of generality, one can impose in the function $U(L_1, L_2, X)$ weak separability between the two labor-supply variables and the vector of consumption X. This would allow one to postulate the existence of a composite commodity $L(L_1, L_2)$ and to estimate an aggregate labor supply. This is not equivalent to a recursive model, however, because in order to estimate an aggregate labor-supply equation, one would have to construct an aggregate labor price that is in general different from w_2. This aggregate labor price is a combination of the shadow price of L_1 and L_2. Since the shadow price of L_1 is endogenous, the aggregate labor price will also be endogenous. Moreover, the shadow price of L_1 is usually not known and, hence, the aggregate labor price would be extremely difficult to determine. Thus, although a composite aggregate labor supply commodity exists, its estimation appears to be infeasible.

5. The unconditional effect of a change in net output price q_j on Q_i can be readily derived:

$$\frac{\partial Q_i}{\partial q_j} = \frac{\partial^2 \pi}{\partial q_i \partial q_j} L_1 + \frac{\partial \tilde{\pi}}{\partial q_i} \frac{\partial L_1}{\partial q_j}.$$

References

Barichello, R. R. 1979. "The Schooling of Farm Youth in Canada." Ph.D. dissertation. University of Chicago, Chicago, Ill. Processed.

Barnum, H. N., and L. Squire. 1979. "An Econometric Application of the Theory of the Farm-Household." *Journal of Development Economics*, vol. 6, pp. 79–102.

Baxter, N. D., and J. Cragg. 1970. "Corporate Choice among Long-Term Financing Investments." *Review of Economic Studies*, vol. 52, pp. 259–61.

Benewitz, M. C., and A. Zucker. 1968. "Human Capital and Occupational Choice: A Theoretical Model." *Southern Economic Journal*, vol. 33, pp. 406–9.

Binswanger, H. P. 1974. "The Measurement of Technical Change Biases with Many Factors of Production." *American Economic Review*, vol. 64, pp. 964–76.

Blackorby, C., R. Boyce, and R. Russell. 1981. "Estimation of Demand Systems Generated by the Gorman Polar Form: A Generalization of the S-Branch Utility Tree." *Econometrica*, vol. 46, pp. 265–82.

Chambers, R., and R. E. Lopez. 1984. "Equity Formation and the On-farm, Off-farm Labor Choice." University of Maryland, Department of Agricultural and Resource Economics, College Park, Md. Processed.

Chan, M. W. 1981. "An Econometric Model of the Canadian Agricultural Economy." *Canadian Journal of Agricultural Economics*, vol. 29, pp. 265–82.

Davidson, R., and J. G. MacKinnon. 1981. "Several Tests for Model Specification in the Presence of Alternative Hypotheses." *Econometrica*, vol. 49, pp. 781–93.

Diewert, W. E. 1971. "Choice on Labour Markets and the Theory of Allocation of Time." Ottawa: Department of Manpower and Immigration.

———. 1974. "Applications of Duality Theory." In *Frontiers of Quantitative Economics*, ed. M. D. Intriligator and D. A. Kenrick. Vol. 2. London: North-Holland.

Fieldings, G. S., and J. Hoseck. 1973. "Human Investment Decisions, Labour Market Choice, and Unemployment." Rand #P-5144, Los Angeles, Calif.

Goldfeld, S. M., and R. E. Quandt. 1972. *Nonlinear Methods in Econometrics*. London: North-Holland.

Gorman, W. M. 1953. "Community Preference Field." *Econometrica*, vol. 21, pp. 63–80.

Hotelling, H. 1932. "Edgeworth's Taxation Paradox and the Nature of Demand and Supply Functions." *Journal of Political Economy*, vol. 40, pp. 577–616.

Lau, L. J., W. L. Lin, and P. A. Yotopoulos. 1978. "The Linear Logarithmic Expenditure System: An Application to Consumption-Leisure Choice." *Econometrica*, vol. 46, pp. 843–68.

Lopez, R. E. 1980. "The Structure of Production and the Derived Demand for Inputs in Canadian Agriculture." *American Journal of Agricultural Economics*, vol. 62, pp. 38–45.

———. 1982. "Applications of Duality Theory to Agriculture." *Western Journal of Agricultural Economics*, vol. 7, pp. 353–66.

———. 1984. "Estimating Labor Supply and Production Decisions of Self-Employed Farm Producers." *European Economic Review*, vol. 24, pp. 61–82.

Malinvaud, E. 1976. *Lectures on Microeconomic Theory*. London: North-Holland.

Rottenberg, S. 1956. "On Choice in Labour Markets." In *Readings in Labour Markets*. Edited by J. Burton. London.

Theil, H. 1971. Principles of Econometrics. New York: John Wiley & Sons.

Tweeten, L. B., and L. C. Quance. 1969. "Positivistic Measures of Aggregate Supply Elasticities: Some New Approaches." *American Journal of Agricultural Economics, Proceedings*, vol. 51, pp. 475–89.

Wales, T. J., and A. D. Woodland. 1977. "Estimation of the Allocation of Time for Work, Leisure and Housework." *Econometrica*, vol. 45, pp. 115–25.

Index